ISABELLA D'ESTE

VOL. I

AMS PRESS

NEW YORK

Walker & Cockerell, Ph. Sc.

Isabella d'Este
by Leonardo da Vinci (Louvre)

ISABELLA D'ESTE
MARCHIONESS OF MANTUA
1474–1539
A STUDY OF THE RENAISSANCE
BY JULIA CARTWRIGHT (Mrs. ADY)

AUTHOR OF "BEATRICE D'ESTE," "THE PAINTERS
OF FLORENCE," "MADAME," ETC.

" La prima donna del mondo."
NICCOLO DA CORREGGIO.

" D'opere illustri e di bei studi amica,
Ch' io non so ben se più leggiadra e bella,
Mi debba dire, o più saggia e pudica
Liberale e magnanima Isabella."
ARIOSTO.

VOL. I

NEW YORK
E. P. DUTTON AND COMPANY
1907

Library of Congress Cataloging in Publication Data

Ady, Julia Mary (Cartwright) d. 1929.
  Isabella d'Este, Marchioness of Mantua, 1474-1539.

  "List of the chief authorities on the life and
times of Isabella d'Este": p.
  1. Isabella d'Este, Consort of Francis II,
Marquis of Mantua, 1474-1539. 2. Italy—History—
1492-1559.
DG540.8.17A66 1974   945'.05'0924 [B]   79-154139
ISBN 0-404-09214-4

Reprinted from the 1907 edition, New York.
First AMS edition published in 1974.
Manufactured in the United States of America.

International Standard Book Number:
Complete Set: 0-404-09214-4.
Volume 1: 0-404-09215-2.

AMS PRESS INC.
NEW YORK, N. Y. 10003.

PREFACE

THE life of Isabella d'Este has never yet been written. After four hundred years, the greatest lady of the Renaissance still awaits her biographer. An unkind fate has pursued all the scholars, whether French, German, or Italian, who have hitherto attempted the task. Their labours have been hindered and interrupted, or their lives prematurely cut short by death. More than fifty years ago an interesting study on the famous Marchesa, from the pen of a Mantuan scholar, Carlo d'Arco, was published in the *Archivio Storico Italiano* (1845), based upon documents preserved in the Gonzaga Archives. In 1867, a distinguished Frenchman, M. Armand Baschet, wrote a remarkable essay on Isabella d'Este's relations with the great Venetian printer, Aldo Manuzio, but died before he could execute his intention of publishing a life of this princess. A mass of documents, which he had copied from the Mantuan Archives, remained in the hands of the late M. Charles Yriarte, who wrote several interesting chapters on Isabella d'Este's relations with the great painters of her age, in the *Gazette des Beaux Arts*, and was preparing a fuller and more complete work on the subject when he died. M. Firmin Didot, Dr. Janitschek, Dr. Reumont, and Ferdinand Gregorovius have all in turn given us sketches of Isabella in their historical works, while deploring the absence of any biography which should do full justice to so attractive and important a figure.

Meanwhile, Italiàn students have not been idle. Twenty years ago a learned Mantuan ecclesiastic, Canonico Willelmo Braghirolli, made a careful study of Isabella's correspondence with Giovanni Bellini and Perugino, and published many of the letters relating to these artists. But he too died before his time, leaving her life still unwritten. Other well-known scholars, Ferrato, Bertolotti, Campori, Signor Vittore Cian, and Cavaliere Stefano Davari, the present Director of the Archivio Gonzaga, have turned their attention to different aspects of the theme, and have published studies on the Gonzaga princes, or on the scholars and artists attached to their court. Above all, Dr. Alessandro Luzio, the present Keeper of the State Archives of Mantua, and his former colleague, Signor Rodolfo Renier, have devoted years of patient and untiring labour to the examination of the vast mass of Isabella d'Este's correspondence, amounting to upwards of two thousand letters, which had been fortunately preserved. During the last fifteen years these indefatigable workers have published a whole series of interesting articles and pamphlets containing the results of their researches, as well as one valuable volume, in which the intercourse between the courts of Mantua and Urbino, in the lifetime of Isabella and her sister-in-law, Elisabetta Gonzaga, is fully described. In an essay which Signor Renier contributed to the *Italia*, fifteen years ago, he informed his readers that he and Dr. Luzio would shortly publish a monograph on the great Marchesa, but these distinguished scholars have as yet been unable to fulfil their promise, and the appearance of this important and long-expected work is still delayed.

Meanwhile, the following study, without pretending to be an exhaustive biography, may interest those of our readers who are already familiar with Isabella through the Life of her sister, Beatrice d'Este.[1] The history of these two princesses was closely interwoven during the early days of their wedded life, and Isabella's visits to Milan, and her correspondence with Lodovico Sforza and his young wife naturally filled a large share of her time and thoughts. But these six brilliant years which made up the whole of Beatrice's married life formed only a brief episode in Isabella's long and eventful career. During the next forty years she played an important part in the history of her times, and made the little court of Mantua famous in the eyes of the whole civilised world. Her close relationship with the reigning families of Milan and Naples, of Ferrara and Urbino, and constant intercourse with Popes and monarchs made her position one of peculiar importance, while the wisdom and sagacity which she showed in political affairs commanded universal respect. Both during the lifetime of her husband and son she was repeatedly called upon to administer the government of the state, and showed a coolness and dexterity in the conduct of the most difficult negotiations that would have excited the admiration of Machiavelli himself. By her skilful diplomacy this able woman saved the little state of Mantua from falling a prey to the ambitious designs of Cæsar Borgia, or the vengeance of two powerful French monarchs, Louis XII. and Francis I. At the same time she helped her brother, Duke Alfonso of Ferrara, to resist the furious assaults of Julius II.

[1] Beatrice d'Este, Duchess of Milan, by Julia Cartwright. (Dent & Co., 1899.)

and the tortuous policy of Leo X., and to preserve
his duchy in the face of the most prolonged and
determined opposition. Isabella lived to see the
fulfilment of her fondest wish, when, in 1531, the
newly-crowned Emperor, Charles V., visited Mantua
and raised her eldest son to the rank of Duke, while
Pope Clement VII. bestowed a Cardinal's hat on her
second son Ercole.

But it is above all as a patron of art and letters
that Isabella d'Este will be remembered. In this
respect she deserves a place with the most enlightened princes of the Renaissance, with Lorenzo dei
Medici and Lodovico Sforza. A true child of her
age, Isabella combined a passionate love of beauty
and the most profound reverence for antiquity with
the finest critical taste. Her studios and villas
were adorned with the best paintings and statues by
the first masters of the day, and with the rarest
antiques from the Eternal City and the Isles of
Greece. Her book-shelves contained the daintiest
editions of classical works printed at the Aldine
Press, and the newest poems and romances by living
writers. Viols and organs of exquisite shape and
tone, lutes of inlaid ivory and ebony, the richest
brocades and rarest gems, the finest gold and silver
work, the choicest majolica and most delicately
tinted Murano glass found a place in her *camerini*.
But everything that she possessed must be of the
best, and she was satisfied with nothing short of
perfection. Even Mantegna and Perugino sometimes failed to please her, and Aldo's books were
returned to be more carefully revised and printed.
To attain these objects Isabella spared neither time
nor trouble. She wrote endless letters, and gave the

artists in her employment the most elaborate and
minute instructions. Braghirolli counted as many
as forty letters on the subject of a single picture
painted by Giovanni Bellini, and no less than fifty-
three on a painting entrusted to Perugino. Especial
attention has been devoted to this portion of Isabella's
correspondence in the present work. The vast number of letters which passed between her and the chief
artists of the day have hitherto lain buried in foreign
archives or hidden in pamphlets and periodicals, many
of them already out of print. All these have been
carefully collected, and are for the first time brought
together here.

If Isabella was a fastidious and at times a
severe critic, she was also a generous and kindly
patron, prompt to recognise true merit and stimulate
creative effort, and ever ready to befriend struggling
artists. And poets and painters alike gave her freely
of their best. Castiglione and Niccolo da Correggio,
Bembo and Bibbiena, were among her constant
correspondents. Aldo Manuzio printed Virgils and
Petrarchs for her use, Lorenzo da Pavia made her
musical instruments of unrivalled beauty and sweetness. The works of Mantegna and Costa, of Giovanni
Bellini and Michelangelo, of Perugino and Correggio,
adorned her rooms. Giovanni Santi, Andrea Mantegna, Francesco Francia, and Lorenzo Costa all
in turn painted portraits of her, which have alas!
perished. But her beautiful features still live in
Leonardo's perfect drawing, in Cristoforo's medal,
and in Titian's great picture at Vienna. Nor were
poets and prose-writers remiss in paying her their
homage. Paolo Giovio addressed her as the rarest of
women; Bembo and Trissino celebrated her charms

and virtues in their sonnets and *canzoni*. Castiglione
gave her a high place in his courtly record, Ariosto
paid her a magnificent tribute in his "Orlando,"
while endless were the songs and lays which minor
bards offered at the shrine of this peerless Marchesa,
whom they justly called the foremost lady in the
world—"*la prima donna del mondo.*"—"Isabella
d'Este," writes Jacopo Caviçeo, "at the sound of
whose name all the Muses rise and do reverence."

In her aims and aspirations Isabella was a typical
child of the Renaissance, and her thoughts and actions
faithfully reflected the best traditions of the age.
Her own conduct was blameless. As a wife and
mother, as a daughter and sister, she was beyond
reproach. But her judgments conformed to the
standard of her own times, and her diplomacy followed the principles of Machiavelli and of Marino
Sanuto. She had a strong sense of family affections,
and would have risked her life for the sake of advancing the interests of her husband and children
or brothers, but she did not hesitate to ask Cæsar
Borgia for the statues of which he had robbed her
brother-in-law, and danced merrily at the ball given
by Louis XII. while her old friend and kinsman
Duke Lodovico languished in the dungeons of
Loches. Like others of her age, she knew no
regrets and felt no remorse, but lived wholly in the
present, throwing herself with all the might of her
strong vitality into the business or enjoyment of the
hour, forgetful of the past and careless of the future.

Fortunate in the time of her birth and in the circumstances of her life, Isabella was above all fortunate
in this, that she saw the finest works of the Renaissance in the prime of their beauty. She knew

Venice and Milan in their most triumphant hour,
when the glowing hues of Titian and Giorgione's
frescoes, of Leonardo and Gian Bellini's paintings,
were fresh upon the walls. She visited the famous
palace of Urbino in the days of the good Duke
Guidobaldo, when young Raphael was painting his
first pictures, and Bembo and Castiglione sat at the
feet of the gentle Duchess Elisabetta. She came
to Florence when Leonardo and Michelangelo were
working side by side at their cartoons in the
Council Hall, and she was the guest of Leo X., and
saw the wonders of the Sistina and of Raphael's
Stanze, before the fair halls of the Vatican had been
defaced by barbarian invaders.

Many and sad were the changes that she witnessed
in the course of her long life. She saw the first
"invasion of the stranger, and all Italy in flame and
fire," as her own Ferrara poet sang in words of
passionate lament. She saw Naples torn from the
house of Aragon, the fair Milanese, where the Moro
and Beatrice had reigned in their pride, lost in a
single day. She saw Urbino conquered twice over
and her own kith and kin driven into exile, first by
the treacherous Borgia, then by a Medici Pope,
who was bound to the reigning house by the closest
ties of friendship and gratitude. And in 1527, she
was herself an unwilling witness of the nameless
horrors that attended the siege and sack of Rome.
Three years later, she was present at the Emperor
Charles V.'s coronation at Bologna, and took an
active part in the splendid ceremonies that marked
the loss of Italian independence and the close of
this great period. But to the last Isabella retained
the same delight in beauty, the same keen sense of

enjoyment. She advanced in years without ever growing old, and in the last months of her life, one of the foremost scholars of the age, Cardinal Bembo, pronounced her to be the wisest and most fortunate of women. The treasures of art and learning which she had collected were sold by her descendants to foreign princes or destroyed when the Germans sacked Mantua ninety years after her death, and the ruin of her favourite palaces and villas was completed by the French invaders of 1797, who did not even spare the tomb which held her ashes. But Isabella herself will be long remembered as the fairest and most perfect flower of womanhood which blossomed under the sunny skies of Virgil's land, in the immortal days of the Italian Renaissance.

JULIA CARTWRIGHT.

I add a list of the chief authorities on the life and times of Isabella d'Este :—

ITALIAN.

Notizie di Isabella Esteuse. Carlo d'Arco (Archivio Storico Italiano, Appendice. Tom. ii.). 1845.

Dell' Arte e degli Artefici di Mantova. Carlo d'Arco. 2 tom. 1857.

Discorso intorno le Belle Lettere e le Arte Mantovani. Abate Bettinelli. 1774.

Cronaca di Mantova. A. Schivenoglia. 1445–1484. Müller. Raccolta. 1857.

Storia di Mantova. Mario Equicola. 1610.

Storia ecclesiastica di Mantova. Donesmondi. 1613–1616.

Diario Ferrarese. Italicarum Rerum Scriptores. xxiv. L. A. Muratori. 1750.

Storia di Ferrara. A. Frizzi. Tom. iv., v. 1791.

Compendio della Storia di Mantova. Volta. 1807–1838.

Lettere inedite di Artisti cavate dall' Archivio Gonzaga. W. Braghirolli. 1878.

Isabella d'Este e Giovanni Bellini. W. Braghirolli (Archivio Veneto, xiii.). Mantova. 1877.

Notizie inedite di P. Vannucchi. W. Braghirolli. Perugia. 1874.

Tiziano alla Corte dei Gonzaghi. W. Braghirolli. 1881.

Notizie e Documenti intorno al ritratto di Leon X. W. Braghirolli e C. d'Arco (Archivio Storico Italiano, vii.). 1868.

Lettere inedite di donne Mantovane del secolo XV. P. Ferrato. 1878.

Alcune lettere di Principesse di Casa Gonzaga. P. Ferrato. Imola. 1879.

Mantova e Urbino. Isabella d'Este ed Elisabetta Gonzaga. Narrazione storica documentata di A. Luzio e R. Renier. 1893.

I Precettori d'Isabella d'Este. A. Luzio. 1887.

Federico Gonzaga, Ostaggio alla Corte di Giulio II. 1887.

Delle Relazioni d'Isabella d'Este.—Gonzaga con Lodovico e Beatrice Sforza. Luzio e Renier (Archivio Storico Lombardo, xvii.). Milano. 1890.

Isabella e la Corte Sforzesca. Luzio (Archivio Storico Lombardo, xxviii.). Milano. 1901.

Francesco Gonzaga alla battaglia di Fornovo (Archivio Storico Italiano, Serie V., v. vi.). Luzio e Renier. Firenze. 1890.

Gara di viaggio fra due celebri dame del Rinascimento. Luzio e Renier. Alessandria. 1890.

Isabella d'Este. Rivista Italia, i. R. Renier. Roma. 1888.

Niccolo da Correggio. Luzio e Renier (Giornale Storico della Letteratura Italiana, tom. xxi. e xxii.). Torino. 1893.

Buffoni, nani e schiavi dei Gonzaga ai tempi d'Isabella d'Este. Luzio e Renier (Nuova Antologia). Roma. 1891.

Il Lusso d'Isabella d'Este. Luzio (Nuova Antologia). Roma. 1896.

Lettere inedite di Fra Sabba da Castiglione. Luzio (Archivio Storico Lombardo, xiii.). Milano. 1886.

Vittoria Colonna. Luzio (Rivista Storica Mantovana, i.). Mantova. 1885.

Il Palazzo di Mantova. Stefano Davari (Archivio Storico Lombardo, xxii.). 1895.

La Musica in Mantova. Stefano Davari (Rivista Storica Mantovana, i.). 1885.

Le Arte Minori alla Corte di Mantova. A. Bertolotti (Archivio Storico Lombardo, v.).

Artisti in relazione coi Gonzaga. A. Bertolotti. Modena. 1885.

Il Palazzo del Tè. G. B. Intra (Archivio Storico Lombardo, xiv.). 1887.

Notizie intorno allo studio publico in Mantova. S. Davari. 1876.

Il Matrimonio di Dorotea Gonzaga. S. Davari.

Il Matrimonio di Federico Gonzaga(Arch. Storico Lombardo). 1887.

Lorenzo Gusnasco. Dr. Carlo dell' Acqua. Milano. 1886.

G. C. Romano. A. Venturi (Archivio Storico dell' Arte, i.). 1888.

Lorenzo Costa. A. Venturi (Archivio Storico dell' Arte, i.). 1888.

Notizie da Raffaelle e Giovanni Santi. G. Campori. Modena. 1870.

La Coltura e le Relazioni Letterarie di Isabella d'Este Gonzaga. Luzio e Renier (Giornale Storico della Letteratura Italiana, xxxiii.). Torino. 1899–1901.

Pietro Bembo. V. Cian (Giornale Storico di Letteratura Italiana, ix.). Torino. 1887.

Un decennio nella vita di P. Bembo. V. Cian. 1885.

Nuovi Documenti su Pietro Pomponazzi. V. Cian. Venezia. 1887.

Ercole Gonzaga a Bologna. Luzio (Giornale Storico della Letteratura Italiana, viii.). Torino. 1886.

La Madonna della Vittoria del Mantegna. Luzio (Emporium, x.). Bergamo. 1899.

La Chiesa e la Madonna della Vittoria. Portioli. 1883.

I Ritratti d'Isabella d'Este. Luzio (Emporium,xi.). Bergamo. 1900.

Viaggio d'Isabella d'Este sul Lago di Garda. A. Pedrazzoli (Archivio Storico Lombardo, xxii.). 1890.

Carteggio inedito d'Artisti. Gaye, tom. ii. e iii. Firenze. 1837.

La Vita di Benvenuto Cellini.

Le Vite dei più Eccellenti Pittori, Scultori ed Architettori, scritte da Giorgo Vasari con nuove annotazioni di Gaetano Milanesi. Firenze. 1878.

Leonardo da Vinci. Edmondo Solmi. Firenze. 1900.

Leonardo da Vinci. Luzio (Archivio Storico dell' Arte, i.). 1888.

Lettere di Pietro Bembo. Verona. 1743.

Dell' Imprese. Paolo Giovio. 1555.

Lettere di Baldassarre Castiglione. Edizione Serassi. 1769.

Lettere diplomatiche di Castiglione. Ed. Contini. Padova. 1875.

Delle esenzioni della famiglia di Castiglione. Coddè. Mantova. 1780.

Notizie biografiche intorno al Conte Baldassarre Castiglione. Martinati, 1890.

Un Giudizio di lesa romanità. D. Gnoli. Roma. 1891.

Renata di Francia. B. Fontana. Roma. 1889.

Gian Giacomo Trissino. B. Morsolin. Vicenza. 1894.

Francesco Chiericati. B. Morsolin. Vicenza. 1873.

Opere del Trissino. Ed. Maffei. Verona. 1729.

Origini del Teatro Italiano. Alessandro d'Ancona. 2 tom. Torino. 1891.

Cesare Borgia. Ed. Alvisi. Imola. 1878.

Vittoria Colonna. A. Reumont. Torino. 1883.

Veronica Gambara. Rime e lettere raccolte. F. Rizzardi. Brescia. 1759.

Lettere inedite di V. Gambara. R. Renier (Giornale Storico della Letteratura Italiana, xiv.). Torino. 1889.

Vita di Luigi Gonzaga Rodomonte. Affò. Parma. 1780.

Storia di Gazolo. Bergamaski. Casalmaggiore. 1883.

Famiglie celebri Italiane. P. Littà. 8 tom. Milano. 1819-1858.

Storia d'Italia. Fr. Guicciardini. Firenze. 1822.

Opere Inedite. Fr. Guicciardini. 10 tom. Firenze. 1857-1867.

Vita di Vittorino da Feltre. Rosmini. 1845.

Dispacci Giustiniani, 1502-1505. Ed. Villari. 3 tom. Firenze. 1876.

Fonti italiane per lo scoperto del Nuovo Mondo. W. Berghet. Roma. 1892,

Lettere storiche, 1509-1528. Luigi da Porto. Firenze. 1857.

Storia dei Conti e Duchi da Urbino. J. Ugolini. Firenze. 1859.

Sacco di Roma. Narrazioni di Contemporanei. Ed. Milanesi. Firenze. 1867.

Della venuta e dimora in Bologna del S. Pontefice Clemente VII., per la Coronazione di Carlo V. Imperatore. G. Giordano. 1842.

I Diarii di Marino Sanuto, 1496-1535. Stefano Berghet. Venezia. 1885-1900. 58 tom.

Le Novelle del Bandello. Ed. Busdrago. Lucca. 1554.

Il Cortigiano di B. Castiglione, annotato da V. Cian. Firenze. 1894.

Caterina Sforza. P. D. Pasolini. 3 tom. Rome, 1893.

FRENCH.

Les Relations de Leonardo da Vinci avec Isabelle d'Este. Charles Yriarte (Gazette des Beaux Arts). 1888.

Isabelle d'Este et les Artistes de son temps. Charles Yriarte (Gazette des Beaux Arts). 1895 et 1896.

Andrea Mantegna. Charles Yriarte. Paris. 1901.

Alde Manuce et l'Hellénisme à Venise. Ambroise Firmin Didot. Paris. 1875.

Alde Manuce. Lettres et Documents. Armand Baschet. Venise. 1867.

Recherches des Documents dans les Archives de Mantoue. Armand Baschet (Gazette des Beaux Arts). 1866.

Documents inédits tirés des Archives de Mantoue. Armand Baschet (Archivio Storico Italiano, iii.). 1886.

Les Médailleurs Italiens des quinzième et seizième siècles.
Armand. Paris. 1883-1887.

Leonardo da Vinci. Eugène Müntz. Paris. 1898.

Histoire de l'Art pendant la Renaissance. Italie. Paris. Eugène
Müntz. Tom. ii. 1891.

L'Art ferrarais à l'époque des Princes d'Este. Gustave Gruyer.
Paris. 1877. 2 tomes.

Louis XII. et L. Sforza. Louis Pélissier. 1498-1500.

Les Amies de Ludovic Sforza (Revue historique). L. Pélissier. 1891.

César Borgia, sa vie, sa captivité, sa mort. C. Yriarte. Paris. 1887.

Autour des Borgias. C. Yriarte. Paris. 1891.

GERMAN.

Geschichte der Stadt Rom im Mittelalter, Bände vii. und viii.
F. Gregorovius. Stuttgart. 1880.

Geschichte der Stadt Rom. A. Reumont. Leipzig. 1872.

Geschichte der Päpste. Dr. Ludwig Pastor. English edition, 6
vols. 1888.

Andrea Mantegna. Paul Kristeller. English edition by S. A.
Strong. 1901.

Barbara von Brandenburg ("Hohenzollern Jahrbuch," 1897).
Paul Kristeller. 1901.

Barbara von Hohenzollern, Markgräfin von Mantua. B. Hofmann.
Anspach. 1881.

Lucrezia Borgia. F. Gregorovius. Stuttgart. 1875.

Papst Julius II. Moritz Brosch. 1878.

Kunst und Künstler. Dohme. Leipzig. 1878, &c.

Die Gesellschaft der Renaissance in Italien und die Kunst. H.
Janitschek. Stuttgart. 1879.

Der Cultur der Renaissance in Italien. J. Burckhardt. Basel. 1860.

ENGLISH.

Memoirs of the Dukes of Urbino. Dennistoun. 3 vols. 1851.

Life and Works of Raphael. Crowe and Cavalcaselle. 1882.

Life and Works of Titian. Crowe and Cavalcaselle. 1881.

The Renaissance in Italy. J. A. Symonds. 1886.

History of the Papacy. Dr. Creighton. 1897.

Il Principe, by N. Machiavelli. Ed. by L. Burd, with an introduc-
tion by Lord Acton. Oxford, 1891.

The Cambridge Modern History. Ed. by A. W. Ward, G. W.
Prothero and Stanley Leathes. Vol. I. The Renaissance.
1902.

The Emperor Charles V. By Edward Armstrong. 1902.

CONTENTS

CHAPTER I

1474—1490

PAGE

Birth of Isabella d'Este—Her betrothal to Francesco Gonzaga—Visit of the Mantuan envoy to Ferrara—Her letters to the Marquis—Mantegna's Madonna—Elisabetta Gonzaga visits Ferrara—Personal charms of Isabella—Her education and teachers—Classical studies and love of music—Cultured tastes of her parents—Music and art at their court—Cosimo Tura and Ercole Roberti—Marriage of Isabella — Her reception at Mantua 1–18

CHAPTER II

1328—1478

The court of Mantua and house of Gonzaga—Gianfrancesco II., the first Marquis—Vittorino da Feltre and the Casa Zoiosa—Cecilia Gonzaga—Reign of Lodovico Gonzaga and Barbara of Brandenburg—Their patronage of art and learning—Marriage of Federico to Margaret of Bavaria—Betrothal of Dorotea Gonzaga to Galeazzo Sforza—Frescoes of the Camera degli Sposi . . 19–36

CHAPTER III

1478—1490

Reign of Federico Gonzaga—Death of his wife and mother—His love for his daughters — Visit of Lorenzo dei Medici—Accession of Francesco Gonzaga—His character and warlike tastes—Betrothal of Elisabetta Gonzaga to Guidobaldo, Duke of Urbino—His visit to Mantua—Marriage of Elisabetta—Her return to Mantua for

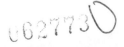

PAGE

Francesco's wedding—Her friendship with Isabella
d'Este—Excursion to the Lago di Garda—Visits to
Ferrara 37–53

CHAPTER IV

1490—1493

Marriage of Beatrice d'Este to Lodovico Sforza—Isabella's
preparations for the wedding—Journey to Pavia and
Milan—Marriage of Alfonso d'Este to Anna Sforza—
Fêtes at Ferrara — Correspondence of Isabella with
Lodovico and Beatrice Sforza — Isabella administers
affairs of State—Galeotto's dyke—Visits to Ferrara,
Milan, and Genoa—The Duchess of Urbino comes to
Mantua—Isabella's affection for Elisabetta . . 54–69

CHAPTER V

1491—1493

Correspondence of Isabella with her family and friends;
with merchants and jewellers—Her intellectual in-
terests — Love of French romances and classical
authors — Greek and Hebrew translations and de-
votional works — Fra Mariano and Savonarola—
Antonio Tebaldeo—Isabella's friendships—Niccolo da
Correggio—Sonnets and eclogues composed for her—
Her love of music—Songs and favourite instruments—
Atalante Migliorotti's lyre—Isabella's *camerino* in the
Castello—Liombeni decorates her *studiolo*—Mantegna
returns from Rome — Paints Isabella's portrait—
Giovanni Santi at Mantua 70–93

CHAPTER VI

1493—1494

Discovery of the New World—The news reaches Mantua—
Birth of the Moro's son—Isabella's journey to Ferrara
and Venice—Reception by the Doge and Signory—
Her relations with Gentile Bellini—Return to Mantua
Francesco Gonzaga at Venice — Death of Duchess

CONTENTS

PAGE

Leonora—Birth of Leonora Gonzaga—Departure of the Duke and Duchess of Urbino—Decorations of Marmirolo and Gonzaga . . . 94–107

CHAPTER VII

1494—1495

Journey of Isabella to Loreto and Urbino—Letters from Gubbio and Urbino—Charles VIII. enters Italy—The Marquis of Mantua refuses his offers—Visit of Isabella to Milan—Conquest of Naples by the French—League against France—Francesco Gonzaga, captain of the armies of the League—Isabella governs Mantua— Battle of the Taro—Heroism of Francesco Gonzaga— Rejoicings at Venice and Mantua—The Jew Daniele Norsa and Mantegna's Madonna della Vittoria. 108–127

CHAPTER VIII

1496—1497

Campaign of Naples—Ferrante recovers his kingdom— Francesco Gonzaga commands the Venetian army— Isabella governs Mantua—Her correspondence and friendship with Lorenzo da Pavia—Birth of her second daughter—Illness of the Marquis—His return to Mantua, and visit to Venice—Death of Ferrante of Naples, of Gilbert de Montpensier, and Beatrice d'Este—Francesco Gonzaga deprived of the office of captain-general of the Venetian armies—Death of Anna Sforza 128–144

CHAPTER IX

1498—1499

Intrigues of Francesco Gonzaga with Venice and Milan— Isabella seeks to reconcile him with Lodovico Sforza— The Marquis goes to Milan and is appointed captain- general of the League—Visit of the Duke of Milan to Mantua—Correspondence of Isabella with Lodovico —Conquest of Milan by the French and flight of the

PAGE

Duke—Louis XII. enters Milan—Isabella pays court
to the French—Receives the Milanese exiles—The
Moro's return and his final surrender at Novara   145–156

CHAPTER X

1497—1500

Isabella's literary and artistic interests—Foundation of the
Studio of the Grotta in the Corte Vecchia—Mantegna's
paintings for the Grotta—Cristoforo Romano comes to
Mantua—Works for the studio—His medal of Isabella
—Correspondence with Niccolo da Correggio—Leon-
ardo da Vinci visits Mantua—Draws Isabella's portrait
—Shows it to Lorenzo da Pavia at Venice—Isabella
intends to raise a monument to Virgil—Her letter to
Jacopo d'Atri   157–176

CHAPTER XI

1500—1502

Birth of Isabella's son Federico—Cæsar Borgia his god-
father—Relations of the Gonzagas with him—Elisabetta
of Urbino goes to Rome — Letters of Sigismondo
Cantelmo—Comedies at Ferrara and Mantua—Treaty
of Granada and partition of Naples—Cæsar Borgia con-
quers Romagna—Abdication and exile of Federico,
King of Naples — Betrothal of Alfonso d'Este to
Lucrezia Borgia — Preparations for the marriage in
Rome — Il Prete's letters to Isabella — Wedding of
Lucrezia and her journey to Ferrara .   .   177–197

CHAPTER XII

1502

Isabella presides at Lucrezia Borgia's marriage festivities—
Reception of the bride at Ferrara—Isabella's letters
to her husband — Comedies, balls, and fêtes — The
ambassadors' gifts — Isabella entertains the French
ambassador—Her interview with the Venetian envoys
—Return to Mantua—Lucrezia Borgia's life at Ferrara
—Her relations with Isabella and the Marquis.   198–216

CHAPTER XIII

1502

PAGE

Isabella's visit to Venice—Her letters to the Marquis—
Courtesy of the Doge and Signory—Her income and
expenditure—Proposed marriage between Federico
Gonzaga and Cæsar Borgia's daughter—Elisabetta of
Urbino goes with Isabella to Porto—Cæsar Borgia
seizes Urbino—Flight of Duke Guidobaldo to Mantua
—Isabella asks for the Venus and Cupid of Urbino—
Cæsar Borgia sends them to Mantua—Michel Angelo's
Cupid sold to Charles I. and brought to England   217–234

CHAPTER XIV

1502—1503

Louis XII. at Milan—He receives the exiled princes and
the Marquis of Mantua—Cæsar Borgia arrives at Milan
and concludes an agreement with the king—Isabella's
warnings to her husband—The Duke and Duchess of
Urbino forced to leave Mantua and take shelter at
Venice—Francesco Gonzaga goes to France—Isabella
governs Mantua—Her negotiations with Borgia regarding her son's marriage—Cæsar's campaign in
Romagna—Treacherous murder of Vitellozza and his
companions—Isabella sends Valentino a present of
masks—Death of the Pope and sudden revolution in
Rome—Return of Duke Guidobaldo to Urbino—Election of Pope Pius III. .   .   •   •   235–257

CHAPTER XV

1503—1505

Death of Pius III.—Election of Julius II.—Return of
Elisabetta to Urbino—Cæsar Borgia sent to Spain, and
his capture—Birth of Isabella's daughter Ippolita—
Francesco Gonzaga resigns his command of the French

PAGE

armies—Returns to Mantua—The French lose Naples—
Comedies at Urbino, Mantua, and Ferrara—Death of
Duke Ercole—Quarrels and plots of the Este brothers
—Marriage of Francesco Maria della Rovere and
Leonora Gonzaga—Sigismondo Gonzaga raised to the
Cardinalate—Letters of Emilia Pia—Castiglione and
Bembo—Death of Suor Osanna—A Dominican vicar-
general—Birth of Isabella's son Ercole.   258–277

CHAPTER XVI

1505—1507

Isabella's visit to Florence—Mario Equicola's treatise, *Nec
spe nec metu*—Ravages of the plague at Mantua—Isa-
bella retires to Sacchetta with her family—Francesco
Gonzaga joins Pope Julius II. at Perugia—Conducts
the papal army against Bologna — Flight of the
Bentivogli—Entry of the Pope—Letters of Isabella—
Frisio sends her antiques from Bologna — Birth of
Isabella's son Ferrante—Visit of Ariosto to Mantua—
Favour shown him by Isabella—Ariosto pays her a
splendid tribute in his *Orlando Furioso* .   278–294

CHAPTER XVII

1507—1508

Louis XII. invites Francesco Gonzaga to help him in the
siege of Genoa—Visit of Isabella to Milan—Fêtes in
the Castello—Isabella's correspondence with Elisabetta
Gonzaga—Her intended journey to France—Death
and funeral of the Duke of Urbino—Visit of Duke
Francesco Maria to Mantua—Birth of Isabella's
youngest daughter—Murder of Ercole Strozzi, and
death of Niccolo da Correggio—Rivalry of Isabella
and Lucrezia Borgia   295–316

CONTENTS

CHAPTER XVIII

1500—1506

PAGE

Isabella's relations with painters during the early years
of the sixteenth century—Her letters to Leonardo da
Vinci—Correspondence with Fra Pietro da Novellara,
Angelo del Tovaglia, Manfredi, and Amadori—She
asks Perugino for a painting for her studio—Description of the Triumph of Chastity composed by Paride
da Ceresara—Perugino's delays—Correspondence with
Malatesta, Tovaglia, &c.   .   •   •   317–340

CHAPTER XIX

1501—1507

Isabella asks Giovanni Bellini for a picture—Her correspondence with Lorenzo da Pavia and Michele Vianello
—The subject changed to a Nativity—Delays of the
painter—Isabella calls in Alvise Marcello—Asks for
her money to be returned—The picture is completed
and sent to Mantua in 1504—Isabella's negotiations
with Giovanni Bellini through Pietro Bembo for
another picture, which is never painted   .   341–361

CHAPTER XX

1504—1512

Mantegna's last works for Isabella d'Este — Illness and
debts—He appeals to Isabella for help, and sells her
his antique bust of Faustina—Calandra's description of
his Comus—Death of Mantegna and tribute of Lorenzo
da Pavia—Pictures in Andrea's workshop—The Comus
finished by Lorenzo Costa — Letters of Antonio
Galeazzo Bentivoglio to Isabella — The Triumph of
Poetry or Court of Isabella—Costa's portrait of the
Marchesa—Francia paints the portrait of her son
Federico and her own—Correspondence on the subject with Casio and Lucrezia Bentivoglio—Death of
Giorgione   •   •   •   •   •   362–392

GENEALOGICAL TABLES   •   •   •   •   393

LIST OF ILLUSTRATIONS

ISABELLA D'ESTE . . . . *Frontispiece*

From the Charcoal Drawing by LEONARDO DA VINCI,
in the Louvre (*Photogravure*)

LODOVICO GONZAGA AND HIS SONS . . . *To face page* 36

By ANDREA MANTEGNA

PONTE SAN GIORGIO, CASTELLO E DUOMO, MAN-
TOVA . . . . „ 70

THE DEATH OF THE VIRGIN, WITH MANTUA IN
THE BACKGROUND . . . . . „ 90

By ANDREA MANTEGNA

THE MADONNA DELLA VITTORIA, WITH THE KNEELING
FIGURE OF THE MARQUIS FRANCESCO . . „ 126

By ANDREA MANTEGNA, in the Louvre (*Photogravure*)

PARNASSUS . . . . „ 158

From the Picture by ANDREA MANTEGNA, in the
Louvre (*Photogravure*)

THE PORTRAIT MEDAL OF ISABELLA D'ESTE . . „ 170

By CRISTOFORO ROMANO, from the Impression set in
Jewels, now in the Imperial Museum, Vienna
(*Photogravure*)

LA BEATA OSANNA . . . . „ 276

By F. BONSIGNORI

CASTELLO DI MANTOVA . . . . . . „ 362

ISABELLA D'ESTE

CHAPTER I

1474—1490

Birth of Isabella d'Este—Her betrothal to Francesco Gonzaga—
Visit of the Mantuan envoy to Ferrara—Her letters to the
Marquis — Mantegna's Madonna—Elisabetta Gonzaga visits
Ferrara—Personal charms of Isabella—Her education and
teachers—Classical studies and love of music—Cultured tastes
of her parents—Music and art at their court—Cosimo Tura
and Ercole Roberti—Marriage of Isabella—Her reception at
Mantua.

" ON the 18th of May 1474 a daughter was born to
Madonna Leonora and Duke Ercole, and she was
given the name of Isabella, and baptized by the
Bishop of Cyprus, the Venetian Ambassador in
Ferrara." [1]

So a contemporary Ferrara diarist, whose chronicle
was published by Muratori, records the birth of Duke
Ercole's elder daughter, Isabella d'Este. The event
took place in the ancient palace on the Cathedral
square which had been the home of the Este
princes long before Bartolino da Novara reared the
massive walls and crenellated towers of the Castello
Rosso at the close of the fourteenth century. There
Giotto and Petrarch had both been entertained as
the guests of princes who, even in those early days,

[1] Muratori, *Italicarum Rerum Scriptores,* vol. xxiv. p. 250.

showed the love of art and letters that distinguished this illustrious race.   There Pisanello and Piero della Francesca painted at the Court of Duke Ercole's elder brothers, Leonello and Borso, and the Venetian master, Jacopo Bellini, introduced the picturesque loggia of the old palace in the background of his drawing of the Queen of Sheba's visit to Solomon. Duke Ercole added the grand marble staircase of the inner court, and the great hall where Ariosto's comedies were performed, which was burnt down just before the poet's death.

Three passions, says Frizzi, the historian of Ferrara,[1] ruled the Duke's heart, the love of building, of the theatre, and of travel. All three were inherited, in no small measure, by his daughter Isabella.   But the execution of Ercole's favourite plans was hindered during the early part of his reign by frequent wars and political troubles.   One night, when Isabella was only two years old, and her brother Alfonso was still an infant, the Duke's nephew, Niccolo d'Este, suddenly attacked the palace at the head of a band of armed conspirators, and Duchess Leonora and her three children had barely time to escape by the covered way into the Castello ; and before she was eight the Venetian armies invaded her father's dominions, and planted the Lion of St. Mark in the park of his villa at Belfiore, while the Duke himself lay at the point of death in the Castello.   All these dangers, however, were safely overcome by the valour and skilful diplomacy of the Duke, loyally supported by his brave wife and faithful subjects, and the treaty concluded at Bagnolo in 1484 was followed by a long period of peace and prosperity.

[1] *Storia di Ferrara,* vol. iv.

Meanwhile, Isabella grew up under her good mother's watchful eyes. When, in the summer of 1477, Leonora took her young family to visit her old father, King Ferrante, at Naples, her three-year-old daughter was already a fascinating child, and her uncle Federico, afterwards King of Naples, was heard to say that if she were not his niece he would like to make her his bride! At the old king's urgent request, the Duchess consented to leave her younger daughter Beatrice at her grandfather's court for the next eight years, but brought Isabella back with her to Ferrara. Three years afterwards the child-princess was betrothed to young Giovanni Francesco Gonzaga, the eldest son of Federico, Marquis of Mantua.

The two houses were already closely connected, both by friendship and marriage. Leonello, the accomplished Duke, whose hooked nose and low forehead are familiar to us in Pisanello's medals and portraits, had married Federico's aunt, Margherita Gonzaga, and his own sister Lucia had been the wife of Margherita's brother, Carlo Gonzaga. Margherita, whose charming portrait, with its background of columbines and butterflies, painted by Pisanello at the time of her wedding, is still preserved in the Louvre, died in July 1439, only four years after her marriage. But her brother, the Marquis Lodovico, had proved a loyal friend to Duke Ercole, and had refused to support his nephew Niccolo in his plot to seize the Duchess and her children. His son and successor, Federico, showed the same cordial feeling for his neighbour, and paid several visits to Ferrara. Early in April 1480, he sent his trusted servant, Beltramino Cusatro, to propose a marriage between his eldest son, a boy of fourteen, and the Duke's little daughter, Isabella, now a child of five years. Ercole, who had good reason to fear the enmity of Venice, and was the more anxious to strengthen his alliance with this near neighbour, gladly accepted his proposals, and as soon as preliminary matters had been arranged with the envoy, the Duke sent for his little daughter.

" Madonna Isabella," wrote Cusatro to his master, " was then led in to see me, and I questioned her on many subjects, to all of which she replied with rare good sense and quickness. Her answers seemed truly miraculous in a child of six, and although I had already heard much of her singular intelligence, I could never have imagined such a thing to be possible."

A few days afterwards the envoy sent a portrait of the youthful princess by Cosimo Tura, the Duke's court-painter, to Mantua, with the following note : " I send the portrait of Madonna Isabella, so that Your Highness and Don Francesco may see her face, but I can assure you that her marvellous knowledge and intelligence are far more worthy of admiration."

The excellent impression which the little bride made upon Cusatro was confirmed by another Mantuan envoy, who informed the Marquis that he had seen Madonna Isabella dance with her master Messer Ambrogio, a Jew in the Duke of Urbino's service, and that the grace and elegance of her movements were amazing in one of her tender age.[1]

On the Feast of St. George, always a great day at the Court of Ferrara, another envoy arrived from Duchess Bona of Milan, and her brother-

[1] A. Luzio, *I Precettori d'Isabella d'Este*, p. 12.

in-law, the Regent Lodovico Sforza, asking for
Madonna Isabella's hand on behalf of the said Signor
Lodovico. Since, however, his elder daughter was
already betrothed, the Duke offered to give Lodovico
the hand of his younger daughter, Beatrice, with
the consent of her grandfather, the King of Naples,
who warmly approved of the Milanese alliance. So
on the 28th of May, the betrothal of the Duke's
two daughters was publicly proclaimed on the Piazza
in front of the Castello.

In the following spring, the Marquis of Mantua
brought his son Francesco to spend the Feast of St.
George at Ferrara, and make acquaintance with his
bride and her family. The Mantuan chronicler,
Schivenoglia, relates how on this occasion the Marquis and his suite of six hundred followers sailed
down the Po in four bucentaurs, how Duke Ercole,
in his anxiety to do his guests honour, fed the whole
party on lamb and veal and similar delicacies during
the four days which they spent in Ferrara, and how
his master's famous Barbary horses won the race, and
carried back the *palio* of cloth of gold in triumph to
Mantua. After this first meeting with her future
husband, Isabella frequently exchanged letters with
Francesco, who sent her presents and verses written
in her honour by the poets at his court. Some of
these formal little notes, in Isabella's own hand-
writing, are still preserved, Dr. Luzio tells us, in the
Gonzaga Archives. On the 22nd of May 1483, the
little princess writes from Modena, where the Duke's
children had been sent for safety during the war with
Venice, thanking Francesco for his inquiries after her
health. " Although when your letters and presents
reached me I was ill, their arrival has made me

suddenly well. But when I heard that if I were still suffering from illness Your Highness thought of coming to Modena, to see me, I almost wished myself ill again, if only to have the pleasure of seeing you."[1]

A year later the Marquis Federico died, and Isabella wrote to condole with Francesco on his father's death, begging him to dry his tears and take comfort for her sake. The new Marquis from the first showed himself an ardent lover, and neglected no opportunity of paying attention to his bride's family. Hearing that the Duchess of Ferrara was anxious to possess a certain Madonna by the hand of Andrea Mantegna, the loyal servant and court-painter of the Gonzagas, he wrote to that master on the 6th of November 1485, enclosing Leonora's letter, and begging him to comply with her request.

" *Carissime noster.* Our most illustrious Madonna the Duchess of Ferrara, as you will see by the letters which we enclose in order that you may the better understand her wishes, is very anxious to have a certain picture by your hand. We trust that you will satisfy this lady, and use the utmost diligence to finish the said picture, and beg of you to put forth all your powers, as we feel sure you will do, and that as quickly as possible, since we are most desirous to gratify the said illustrious Madonna." Goïto, Nov. 6, 1485.

On the same day Francesco wrote to his future mother-in-law :—

" Hearing that Your Excellency desires to have a picture of the Madonna with some other figures that is still unfinished by the hand of Andrea Mantegna,

---

[1] A. Luzio, *I Precettori d'Isabella d'Este*, p. 13.

I have told him to finish it with the utmost care, and hope to bring it with me, when I come, as I hope, before long, to visit Your Illustrious Highness. If not, I will send it you, as it is my greatest pleasure to be able to do anything for you. To whom I commend myself, praying that you may fare well."

A week later, the impatient young Prince wrote again to Mantegna on the subject :—

" *Carissime noster.* We wrote before to beg you to finish a picture of the Madonna with other figures, at the prayer of that illustrious Madonna the Duchess of Ferrara, but do not know if you have yet put your hand to the work, so now we repeat that you must finish it as quickly as possible, seeing that we greatly desire this thing, in order to be able to satisfy the wish of the said lady as soon as possible." Goïto, Nov. 14, 1485.

Again on the 12th December he returned to the charge :—

" We must remind you to lose no time in finishing the picture which you have begun, and which we wish to give the Duchess of Ferrara, and hope you will use such diligence that we may be able to present it to her this Christmas, and we will take care that you are well rewarded, and that your labour is not thrown away."

Mantegna did not fail to obey his young lord's command, and on the 15th Francesco wrote as follows :—

" We are sure that in finishing this picture you will use such diligence as will do you honour, and that it will bring you no small glory. And as Lodovico of Bologna is going to Venice, you had better see him about that varnish, if you have not already spoken to him, that he may bring or send you some without delay."[1]

Leonora on her part wrote to express her joy not only at the prospect of receiving Messer Andrea's Madonna, but of seeing Francesco himself, and the young Marquis met with a cordial welcome when he reached Ferrara with his precious picture. Mantegna's Madonna was given a place among Leonora's choicest treasures, and is mentioned in the inventory of her pictures, taken after her death, as "a painting on panel of Our Lady and her Son with seraphim, by the hand of Mantegna." The picture now hangs in the Brera, and its smiling cherub faces and glowing tints are almost as fresh and fair as on the day on which they left Andrea's workshop.

It is uncertain if Leonora herself brought her daughter to visit her affianced husband at Mantua, and there saw Mantegna at work on the great series of Triumphs which he was painting for the Marquis, but we know that, in February 1488, Francesco's sister Elisabetta visited Ferrara on her way to celebrate her marriage at Urbino, and received the rite of confirmation from the Bishop of Ferrara in the chapel of the ducal palace in the presence of the Duke and Duchess and their family. There Isabella met the sister-in-law who was to become her dearest and closest friend, and the warm welcome which the motherless young Princess received from the kind Duchess Leonora, and the sisterly affection of the Marchesana, were a great consolation to her in the grief which she felt at parting from her brothers

---

[1] *Archivio Gonzaga, Copialettera,* 126, quoted in *Andrea Mantegna,* by Paul Kristeller, App., p. 482.

and sister and leaving the happy home of her childhood.[1]

By this time Isabella herself had reached the age of fourteen, and was growing up a beautiful and accomplished maiden. She inherited her mother's regular features, but, unlike her sister Beatrice, had the fair hair and white skin which we see in Titian's portrait at Vienna. According to Mario Equicola, who spent many years in the Marchesa's service, her eyes were black and sparkling, her hair yellow, and her complexion one of dazzling brilliancy. Trissino, the great Vicenza humanist, in his *Ritratti*, describes the rippling golden hair that flowed in thick masses over her shoulders, recalling Petrarch's lines, "*Una donna più bella assai che'l sole;*" and tells us that, although only of middle height, she was remarkable for the dignity of her carriage and stately grace of her head and neck. But, as the Mantuan envoy told his master, her gifts of mind were still more striking than those of her person. Like other princesses of the day, Isabella received a classical education, and in after years acquired the reputation of speaking the Latin tongue better than any woman of her age. Battista Guarino, a son of the famous Verona scholar who taught her uncle Duke Leonello, and lectured in the University to the most distinguished students in Italy, was her first teacher, and during the famine of 1482 begged the Marquis of Mantua for a grant of wheat, in order that he might the better instruct Donna Isabella, "who is now," he adds, "thank God, in perfect health, and learns with a marvellous facility far beyond her years." Guarino was succeeded by another tutor, Jacopo Gallino, who became

[1] A. Luzio e R. Renier, *Mantova e Urbino*, p. 16

fondly attached to his clever pupil, and often reminded the Marchesana in later years of the happy
days when they studied the grammar of Chrysolaras
together, and she repeated the Eclogues of Virgil
and the Epistles of Cicero by heart, or construed
the Æneid with such rare grace and fluency. At
the same time the more womanly arts were not
neglected in Isabella's education. She learnt to
dance, as we have already seen, from her baby-
hood, and two bone needles and one gold needle,
for Madonna Isabella's embroidery, are found among
the entries in the household accounts of the ducal
family.[1] At an early age she showed signs of the
musical tastes for which she was afterwards distinguished, and which she shared with the other
members of her race. Duke Leonello played the
guitar, and her own brother Alfonso was an excellent violinist and frequently took part in public
performances. Duchess Leonora played the harp,
and both her daughters learnt the lute and clari-
chord. As a child, Isabella studied music under
Don Giovanni Martino, a German priest who had
been brought from Constance to train the singers
of the ducal chapel. After her marriage she had
many masters, and often said laughingly that she
was but a poor pupil, who did her teachers little
credit.[2] But she had a beautiful voice, and accompanied herself on the lute with exquisite skill; and
the favoured guests who were privileged to hear her
sing and play all went away charmed. Many were

---

[1] *Registro de' Mandati,* c. 48, quoted by Luzio and Renier in
Giorn. St. d. Lett. It., vol. xxxvii. p. 2.

[2] S. Davari, *Musica in Mantova, Rivista Stor. Mants.,* i. 61;
Bertolotti, *Musica alla Corte dei Gonzaga.*

the lines from Virgil and the sonnets of Petrarch which Niccolo da Correggio or Pietro Bembo set to music for her benefit, and Trissino declares that the sweetness of her voice lured the Sirens from their rocks, and charmed the wild beasts and stones with the magic of Orpheus.

But the atmosphere of culture and refinement in which Isabella grew up helped to develop her powers more than the teaching of any masters. Under the rule of three accomplished Dukes, Ferrara had become a centre of art and learning. The foremost scholars and the best poets were attracted to a court where Matteo Boiardo wrote his *Orlando Innamorato*, and Francesco Bello, the blind improvisatore, charmed all men by his poetic recitations. Above all, Isabella had the example of her own parents before her eyes. Duke Ercole's youth had been spent at the court of Naples, where he was sent after his father's death, and early acquired distinction as a valiant soldier. But one day, during a serious attack of illness, he happened to read a translation of Quintus Curtius, which interested him so deeply that from that time he devoted all his leisure hours to classical studies. When Lodovico Sforza asked him for the loan of his translation of Dionysius Cassius he replied that he could not part with the manuscript, which he read almost every day, but would have it copied for his son-in-law. Plutarch and Xenophon, Euripides and Seneca were among his favourite authors, and the comedies of Plautus and Terence were translated into Italian verse and acted at Ferrara under his direction. He added largely to the ducal library founded by his brother Leonello and kept a careful register of all the books which his friends borrowed. His wife Leonora had a private collection of her own favourite authors, which included many Italian versions of French and Breton romances, of Spanish tales such as *Il Carcer d'Amore*, which she brought with her from Naples, and of Pliny's "Letters" and Cæsar's "Commentaries," as well as the *Fioretti* of St. Francis and the *De Consolatione* of Boethius.

From her birth, Isabella was surrounded by the finest works of art. The walls of her mother's rooms were covered with paintings by the best Flemish and Italian masters; a crucifix by Jacopo Bellini hung over her father's writing desk. The frescoes of Pisanello and Piero della Francesca, the medals of Sperandio, the richest tapestries and the finest majolica from Faenza and Urbino adorned the palaces and villas of Ferrara. Much of Isabella's childhood was spent in her father's favourite country house, the Schifanoia or Sans Souci of the Este princes, which the Ferrarese master Francesco Cossa and his followers had decorated with a famous series of hunting and pastoral subjects. And during these years architects and painters were continually at work both in the Castello and in the beautiful villa of Belriguardo on the banks of the Po, which was said to contain as many rooms as days in the year. The chapel was decorated with frescoes by Cosimo Tura, who also, in his capacity of court-painter, executed the portraits of Isabella and Beatrice for their affianced husbands. When, in 1487, Cosimo became too old and infirm for his work, another excellent Ferrara painter, Ercole Roberti, originally the son of a porter in the Castello, took his place and was employed to decorate the new halls which the Duke had lately built at Belriguardo. A new chapel

was also added to the Castello, and amongst the
works of art which adorned its walls was a stucco
group by a Ferrara sculptor representing the Duchess
with her daughter Isabella kneeling on a brocade
cushion at her feet.[1]

Thus, from early youth, Isabella not only learnt
how to appreciate the finest art, but to see the enlightened patronage which her parents bestowed alike
on native and foreign masters.   She heard her father
discuss with keen interest the latest plans for the
decoration of villas and churches, and watched Italian
and Spanish embroiderers at work under her mother's
superintendence.   She saw Duke Ercole's Italian
version of the *Menœchmi*, and her cousin Niccolo da
Correggio's pastoral romance of *Cefalo* acted on a
stage fitted up in the old Palazzo della Ragione.
She met the most brilliant men and women of the
day at her father's table, and heard the best conversation and the most refined criticism from their
lips.   And she grew up a charming and graceful
maiden, adored by her parents and teachers and
beloved by all around her.

In 1487, the Duke's illegitimate daughter Lucrezia
was married to Count Annibale, a son of Giovanni
Bentivoglio, lord of Bologna, and Francia, the famous
goldsmith of that city, who often worked for Leonora,
was employed to design the gold and silver *credenza*
or dinner-service used on this occasion, with lamps
encrusted with flowers and foliage, and goblets
studded with precious gems.   The marriage of
Isabella, who was three years younger than her
half-sister, was delayed for a time.   The Duke and

[1] Gustave Gruyer, *L'Art Ferrarais à l'époque des Princes d'Este,*
vol. ii. p. 136.

Duchess were reluctant to part from their beloved child, and wished the wedding of their two daughters to take place at the same time. But Lodovico Sforza showed little inclination to fix the date of his marriage, while Francesco Gonzaga pressed his suit eagerly, and Leonora finally agreed that Isabella's wedding should take place in the spring of 1490, before she had completed her sixteenth year. Great preparations were made both at Mantua and Ferrara for the coming event. All through the year painters, carvers, and goldsmiths were engaged in preparing the bride's trousseau, under her mother's watchful eye. Early in 1489 [1] Ercole Roberti was sent to Venice, to buy gold-leaf and ultramarine for the decoration of the wedding chests. On his return he painted thirteen cassoni, for which he employed eleven thousand gold leaves, and designed the nuptial bed, as well as a magnificent chariot and gilded bucentaur which the Duke presented to his daughter. The tapestries and hangings for her rooms were made in Venice, seals and buttons and silver boxes for her use were engraved by Ferrarese artists, and a portable silver altar, richly chased and embossed, together with ornaments and office-books to match, were ordered from the skilled Milanese goldsmith Fra Rocco. The girdle or *majestate*, worn by royal brides and elaborately worked in gold and silver, was also ordered from Fra Rocco, who devoted many months to the task, and received 600 ducats from the Duke. No less than 2000 ducats were paid him for a similar belt which he made the next year for Beatrice, and which is described by contemporaries as a still greater marvel of workmanship. Isabella's

---

[1] Gruyer, *op. cit.*, ii. 153.

dowry had been fixed at 25,000 ducats, while her trousseau was valued at 2000 ducats, and the jewels and other costly objects given her by the Duke were held to be worth another 3000, so that the whole of her marriage portion and outfit did not exceed 30,000 ducats, a modest fortune compared to her mother's dowry of 80,000 ducats and the 150,000 ducats that were settled on her sister-in-law Anna Sforza.

The wedding was celebrated at Ferrara on the 11th of February 1490, and after the ceremony in the ducal chapel, the bride rode through the streets of the city in her fine new chariot draped with cloth of gold, with the Duke of Urbino on horseback on her right and the Ambassador of Naples on her left. The banquet which followed was one of the most sumptuous ever held in the Castello of Ferrara. The walls of the Sala Grande were hung with the Arras tapestries brought from Naples by Duchess Leonora, including the "Queen of Sheba's Visit to Solomon," and six pieces known as "La Pastourelle," worked by hand in gold and silver and coloured silks of exquisite delicacy. These priceless hangings originally came to Naples with Queen Joan, and it was said that Flemish workers had been employed upon them during more than a hundred years. The Este princes held the tapestries among their choicest possessions and only used them on great occasions; and in after years they excited the admiration of the Emperor Charles V. when he visited Reggio as the guest of Alfonso d'Este, and insisted on examining each piece separately by torchlight. The magnificent dinner-service used at Isabella's wedding had been made in Venice by a renowned goldsmith, Giorgio da Ragusa, from Cosimo Tura's designs. Crystal flagons and dishes of gold and enamel were supported by griffins and satyrs, dolphins and satyrs, the handles of golden bowls and cornucopias laden with fruit were adorned with genii or the eagles of the house of Este, while two hundred and fifty little banners, painted by Ferrara artists with the Este and Gonzaga arms, adorned the temples and pyramids of gilt and coloured sugar that were a triumph of the confectioner's art.[1]

On the following day the wedding party set out in the richly carved and gilded bucentaur, attended by four galleys and fifty boats, for Mantua, and sailed up the Po. The bride was accompanied by her parents, with their three young sons, Alfonso, Ferrante, and the future Cardinal Ippolito, as well as by her cousins, Alberto d'Este, Niccolo and Borso da Correggio, and a hundred chosen courtiers, who escorted her to the gates of Mantua. On the 15th of February she made her triumphal entry into the city, riding between the Marquis and the Duke of Urbino, and followed by the Ambassadors of France, Naples, Milan, Venice, Florence, Genoa, Pisa, and other Italian States. The loyal citizens of Mantua hailed their young Marchesana with enthusiasm, and it is said that as many as 17,000 spectators were assembled in the town that day. The streets were hung with brocades and garlands of flowers. At the Porta Pradella a choir of white-robed children welcomed the bride with songs and recitations. At the Ponte S. Jacopo, on the Piazza in front of Alberti's church of S. Andrea, at the

---

[1] Gruyer, *op. cit.*, ii. 83.

gates of the park, and on the drawbridge of the
Castello, pageants and musical entertainments were
prepared in her honour. At one point the seven
planets and nine ranks of angelic orders welcomed
her coming, and a fair boy with angel wings recited
an epithalamium composed for the occasion at the
foot of the grand staircase of the Castello di Corte.
There Elisabetta Gonzaga received the bride, and
the princely guests sat down to a banquet in the
state rooms, while the immense crowds assembled
on the Piazza outside were feasted at the public
expense, and the fountains and cisterns ran with
wine. The Marquis had borrowed large stores of
gold and silver plate, of carpets and hangings from
all his friends and kinsfolk. Giovanni Bentivoglio,
Marco Pio of Carpi, the Gonzagas of Bozzolo, and
many of Isabella's relatives had placed their treasures
at his disposal for the occasion, and his brother-in-
law, Duke Guidobaldo, had lent him the famous
tapestries of the Trojan war, which were the glory
of the palace of Urbino. The festivities were prolonged until the last day of the carnival. Tourna-
ments and dances and torchlight processions followed each other in rapid succession, and each day
a fresh banquet was spread on tables in the Piazza,
and *confetti*, representing cities, castles, churches,
and animals in endless variety, were distributed to
the delighted populace.[1]

Only one thing was wanting to complete the
splendour of the festival. This was the presence of
Andrea Mantegna, the great master who had spent
thirty years in the service of the Gonzagas, and
whose genius was so highly esteemed by the young

---

[1] D'Arco, *Notizie d'Isabella Estense*, p. 31.

Marquis. In June 1488, Francesco had given him leave to go to Rome, at the earnest request of Pope Innocent VIII., who employed him to paint his new chapel of the Belvedere. The artist, however, was not happy at the Vatican, and complained bitterly in his letters to the Marquis of the irregular payments and indifferent treatment which he received from the Pope, declaring that he was a child of the house of Gonzaga, and wished to live and die in their service. He was uneasy too about his unfinished Triumphs in the Castello of Mantua, and begged the Marquis to see that the rain did not come in through the windows and damage these canvases, which were his best and most perfect works. Francesco replied in a friendly letter, assuring him that his Triumphs were perfectly safe, and wrote again at Christmas 1489, begging the painter to return as soon as possible, since his help was indispensable in preparing the pageants and decorations for the wedding. But the messenger who brought the letter found Andrea ill in bed and the Pope's frescoes unfinished, and the Marquis was forced to celebrate his marriage without the presence of his favourite painter.

CHAPTER II

The court of Mantua and house of Gonzaga—Gianfrancesco II.,
the first Marquis—Vittorino da Feltre and the Casa Zoiosa—
Cecilia Gonzaga—Reign of Lodovico Gonzaga and Barbara of
Brandenburg—Their patronage of art and learning—Marri-
age of Federico to Margaret of Bavaria—Betrothal of Dorotea
Gonzaga to Galeazzo Sforza—Frescoes of the Camera degli
Sposi.

MANTUA, which now became the home of Isabella
d'Este, was a comparatively small city. The population only numbered 28,000, and the domains of the
Marquis Francesco were both poorer and smaller than
the Duchy of Ferrara. But under the rule of the
Gonzaga family this little state had already acquired
an important position in North Italy. Since the hard-
fought day in 1328, when Lodovico Gonzaga defeated
the rival family of the Buonacolsi, and was chosen captain of the people, and afterwards appointed Vicar-
General by the Emperor, Mantua had rapidly increased
in power and prosperity. His successors not only won
the love of their subjects by their wise and paternal
government, but by their hereditary valour and
skilful diplomacy succeeded in maintaining their
independence against their two powerful neighbours,
Venice and Milan. There was less splendour and
luxury at the court of Mantua than at Ferrara, but
the Gonzagas showed as genuine a love of art and
learning as the princes of the house of Este.
Gianfrancesco I., the fourth prince of his race to bear

sway in Mantua, employed Bartolino da Novara, the
architect of the Castello Rosso of Ferrara, to build
the strong Castello, with the four massive towers at
each angle, overlooking the lakes formed by the
waters of the Mincio, on the east side of the city.
He also rebuilt the old bridge of San Giorgio, which
crosses the Lago di Mezzo opposite the Castello, and
the fine Lombard-Gothic Duomo on the neighbouring Piazza di San Pietro, which Giulio Romano
transformed into a late Renaissance building in the
reign of Isabella d'Este's grandson. The same
prince paid a visit to the south of France in 1389,
and during his residence in that country added sixty-
seven French books to his library, which at his death
numbered 400 volumes.[1]

Gianfrancesco II., who succeeded his father in
1407, was raised to the dignity of Marquis when the
Emperor Sigismund visited Mantua in 1433. This
wise and enlightened prince strengthened the fortifi-
cations of the city, drained the neighbouring marshes,
and did his best to encourage agriculture, and the
manufacture of cloth, which remained the staple
industry of Mantua until the sack of 1630. Like
most of the Gonzaga princes, he served the rival
States of Venice and Milan alternately, but was a
liberal patron of learning, and attracted the best
foreign artists to his court. Brunellesco came to
Mantua twice, in 1432 and in 1436, to give him advice
as to the construction of dykes. Alberti, the distinguished architect, dedicated his " Treatise on
Painting " to him, and even that greedy and querulous
humanist, Filelfo, extolled him as the most generous
of patrons. His excellent wife, Paola Malatesta,

1 W. Braghirolli in *Romania*, 1880.

shared his cultured tastes, and trained her numerous
sons and daughters in habits of virtue and piety.   To
her even more than to her husband was due the
choice of Vittorino da Feltre as tutor to the Gonzaga princes.   This remarkable man became renowned
among living scholars, not only for his knowledge of
Greek, but for the high ideal of education which he
held up before the age.   In his eyes there was no
loftier mission than that of the schoolmaster, and all
his powers were devoted to this high calling.   The
Casa Zoiosa or *Maison Joyeuse*, where he settled in
1425, at Gianfrancesco's invitation, close to the
Castello, soon became famous throughout Italy.
Here, in these fair halls, on the banks of the lake,
adorned with frescoes and surrounded with avenues
of plane trees and acacias, the high-born youths and
maidens in Vittorino's charge received that complete
training of body and mind which he held to be the
best preparation for life.   He began by making a
few necessary reforms.   His pupils' superfluous servants were dismissed, the use of gold and silver plate
and of highly spiced dishes at their table was pro-
hibited, and simple but abundant fare was provided.
All swearing and bad language was forbidden, lying
was treated as the blackest of crimes, good manners
were especially encouraged, and Church festivals and
fasts were strictly observed, since in Vittorino's eyes
true learning was inseparable from virtue and re-
ligion.   His course of instruction included Latin and
Greek, mathematics, grammar, logic, philosophy,
music, singing and dancing, and the hours of
study were pleasantly varied by games at *palla* in the
meadows along the Mincio, and shooting, swimming,
and fencing matches, as well as occasional fishing and

hunting expeditions.   He began by reading carefully
chosen selections from Virgil and Cicero, Homer and
Demosthenes aloud to his scholars, explaining the
meaning as he went along, and made them learn these
passages by heart as the best way of forming their
style.   Afterwards he laid down a few simple rules for
their guidance in composition, telling them to be sure,
first of all, that they had something to say, and then
to see that they said it frankly and simply, avoiding
the subtleties of the schools.   " I want to teach my
pupils how to think," he said, "not to split hairs."
Vittorino himself always paid special attention to
backward pupils, and received many poor scholars
who could not afford to pay the usual fees, teaching
them, as he said, "for the love of God."   On summer
days he often took his scholars to a small country
house on the height of Andes or Pietola, the birth-
place of Virgil, which was the only property that he
ever acquired, and told them stories of Perseus and
Hercules, while they rested on the grass after their
games ; and once or twice in the season more distant
expeditions were made to the shores of the Lake of
Garda or the Alps of Tyrol.[1]

Soon the fame of Vittorino's gymnasium brought
him pupils from all parts of Italy.   One of these
was Federico di Montefeltro, the great and good
Duke of Urbino, who placed his beloved teacher's
portrait in his palace, with the following inscription : " In honour of his saintly master Vittorino da
Feltre, who by word and example instructed him in
all human excellence, Federico has set this here."
Lodovico Gonzaga, the eldest of Gianfrancesco's

---

[1] *Vittorino da Feltre, Prendilacqua ;* Benoit, *Vittorin de Feltre ;*
S. Paglia in *Archivio Storico Lombardo,* xi. 150.

sons, retained the deepest respect for his master all through his life, and after he succeeded his father as Marquis, would never sit down in his old teacher's presence. His brothers Gianlucido and Alessandro, who were cut off from public life by a spinal disease which they inherited from their mother Paola, found their best consolation in literary pursuits, and Gianlucido is said to have known the whole of Virgil by heart. Their sister Margherita charmed her cultured husband, Duke Leonello d'Este, by the elegance of her Latin letters, and he wrote to tell her how much he rejoiced to think that she enjoyed the advantage of Vittorino's instruction, being persuaded that for " virtue, learning, and a rare and excellent way of teaching good manners," this master surpassed all others. But the most accomplished of Vittorino's pupils was the Marquis's youngest daughter, Cecilia Gonzaga. At eight years she read the works of Chrysostom, and amazed learned visitors to Casa Zoiosa by the ease with which she recited Latin verse. As she grew up her charms and sweetness of nature captivated young and old, but trouble arose when her hand was sought by Odd' Antonio di Montefeltro, the elder brother of Federico, who, unlike him, was a prince of notoriously bad character. In vain Cecilia pleaded her wish to take the veil and devote herself to a life of contemplation, and the papal protonotary Gregorio Correr, who, as Abbot of S. Zeno of Verona, employed Mantegna to paint his noble triptych in that church, dedicated to her his treatise *De Fugiendo Sæculo.* Her father was bent on the marriage, and punished Cecilia with blows and imprisonment. At length Paola's tears and Vittorino's remonstrances brought the Marquis

to a better mind, and with his sanction Cecilia
entered the convent of Corpus Domini, a community
of Poor Clares founded by her mother, who came to
end her own days there, after Gianfrancesco's death in
1444.   When Pisanello visited Mantua three years
afterwards, he designed the beautiful medal inscribed
with the words *Cecilia Virgo*, showing on one side
a profile portrait of her delicate and refined features,
and on the other her seated figure, with the crescent
moon and unicorn as emblems of her maidenhood.
Four years after this she died, before she was quite
twenty-five.[1]

Vittorino's good offices were exerted on behalf of
another of his pupils, Lodovico Gonzaga, who in a fit
of anger at seeing his younger brother Carlo preferred to him, fled to the camp of Filippo Visconti,
Duke of Milan, and took up arms against his father.
Gianfrancesco vowed that he would disinherit this
undutiful son, and it was only at the end of three
years, in deference to Paola and Vittorino's entreaties,
that he consented to a reconciliation and publicly recognised Lodovico as his heir.   Meanwhile the young
prince's little German bride, Barbara von Brandenburg, was growing up in his mother's charge, and
profiting by Vittorino's instructions.   The marriage
had been arranged by the Emperor Sigismund when
he visited Mantua in 1433, and that autumn an
escort of 200 Mantuan courtiers was sent to Augs-
burg to bring back the ten-year-old princess, with a
golden chariot drawn by four horses, and a robe of
gold brocade so stiff and splendid that the German
ladies exclaimed "it stood up of itself!"   Soon after
Lodovico's return, in 1440, the marriage was solem-

[1] Paglia, *op. cit.*; Pastor, "History of the Popes," i. 46.

nised, and Barbara proved the best of wives and
mothers and the most admirable helpmeet to her
husband during the thirty-four years of his long
reign.[1]

Amidst the cares of state and perils of war,
Lodovico did not forget the lessons which he had
learnt in the Casa Zoiosa, and while, as captain of
the Florentine and Milanese armies, he proved his
valour on many a hard-fought field, he ruled his
people wisely and well, and showed a zeal for
learning and an enlightened love of art worthy of
Vittorino's scholar. Mindful of the happy days
when he and his comrades played together in the
fields of Pietola, he collected all the manuscripts of
Virgil that he could obtain, and Platina, whom he
employed to revise the text, wrote a poem called
"The Dream of the Marquis," in which Virgil
returns from the Elysian fields and begs Lodovico
to complete his great work and purge his text from
the errors of the copyists. Petrarch and Dante were
as dear to him as the classical poets. He employed
artists to illuminate the Æneid and *Divina Com-
media*, and a richly illustrated MS. of the *Filocolo*
of Boccaccio from his collection, bearing the black
eagles and lions of the Gonzagas, is now preserved in
the Bodleian Library at Oxford. One autumn, when
he was taking the baths at Petriolo, he begged his wife
to send him his St. Augustine, Quintus Curtius and
Lucan, which had been left behind at Mantua.
Another time he borrowed Borso d'Este's precious
Codex of Pliny, while his wife begged the Duke to
lend her S. Caterina of Siena's prayers. Lodovico

[1] B. Hoffmann, *Barbara von Hohenzollern Markgräfin von Mantua;*
P. Kristeller in *Hohenzollern Jahrbuch*, 1899, p. 66, &c.

was also much interested in natural history, and
made a valuable collection of books with illustrations
of birds and animals.   Under his patronage a printing-
press was set up in Mantua, and Boccaccio's *De-
camerone* was the first book published there in 1473.

The decoration of his capital was another object
to which this admirable prince devoted his best
attention.   At his invitation Alberti paid repeated
visits to Mantua, and designed the chapel of the
Incoronata in the Duomo, and the churches of S.
Sebastian and S. Andrea.   This last church, which
was founded in 1472, to receive the sacred blood said
to have been brought to Mantua by the centurion
Longinus, was justly admired as one of the earliest
and most successful examples of ecclesiastical architecture in the classical style.   Alberti's designs were
mostly carried out by Luca Fancelli, another Tuscan
architect, who entered Lodovico's service in 1450,
and built or improved the beautiful ducal villas at
Goïto, Cavriana, Gonzaga, and Revere, which are so
often mentioned in Isabella d'Este's letters.   The
best sculptors and painters were employed by
Lodovico to decorate these sumptuous country
houses.   Pisanello adorned a hall in the Castello
with frescoes, and remained at Mantua until he
received an imperious summons from Leonello
d'Este, threatening him with the forfeiture of all
his property in Ferrara if he did not return immediately.   Donatello spent nearly two years at Mantua,
where he executed the noble bronze bust of Lodovico,
now at Berlin, and began the Arca of St. Anselm in
the Duomo.   The Marquis often employed the great
Florentine sculptor to send him antiques, but complained bitterly how difficult it was to induce him to

finish anything. He was more fortunate with Mantegna, who, after repeated and urgent invitations,
at length came to Mantua in the summer of 1459,
and remained there until his death, half-a-century
later.

That love of antiquity with which Vittorino had
inspired him in early youth, and which he admired
in Alberti's architectural designs, first led him to
appreciate the genius of this great Paduan master,
who was animated with the true classical spirit. He
treated Andrea with unalterable kindness, gave him
a liberal salary of fifteen ducats a month, with
supplies of corn, wood, wine, and lodgings for his
family, and bore patiently with the irritable master's
frequent complaints against the tailor who had spoilt
his new coat, or the neighbour who had robbed his
orchard of five hundred quinces. And when in the
last years of his reign the treasury was exhausted
by a long war, and the plague was raging in Mantua,
the good Marquis replied to Andrea's bitter re-
proaches in the following noble and kindly letter:

" Andrea," he wrote from Goïto, " we have received a letter from you which it really seems to us
that you need not have written, since we perfectly
remember the promises we made when you entered
our service, neither, as it seems to us, have we
failed to keep these promises or to do our utmost
for you. But you cannot take from us what we
have not got, and you yourself have seen that, when
we have had the means, we have never failed to do
all in our power for you and our other servants,
and that gladly and with good will. It is true that,
since we have not received our usual revenues during
the last few months, we have been obliged to defer

certain payments, such as this which is due to you, but we are seeking by every means in our power to raise money to meet our obligations, even if we are forced to mortgage our own property, since all our jewels are already pawned, and you need not fear but that before long, your debt will be paid gladly and readily." [1]

In the government of his people and in the administration of his affairs Lodovico was ably assisted by his excellent wife Barbara, the Hohenzollern princess who, leaving her own land at so early an age, brought the solid and domestic virtues of the Teutonic race to blend with the refined tastes of the Gonzagas. A prudent housewife and devoted mother, she watched over the education of her children with unwearied care. When Platina, who became her son Federico's tutor, after the death of Vittorino in 1446, was sent on a journey to Greece, she looked out at once for another master, saying it was a pity the boy should waste his time ; and when his successor, Filelfo, complained that Federico was lazy and indifferent, and had no real love of books, she counselled patience, and remarked that he would probably develop later. Under her vigilant eye no foolish luxury or wasteful expenditure was allowed. A refined simplicity marked the daily life of the court, and display was reserved for state occasions. At the same time Barbara took a lively interest in the welfare of her husband's subjects. She encouraged the cloth manufacture by her example and influence, and large quantities of this fabric were yearly exported to Germany. When her sister, Queen Doro-

---

[1] *Archivio Gonzaga*, lib. 86, quoted by A. Baschet, *Gazette des Beaux Arts*, 1866.

thea of Denmark, visited Mantua in 1475, a great fair
was held in her honour, and as many as 5000 pieces
of cloth were offered for sale.

Barbara's love for her adopted country did not
weaken the ties which bound her to her old German
home. She kept up an active correspondence with
her kinsfolk beyond the Alps, and entertained her
father the Elector John and her uncle the Margrave
Albert of Brandenburg repeatedly at Mantua.   Her
third and favourite son, the tall and handsome Gianfrancesco, was sent to be educated under the Margrave's eye at Anspach, while Rodolfo, her fourth
son, the gallant soldier who afterwards fell at Fornovo,
completed his knightly training at the court of Charles
the Bold, Duke of Burgundy.   But the proudest day
of Barbara's life was that of the opening of the General Council which Pope Pius II. summoned to meet
at Mantua in 1459.   It was Albert of Brandenburg
who, at Barbara's suggestion, had advised the Pope
to choose Mantua for the meeting of this Council,
which was to restore peace to Christendom and pro-
claim a crusade against the Turk.   Only England,
distracted by the Wars of the Roses, and Scotland,
" buried in the far northern seas," sent no answer to
the Pope's appeal.   Princes and ambassadors arrived
from all parts of Italy and Germany.   Pius II.
and his eight Cardinals, Francesco Sforza, Duke of
Milan, Albert of Brandenburg, and Duke Sigismund
of Austria were among the guests who were entertained in the Castello. The Pope, who spent four
months at Mantua, was greatly impressed by the
noble character of the Marchioness, whom he described in one of his letters as " distinguished among
all other matrons of the age by her shining graces of

body and mind." Two years afterwards, he gratified
Barbara's fondest wish by bestowing a Cardinal's hat
on her second son Francesco, a boy of seventeen,
who was still studying at the University of Pavia.
Her maternal pride was equally pleased when, in
1462, the Emperor Frederick III. arranged a marriage for her eldest son Federico with Margaret,
daughter of Duke Sigismund of Bavaria. But the
bad manners and rude habits of the German envoys,
who came to Mantua to draw up the marriage contract, shocked the Italians, who declared that they
behaved like cooks and scullions; and Federico, who
is said to have been in love with another maiden,
fled to Naples rather than marry this foreign bride.
For several months nothing was heard of him, but
at last he was discovered by King Ferrante, living in
a destitute condition under an assumed name in the
poor quarters of the city, and some time passed
before his mother could induce him to return home
and crave his father's forgiveness. In March 1463,
Gianfrancesco and Rodolfo Gonzaga were sent to
bring home the bride, who entered Mantua in state
on the 7th of June. The chronicler Schivenoglia,
who was Federico's secretary, evidently shared his
master's dislike for the Germans, and describes the
bride as short of stature, blonde and plump, and
unable to speak a word of Italian; while her attendants were clad in coarse red clothes of ugly shape
and colour. "As to their customs and manners," he
adds significantly, "I will say nothing."[1] Margaret
herself, however, soon learnt to appreciate the refinement of Italian manners, and when some years later
she paid a visit to her old home took a troop of

[1] A. Schivenoglia, *Cronaca di Mantova*, 1445-1484.

richly attired singers and minstrels with her to
Bavaria. We hear little else of Federico's bride,
who had neither the vigorous character of the
Marchesa Barbara nor the beauty and charm which
made Isabella d'Este famous. But she was a good
wife and mother, and her placid, gentle face, framed
in a quaintly peaked, pearl-trimmed cap, bearing the
Greek motto *Amomos*—spotless—may still be seen
carved in low relief on a block of Carrara marble
which once adorned the portals of the Gonzaga
villa at Revere, and is now in the Academy of
Mantua.

A worse trouble befell Lodovico and Barbara in
the terrible affliction of their two elder daughters,
Susanna and Dorotea, both of whom inherited the
deformity which afflicted Paola Malatesta in her
latter years. When Susanna, who had been betrothed as a child to Galeazzo Maria, the eldest son
of Francesco Sforza, Duke of Milan, grew up hunch-
backed, her younger sister's name was substituted in
the marriage contract. But soon it became rumoured
abroad that Dorotea, although a fair and attractive
maiden, had one shoulder higher than the other, and
before the wedding took place, the Duke demanded
a medical certificate of her state of health. Rather
than comply with this insulting condition, Lodovico
broke off the negotiations and resigned his own
appointment as captain of the Milanese forces. Both
Galeazzo, who seems to have been really attached
to his affianced bride, and his mother, Duchess
Bianca, who was a personal friend of Barbara,
endeavoured to reopen communications. But the
Marquis declined all further correspondence on the
subject, and in May 1465, refused the Duke's invita-

tion to attend the wedding of his daughter Ippolita
with the King of Naples's son, Alfonso, Duke of
Calabria. When, however, the newly wedded pair
were on their way to Naples, the Marquis and his
family met them at Reggio, and Dorotea saw her
old lover again. The minute directions which Barbara gave her son Federico on this occasion prove
that she had not yet abandoned all hopes of the
marriage.

"We do not yet know," she wrote on the 14th of
June, "whether Signor Galeazzo will be present, but
if he should come to Reggio, I think it well to warn
you how to behave. First of all, as soon as you see
the Milanese party approach, you and your wife must
dismount and advance to meet them with out-
stretched hands and courteous reverence. Be careful not to bend your knee before them, but salute
the illustrious Duke and Duchess, and shake hands
with Filippo and Lodovico, and also with Galeazzo,
if he is present and offers to shake hands. Dorotea
must also give him her hand and curtsey to him, but
if he does not come forward let her not move a step.
Then we will take the Duchess up in our chariot,
and you must all three of you pay her reverence.
Dorotea must either wear her *camora* of black and
silver brocade, or her crimson or gold-embroidered
one, whichever of the three she chooses. Your wife
may shake hands with the princes or not, as she
pleases, for in her condition whatever she does will
be excused. But I hope you will take a little
trouble in the matter, and explain all this clearly to
Dorotea, and see that she makes no mistake. If we
could be present at the interview, I would not
trouble you, but I fear our chariot may be delayed

and we may arrive too late to receive the Milanese princes."[1]

The meeting passed off happily, and Barbara wrote to her absent son, Cardinal Francesco, saying that Dorotea had played her part well, and that Galeazzo had treated her with marked attention. Early in the next year the Duke of Milan died, and Galeazzo's first act was to renew his suit. Already the preliminaries of the contract were drawn up, when Dorotea fell suddenly ill of fever, and died in a few days. Ill-natured persons said that the new Duke had poisoned his bride to be rid of the bargain, but Galeazzo himself expressed the deepest grief, and after his marriage to Bona of Savoy brought his wife to stay at Mantua.

Two of Lodovico's remaining daughters married German princes, one of whom, the Count von Görtz, treated his wife so badly that she came back to Mantua a year after her marriage, while the other, Barbara, became, in 1474, the spouse of Count Eberhard von Würtemberg, the founder of the University of Tübingen.

Fortunately all Lodovico's sons grew up tall and strong. Three of them were valiant soldiers, who distinguished themselves in the service of the Pope and the King of Naples, while the youngest, Lodovico, born in 1458, became Bishop of Mantua, and his brother, Cardinal Francesco, rose to still higher distinction in the Church. This young ecclesiastic was a refined connoisseur, and early showed his passion for music and antiques. When, after his appoint-

[1] Stefano Davari, *Il Matrimonio di Dorotea Gonzaga;* Paul Kristeller, *Barbara von Brandenburg, Hohenzollern Jahrbuch,* vol. iii. p. 66, &c.

ment as papal legate in 1472, he stayed at the baths of Porretta, in the Apennines, on his return from Rome, to recruit his health, he sent his father the following letter, begging that the painter Mantegna and the musician Malagista might be sent to keep him company:—

"Most honoured and illustrious Father,—I hope to arrive at Bologna on the 5th or 6th of August, but shall not stay there more than two or three days, and intend to go on to the baths, where I beg Your Highness to be pleased to order Andrea Mantegna and Malagista to stay with me, in order that I may have some distraction and amusement to enable me to avoid sleep, as is necessary for my cure. It will be a great pleasure to show Andrea my cameos and bronzes, and other fine antiques, which we can examine and discuss together, and Malagista's playing and singing will make it easier for me to keep awake. So I beg you to let me have these two for my companions. After taking the baths, I will return to Bologna for eight or ten days, and then come to spend all October with Your Excellency at Mantua. . . . I am able, thank God, to ride again since I left the bad air of Rome, and am already much better.— Your most devoted son, FRANCESCO GONZAGA, Cardinal and legate."[1] Foligno, 18th July 1472.

Both artists were sent to join Francesco at Bologna, and on Sunday, the 24th of August, the young Cardinal-legate made his solemn entry into Mantua, bringing in his train the distinguished architect Leo Battista Alberti, and the young Florentine poet Angelo Poliziano, whose famous drama of

---

[1] *Archivio Gonzaga,* quoted by A. Baschet, *Gazette des Beaux Arts,* vol. xx., 1866.

"Orfeo," composed by him in three days, was acted for the first time on this occasion.   The event was commemorated by Mantegna in a still more splendid form in the frescoes of the Camera degli Sposi, which were completed in 1474, as recorded in the proud inscription placed by the painter on a tablet, held by winged boys, over the door: "To the illustrious Lodovico II., Marquis of Mantua, most excellent prince, in the faith invincible, and his illustrious wife, Barbara, the incomparable glory of women. Their Andrea Mantegna of Padua has completed this humble work to their honour.   1474."

Here, in the Marquis's own nuptial chamber, in the corner tower of the Castello, the great master has left us a living record of the Gonzaga family.   The painter's genius has transformed this small room in the heart of the grim old fortress into a fairy bower, decorated with garlands and tapestries, where sportive loves play on a marble parapet under the blue sky. On one wall the reception of a foreign ambassador, probably the envoy sent by the Duke of Würtemberg to ask for the hand of Lodovico's daughter Barbara, is represented.   A secretary is seen handing the letter to the good prince, who, with his wife at his side, is seated in true patriarchal fashion under an open loggia on the garden terrace, surrounded by his children and grandchildren, his courtiers and pet dwarfs.   His eldest son, Federico, advances to receive the German ambassador, while the bride-elect, standing behind her mother's chair, turns her eyes with eager gaze in the same direction.   On the opposite wall of the nuptial chamber, a second fresco commemorates the arrival of the young Cardinal and his suite of servants on his return from Rome.   The

Marquis goes out to welcome him, with his sons,
Federico and Gianfrancesco, and his two little grand-
sons, Francesco, afterwards the husband of Isabella
d'Este, and Sigismondo, the future Cardinal. In
both of these family groups the striking personality
of the different personages has been clearly brought
out by the painter. We see the gallant bearing of
the soldier-sons, the culture and wisdom of the man
of the world mingled with the sober gravity of the
ecclesiastic in the sleek face and portly figure of the
young Cardinal, while all the strength and goodness
of Barbara's character lives in the sensible German
face that looks out from under the quaint square
head-dress, and in the grave, black eyes that are fixed
on her lord's face, and seem to express her readiness
to help him with her sympathy and advice. The
sunny landscape, with the Pantheon and Coliseum
among the seven hills, recalls the Eternal City from
which Francesco had lately returned, and if the
medallions of Cæsars and myths of Hercules and
Orpheus are emblems of Lodovico's taste for classical
history and love of music, the peacock on the balus-
trade, the tame lion crouching at his feet, and the
favourite greyhound asleep under his chair, remind
us of his interest in birds and animals.

Thus, in these noble frescoes which still light up
the old walls of the Castello with colour and brightness, the great master has not only left us a faithful
picture of Lodovico and his family, but has enabled
us to realise the strong German sense of family
affection and home life, combined with the splendour
and culture of an Italian court, which Isabella found
at Mantua when she became the wife of Francesco
Gonzaga.

LODOVICO GONZAGA AND HIS SONS

By Andrea Mantegna

(*Sala degli Sposi. Mantua*)

To face p. 36, vol. i

CHAPTER III

1478—1490

Reign of Federico Gonzaga—Death of his wife and mother—His love for his daughters — Visit of Lorenzo dei Medici — Accession of Francesco Gonzaga—His character and warlike tastes—Betrothal of Elisabetta Gonzaga to Guidobaldo, Duke of Urbino—His visit to Mantua—Marriage of Elisabetta— Her return to Mantua for Francesco's wedding—Her friendship with Isabella d'Este—Excursion to the Lago di Garda— Visits to Ferrara.

LODOVICO GONZAGA died at the age of sixty-four on the 12th of June 1478, at his villa of Goïto, less than a month after writing his kind and dignified reply to Mantegna's remonstrances, while the plague was still raging at Mantua. On his deathbed he was induced by his wife, whose affection for her younger children overcame her natural wisdom, to divide his State, and leave her favourite son, Gianfrancesco, the principality of Bozzolo and Sabbioneta, while Castiglione was bequeathed to Rodolfo Gonzaga and Gazzuolo to Bishop Lodovico. This division not only weakened the State, but led to serious family dissensions in the future. During Barbara's lifetime, however, all went well. Her eldest son, the new Marquis, Federico, consoled his widowed mother's grief, and treated her with the greatest respect, telling her, in true humanist fashion, that she had lost a lord whom she was bound to obey and kept a son whose duty it was to obey her. A year afterwards his wife, Margaret of Bavaria, died, leaving a young

family of five children, who were tenderly cared for
by their grandmother.   But on the 10th of November 1481, Barbara herself died at the age of fifty-
eight, deeply lamented by all her children.   Fra
Bernardino da Feltre, the eloquent Franciscan friar,
pronounced her funeral oration, and Matteo Bossi,
the learned Abbot of Fiesole, addressed a Latin
epistle of condolence to Cardinal Gonzaga on the
death of this admirable lady.   She was buried by her
husband's side in front of the Arca di S. Anselmo in
the Duomo, and her sons desired Luca Fancelli to
raise a splendid monument over her grave.   But the
Cardinal died in 1483, and although Bishop Lodovico
intended to carry out his scheme, it seems doubtful
if the tomb was ever erected.

Before the good Marchesa died she had the joy
of seeing her granddaughter, Chiara—born in July
1464—married to the King of France's cousin Gilbert,
Duc de Montpensier, and her eldest grandson Francesco, who was two years younger, betrothed to
Isabella d'Este, with whose mother Leonora she had
long been on friendly terms.   Federico himself was
an affectionate father, and took great interest in his
two younger daughters, Elisabetta, whose delicate
health made her an object of especial anxiety, and
Maddalena, who was only seven years old when her
mother died.   On the 14th of August 1481, Violante
de' Preti, the faithful governess in whose charge the
young princesses were spending the summer at the
ducal villa of Porto, wrote the following report to the
Marquis, who was frequently absent from Mantua
during the long war with Venice :—

"Most illustrious Prince and excellent Lord,—
You will be glad to hear that both your illustrious

daughters are well and happy and very obedient, so that it is a real pleasure to see them busy with their books and embroidery. They are very easy to manage, and they enjoy riding their new pony, one on the saddle, the other on pillion. They ride all about the park, but always attended by servants on horseback, and we follow in the chariot. They are quite delighted with this pony, and Your Excellency could not have made them any present which gave them greater pleasure. I hope, my dear lord, by the grace of God, to be able to give you good news every day, in order that Your Highness may rest satisfied, to whose favour I commend myself.—Your devoted servant, VIOLANTE DE' PRETI." [1]

On February 23, 1483, the little princesses received a visit from no less a personage than Lorenzo dei Medici, who spent a night at Mantua on his way to attend a conference at Cremona, where a new league was formed against Venice, and sent word to Violante's pupils by their dancing master that they might expect him after dinner. In her next letter to the Marquis, Violante describes how the little girls came to meet the Magnifico Lorenzo, and led him into their rooms, and how he sat down between them and talked for some time, and told them, when he took his leave, that their father was rich in fair children. The next day their brother, Francesco Gonzaga, who entertained this distinguished guest in his father's absence, wrote and informed the Marquis how he had accompanied the Magnifico Lorenzo on foot to mass at S. Francesco, and how he went on from the church to the house of Andrea Mantegna, "where he greatly admired some of

---

[1] A. Luzio e R. Renier, *Mantova e Urbino*, p. 6.

Messer Andrea's paintings, as well as certain heads in high relief and other antiques in which he seemed to take great delight."[1]

Federico himself treated Mantegna with great kindness, and wrote affectionately to him when he was ill in October 1478, telling him to try and get rid of the fever as soon as he could, but not to trouble his head about the work at present. He employed Andrea to decorate his new villa of Marmirolo, and when in 1484 the Prefect of Rome, Giovanni della Rovere, a brother-in-law of Duke Guidobaldo of Urbino, begged Bishop Lodovico Gonzaga for a picture by Mantegna, that prelate replied that the painter was unable to comply with his request, since his time was entirely engaged in painting a hall in one of the Mantuan palaces. And when Andrea declined to copy a drawing sent him by Bona, Duchess of Milan, who begged that he would "reduce it to a more elegant form," the Marquis excused his somewhat blunt refusal, saying that "these excellent masters are often somewhat fantastic in humour, and that we must be content to take what they choose to give us."[2] Federico intended at one time to make considerable additions to the Castello, and wrote to ask his father's old friend Federico di Montefeltro for a plan of his famous palace of Urbino, but the execution of this project and many others was hindered by the constant wars which exhausted his treasury. His old tutor Filelfo often reproached him with his parsimony, saying that the Marquis had never forgiven him for complaining to

[1] *Archivio Gonzaga*, quoted by A. Baschet, *Gazette des Beaux Arts*, 1866.

[2] *Archivio Gonzaga*, lib. xcix., quoted by A. Baschet, &c.

his parents of his indolence when he was a boy, but Federico appointed one of the querulous old scholar's twenty-four children to be his son's tutor, while Colombino of Verona, the commentator of Dante, instructed his two little daughters. After his visit to Ferrara in 1482, he begged Duke Ercole to send him *L'Asino d'Oro*, an Italian version of Apuleius's poem, and gave Isabella's tutor Battista Guarino a grant of wheat during the famine which prevailed in that city. But when, in 1483, the said Guarino applied for the post of tutor to his sons, the Marquis replied that this was impossible, since in the first place he could not afford to pay him a salary, and in the second place his sons did not require a teacher. Francesco, he explained, was already seventeen and his own master, while Sigismondo, a boy of fourteen, was studying at the University of Pavia, and Giovanni, being only nine, was too young to need a tutor. A year afterwards Federico died, and was succeeded by his eldest son, Francesco, the affianced husband of Isabella d'Este.

Although small of stature, the young Marquis was vigorous and athletic, and from early boyhood showed greater inclination for manly sports and exercises than for study. One of his first tutors complained that he would never sit still and that it was very difficult to induce him to fix his attention on his book. Throughout his life he retained these characteristics. He was passionately fond of hunting, kept hundreds of dogs, and was especially proud of his famous breed of Barbary horses, which carried off prizes at all the races for which they were entered, and were sent by their owner as presents to Kings and Emperors. A brave soldier and shrewd politician,

with the help of his clever wife he raised Mantua to
the foremost rank among the smaller Italian states,
and although he inherited little of his grandfather's
and uncle's taste for letters, he was fully alive to the
lustre and renown which his court and person derived
from great artistic achievements, and became a liberal
patron of scholars and painters. He was naturally
fond of luxurious and splendid surroundings, and
employed Mantegna soon after his accession to paint
his great series of Triumphs for a hall in the Castello.
As a child he had learnt to revere the genius of the
great master who had worked for three successive
generations of his house, and when he sent him to
Rome in 1488, told Innocent VIII. that Andrea
was "a most excellent painter, who had no equal
in the present age." His own letters to Mantegna
during this prolonged absence show the most friendly
regard, and are a proof of the familiar and intimate
relations that existed between the painter and the
members of the Gonzaga family.

Another pleasant feature of Francesco's character
was his affection for his little sisters. In August
1486, he arranged two excellent marriages for these
young princesses. Elisabetta was betrothed to
Guidobaldo, the son and successor of Duke Federico
of Urbino, while Maddalena became the affianced
bride of Giovanni Sforza, lord of Pesaro and cousin
of the reigning Duke of Milan. The young Duke
of Urbino visited Mantua on this occasion, and
Silvestro Calandra, the court chamberlain, wrote on
the 26th of August to the absent Marquis: "To-day
this illustrious Duke went in a boat for his pleasure
after dinner on the lake, but, being little used to the
water, felt unwell and landed at the gate of the

Corte to see the Triumphs of Cæsar, which Mantegna is painting, which pleased him greatly, and
then passed by the Via Coperta into the Castello."[1]
That Christmas Chiara Gonzaga, the young Duchess
of Montpensier, came to visit Mantua for the first
time since her marriage five years before, and the
three sisters prepared a "beautiful *festà*" for their
brother's entertainment, and were sorely disappointed
when three days before the feast they heard that
he had been obliged to put off his visit. "Illustrious
Prince and dearest brother," they wrote in a joint
epistle, "we three sisters, with some other gentle
ladies, had prepared a most beautiful entertainment
for Your Excellency, since we made sure that we
should enjoy your presence at this solemn festival.
But now that we hear our hopes were vain we are
grievously disappointed, and feel very unhappy, and
can enjoy no mirth or pleasure without you, and
indeed it seems to be a thousand years since we have
seen you. So now we pray you earnestly, by that
gentle and brotherly love you bear us, to come and
console us in the New Year and taste the pleasures
that we have prepared for you in our *festà*, which
will certainly gratify you and give us the greatest
possible delight.—Your sisters and servants, CHIARA,
ELISABETTA and MADDALENA GONZAGA."[2]

In February 1488, Elisabetta set out on her
journey to Urbino, and after experiencing terrible
weather on the Po, enjoyed a brief rest at Ferrara,
as the guest of the hospitable Duke and Duchess.
But hardly had the wedding party left Ferrara than
the tempest began again. At Ravenna, where the

---

[1] Luzio e Renier, *Mantova e Urbino*, p. 9.
[2] *Ibid.*, p. 8.

Podestà gave them lodgings, the rain came through the roof in such torrents that it was almost impossible for the princess to find a dry place in her bed, and as they rode on through the Apennines, the roads were so bad and the rivers so much swollen that the attendants often had to carry Elisabetta and her horse bodily in their arms. "If it had not been for their devotion," she wrote to her brother, "I should certainly not have reached Urbino alive."[1] After this perilous journey, in what Francesco's secretary Capilupo calls "the most detestable weather ever known for weddings," Elisabetta found a splendid reception awaiting her at Urbino. The Duke's loyal subjects poured out of the city gates, troops of white-robed children waving laurel boughs came down the hillside to welcome her with shouts of joy, and the splendours of the wonderful palace on the heights, with its gorgeous tapestries and treasures of gold and silver, consoled the Mantuan courtiers for the perils and sufferings of the way. The young Duke Guidobaldo was a very handsome and courteous prince, exactly the same age as his wife and skilled in all knightly exercises, although even at this early age he suffered cruelly from gout. From the first he showed himself a devoted husband, while Elisabetta's charm and goodness soon won all hearts in her new home. But the happiness and splendour of her present surroundings could not make her forget the old home to which she was so fondly attached, and she wept bitterly when her brother Giovanni and the Mantuan escort took their departure. "I was very unhappy at parting from Messer Giovanni," she wrote to the Marquis, "and feel that I am abandoned

[1] Luzio e Renier, *Mantova e Urbino,* p. 27.

by all my own family." But in August she had the joy of seeing Francesco, who paid his sister a flying visit, and showed his affection for her by frequent presents of fish, fruit, and game, as well as antiques and horses for his brother-in-law's acceptance. In 1489, the young Marquis was appointed captain-general of the Venetian armies, a post which he held with distinction during the next nine years, and which occupied his time fully. A few months later, in October, Elisabetta and her husband were present at her sister Maddalena's marriage to Giovanni Sforza at Pesaro. But her health, which was never strong, gave way under the strain of these prolonged festivities, and she fell seriously ill in November.

"We found Madonna, your sister," wrote Francesco's secretary Capilupo, who accompanied the Mantuan doctor sent by the Marquis to Urbino, "looking very thin and pale, with none of the bright and healthy colour that she used to have in her cheeks. . . . It is true there is a grace and gentleness about her which is that of a creature angelic rather than human, and although she will not allow us to say she is thin, and keeps up bravely, her limbs betray her weakness. She is up and dressed all day, but confesses that she is obliged to sit down when she has walked once or twice across the room."[1] The air of Urbino was pronounced to be too keen for the delicate young Duchess in winter, and as soon as she was fit to travel she came to Mantua for change, and remained there for her brother's wedding. She it was, we have already seen, who greeted the youthful bride on the threshold of the Castello di Corte, and whose gentle face and winning smile was the first

[1] Luzio e Renier, *Mantova e Urbino*, p. 50.

sight that met Isabella's eyes as she passed into her new home. A Mantuan chronicler, quoted by Amedei,[1] who was present at the Marquis Francesco's wedding, describes Isabella as the most fascinating child in the world, and the bridegroom as a youth of majestic bearing, with broad forehead, keen eyes, and thick locks. To judge from contemporary portraits, Francesco's appearance could hardly have been called prepossessing. The terra-cotta bust preserved in the Museum at Mantua, and the two portraits by Mantegna, the one painted when he was a boy of eight in the Camera degli Sposi, the other representing him twenty years later kneeling before the Virgin of Victory, all show us the same swarthy complexion, irregular features, and dark bushy locks. He had neither the good looks of his uncles nor the dignity of his father, and his short, stunted figure gives the impression that he had narrowly escaped inheriting the deformity which afflicted the former generation of Gonzagas. But he was young and vigorous, full of courage and activity, and as impetuous in love as he was in war. And he was naturally enough deeply enamoured of his fair young wife. Isabella on her part was fondly attached to her husband, and proud of his valour and unrivalled skill as a bold rider and fearless jouster. Both in character and intellect he was greatly her inferior, but even when in later years estrangements arose between the husband and wife, Isabella resolutely shut her eyes to his open acts of unfaithfulness, while Francesco placed the most absolute confidence in his wife and to the last retained the deepest admiration for her great qualities.

[1] D'Arco, *Notizie d'Isabella d'Este.*

In these early days no shadow dimmed the bright prospects of the young Marchesana. Her joyous nature, her youth and beauty, brought sunshine into the old Castello on the Mantuan lakes, and she was soon as much adored in her new home as she had been in her father's home. Her ready tact and good sense helped to allay the dissensions which had arisen between the young Marquis and his uncles. Bishop Lodovico in particular had incurred his nephew's displeasure after his elder brother's death by his efforts to obtain the Cardinal's hat which Francesco wished to secure for his brother Sigismondo, and held a rival court of his own at Gazzuolo. But soon after Isabella's marriage the Bishop sent to Venice for a costly jewel which he offered her as a wedding present, and the young Marchesana always kept up a friendly intercourse with him and his brother Gianfrancesco, the lord of Bozzolo. This gallant soldier served King Ferrante of Naples for many years, and, during his residence in Southern Italy, married Antonia del Balzo, the beautiful and accomplished daughter of Pirro, Prince of Altamura, the representative of the old Provençal family of Des Baux, who had followed Charles of Anjou to Naples, and bore the star in their coat-of-arms in proud token of their descent from Balthasar, one of the Three Kings.[1] The Gonzagas of Bozzolo shared Isabella's love of romances and plays, and she constantly exchanged books with them or assisted at the dramatic performances in which they took delight. At her request Francesco Bello, the blind improvisatore of Ferrara, who had settled at the court of Bozzolo, came to Mantua on a visit ; but Gianfrancesco, who suffered from increasing infirmities

[1] V. Rossi, *Giorn. St. d. Lett. It.*, vol. xiii.

and became prematurely old during the last years of his life, entreated her to send him back soon, since the poet's recitations were one of the few pleasures that he was still able to enjoy. Antonia remained one of Isabella's intimate friends to the end of her long life, and in August 1492, when the Marchesana passed through the town of Canneto in their dominions on her way to Milan, she wrote back to tell her husband how Madame Antonia had come out to meet her with her two beautiful daughters. "Messer Andrea Mantegna," she exclaimed, "could not paint fairer maidens!" [1]

With the more immediate members of her husband's family Isabella soon became a great favourite. Both her brother-in-law, *Monsignore il protonotario*, as Sigismondo was styled, and the young Giovanni, a merry lad of sixteen, were from the first her devoted slaves. Giovanni especially took part in all Isabella's amusements, and kept up a lively correspondence with her when she was absent from Mantua. But, of all her new relations, the one whom Isabella admired the most and loved the best was her sister-in-law, Elisabetta. From the day when the young Marchesana arrived at Mantua, a fast friendship sprang up between these two princesses, which was destined to prove as enduring as it was deep and strong. "There is no one I love like you," she wrote to Elisabetta in the ardour of her affection, "excepting my only sister, the Duchess of Bari"— Beatrice d'Este. And through all the changes and turmoil of the coming years, through the political troubles and fears and plots which tore Italy in twain and divided households against each other,

---

[1] Luzio e Renier in *Archivio Storico Lombardo,* vol. xvii. p. 344.

Isabella's friendship for her beloved sister - in - law never altered.

The two princesses had much in common. Both of them took especial delight in music and singing. Both were studious in their tastes, and showed the same kindly interest in painters and scholars. Isabella was more than three years younger than the Duchess, who had reached the age of nineteen at the time of her brother's wedding. She was more brilliant and witty, quicker at gay repartee and merry jokes. And she was also more talented and many-sided in her tastes. In future years she took an active part in politics, showed herself a skilful and able diplomatist, and was a match for Cæsar Borgia himself. Elisabetta was graver and more thoughtful. She had neither the physical strength nor the striking beauty and high spirits of Isabella. But her sweetness and goodness inspired those who knew her best with absolute devotion. She was adored, not only by her husband and brothers, but by the most brilliant cavaliers and distinguished men of letters of the age, by Baldassarre Castiglione and Pietro Bembo.

On this occasion Elisabetta remained at Mantua, by her sister-in-law's especial wish, till June. During the frequent journeys of the Marquis to Venice, the two princesses were inseparable companions. Together they sang French songs and read the latest romances, or played *scartino*, their favourite game at cards, in the pleasant rooms which Francesco had prepared for his bride on the first floor of the Castello, near the Sala degli Sposi. Together they rode and walked in the park and boated on the crystal waters of the lake, or took excursions to the neighbouring villas of Porto and Marmirolo. By the middle of

March, the Duchess's health was sufficiently improved
to venture on a longer trip, and on the 15th, Isabella
wrote to her absent lord : " To-day, after dinner, with
Your Highness's kind permission, the Duchess of
Urbino and I are going to supper at Goïto, and to-
morrow to Cavriana, where the wife of Signor Fracassa (Gasparo San Severino) will meet us, and on
Thursday we are going on the lake of Garda, according to Your Highness's orders, and I have let the
Rector of Verona know, so that we may find a barge at
Sermione." A few days later she wrote from Cavriana
to inform her husband of the success of their expedition. " The Duchess of Urbino and I, together with
Signor Fracassa's wife, went on Thursday to dine
at Desenzano and to supper at Tuscullano, where we
spent the night, and greatly enjoyed the sight of this
Riviera. On Friday we returned by boat to Sermione, and rode here on horseback. Wherever we
went we were warmly welcomed and treated with the
greatest attention, most of all by the captain of the
lake, who gave us fish and other things, and by the
people of Salò, who sent us a fine present. To-morrow
we go to Goïto, and on Tuesday back to Mantua."[1]
So for the first time Isabella saw the lovely shores of
Garda and the lemon groves of Salò, and lingered in
the classic gardens of Sermione, charmed with the
delights of that fair paradise which she was often to
visit in years to come. "These Madonnas," wrote
one of the gentlemen-in-waiting, Stefano Sicco, from
Cavriana on the 20th, "have been indefatigable in
making excursions by boat and on horseback, and
have seen all the gardens on the lake with the
greatest delight. The inhabitants have vied with

---

[1] Luzio e Renier, *Mantova e Urbino,* p. 54.

each other in doing them honour, and one Fermo of Caravazo caused his garden to be stripped for the Marchesana and her party and loaded them with lemons and pomegranates." [1]

Meanwhile the blank which Isabella's departure had left at Ferrara made itself daily felt. Her old tutor Jacopo Gallino wrote that he could not keep back his tears when he thought of those happy days when she read Virgil at his side, and repeated the Eclogues in her clear voice. At Isabella's request he sent her old Latin books to Mantua that she might pursue her studies and sometimes remember her poor old tutor. Another servant, Brandelisio Trotti, describes in his letters how he wanders, from room to room, through the desolate chambers where her angelic face once smiled upon him, recalling each word and act, and saying to himself: " There my divine lady lived — here she spoke those sweet, thoughtful words." " In the whole palace," wrote Leonora's chamberlain, Bernardino dei Prosperi, " there is not a single courtier or serving woman who does not feel widowed without Your Highness. Even the tricks and jests of the dwarfs and clowns fail to make us laugh." Most of all to be pitied was the poor Duchess, who would not even allow the little window-shutters of Isabella's apartment to be opened, saying that she had not the heart to visit those empty rooms, knowing how great was the blank that she would find there.

Isabella, to do her justice, did not forget her old friends. She wrote kind letters to her old tutors, Battista Guarino and Jacopo Gallino, and sent them presents of black damask and velvet in gratitude

[1] Luzio e Renier, *Mantova e Urbino*, pp. 54–56.

for their past services.   She even remembered the
clown Fritella, and sent a ducat and three yards of
tan-coloured satin to this pet dwarf, who remained
deeply attached to the young Marchesana, and
whose blotted, ill-spelt letters are still preserved in
the Gonzaga archives.[1]   Early in April the Marquis
took her back to Ferrara for a short visit, and in
July, after the Duchess of Urbino had left Mantua,
she returned to spend another fortnight with her
parents.   The sudden death of Maddalena Gonzaga,
the young wife of Giovanni Sforza, on the 8th of
August, within a year of her marriage, was a great
shock to all her family, and Isabella grieved most
of all for the sake of Elisabetta, whose health was
severely affected by this unexpected sorrow.   Isabella herself was suffering from a slight attack of
fever at the time, and Beatrice dei Contrari, the
faithful Ferrara lady whom Leonora had solemnly
charged to watch over her young mistress's welfare,
would not allow the sad news to be told her for
some days, " knowing her cordial affection for Madonna Maddalena, and fearing," as she wrote to the
Marquis, " lest we should add ill to ill." [2]   A month
later the Marchesana and her ladies took another
excursion to the shores of Garda, and wrote to tell
Elisabetta how much she missed her in these fair
regions and how ardently she wished for her to
enjoy the good fish and the delights of the arch-
priest's garden at Tuscullano.   After her return
to Mantua, she received a visit from her brothers
Alfonso and Ferrante, and intended to accompany
them to Ferrara, as her mother was suffering from

[1] A. Luzio, *I Precettori d'Isabella d'Este*, pp. 13, 17.
[2] Luzio e Renier, *Mantova e Urbino*, p. 55.

fever, but in deference to Francesco's wish put off the visit till November. On arriving at Ferrara, Isabella found the Duchess engaged in active preparations for Beatrice's wedding, which was to take place at Pavia in January, but amid the stir and excitement around her she managed to write the following affectionate little note to her husband :—

" My dearest lord,—If I have not written before, it is not that you have not been continually in my heart, but that I had simply not a moment to spare as long as the Milanese ambassador was here. Now I must do my duty and tell you that I can have no pleasure when I am away from Your Highness, whom I love more than my own life.— One who loves Your Highness more than herself, ISABELLA DA ESTE DA GONZAGA." Ferrara, November 25, 1490.

On the 28th Francesco replied to this loving little note in similar terms :—

" Since you feel that you cannot be happy away from me any longer, which is only natural, considering the immense love which we both feel for each other, it seems to me that, now you have satisfied your illustrious father and mother's wishes, as well as your own affection for your family, you might return home for our own happiness, and so I shall look forward to your arrival with impatience."

And on the same day Beatrice dei Contrari wrote to the Marquis :—

" My illustrious lady is as beautiful, well and gay as possible, and wants nothing but the presence of Your Excellency to make her perfectly happy." [1]

[1] Luzio e Renier in *Archivio Storico Lombardo,* vol. xvii. p. 81.

CHAPTER IV

1490—1493

Marriage of Beatrice d'Este to Lodovico Sforza—Isabella's preparations for the wedding—Journey to Pavia and Milan—Marriage of Alfonso d'Este to Anna Sforza—Fêtes at Ferrara —Correspondence of Isabella with Lodovico and Beatrice Sforza — Isabella administers affairs of State — Galeotto's dyke—Visits to Ferrara, Milan, and Genoa—The Duchess of Urbino comes to Mantua—Isabella's affection for Elisabetta.

THE next few weeks after Isabella's return were spent in preparations for her journey to Milan. She had gladly accepted the courteous invitation sent her by Lodovico Sforza to accompany her mother and sister to the wedding, although her husband thought it best to decline for his part, fearing to offend the Signory of Venice, who looked with suspicion on this alliance between the Sforzas and Estes. The young Marchioness was determined to make a brave show on this occasion, and all the merchants in Venice and Ferrara were required to ransack their stores and supply her with furs, brocades, and jewels. Zorzo Brognolo, the Gonzagas' trusted agent in Venice, was desired to search all the shops in Venice for eighty of the very finest sables to make a *sbernia* or mantle. " Try to find one skin with the head of the animal, Isabella adds, " to make a muff, which I can carry in my hand. Never mind if it costs as much as ten ducats ; I will give the money gladly as long as it is really a fine fur. You must also buy eight yards of the best crimson satin which you can

find in Venice to line the said *shernia,* and for God's
sake use all your accustomed diligence, for nothing, I
assure you, will give me greater pleasure." [1]   A few
days later she entreats Giacomo Trotti, the Duke of
Ferrara's ambassador at Milan, to send her two skins of
Spanish cat, the best and finest that are to be found
in that city, to trim this sumptuous mantle; and in
January 1491, when she had already started on her
journey, she writes to Genoa and orders another
shernia of costly brocade to be sent by express
courier to await her arrival at Pavia.

The cruel hardships to which the Marchioness
and her ladies were exposed during their journey in
barges up the Po, the actual cold and hunger which
they suffered, are vividly described in Beatrice dei
Contrari's letters to the Marquis, while Isabella herself has left a lively narrative of the brilliant festivities
with which the Moro's wedding was celebrated in her
letters to her young brother-in-law Giovanni Gonzaga.[2]   The young princess threw herself with ardent
enthusiasm into the pleasures of the hour, and the
friendship which she formed on this occasion with
her new brother-in-law Lodovico Sforza was destined
to prove an important factor in North Italian politics.

The espousals of her brother Alfonso with Anna
Sforza, niece of Lodovico and sister of the reigning
Duke of Milan, Giangaleazzo, were solemnised in the
ducal chapel at Milan on the 23rd of January, but
the final nuptial benediction was deferred for the
present, and, on the 1st of February, the bridal pair

[1] Luzio in *Nuova Antologia,* 1896, p. 455.

[2] For details of the wedding and the later visits of Isabella to
Milan, as well as the correspondence between the sisters, &c., see
my work on "Beatrice d'Este, Duchess of Milan," chaps. v. and vi.
(Dent & Co., 1899).

set out on the return journey to Ferrara, accompanied
by Duchess Leonora, Isabella, and their respective
suites, and escorted by 200 Milanese knights and
nobles.   On their way to Pavia the distinguished
travellers paid a visit to the famous Certosa, which
the Dukes of Milan justly counted one of the finest
jewels in their crown, and which both Isabella and
her mother had expressed their wish to see.   At
first the Prior raised objections, and told the
Regent that no women might be admitted into the
convent precincts without a dispensation from the
Pope.   But Lodovico overruled his scruples, saying
that he would take the responsibility upon himself,
and gave peremptory orders that church and convent
should be thrown open on this occasion, and that
the Duchess and her party should be feasted with
"an abundance of lampreys" and other delicacies.
After this no further objection was raised by the
Prior, and the archives of the Certosa record how,
on the 6th of February 1491, "there came to this
monastery the wife of the Duke of Ferrara, with the
Marchioness of Mantua and the brother and sister of
the Duke of Milan, together with a suite of 400
horses and 800 persons, and the expense of supplying
them with confectionery, fish and Malvasia wine
amounted to 400 lire." [1]

That winter was exceptionally severe; the streets
of Milan and the park of Pavia lay deep in snow, and
when the wedding party reached Ferrara the Po was
still frozen over and hundreds of workmen were employed to break the ice and make a passage for the
bucentaur.   On the 12th of February, the bride
entered the city on horseback, escorted by the Duke

[1] Carlo Magenta, *I Visconti e Sforza nel Castello di Pavia.*

and Alfonso, and followed by the Marquis and
Marchioness of Mantua, Annibale Bentivoglio and
his wife, Lucrezia d'Este, Ercole's learned sister
Bianca d'Este, with her husband Galeotto della
Mirandola, and the Ambassadors of Milan, Venice,
and Naples.   Four triumphal arches, adorned with
mythological groups, had been erected along the
route by the ducal architect Biagio Rosetti, the
builder of the Campanile of the Duomo and of the
famous Palazzo Diamante.   The Sun-god was seen
driving his chariot on the arch opposite the
Schifanoia palace, Cupid rode in his car drawn by
doves in front of the Franciscan church, the Great
Twin Brethren with their prancing steeds were represented on the arch before the Duomo, while all the
chief gods of Olympus welcomed the bridal pair at
the gates of the Castello.   Here Leonora received
the bride, and the nuptial blessing was pronounced
by the Archbishop in the ducal chapel, while the
German Kapellmeister, Don Giovanni Martini, played
exquisite organ melodies, and the choir boys sang
their sweetest strains.   This was followed by a
banquet and a representation of the *Menœchmi* with
scenery painted for the occasion by a Ferrara master,
Niccolo del Cogo, and a ball in which the Marquis of
Mantua danced with the bride and Alfonso with the
Marchioness.   Later in the evening Isabella and
Anna Sforza danced country dances together amidst
the applause of the assembled company, after which
the bride was escorted to her chamber by her family
and courtiers, with lighted torches and much noisy
merriment.[1]

The concourse of guests assembled at Ferrara

[1] Luzio e Renier in *Arch. St. Lomb.,* vol. xvii. p. 96.

on this occasion was enormous. The Venetian Ambassadors, Zaccaria Barbaro and Francesco Capello, brought as many as 150 persons in their suite, and the Duke's steward records that upwards of 45,000 pounds of meat were consumed at court during the week.[1]

On the 17th of February, Isabella wrote a detailed account of these festivities to her sister Beatrice, whose absence from Ferrara at this eventful time was the only thing she regretted, and promised to keep her better supplied with letters now that the fêtes were over and she was quietly at home again. Lodovico, in his anxiety to gratify his sister-in-law, agreed to send a weekly courier to Mantua, and seldom failed to write himself, while Beatrice's Ferrarese ladies-in-waiting, Teodora degli Angeli and Polissena d'Este, kept Isabella well informed of all that happened at the court of Milan. Both the Duke and Duchess of Bari were exceedingly anxious that Isabella should join their hunting parties at Pavia and Vigevano that summer, but the Marchesa was unable to leave home, since her husband visited Bologna in June for his brother Giovanni's wedding to Laura Bentivoglio and afterwards went on to see his sister at Urbino. Money was short at Mantua, and Isabella could ill afford the expense of another journey to her sister's brilliant court. So she reluctantly declined her pressing invitations, and like a good wife devoted herself to the management of her lord's public and private affairs.

The long letters which Isabella addressed to Francesco in his absence show how seriously she applied herself to public business and how anxiously

[1] Muratori, *R. I. S.*, vol. xxiv.

she considered the good of his subjects. She often consulted her father and her brother-in-law Lodovico Sforza, on questions which concerned them as neighbouring Powers. That summer she was much troubled about a certain dyke which her uncle Galeotto della Mirandola had constructed in his dominions whereby the waters of the river Secchia were diverted from Mantuan territory, and many farmers and peasants were threatened with ruin. In August, the Marchesa addressed an urgent entreaty to Lodovico, complaining that Galeotto had not only refused to attend to her request, but that, when she proposed to refer the question to the Regent of Milan, he had actually boasted that the Moro was far more friendly to him than to the Gonzagas, " although," she added indignantly, " our two houses are not only connected by ties of blood and marriage, but united by the closest friendship, and all the world knows the great kindness and paternal affection which you have shown to my lord and in a still higher degree to myself, so that Messer Galeotto need not presume to think himself more highly favoured than we are."

Galeotto however remained obdurate, and Duke Ercole at his daughter's request sent a shrewd lawyer, Pellegrino Prisciani, to examine the case and give her the benefit of his advice. In a letter dated the 13th of September, written from her favourite villa of Porto, she gives her father an amusing account of Messer Pellegrino's visit, and describes how the advocate listened attentively while she laid the case before him and took down notes of all that she said, after which he went on to Mirandola to hear Galeotto's defence and report both sides of the question.

" Messer Pellegrino," she writes in her lively style,

" began by making me a long *exordium* which to
my mind altogether surpassed the speech which he
addressed to you. For in haranguing Your Excellency he only quoted Pliny, whereas in speaking to
me he quoted Ptolemy, Vitruvius, Homer, Horace,
as well as an innumerable quantity of other authors
about whom I knew as little of the one as of the
other! One thing however really pleases me. It is
that after seeing and examining all these plans I have
begun to learn something about architecture, so that
in future when you tell me about your buildings I
shall be able to understand your explanations better."
And in a postscript she adds: " M. Pellegrino
departed yesterday, so well primed with our argu-
ments regarding the dyke of Secchia that I cannot
imagine how Messer Galeotto will be able to answer
him, unless, as is generally the case, he persists in
denying the truth!"[1] Unfortunately we do not
learn the result of the lawyer's mission, but as we
hear no more on the subject can only conclude that
the Prince of Mirandola was brought to reason and
that the fair Marchesa won her case.

In November, Isabella spent some weeks at
Ferrara, and while she was there heard to her sur-
prise that her husband had suddenly gone to Milan.

" My dearest lord," she wrote to him on the 4th
of December, " I hear that you are gone to Milan
and am vexed not to have known of this before your
departure, as I would have left all the pleasures
which I am enjoying here in the company of my
father and mother, and would have come to Mantua
at once to see Your Highness. But, as I did not
know this in time, I send these few lines by a courier

[1] Luzio e Renier in *Giorn. St. d. Lett. It.*, 1900.

on horseback to satisfy my anxiety as to your welfare, begging you to commend me to Signor Lodovico and the Duchess.—From her who longs to see Your Highness, ISABELLA D' ESTE, with her own hand."

Francesco explained in a letter from Milan that he had informed his wife of his intended journey in a note which never reached her. Now he told her of the kindly reception which he had received from Lodovico and Beatrice, and of the honours and attentions with which he was loaded, "all of which," wrote Isabella in reply, "gave me incredible consolation, and were no less delightful to me than if I had been there in person."[1]

It was only in the following summer that Isabella herself was able to accept the Moro's repeated invitations and pay her long-deferred visit to Milan. A series of fêtes and dramatic representations were to be given at Pavia in honour of Duke Ercole, and Francesco Gonzaga wrote from Venice urging his wife to accompany her father. This, Isabella declared, was absolutely impossible. " I have received your letter," she wrote on the 25th of July, " and understand that you wish me to go to Milan. Certainly that is my own wish also, especially since I hear the idea gives you pleasure, which is my sole object in life, so that now I should go there with the greatest good-will. But it is quite impossible that I should accompany my father, or even start soon after him, as I have not the means. Half of my household are ill, and I must wait till they have recovered, and Your Highness can choose the gentlemen who are to accompany me. Meanwhile I will arrange my affairs so as to be ready to start as soon

[1] Luzio e Renier in *Arch. St. Lomb.*, vol. xvii. p. 116.

as possible. But, of course, if Your Highness thinks differently, I will set out to-morrow, even if I have to travel alone and in my chemise. If, however, you are agreeable, I will write to Signor Lodovico and accept his invitation, and will let him know the date of my departure later on."

The proud young princess had certainly no intention of appearing at the splendid court of Milan " in her chemise," as she described it. During the next few days letters were written and couriers were sent flying in all directions to order new clothes and jewels, not only for herself, but for the members of her suite. " Since we have to go to Milan in the middle of this month," the Marchioness wrote to her old servant, Brandelisio Trotti, at Ferrara, " I am anxious that the necklace of a hundred links should be finished by then, and I beg and implore you by the love you bear me to see it is ready in time. And since I am anxious that the few persons who accompany me should be honourably adorned with chains, I should be very glad if you would kindly lend your son Negro one of your own, as you did at my wedding." At length all the final preparations were made, and Isabella set out on her journey on the 10th of August. But half-way to Pavia she suddenly found that her best hat and jewelled plume had been forgotten, and sent back the key of her black chest with orders to one of her servants to send it post haste.[1]

The visit proved a great success, and Isabella's letters to her husband dwell with delight on the brilliant round of entertainments, hunting parties, and theatricals provided for her amusement, on the affectionate kindness of Lodovico and Beatrice, and

[1] Luzio e Renier, *op. cit.*, pp. 348–350.

the enthusiastic welcome given her by the people of
Milan and Pavia. Political events also occupy a
prominent place in her correspondence at this time.
Alexander Borgia had just been elected Pope in
great measure owing to the powerful support of
Lodovico's brother, Cardinal Ascanio Sforza, and
Isabella faithfully reports the latest news from Rome
and the satisfaction of the Moro at the elevation of
this Pontiff, who was to become ere long his most
bitter enemy. But, in the midst of all these pleasures
and distractions, Isabella often sighed for her husband's presence. "I will not deny," she wrote
affectionately to him, "that I am enjoying the
greatest pleasures; but, when I think how far off I
am from Your Excellency, I feel they are not half as
delightful as they would be if you were here." The
Marquis, however, was engaged in attending the
public races at Brescia, Siena, Lucca, and other
cities, and gladly gave his wife leave to visit Genoa
before her return home. New and warmer clothes
were necessary for this expedition now the summer
was over, and Isabella wrote to her chamberlain,
Alberto da Bologna, desiring him to have a new
grey satin *camora*, with black velvet sleeves, made
for her without delay.[1] Some misunderstanding,
however, arose on the subject, for a week afterwards Isabella wrote again, this time in very imperious fashion, telling Alberto that he must have
lost, not only his memory, but his brain and
eyesight by the fall of which he complained, and
repeating her orders with greater minuteness than
before. But no sooner had she sent this letter than
she repented of her hasty temper, and with her usual

[1] Luzio e Renier, *Nuova Antologia*, 1896, p. 451.

kindness she wrote another note, assuring her old
servant that she had only been joking! On the 1st
of October, the Marchioness went to Genoa, attended
by two of Lodovico's favourite courtiers, Girolamo
Tuttavilla and the Marchesino Stanga, and was
received by the governor, Adorno, who rode out to
meet her with an escort of Genoese nobles, mounted
on richly draped mules, " which made a fine show."
But, as Isabella herself tells us, the splendour of her
reception was marred by a curious incident which is
highly characteristic of the times. " At six o'clock,"
she writes, " we entered Genoa, amid the noise of
guns and trumpets, and I was conducted to the house
of Messer Cristoforo Spinola, where the governor's
wife and sister-in-law and other noble ladies were
waiting to receive me. Before I had time to dismount, a crowd of workmen gathered round me, and
seized my mule, according to their custom here.
They snatched the bridle and tore the trappings
to pieces, although the governor interfered, and I
willingly gave it up to them. I was never so much
frightened in my life, and was really afraid of some
accident, but fortunately I did not lose my head.
At length I was released from their hands, leaving
my steed, a mule which Signor Lodovico had lent
me, to be their prey. I must redeem it at a fair
price, and shall have to buy a new set of trappings ! " [1]

Isabella was summoned back to Milan by her
sister's sudden illness, and as soon as she could leave
Beatrice hastened home. Francesco was growing
impatient at her prolonged absence, and wrote urgent
letters desiring her to return, as his presence was required in another part of his dominions, and he had sent

[1] Luzio e Renier, *op. cit.*, p. 359.

Giovanni to Rome to congratulate the new Pope on his accession. Unluckily, Beatrice dei Contrari fell dangerously ill on the return journey, and during some weeks Isabella was very anxious about this favourite companion. When she went to Ferrara in the end of November, she begged Beatrice to send her daily reports of her condition, " for, loving you as I do," she wrote, " I long to hear every hour how you are." Happily the lively maid-of-honour's high spirits did not desert her, and she wrote amusing letters to Isabella, telling her how the Marquis had paid her a visit and spent two hours in her company, lamenting his wife's absence. " After discussing all manner of subjects," adds the writer, "he ended by saying that he should have to take me for his wife in your absence, to which I replied that I feared he would have a bad bargain, since Your Illustrious Highness is young and beautiful, and I am old and ugly and nothing but a bag of bones ! "[1]

The Marchesa however could not leave her mother, who had been in bad health all the summer, and remained at Ferrara until the end of the year, when Leonora set out for Milan and Isabella accompanied her to the borders of the Mantuan territory. Here the mother and daughter parted. The Duchess went on to Milan, where she was present at the birth of Beatrice's first-born son, while Isabella returned home to devote herself to her studies, and make up for lost time, as she told her mother, by fresh zeal and assiduity.

In spite of the manifold occupations and distractions of the last two years, the young Marchesa had by no means given up her classical studies.

---

[1] Luzio e Renier, *op. cit.*, p. 360.

In a Latin letter which she addressed to her old
teacher Guarino, in January 1492, she deplores the
cares of state which interfere with her good intentions, and at the same time tells him that it is quite
unnecessary to commend his daughter to her notice,
since she already loves the girl both for her own sake
and that of her father. A few months later she began
to read Latin again with a new tutor, and in another
letter Guarino exhorts her to persevere in the acqui-
sition of that learning which cannot fail to bring
her fame, since a truly cultured woman is as rare as a
phœnix. For a time the Mantuan scholar Sigismondo
Golfo helped the Marchesa in her studies, and sent
her long letters retailing the court gossip, when she
was at Milan or Ferrara. Since, however, she was no
longer as familiar with Latin as she had been in her
girlhood, she begged him to write to her in Italian for
the present, in spite of the humanist's protests at this
unworthy practice. By the end of the year, however,
Golfo left Mantua, and in his stead Guarino sent
Isabella one of his best scholars, Niccolo Panizzato,
whom Leonora had chosen to accompany her son
Ferrante on a journey to Hungary, and who was now
a public lecturer in the University of Ferrara. The
Marchioness agreed to give him the modest salary of
three ducats a month and to provide for his family, and
desired Niccolo to come to Mantua by the first boat
that was available after the carnival fêtes were over,
in order that she might lose no time in setting to
work. But hardly had the new teacher set foot in
Mantua, than Isabella sent him back to resume his
work at Ferrara, saying that her time was too fully
occupied for her to resume her studies. Both the
youth himself and Isabella's old master were bitterly

disappointed. "It is really a thousand pities," wrote Guarino, "both for the sake of the poor young man and for ourselves, who hoped to have a Madonna of our own who would become honoured as a tenth muse."[1] But the true reason for this sudden change of mind was the news which Isabella had just received that her beloved sister-in-law Elisabetta was on her way to Mantua. During the last year the Duchess of Urbino's presence had been anxiously expected at her brother's court. But her coming had been repeatedly delayed by protracted illness, and Isabella's letters show how bitterly she had been disappointed in her hopes of once more welcoming this dear companion. When a year before Elisabetta, instead of coming to Mantua, had been ordered to take the baths of Viterbo, the Marquis sent his sister's old friend, the Castellan Silvestro Calandra, to cheer her solitude, with the following letter, which does justice both to the warmth of Isabella's heart and the excellence of her sense:—

"By the love I bear you, my dearest sister, I must say this one thing, that I hope the first bath you take will be a steadfast resolve to avoid all unwholesome things and live on those which give health and strength. Above all, I hope you will force yourself to take regular exercise on foot and horseback, and to join in pleasant conversation, in order to drive away melancholy and grief, whether they arise from mental or bodily causes. And you will, I hope, also resolve to think of nothing but of your health in the first place, and of your own honour and comfort in the second place, because in this fickle world we can do nothing else, and those who

[1] Luzio, *I Precettori d'Isabella d'Este*, p. 25.

do not know how to spend their time profitably, allow their lives to slip away with much sorrow and little praise. I have said all this, not because Your Highness, being most wise yourself, does not know all this far better than I do, but only in the hope that, being aware of my practice, you may the more willingly consent to live and take recreation as I do, and as the Castellan will be able to inform you. And my husband is well content that he should remain with Your Highness until you leave the baths and as long afterwards as you choose, always on the understanding that you will soon come to Mantua, since otherwise he will not only recall the Castellan, but will, if possible, renounce all his love and connection with you!"

Calandra himself was given a letter couched in the same terms, giving him leave to remain with the Duchess as long as she persevered in her intention of coming to Mantua. "If, however, the Duchess changes her mind," wrote the imperious young Marchesa, "not only are you to return at once, but you are also to assure her that neither you, nor any one else, will be sent to her from us, and that the tender love we bear her will undergo a complete change."

But, although Elisabetta returned from Viterbo in somewhat better health, fresh causes arose to delay her visit to Mantua. First Guidobaldo fell ill, then he took his wife with him to Rome, after which she had a fresh attack of her old gastric complaint. When, in January 1493, Isabella heard that, instead of coming to Mantua, the Duchess had been sent to take the baths of Porretta, she began to despair of ever seeing her again, and wrote saying that nothing could give her pleasure this carnival, since all the fine plans which she had made for their mutual amusement were blown to the winds! "And the time which I hoped to spend in joyful intercourse together I will now pass in dreary solitude, sitting alone in my studio lamenting your illness and praying God soon to restore you to health, so that if our desires may not be granted this carnival, they may at least be satisfied before the end of Lent."

This last wish was happily fulfilled. On the 9th of March the Duchess started for Mantua, and Isabella sent the poet Picenardi with his lyre, in the bucentaur which went out to meet her, in order that he might beguile the journey with music and song. The Marchesa herself and the chief citizens went to meet Elisabetta at Revere, and brought her back to Mantua amidst universal rejoicing. "And I really think," wrote Isabella to her mother a few days later, "that she is already beginning to feel the good effects of her native air and of the caresses with which I load her all day." [1]

[1] Luzio e Renier, *Mantova e Urbino*, pp. 58–62.

CHAPTER V

1491—1493

Correspondence of Isabella with her family and friends; with merchants and jewellers—Her intellectual interests—Love of French romances and classical authors—Greek and Hebrew translations and devotional works — Fra Mariano and Savonarola — Antonio Tebaldeo — Isabella's friendships — Niccolo da Correggio—Sonnets and eclogues composed for her—Her love of music—Songs and favourite instruments —Atalante Migliorotti's lyre — Isabella's *camerino* in the Castello — Liombeni decorates her *studiolo* — Mantegna returns from Rome — Paints Isabella's portrait — Giovanni Santi at Mantua.

NOTHING is more remarkable in the history of Isabella than the vast correspondence which she carried on with the most different personages on the greatest variety of subjects. Her appetite for news was insatiable, her curiosity boundless. There was nothing which did not excite her interest, from the most important affairs of state down to the newest fashion in dress or jewellery, from the most recent discoveries in the New World or the last cantos of Ariosto's "Orlando" to the purchase of a carved turquoise or a Persian kitten. And she entered into the smallest details on these subjects with the same keen zest, and gave her orders with the same clearness and minuteness, whether the defence of the State or the painting of an illuminated missal were in question. The correspondence which she kept up with her relatives alone during these first years after her marriage must have occupied many hours. She wrote

Photo, Premi, Mantua

PONTE SAN GIORGIO, CASTELLO E DUOMO

(Mantova)

To face p. 70, vol. i

weekly letters to her mother at Ferrara, to her sister
Beatrice and Lodovico Sforza at Milan, to Elisabetta
Gonzaga at Urbino, and corresponded frequently
with her half-sister Lucrezia Bentivoglio and her
husband, as well as with her own brothers. Alfonso
d'Este, her eldest brother, was deeply attached to this
sister, who was only two years older than himself,
and who shared his literary and artistic tastes. One
day in the autumn of 1490, after paying Isabella a
visit at Mantua, he sent her a long description of a
tournament at Bologna, in which his brother-in-law
Annibale Bentivoglio appeared in the guise of
Fortune and Count Niccolo Rangone figured as
Wisdom. Both princes were attended by pages in
French, German, Hungarian and Moorish costumes,
and recited allegorical verses and broke lances after
the approved fashion of the day. "I cannot tell
you," writes the enthusiastic boy, "how gallantly
Messer Annibale bore himself, but I felt sorry for
Count Niccolo when his horse stumbled and fell."
A few months later he wrote to tell his sister that
a new island had been discovered on the coast of
Guinea, and sent her drawings of the strange race
of men who dwelt there and of their horses and
clothes, as well as of the trees and products of the
country.

The choice of new robes and jewels, of furs and
camoras naturally took up a large part of Isabella's
time and thoughts in these early days. She was in
constant communication with merchants and goldsmiths, with embroiderers and engravers of gems.
Countless were the orders for rings, seals, diamond
rosettes and arrows, rubies, emeralds, and enamels
which she sent to her agents at Ferrara and Venice.

One day she must have a cross of diamonds and pearls
as a gift for her favourite maid-of-honour Brogna, the
next she sends to Genoa for a choice selection of
corals and turquoises. When she hears that her
father has a rosary of black amber beads and gold
and enamelled roses, she desires a Ferrara jeweller
to make her one like it without delay, and when
her sister Beatrice wears a jewelled belt brought
from France, made in imitation of a *cordone di S.
Francesco*, she writes to ask for the pattern in order
that she may copy it. The following letter to her
father's agent, Ziliolo, who was starting on a journey
to France in April 1491, is a characteristic specimen
of the commissions which she gave her servants and
of her eagerness to see her wishes gratified.

" I send you a hundred ducats," she says, " and
wish you to understand that you are not to return
the money if any of it is left, after buying the things
which I want, but are to spend it in buying some
gold chain or anything else that is new and elegant.
And if more is required, spend that too, for I had
rather be in your debt so long as you bring me the
latest novelties. But these are the kind of things
that I wish to have — engraved amethysts, rosaries
of black amber and gold, blue cloth for a *camora*,
black cloth for a mantle, such as shall be without
a rival in the world, even if it costs ten ducats a
yard ; as long as it is of real excellence, never mind !
If it is only as good as those which I see other
people wear, I had rather be without it !" She
goes on to ask Ziliolo not to forget to bring back
some of the finest *tela di Rensa* — the linen made
at Rheims, which was in great request at Italian
courts, and ends by begging him to lose no chance

of hunting out some rare and elegant trifles for her use.[1]

The commissions with which Zorzo Brognolo, the Mantuan envoy at Venice, was charged, were still more varied. Silks and velvets of Oriental manufacture, brocades patterned over with leopards and doves and eagles, perfumes, Murano glass, silver and *niello* work, very fine Rheims linen for the Marquis's shirts, even finer and more delicate than the pattern which she encloses—these are some of the things which he must procure without a moment's delay. Often, indeed, faithful Zorzo found it no easy task to satisfy the demands of his impatient young mistress. Skilled goldsmiths and engravers were slow to move and apt to put off commissions and linger over the work in a way that was very trying to Isabella's patience. " If the bracelets we ordered months ago are not here till the summer is over and we no longer wear our arms bare, they will be of no use," she writes on one occasion when the Jewish goldsmith, Ercole Fedeli of Ferrara, had failed to execute her order punctually. Another time the same artist kept her waiting four years for a pair of silver bracelets, and would, she declared, never have finished them in her lifetime if Duke Alfonso had not thrown him into the Castello dungeon! But the work when it came was so exquisitely finished that Isabella had to forgive him and own that no other goldsmith in the world was his equal. And certainly the scabbard which Ercole worked in *niello* for Cæsar Borgia, now in South Kensington Museum, and the sword of state which he made for the Marquis

[1] *Il Lusso di Isabella d'Este*, A. Luzio in *Nuova Antologia*, 1896, p. 453.

Francesco, now in the Louvre, deserve the high praise which the Marchioness bestowed upon his work. It was the same with Anichino, another Ferrarese jeweller, who spent most of his time in Venice and engraved gems in the most perfect style. "Fortunate are those," sang a contemporary poet, "who are endowed with the genius of Anichino, for over them Time and Death have no power." "I will not fail," wrote Zorzo Brognolo to his mistress in 1492, "to urge Anichino to serve Your Highness quickly, but he is a very capricious and eccentric man, and it is necessary to hold him tight if you mean to get work out of him!" As usual Isabella had to bide the artist's pleasure and wait many weary months before her turquoise was returned engraved with a Victory. But when it came it was so beautifully worked that she forgot her displeasure and sent Anichino another gem to be engraved with a figure of Orpheus, telling him with many flattering words that he might be as slow as he liked, as long as the work came so near to antique art. This time, however, she owned to Brognolo that she was not altogether satisfied, but did not dare tell the artist her opinion for fear of exciting his wrath. "I know," she adds, "the man is the best master in Italy, but unfortunately he is not always in the right mood."[1]

This fine taste and quickness to recognise true excellence naturally attracted the best artists into Isabella's service. She might be hasty and impetuous in her orders; she often grumbled at the cost of pictures and gems, tried to beat down the price, and was undoubtedly difficult to please, but

[1] Gruyer, *L'Art Ferrarais à l'epoque des Princes d'Este*, vol. i. pp. 575, 714, &c.

she was always ready to recognise good work and to give the artist warm praise. Naturally, however, want of money often interfered with the gratification of her wishes, and she was compelled to return precious stones and finely carved gems because, as she told the goldsmiths sorrowfully, they were too dear. For the state of Mantua was small and its revenues could not compare with those of Milan or Ferrara. "Would to God!" Isabella exclaimed when her brother-in-law Lodovico Sforza displayed his treasures before her dazzled eyes — "Would to God that we who spend money so gladly had half as much!" As it was, she often spent more than she could afford, and owed large sums to Taddeo and Piero Albano, the Venetian bankers, who generally advanced money both to the Marchesa and her husband. Often too she was forced to pledge her jewels and even her costly robes to raise money for political objects, to help Francesco in his wars or buy a cardinal's hat for his brother. The Mantuan agent Antonio Salimbeni wrote to her from Venice in 1494, begging that she would send him some money without delay, since he had all the merchants in the city on his shoulders, and could only give them good words, and hope that Her Excellency would soon come to the rescue. But Isabella was no spendthrift, and although she might occasionally be led into extravagance, showed herself to be as practical in the management of her fortune as in everything else. When, in 1491, one of her husband's estates was seized by the Venetian merchant Pagano, Isabella hastened to redeem the land, paying down 2000 ducats and begging the Doge to be her security for the rest. Pagano began by raising objections, and evidently looked with some distrust on the Marchesa's proposals, upon which Isabella lost no time in paying down the money, saying proudly to Brognolo: "He might have trusted us, for, as you know, we would rather die than break our word."

But the raising of loans, and the purchase of rare gems and costly brocades, of elegant trifles and ornaments for her *camerini* were by no means the only commissions which Brognolo had to execute for his young mistress. From the first, intellectual interests played a large part in Isabella's life at Mantua. All through the summer of 1491, she was engaged in an active controversy with the Moro's son-in-law Galeazzo di San Severino, on the respective merits of the Paladins Rinaldo and Orlando, and entered into the lists with her wonted spirit and gaiety. On the one hand, she asked her old friend, Matteo Boiardo, to send her the latter part of his *Orlando Innamorato*, as yet in manuscript; on the other, she wrote to Brognolo on the 17th of September: "We wish you to ask all the booksellers in Venice for a list of all the Italian books in prose or verse containing battle stories and fables of heroes in modern and ancient times, more especially those which relate to the Paladins of France, and send them to us as soon as possible."[1] Zorzo executed this commission with the utmost despatch, and on the 24th, sent her a list of works, containing, amongst others, a Life of Julius Cæsar, the romances of Boccaccio, Piccinino, Fierabraccio, and several translations from the French. Many other French and Breton romances, tales of the San Graal, of King

[1] Luzio e Renier in *Giorn. St. d. Lett. It.*, 1899, p. 8. See also "Beatrice d'Este," p. 68, &c.

Arthur and his Round Table, of Lancelot, Tristan, Amadys, Astolfo, Morgante Maggiore and Rinaldo di Montalbano, belonged to Isabella's library, and are mentioned in the inventory which was drawn up at Mantua in 1542, three years after her death. Her Gonzaga cousins at Gazzuolo shared this taste for French romances which Isabella had brought from the court of the Estes, and many years afterwards, when Gianfrancesco's widow, Antonia del Balzo, was growing old, she begged the Marchesa to lend her the "History of King Arthur and the Round Table" and that of Godefroi de Bouillon. "Now that I am often ill and unable to go out much, I like to have books read aloud to me," she writes, "and find that this passes the time pleasantly, especially when the story is quite new to me." Isabella sent the books without delay, and Antonia gratefully acknowledged the parcel, saying that the French romances were read to her while she was at work every day, and that her brother-in-law Monsignore Lodovico was especially glad to see them, since a youth in his household was writing a book on Orlando, and hoped to find some new incident or idea in them.[1]

But, dear as mediæval romances were to Isabella's heart, classical authors were dearer still. The great Venetian Aldo Manuzio had not yet printed those choice editions which gave her so much delight in later years, but even in these early days her library contained a large proportion of Latin authors, including the works of Virgil and Horace, of Livy and Pliny, and the plays of Seneca, of Plautus and Terence. She never mastered the Greek language,

---

[1] Luzio e Renier, *op. cit.*, pp. 8, 9, 12.

but read the works of Greek writers in Latin or
Italian versions, and employed Demetrius Moschus
to translate the Lives of Plutarch and the Icones
of Philostratus, which as a treatise on painting
was of especial interest to herself and her contemporaries. In 1498, she was seized with a wish to read
Herodotus, and borrowed an Italian translation from
her cousin Alberto d'Este, which she kept over a year,
giving as an excuse for her delay in returning the
volume, that it was such a big one and that she had
not yet finished it. With the true spirit of the biblio-
phile Isabella loved to add rare works to her library,
even when she could not read them, and was especially
proud of a Greek Eustathius, which Pope Clement
VII. was glad to borrow, and which she once lent
as a great favour to her cousin, Cæsar of Aragon,
begging him not to allow too many persons to see
the precious volume, lest its reputation should be
diminished! Even Hebrew literature occupied her
attention, and she employed a learned Jew to translate
the Psalms from the original, in order to satisfy herself that the text was correct. An illustrated Bible
was one of the first books which she desired Brognolo
to procure for her when she came to Mantua, and
some years later she paid Taddeo Albano fifty ducats
for an illuminated copy of the Seven Penitential
Psalms bound in a richly chased gold and silver
cover. A copy of St. Jerome's Epistles, which she
had borrowed from her old tutor Battista Guarino,
interested her so much that she caused the work
to be printed at Mantua in 1497.[1] Even at this
early age the youthful Marchesa was fond of reading
the Fathers and of hearing sermons. Some of the

[1] Luzio e Renier, *op. cit.*, pp. 21–23.

most learned and eloquent friars of the day—the
General of the Carmelites, Fra Pietro da Novellara;
the Mantuan Carmelite Battista Spagnoli, Frate
Francesco Silvestri of Ferrara, afterwards General of
the Dominican Order — were numbered among her
friends and correspondents.

Her relations with the Dominican nun, Osanna
dei Andreasi, were still more intimate. This devout
lady, a kinswoman of the Gonzagas, was regarded
by Francesco and all his family as the protectress of
Mantua, whose prayers they sought in time of war
and plague. She was a wise and noble woman,
whom the learned Francesco Silvestro held in high
esteem, and as she was supposed to have received
the stigmata and to be endowed with prophetic
gifts, her fame extended far and wide. Beatrice
d'Este induced her to visit Milan, where she was
received as an angel of light, and the Queen of
France, Anne of Brittany, asked her prayers that she
might bear a son. Isabella was deeply attached to
the Beata Osanna, to whom she turned in all her
troubles, and after her death, in 1505, raised a splendid
tomb over her ashes and offered a silver head at her
shrine. On one occasion the Marchesa believed the
good nun's prayers had saved her from a dangerous
illness, while on another they brought her instant
relief from a violent headache [1] And in an altar-piece
of the Vision of the Beata Osanna, painted by Bonsignori, now in the Academy at Mantua, the portrait
of Isabella is introduced kneeling with three of her
ladies at the saint's feet.[2]

[1] Donesmondi, *Storia ecclesiastica di Mantova*, ii. 90.
[2] Mr. Berenson first drew my attention to this portrait, which
strongly resembles Leonardo's drawing of Isabella.

In 1492, Fra Mariano da Genazzano, the cultured and popular Augustinian, whose polished oratory at one time made him the rival of Savonarola in Florence, preached a course of Lent sermons at Mantua, which pleased Isabella so much that she insisted on keeping him at her court for Easter. On his return to Ferrara, the friar told Duchess Leonora how deeply he had been impressed with her daughter's intelligence and devotion. "Indeed," wrote the gratified mother, "he praised you so much that he almost made me believe you are really all that he said, and this would give me the greatest pleasure in the world."[1] At the same time, like all the Este princes, Isabella never ceased to follow the career of Fra Mariano's rival with the deepest interest. A volume of Savonarola's sermons was in her library, and six months after his death, she sent to Ferrara for a copy of the Miserere, a commentary on the Fifty - first Psalm, which he had written in prison before his execution. "I send you the Miserere of Savonarola," wrote her brother Alfonso on the 30th of October, "which I have had copied by your wish, and which you will find a worthy and devout book."[2] For the great friar of San Marco was a citizen of Ferrara, and neither Ercole d'Este nor his children ever forgot that his grandfather, Michele Savonarola, had held the post of physician to the ducal family. But wide and varied as was Isabella's interest in all forms of literature, the study of poetry remained her favourite pursuit. She was as indefatigable in her endeavours to obtain the productions of living bards as those of dead

---

[1] Luzio e Renier, *op. cit.*, p. 62.
[2] *Bibliofilo*, i. 26.

authors, and her correspondence in these early years is as much concerned with sonnets and *cauzoni* as with jewels and fine clothes. Antonio Tebaldeo, the young poet who had already acquired considerable reputation at the courts of Ferrara and Bologna, was constantly sending her his *strambotti* and *capitoli*, and the insatiable Marchesa was always begging for more.

"Find out Messer Tebaldeo," she writes in December 1491, to Giacomo Trotti, her father's envoy at Milan, "and beg him to send twenty or twenty-five of the finest sonnets as well as two or three *capitoli* which would give us the greatest possible pleasure." Sometimes she herself tried to express her thoughts in verse, and in one of his letters Tebaldeo speaks with high praise of a certain *strambotto* of her composition on the autumn trees which have lost their leaves, and thanks heaven that one of his disciples has attained an excellence to which he could never aspire, prophesying that she will go far in this direction, and achieve miracles in poetry. Isabella, however, took these flattering words for what they were worth, and although she occasionally wrote verses in private, steadily refused to allow her productions to be handed round among her courtiers, saying that such attempts were more likely to bring her ridicule than fame.[1]

But among all courtly poets of her circle the one whom she admired the most was her kinsman Niccolo da Correggio. From her earliest childhood she remembered him as the handsomest and most accomplished cavalier at the court of Ferrara, distinguished alike by his prowess in war and tourna-

---

[1] S. Davari, *La Musica in Mantova*, in *Riv. St. Mant.*, i. 54; and A. Luzio, *I Precettori d'Isabella d'Este*, p. 53.

ments, and by his polished courtesy and rare gift of poetic invention. His fame was celebrated by the most illustrious poets and writers of the age. Ariosto and Sabbà da Castiglione sang his praises in the next century. Sperandio struck a noble medal in his honour, and Isabella herself spoke of him after his death as the most perfect courtier and finished poet in all Italy. The son of Duke Ercole's sister, that fair Beatrice who was known as the Queen of Feasts, and of a prince of the reigning house of Correggio, who died before his son's birth in 1450, Niccolo grew up at his uncle's court at Ferrara, and was held in high favour by the Duke and all his family. He had been sent to escort Leonora of Aragon to Ferrara on her wedding journey, and had accompanied her when she returned to Naples with her children in 1477. He served with distinction in the wars against Venice, and was taken prisoner and kept in captivity for nearly a year, to the great distress of the Duchess, who entered warmly into the grief of his mother and of his wife, Cassandra, a daughter of the famous captain, Bartolommeo Colleoni.

In 1487, Niccolo's pastoral play of " Cefalo " was performed at Ferrara, and his eclogues and sonnets were in the hands of all lovers of poetry. Isabella frequently alludes to the choice copy of his poems, in white damask embroidered with diamonds, which he had presented to her father, and her own library contained several volumes of his works. A copy of his romances was bound in red velvet, while his eclogues and another book called *Il Giardino* were bound in black leather enriched with gold and silver clasps. Niccolo had been present at Isa-

bella's wedding, and again at that of Beatrice at
Milan, where, although past forty years of age, he
was pronounced by general consent to be the most
splendid figure in all that brilliant company.[1]   After
this, the influence of his mother, who had married the
Moro's half-brother Tristan Sforza, and the marked
favour shown him by Lodovico, induced him to settle
at Milan, where he played a leading part in court
and carnival festivities during Beatrice's lifetime.
But, although he rarely visited Mantua, he still
remained deeply attached to Isabella, whose devoted
slave he professed himself and with whom he kept
up an animated correspondence.   He addresses her
habitually as *Madonna unica mia*, his beloved *patrona*
and *signoria*, and speaks of her in his letters to others
as *la mia Illustrissima Isabella*.   And on one memorable occasion, when a discussion arose at the Moro's
palace of Vigevano on the illustrious women of the
day, Niccolo da Correggio ventured to speak of the
Marchesa as the first lady in the world—*la prima
donna del mondo*.[2]

In February 1491, Niccolo was present at the
fêtes held at Ferrara in honour of Alfonso d'Este and
Anna Sforza's marriage, and on this occasion showed
Isabella a complete collection of his works in manuscript, with a dedicatory epistle to herself, destined to
be published at some future date.   At the same time
he promised her a new poem of his own composition,
as well as a translation of one of Virgil's eclogues.
In the course of that spring he was sent by Lodovico on a mission to France, and before his departure,

[1] T. Chalcus, *Residua*, p. 95.
[2] Luzio, *Niccolo da Correggio*, in *Giorn. St. d. Lett. It.*, vol. xxi.
pp. 239–241.

wrote to the Marchesa assuring her of his devotion
and offering to execute any commission for her
in Paris. On his return, Isabella lost no time in
reminding him of his promise, and ended her letter
with these characteristic words: "Since I am of
an essentially greedy and impatient nature, I hold
those things the most dear, which I can obtain the
soonest." But the young princess had to restrain
her impatience, and it was not until the close of the
year that she received the fable of Psyche—a short
poem in *ottava rima*, with an elaborate dedication
which is still preserved in a few rare editions.
Meanwhile rumours of Niccolo's new fable had
reached Mantua, and a Milanese poet wrote to tell
one of Isabella's favourite courtiers, Jacopo d'Atri,
Count of Pianella, that he would soon see the Psyche
composed for his illustrious Madonna. "It is
finished," he goes on to say, "and will, I feel sure,
please you, but on your honour I beg you not to say
a word to any one, as the author does not wish
the report to precede the presentation of his poem."[1]
Isabella was anxious that her accomplished kinsman
should spend the next carnival at Mantua, but
he was detained at Milan, to organise the festivities at the Moro's court, and she did not see
him until she went to Pavia and Milan that
summer. Early in 1493, Niccolo sent her a copy of
the Rime composed by his friend Gasparo Visconti,
one of the sweetest singers of Beatrice's court,
but the Marchesa received the gift coldly, remarking that she should have much preferred to have
the poems before they were printed, and begging
Niccolo to send her anything new of his own, "for

[1] Luzio, *op. cit.*, p. 250.

without flattery I may say that your verses please me better than any other poems of the present day."[1]

But Isabella did not only turn to Niccolo da Correggio for verses and eclogues. She consulted him on many subjects and asked him to gratify many different fancies. When they met at Milan in the autumn of 1492, he invented a new design of cunningly interlaced links with which she proposed to adorn her next *camora*. This was the famous *fantasia dei vinci*, which her sister Beatrice borrowed with her permission, and wore, worked in massive gold, on a purple robe, at the wedding of Bianca Sforza and the Emperor Maximilian.[2] And when the Duchess of Urbino was spending the following summer at Mantua, and the two young princesses constantly sang and played together, Isabella, seized with a wish to learn some new instrument, wrote to beg Niccolo for the loan of a wonderful silver lyre which had been lately made for him by the renowned Florentine, Atalante Migliorotti. As usual, this courteous gentleman expressed his eagerness to comply with her request, and wrote, from Correggio, saying that his silver lyre should be sent to her as soon as he returned to Ferrara. " If you had not asked for Atalante's lyre," he remarks, " I would have sent you a smaller one, better fitted for a beginner, but since you wish for this one, I hope the name of Atalante and the memory of the giver will dispose you to learn the art with the greater readiness and affection." He goes on to explain the meaning of

[1] Davari, *Riv. St. Mant.*, i. p. 54.
[2] " Beatrice d'Este," p. 208, &c.

a new cantata entitled "Mopsa and Daphne," which had been performed at Milan last carnival, and which he is now sending her, but if she does not like it, promises to let her have another and a more attractive one, adding that she has only to ask, for he will be never weary of doing her service.[1]

The lute, as we know, was Isabella's favourite instrument, on which she accompanied herself with rare skill and charm. A few months after her marriage her father allowed his favourite musician, the Constance organist Giovanni Martini, to pay a visit to Mantua and give her singing lessons. After his return to Ferrara the German priest sent his pupil a book of songs, begging her to remember his directions and practise them daily. At the same time Duke Ercole sent Isabella his own book of songs, in order that she might transcribe her favourite melodies, begging her not to keep it too long, but return it as soon as possible. In 1491, another Ferrarese musician, Girolamo da Sestola, came to Mantua to give her singing lessons, and after his return to Ferrara, remained one of her most constant correspondents. Now, however, a sudden fancy to learn other instruments seems to have seized her, and this same summer she wrote to the great musician Atalante himself, begging him to send her a silver *citarra* or lute, with as many strings as he chooses, but which shall be a " fair and gallant thing to see." Atalante, it appears, had visited Mantua in 1491, at the pressing entreaty of the Marquis, to take the leading part in a performance of Polizianio's " Orfeo," which took

---

[1] Luzio, *op. cit.*, p. 243.

place at Marmirolo. In 1494, the Marchesa gave the Florentine musician a special token of favour by standing sponsor to his new-born child, who was held at the font by the Ferrarese envoy Manfredi, and named after her.[1]

The decoration of her rooms in the Castello was another subject which occupied much of the young Marchesa's thoughts at this time. Since the death of the Marchesa Barbara, ten years before, there had been no lady to reign over the court of Mantua, and Isabella may well have longed to bring some of the grace and beauty of her mother's *camerini* to brighten her new home in the grim old Castello di Corte. The apartments which she occupied during the greater part of her married life, were on the Piano Nobile of the Tower, close to the Camera Dipinta, as the nuptial chamber decorated with Andrea's frescoes was commonly called. These rooms looked over the waters of the lake and the long bridge of San Giorgio, and a staircase in the corner close to the Sala degli Sposi, led to her husband's apartments on the ground floor. Unfortunately these *camerini*, which Isabella occupied for more than thirty years, have undergone many alterations, and were mostly stripped of their decorations under the Austrian rule, when the Castello was inhabited by soldiers for a hundred and fifty years. But one little room looking towards the lake, in the corner of the Castello, near the Palazzina or annexe added on by Isabella's son, Federico, at the time of his own marriage, still retains traces of the original

[1] D'Ancona, *Origini del Teatro Italiano*, vol. ii. ; and Davari, *op. cit.*

decorations planned by the young Marchesa. Here we still find remains of gilding and ultramarine on the barrel-vaulted ceiling, and recognise the Gonzaga devices carved on the frieze of delicately inlaid wood-work. Here too, finely wrought in gold on an azure ground, are the musical notes and rests which were Isabella's favourite emblem, the *impresa* or device which she loved to wear on her embroidered robes, and the playing cards tied in packs together with the mystic numbers to which Paolo Giovio and other contemporaries allude. This charmingly decorated little room was, there can be little doubt, the *studiolo* which is so often mentioned in Isabella's letters, the peaceful retreat where she and Elisabetta Gonzaga spent their happiest days, surrounded by the books and pictures, the cameos and musical instruments which they loved.

At her first coming to Mantua, Isabella brought a whole train of artists, but most of these soon returned to Ferrara, and the court-painter, Ercole Roberti, suffered so much from sea-sickness on the journey up the Po, and was so much exhausted with his labours before the wedding, that he left suddenly, without even bidding the Marchesa fare-well.[1] A Mantuan painter, Luca Liombeni, was the artist whom she entrusted with the decoration of her *studiolo*, as we learn from an imperious letter which she addressed to him from Ferrara, on the 6th November 1491.

" Since we have learnt, by experience," wrote the impatient young princess, "that you are as slow in finishing your work as you are in everything else, we send this to remind you that for once you

[1] Gruyer, *op. cit.*, ii. 154.

must change your nature, and that if our *studiolo* is not finished on our return, we intend to put you into the dungeon of the Castello. And this, we assure you, is no jest on our part."

Upon this the terrified painter offered the humblest apologies to his mistress, who replied on the 12th of November :—

" In answer to your letter, we are glad to hear that you are doing your utmost to finish our *studiolo*, so as not to be sent to prison. We enclose a list of the devices which we wish to have painted on the frieze, and hope that you will arrange them as you think best, and make them appear as beautiful and elegant as possible. You can paint whatever you like inside the cupboards, as long as it is not anything ugly, because if it is, you will have to paint it all over again at your own expense, and be sent to pass the winter in the dungeon, where you can, if you like, spend a night for your pleasure now, to see if the accommodation there is to your taste ! Perhaps this may make you more anxious to please us in future. On our part, we will not let you want for money, and have told Cusatro to give you all the gold that you require." [1]

Meanwhile Mantegna had returned from Rome in September 1491, after two years' absence from Mantua. He brought with him a letter from Isabella's old tutor, Battista Guarino, whom he had formerly known at Verona, begging the Marchesa to look graciously on this master, whose excellent genius was indeed too well known to need any recommendation, and assuring her that he was as charming by nature as he was gifted in his art,

[1] Luzio, *I Precettori*, &c., pp. 18, 19.

"*Egh e tutto gentile.*"[1] This description, it must be owned, hardly agrees with all that we hear of Andrea's irritable and suspicious temper. But from the first, Isabella appreciated his rare talent and proved a kind patron and faithful friend to the great master. The whole of the next year was devoted to his unfinished Triumphs, and by a decree of February 1492, the Marquis bestowed a fresh gift of land upon the painter, " as a reward for the admirable works which he formerly painted in the Chapel and Camera of our Castello, and which in the Triumph of Cæsar he is now painting for us, in pictures which seem almost to live and breathe."[2] The works in the Chapel here mentioned were in all probability the noble Triptych now in the Uffizi, containing the Adoration, Circumcision, and Ascension, and the small altar-piece of the Death of the Virgin, with the view of the lake and bridge of S. Giorgio as seen from the Castello. This last-named picture came to England in 1627, with the chief treasures of the Gonzaga gallery, and is described in Van der Doort's catalogue of Charles the First's pictures as "a little piece of Andrea Montania, being the dying of Our Lady, the Apostles standing about with white candles lighted in their hands; and in the landskip where the town of Mantua is painted is the water-lake, where a bridge is over the said water towards the town. In a little ebony wooden frame." This precious little painting, on which Isabella's eyes must often have rested and which bore the words " Mantua piece" in the King's own writing, was

---

[1] W. Braghirolli, in *Giorn. di Erud. Art.*, i. p. 202.

[2] *Archivio Gonzaga, Libro dei Decreti,* 24, fol. 56, quoted by Kristeller, *op. cit.,* App. p. 486.

THE DEATH OF THE VIRGIN

By Andrea Mantegna

(*Madrid*)

To face p. 90, vol. i

bought at the sale of his pictures after his execution by the Spanish Ambassador Cardenas, and now hangs in the Prado at Madrid.

By the end of 1492, the Triumphs were finally completed, and Andrea was at length able to execute a commission for Isabella. This was a portrait of herself which she wished to send to Isabella del Balzo, Countess of Acerra, the younger sister of Gianfrancesco Gonzaga's wife, Antonia del Balzo, who was apparently one of her intimate friends.

In January 1493, Isabella d'Este wrote the following letter to Jacopo d'Atri, her lord's envoy at Naples :—

" In order to satisfy the most illustrious Madonna, the Countess of Acerra, whom we love tenderly, we have arranged to have our portrait taken by Andrea Mantegna, and will ask him to send it to you in order that you may present it to her before you leave, and we hope that you will bring back the portrait of the said Countess, since she has asked for ours."

Jacopo d'Atri returned to Mantua in April with a drawing of the Countess, which Isabella acknowledged gratefully in the following letter :—

" The sight of your picture gave us the liveliest joy, since you are as dear to us as our only sister Beatrice. If Our Lord God would only grant that we might see you once more and embrace you, it would make us happier than anything in the world. This feeling prompted our urgent desire to possess your portrait and thus in some measure satisfy the longing of our heart. Now that we have your image both on paper and in wax, we shall hold it very dear

and often look at it, although, from what Jacopo
says and from our own recollection, neither portrait
resembles you very much. But we know how
difficult it is to find painters who take good likenesses from life, and shall try to supply the artist's
deficiencies with the help of the information given
us by Margherita, Jacopo, and others who have lately
seen you, so that we may not be deceived in our idea
of you. We thank you exceedingly for your kindness, and beg you to keep the promise made us
through Jacopo, that you will send us another on
panel, and we will do the same in compliance with
your request. We do not say that you will see a
beautiful picture, but at least you will have in your
house a portrait of one who is your most loving
sister."

But when, a fortnight later, Andrea's portrait was
finished, it failed to satisfy Isabella's critical taste.

" We are much vexed," she writes on the 20th of
April, " that we are unable to send you our portrait,
because the painter has done it so badly that it does
not resemble us in the very least. But we have
sent for a foreign artist who has the reputation of
taking excellent likenesses, and as soon as it is ready
we will send it to Your Highness, who will not forget
that we are altogether devoted to you."

The foreign master was Giovanni Santi, the father
of Raphael, who had been evidently recommended to
Isabella by her sister-in-law, the Duchess of Urbino.
Elisabetta sent him without delay, and he spent some
time at Mantua that summer painting a series of family
portraits—probably for the decoration of some hall in
one of the Gonzaga villas—and began a picture of
Isabella. Unluckily, before it was finished he fell ill

of fever, and was compelled to return to the healthier climate of Urbino. Some months passed before Isabella was able to inform her friend that the portrait was ready, and would be scnt to her straight from Urbino.

"Most illustrious Madonna and dearest sister, in order to satisfy Your Highness—not because our countenance is so beautiful that it deserves to be painted—we send you, by Simone da Canossa, chamberlain to the illustrious Duke of Calabria, a panel portrait by the hand of Zohan de Sancte, painter to the Duchess of Urbino, who is said to make good likenesses, although from what we hear it seems that this one might resemble us more."[1]

This Contessa d'Acerra, to whom Isabella was so fondly attached, became the second wife of her uncle Federico, the last king of the house of Aragon who reigned over Naples. After that monarch died in France, his widow came back to Italy with her daughters and ended her days at the court of his nephew, Alfonso, Duke of Ferrara.

[1] A. Luzio, *I Ritratti d'Isabella d'Este* in *Emporium*, 1900, p. 347.

CHAPTER VI

1493—1494

Discovery of the New World—The news reaches Mantua—Birth of the Moro's son—Isabella's journey to Ferrara and Venice—Reception by the Doge and Signory—Her relations with Gentile Bellini—Return to Mantua—Francesco Gonzaga at Venice — Death of Duchess Leonora — Birth of Leonora Gonzaga—Departure of the Duke and Duchess of Urbino —Decorations of Marmirolo and Gonzaga.

WHILE the young Gonzaga princesses were spending the spring days together, singing Petrarch and Virgil to the lute, or playing their favourite game of *scartino*, great events were happening in the outer world. On the 15th of March Columbus landed at Palos on his return from his first voyage, and told the wondering Spaniards of the New World which had been discovered beyond the seas. Soon the news reached the little blue and gold *studiolo* looking over the Mantuan lakes, and we can picture to ourselves the breathless excitement with which Isabella and her sister-in-law read the marvellous traveller's tales that came from Spain. On the 22nd of April, Luca Fancelli, the old architect who had spent his last forty years in the service of the Gonzagas, wrote from Florence to tell his lord and master, Marquis Francesco, these wonderful things.

" Your Highness," he says, " may have heard that we have had letters here telling us that the King of Spain sent some ships over the seas, which, after a voyage of thirty-six days, discovered certain islands, amongst others a very big one lying east, with broad rivers and terrible mountains, and a very fertile land, inhabited by handsome men and women, who go naked or only wear a cotton leaf round the waist. This country abounds in gold, and the people are very courteous and liberal of their property, and there are quantities of palms of more than six different kinds, and some wonderfully tall trees. There are other islands, five of which have been given names, and one which is nearly as large as Italy. And the rivers there run with gold, and there is plenty of copper but no iron, and many other wonders, and you can neither see the Arctic nor the Antarctic poles."

Further particulars came from two of Francesco's servants, Giovanni dei Bardi and Giambattista Strozzi, who had been sent to buy horses in Spain, and who now wrote from Cadiz, saying: " A Savona sailor named Columbus has landed here, bringing 30,000 ducats in gold, as well as pepper and other spices, and parrots as big as falcons and as red as pheasants. They found trees bearing fine wool, and others which produce wax and linen fibres, and men like Tartars, tall and active, with long hair falling over their shoulders. They eat human flesh, and fatten men as we do capons, and are called cannibals. . . . It is certain that these sailors have brought back a great quantity of gold, sandal-wood, and spices, and what I myself have seen—sixty parrots of variegated colours, eight of them as big as falcons—as well as twelve Indians, who have been sent to the King. And in that land they found great forests in which the trees grow so thickly you could hardly see the sky, and if some men had not climbed to the top of the trees they would never have got out again, and many other things of which I have not time to tell."

A few months later, Isabella herself received the following letter from a Cremona scholar at Ferrara named Ponzone: " I hear that a man named Columbus lately discovered an island for the King of Spain, on which are men of our height but of copper-coloured skin, with noses like apes. The chiefs wear a plate of gold in their nostrils which covers the mouth, the women have faces as big as wheels, and all go naked, men and women alike. Twelve men and four women have been brought back to the King of Spain, but they are so weakly that two of them fell ill of some sickness which the doctors do not understand, and they had no pulse and are dead. The others have been clothed, and if they see any one who is richly clad they stroke him with their hands and kiss his hands to show how much they admire him. They seem intelligent, and are very tame and gentle. No one can understand their language. They eat of everything at table, but are not given wine. In their own country they eat the roots of trees and some big kind of nut which is like pepper but yields good food, and on this they live." [1]

Meanwhile affairs nearer home claimed Isabella's attention. Her mother's ladies wrote long letters from Milan giving full particulars of the birth of Beatrice's son, and of the splendid festivities and rejoicings with which this event had been hailed. Isabella's warm heart glowed with affection when she heard of the *bello puttino*, and she told her sister how she longed to hold the babe in her arms and cover

---

[1] G. Berghet, *Fonti Ital. per la Storia della Scoperta del Nuovo Mondo*, pp. 165, 169.

him with kisses, but she was, not unnaturally,
inclined to wish for the same blessing herself, and to
envy Beatrice's prosperity. When Francesco Gonzaga, on his return from Venice in April, brought
his wife an invitation from the Doge to attend the
Ascension-tide festivities in that city and witness the
yearly ceremony of the espousals of Venice with the
sea, Isabella accepted the offer joyfully. But when,
a few days later, she heard from her mother that
Lodovico and his wife were coming to Ferrara in
May, and that Beatrice was to accompany Duchess
Leonora to Venice, she told her husband that nothing
would induce her to visit Venice at the same time.
And since it was impossible to vie with the splendour
of her sister's train, she begged to be allowed to
appear without ceremony before the Doge as his
humble servant and daughter. Fortunately the
Moro's journey was delayed, and Isabella left Mantua
early in May and travelled by boat to Ferrara. On
her arrival she sent an affectionate note to her
sister-in-law Elisabetta, from whom she had parted
with much regret.

" When I found myself alone in the boat, without
your sweet company, I felt so forlorn I hardly knew
what I wanted or where I was. To add to my
comfort, the wind and tide were against us all the
way, and I often wished myself back in your room
playing at *scartino !* " [1]

On the same day Elisabetta wrote saying that
the weather had been so bad since the Marchesa's
departure that she had never left her room, and
complaining that she only felt half-alive now that

---

[1] *Copialettera d'Isabella,* lib. iii., quoted by Luzio, *Mantova
e Urbino,* p. 63.

she was deprived of her sister's charming conversation.[1]　After assisting at the wedding of Guido, the son of the accomplished poet Tito Strozzi, and at a dramatic representation in honour of the occasion, which afforded her great delight, Isabella continued her journey, accompanied by her brother-in-law, the papal protonotary, Sigismondo, and reached Chioggia on the 13th of May.　Here she was lodged in the palace of the Podestà, and sumptuously entertained at the Signory's expense.　After supper three Venetian patricians who had been present at her wedding— Zorzo Pisano, Zaccaria Contarini, and Francesco Capello — waited on her to bid her welcome in the Doge's name, and escorted her to the palace near San Trovaso occupied by her husband as captain of the Republic's armies.　Early the next morning Isabella entered the port of Venice, passing between the forts of Malamocco so quietly that she hardly saw them, and was received at Santa Croce by the Doge and Signory, together with the ambassadors of Naples, Milan, and Ferrara.[2]　The scene that followed is best described in her own words.

"Here I landed and met the Prince and ambassadors coming out of the church, and kissed His Serene Highness's hand and exchanged courteous greeting, after which he led me to his bucentaur, which was loaded with gentlemen and ladies.　There were ninety-three of these last, all richly attired and glittering with jewels, and I am sure that not one among them had less than 6000 ducats worth of precious stones upon her person.　I sat on the

[1] P. Ferrato, *Lettere inedite di Donne Mantovane del Secolo*, xv. p. 56.

[2] Luzio e Renier in *Arch. St. Lomb.*, xvii. 366–372.

Prince's right, and so, talking of many things, we rowed up the Canal Grande to the sound of bells, trumpets, and guns, accompanied by such a crowd of boats and people that it was impossible to count them. I cannot tell you, my dear lord, what loving attention and great honour are paid me here. The very stones of Venice seem to rejoice and be glad of my coming, and all for the love which they bear Your Excellency. Not only my own expenses, but those of my whole suite, are liberally defrayed, and two gentlemen have been deputed to provide for us. . . . To-morrow the Doge and Signory are to give me an audience, and I will reply as you desired to the best of my ability. I do not describe the beauties of this place as you have been here so often, and will only say that it seems to me, as it does to you, the finest city which I have ever seen."

The next day forty gentlemen escorted the Marchesa to the Sala del Collegio, and the Doge, taking her by the hand, placed her on a seat on the tribunal on his right hand, while Sigismondo Gonzaga sat on his left. Then, rising and bowing with charming grace towards the Doge, Isabella expressed her joy at being allowed to assure His Serenity of her reverence and loyalty for him and this illustrious Signory under whose shadow and protection her lord wished to live and die, and begged to commend the Marquis, his State, and herself to their protection. The Doge replied in gracious words, and invited her to attend vespers in San Marco, a function which Isabella, tired with the heat and length of these ceremonies, found very tedious. "I know," she wrote to Francesco, "that to-morrow's ceremony will be no less wearisome, but I will bear it cheerfully for the sake of seeing so many fine things and doing honour to Your Excellency."

The solemn espousals of Venice with the sea, and the state banquet which followed, proved even more fatiguing than Isabella expected. "Have pity on me," she wrote that evening, "for I was never more tired and bored than I am with all these ceremonies. . . . It seems to me a thousand years until I can get back to Mantua! For, although Venice is a glorious city and has no rival, to have seen it once is quite enough for me."[1] The concluding days of her visit, however, were spent more pleasantly. She visited Queen Caterina Cornaro in her beautiful home at Murano, assisted at a sitting of the Great Council, and went to the Church of S. Zaccaria to hear the nuns sing. She spent one afternoon with her husband's uncle, the Duke of Bavaria, who was staying in Venice and showed her the most cordial affection; and she visited the ducal palace and saw the noble frescoes which Gentile and Giovanni Bellini were painting in the Council-hall. On this occasion she probably made the acquaintance of the painters themselves, whose sister Niccolosia was the wife of Andrea Mantegna, and saw the wonderful portrait of Sultan Mahomet II. which Gentile had lately brought back from Constantinople. At the same time she expressed a great wish to have a portrait of the Doge Agostino Barbarigo upon which Gentile was engaged, and, after her return to Mantua, she desired Antonio Salimbeni to remind the painter of her request, and to beg that he would send the Marquis plans of Cairo and Venice. On the 1st of October the Mantuan agent informed his lord that Gentile would gladly

[1] Luzio e Renier, *op. cit.*, p. 371.

oblige him and his illustrious lady, but three weeks later he excused himself on the plea of pressing engagements and begged the Marchesa to write to the Doge herself on the subject. Accordingly Isabella addressed a letter to the Doge, which was duly delivered by her envoy Battista Scalona, begging him to gratify her earnest desire to possess his portrait. "The Most Serene Prince," wrote Scalona, "called one of his secretaries and bade him give the Marchesa the most gracious answer, explaining that Gentile's portrait was already promised to his nephew, but that he would desire the painter to have it copied for her without delay." Since, however, we find no mention of a picture by Gentile Bellini in Isabella's collection, it is doubtful if the work was ever executed. But the plan of Cairo which Gentile had promised "on the faith of a cavalier" to let the Marquis have was really brought to Mantua by Scalona on the 22nd of December, together with an old plan of the Piazza di San Marco and the ducal palace, by the hand of his father, Jacopo Bellini.[1]

On the 20th of May, Isabella left Venice, and spent the night at Padua. After paying her vows at the famous Basilica of Il Santo, she went on to Vicenza and Verona, where she was received with great honour, and entertained at the expense of the Signory. Meanwhile her return was impatiently awaited by Elisabetta, who wrote charming letters to her absent sister, saying how much she missed her sweet companionship, greatly as she rejoiced to hear of the honours which had been paid her in Venice, and begging her to return quickly, lest the

[1] Yriarte, *Isabelle d'Este et les Artistes de son temps; Gazette des Beaux Arts*, xv. p. 216.

excessive heat should injure her health.[1] The Marquis was superintending the works at his favourite villa of Marmirolo, and only paid his sister flying visits, so that the Duchess gladly obeyed Isabella's invitation to meet her at Porto, outside Mantua, " where," she wrote, " we may together enjoy the pure country air and tell each other all that has happened since we parted." [2]

The two princesses spent the next six weeks in this villa, which Francesco had lately bestowed on his wife, and which she was to improve and beautify so much in future years. Here they read and sang together, in the terraced gardens on the Mincio and Jacopo di San Secondo, the accomplished viol-player, who had been sent from Milan as a special act of courtesy on Lodovico Moro's part, serenaded them with exquisite music through the long summer evenings. Isabella was blissful, and not even the accounts which the Marquis sent from Venice of the splendid fêtes in honour of her mother and sister could make her wish to be there. " To say the truth," she wrote to Duchess Leonora, " all these fêtes and ceremonies are very much alike." She was better pleased to hear from her husband of the excellent impression which she herself had made on the Doge and Senators. Wherever he went, the praises of her charms rang in his ears. Everywhere he heard how honourably she had been entertained, and with what infinite tact and skill she had behaved. He himself could not commend her wisdom and discretion too highly, and all he now begged was that his wife would take great care of her health and

<hr>

[1] Ferrato, *op. cit.*, p. 85.
[2] Luzio e Renier, *Mantova e Urbino*, p. 67.

be of good courage for his sake. The warmth of
Francesco's affection for Isabella was evidently increased, not only by gratitude for her good offices
with the Venetian Signory, but by the hopes of an
heir which she had begun to entertain.

In July, the Marchesa tore herself reluctantly
away from her sister-in-law to visit her mother,
whose health was giving her family anxiety, and
spent a month at Ferrara. It was the last time
that she ever saw the good Duchess, who died on
the 11th of October of a gastric fever which carried
her off in a few days. Francesco Gonzaga hastened
to Ferrara, but gave orders that the sad news should
be kept from the Marchesa until his return. But
when no letters came from the Duchess for a whole
week, Isabella's fears were aroused, and she heard
from a Milanese correspondent, "who," as Capilupi
wrote to the Marquis, "must have been either very
imprudent or still more wicked," that her beloved
mother had been dead three days. Happily no harm
was done, and after the first outburst of grief Isabella
showed her usual good sense and self-control. The
highest honours were paid to the dead Duchess both
at Ferrara and at Mantua. The saintly friar, Bernardino da Feltre, preached the funeral sermon, young
Ariosto wrote an elegy on her death, and Latin
orations were pronounced by some of the most distinguished humanists of the day. But more touching than any of these pompous tributes was a letter
in which Battista Guarino poured out the grief of
his soul to his old pupil.

"If I had a hundred tongues, dearest lady," he
wrote, "I could not express the grief which I feel at
the death of our Madonna. I long to fly to you and

comfort you, but am myself in sore need of consolation. The whole city is weeping for our dead lady,
and I, who received so much kindness from her, am
more unhappy than any one, and can only take
comfort in feeling that this is the will of God.
I am sure that none of those saints whom the
Church has canonised, ever made a better or more
devout end than she did, as you will learn from
a few words which I spoke over her grave, which
I will send you, in memory of this virtuous and
excellent lady. And I will see that Your Excellency is not the last to receive a copy, for I have
always looked upon you as my mistress, but how
much more now that I have lost her who was my
sole hope and refuge! Forgive me if I cannot say
more, but tears will not allow me to write.—Your
faithful servant, BATTISTA." [1]

Fortunately for the Marchesa's happiness, she was
able to forget her grief in her new hopes, and on the
last day of the year 1492, she gave birth to her first
child—a daughter, in whom, as she wrote to her aunt
Beatrice, the wife of Matthias Corvinus, King of
Hungary, "the name and blessed memory of my
mother shall live again." Congratulations poured
in from all sides. Fra Mariano and the holy nun
Osanna sent the mother and child their blessing, and
the poor fool Mattello wrote in his maddest and
merriest mood, telling his dear Madonna not to have a
thought or care in the world, now that she had given
birth to a lovely daughter. He proceeded to address
the new-born princess as *Leonora zentile—Leonora
mia bella—Leonora mia cara*, informed her that he
was coming from Marmirolo to her christening, and

[1] Luzio e Renier in *Giorn. St. d. Lett.*, vol. xxxv.

ended by begging her father the Marquis for a dole
on this happy occasion. Isabella herself however did
not conceal her disappointment at the sex of the
child, as we learn from the letter which she wrote
to her sister on New Year's Day. "You will have
heard that I have a daughter and that both she and
I are doing well, although I am sorry not to have
a son. But since this is the will of God, she will be
dear to me."[1] The child received the names of
Leonora Violante Maria, and Lodovico Sforza, his
wife Beatrice, the Doge of Venice, and Lorenzo di
Pierfrancesco dei Medici were among the sponsors.
None of these illustrious personages, however, were
able to be present at the christening, but Lorenzo
dei Medici wrote a courteous letter to the Marquis,
thanking him for the honour which he had paid him
and congratulating him and the Marchesa on the
happy event. "I hope," he adds, "that this new-
born daughter may grow up to be a great joy to
you, and that God will give you sons in future."
Since he was unfortunately too unwell to attend the
christening, he promised to send his brother, Giovanni
dei Medici, to take his place. This prince, who
soon afterwards became the third husband of Caterina Sforza, the famous Madonna of Forli, visited
Mantua on the 2nd of March, and was entertained
by Isabella, as we learn from the following note to
her absent lord:—

"The Magnificent Giovanni dei Medici arrived
this morning in time for dinner. I have given him
rooms in the Corte and sent Giovanni Pietro Gonzaga
and Lodovico Uberti to wait on him. After dinner
he paid me a visit, and I entertained him and showed

[1] Luzio e Renier, *Mantova e Urbino*, p. 69.

him the Camera and the Triumphs and afterwards took him to see our little girl." [1]

The Camera was the Sala degli Sposi, decorated with Mantegna's frescoes, while his newly completed Triumphs hung in a hall in that portion of the Castello known as the Corte Vecchia, and were not removed to Francesco's new palace of San Sebastiano until the year 1506.

Elisabetta Gonzaga had been induced to remain with Isabella for her confinement, and only returned to Urbino on the 20th of January, with her husband Duke Guidobaldo, who came to spend Christmas at Mantua. Her departure was greatly lamented by the Marchesa, who sent her a tender little note on the same day, saying how sadly she missed her sweet and loving conversation. "It seems strange enough," she adds, "to be without you as long as I am in bed, but it will be much worse when I leave the house— for there is no one whom I love like you, excepting my only sister, the Duchess of Bari." Her recovery, however, proved rapid. A week later she rode out through the town, to the joy of all the people, and the next day went to pay her vows at S. Maria delle Grazie, a favourite sanctuary of the Gonzaga princes, on the other side of the lakes, five miles from Mantua.

Early in February, we find her enjoying hunting parties and theatricals, at Marmirolo, that superb country-house which Francesco Gonzaga delighted to adorn. For the last three years architects and artists had been busy here. Mantegna's son Francesco had painted a series of Triumphs on canvas, in

[1] *Archivio Gonzaga,* quoted by P. Kristeller, *Andrea Mantegna,* App.

imitation of his father's great works, and both this artist and the Veronese master Bonsignori, who had entered the Marquis's service in 1488, were now engaged in decorating certain halls with views of Greek and Turkish cities. Constantinople, Adrianople, Gallipoli and Rhodes were all represented in the *Camera greca*, and groups of Turkish women bathing and going to mosque, as well as a portrait of the Sultan's ambassador, were painted on one of the walls. The plans provided by Gentile Bellini were evidently destined to hang in three rooms, and one hall, we are told, contained a *Mappamondo* drawn in charcoal. In 1496, the Marquis applied to Giovanni Bellini for a map of Paris, and the painter promised to do his best to satisfy His Excellency, but said he could not vouch for its correctness, since he had never been in France. Francesco addressed the same request to Lorenzo dei Medici when he asked him to stand godfather to his infant daughter, but such a thing, it appeared, was not to be found in the whole of Florence. Isabella, as might be expected, shared her husband's taste for topographical plans and maps. Many years afterwards, she ordered copies to be made of a celestial and terrestrial globe in the Vatican Library, and sent to Venice for the latest plans of Constantinople and Cairo.

CHAPTER VII

1494—1495

Journey of Isabella to Loreto and Urbino—Letters from Gubbio and Urbino—Charles VIII. enters Italy—The Marquis of Mantua refuses his offers—Visit of Isabella to Milan—Conquest of Naples by the French—League against France—Francesco Gonzaga, captain of the armies of the League—Isabella governs Mantua—Battle of the Taro—Heroism of Francesco Gonzaga—Rejoicings at Venice and Mantua—The Jew Daniele Norsa and Mantegna's Madonna della Vittoria.

As soon as the carnival fêtes at Marmirolo were ended and her infant daughter had been christened, Isabella set out on a pilgrimage to Loreto, to fulfil a vow which she had made to Our Lady before the birth of her child. She started on the 10th of March, taking with her an offering of chased gold ornaments, worked by the skilful Mantuan goldsmith, Bartolommeo Meliolo, who had lately been appointed Master of the Mint, and whose medals of the Gonzaga princes are well known. Her original intention had been to spend Holy Week at Urbino with her sister-in-law, but the Duchess begged her to put off her visit till after Easter, since it was difficult to obtain sufficient supplies of fish at Urbino to feed a large number of guests. So after spending a few days at Ferrara and a night at Ravenna, where she visited the ancient churches and admired the mosaics, the Marchesa travelled by Pesaro and Ancona to Loreto. Here she

arrived on Wednesday in Holy Week, and confessed and communicated at the altar of the Santa
Casa on Maundy Thursday. In a letter to her
husband from Ravenna she informed him that she
intended to spend Easter at Gubbio, and then
devote one day to Assisi, and another to Perugia,
" both in order to see that noble city, and because,
if I am to hear mass and dine at Assisi, there
would not be time to return to Gubbio the same
day. From Assisi to Perugia, I hear, it is only
ten miles, through a most beautiful valley, and
twelve more from Perugia to Gubbio." [1]

But when the Marchesa reached Gubbio she
found the Duke and Duchess of Urbino awaiting
her, and was induced to spend ten days with them
at Gubbio, and another fortnight at Urbino. From
Gubbio she visited Assisi, where she saw Giotto's
frescoes and paid her vows at the tomb of St. Francis,
and Camerino, where her cousins, the Varani, gave
her a warm welcome, and would gladly have detained her longer. But she was eager to return to
Gubbio, and was as much struck with the beauty
of the spot as the splendour of the ducal palace,
which had been the favourite abode of the last
Duchess, Battista Sforza, where her son Guidobaldo
was born, and where she herself died. " This
palace," she wrote on the 30th of March to her
husband, " is magnificently furnished, besides being
a noble building, and is so finely situated that I
do not think I have ever seen a place which pleased
me better. It stands on a height overlooking the
town and plain, and has a delightful garden, with
a fountain in the centre." To-day the fair gardens

are desolate, and the sumptuous fittings of the palace are gone, but a considerable portion of Duke Federico's building still remains. We can look down from the beautiful loggia on the view which Isabella admired, and breathe the health-giving breezes which Elisabetta praised in her letters.

But the famous palace of Urbino inspired the young Marchesa with still greater enthusiasm. "This palace," she writes to her husband, "is far finer than I ever expected. Besides the natural beauty of the place, it is very richly furnished with tapestries, hangings, and silver plate; and I must tell you that in all the different rooms which I have occupied in this Duke's different homes, the hangings have never been moved from one place to another, and from the first moment when I arrived at Gubbio until now, I have been entertained more and more sumptuously every day: indeed I could not have been more highly honoured if I had been a bride! I have repeatedly begged my hosts to reduce these expenses and treat me in a more familiar way, but they will not listen to this. This is, no doubt, the doing of the Duke, who is the most generous of men. He holds a fine court now, and lives in royal splendour, and governs the State with great wisdom and humanity, to the satisfaction of all his subjects."

It was not till the 25th of April that Isabella finally took leave of the Duke and Duchess, who was inconsolable at parting from her dearly-loved friend, and wrote the following note within the next twenty-four hours:—

"Your departure made me feel not only that I had lost a dear sister, but that life itself had gone from me. I know not how else to soften my grief, except by writing every hour to you, and telling you on paper all that my lips desire to say. If I could express the sorrow I feel, I believe that you would come back out of compassion for me. And if I did not fear to vex you, I would follow you myself. But since both these things are impossible, from the respect which I owe Your Highness, all I can do is to beg you earnestly to remember me sometimes, and to know that I bear you always in my heart."

The tender-hearted Duchess experienced a fresh sorrow that summer in the death of her favourite painter, Giovanni Santi. He had never recovered from the fever which he caught at Mantua in the previous autumn, and died on the 1st of August. "About twenty days ago," wrote Elisabetta to her sister-in-law on the 19th, "our painter, Giovanni dei Sancti, passed out of this life, being in full possession of his senses, and in the most excellent disposition of mind. May God pardon his soul!" On hearing of Santi's death, the Marquis Francesco wrote at once to ask his sister to send him the portraits on *tondi* which he began at Mantua, and, on the 13th of October, Elisabetta replied: "In answer to your letter, I must tell you that Giovanni dei Sancti was unable, owing to his illness at Mantua, to finish the portrait of Monsignore (Sigismondo Gonzaga); and after his return here, his illness increased so rapidly that he could not go on with mine, but if Your Excellency will send me a round of the same size as the others, I will have my portrait painted by a good artist here, and send it you as soon as possible. I am well, and have good news of my illustrious consort, from whom I hear constantly." And in a postscript she adds: "I have made Giovanni's assistant search everywhere, but he says that he can find nothing."[1]

Meanwhile Isabella travelled northward through Romagna to Bologna, where she was hospitably entertained by Annibale Bentivoglio and her sister Lucrezia; and after paying a short visit to her father and brother at Ferrara, reached Mantua towards the middle of May. During her absence from home she received daily accounts of her little daughter's well-being from Violante de' Preti, and the Marquis himself gave her constant news of the child, to whom he was tenderly attached. "Yesterday we went into our little daughter's room," he writes in one letter to Urbino, "and were glad to see her so well and lively. We had her dressed before us, as you desired, in her white damask robe, which suits her charmingly, and of which she was very proud. This morning we have been to see her again, but finding her asleep, would not wake her."[2] Neither did Francesco fail to give his wife private information of the important political events which had been happening at Milan and Mantua in the last few weeks. In a long letter to Bologna, intended for her eyes alone, he told her that Monseigneur de Migni, as he called D'Aubigny, and three other French ambassadors had arrived at Mantua on the 22nd of April, with eighty-five horsemen, to ask a free passage through his dominion for the Most Christian King's troops on the way to Naples. More than this, they had

[1] Campori, *Notizie di Giovanni Santi*, Modena, 1870.
[2] Luzio e Renier, *Mantova e Urbino*, pp. 75–77.

secretly invited him to enter Charles the Eighth's service, offering him the title of Captain-General and Grand Chamberlain. These proposals, however, Francesco felt compelled to refuse, since he was already pledged to the Signory of Venice. In the same letter he informed Isabella that he had sent an envoy to visit the Grand Turk's ambassador at Venice, and had heard from him that the Sultan would gladly give him the relic of the Holy Shirt, worn by Our Lord Christ, as well as forty good horses, for which he was about to send to Constantinople.[1]

In September, the French king entered Italy, and was met at Asti by Lodovico Sforza and Duke Ercole of Ferrara, and sumptuously entertained at Vigevano by Duchess Beatrice. Isabella herself, whose sympathies, like those of all her family, were strongly on the side of France, went to Parma at her brother-in-law's request to see the first French cavalry pass through the town, and afterwards wrote to her brother Ferrante, congratulating him on his triumphal entry into Florence with the king, and expressing her regret that she had not witnessed this splendid sight. The presence of her sister-in-law, Chiara Gonzaga, who came to Mantua in December, while her husband, Gilbert, Duke of Montpensier, was leading the French armies against Naples, helped to enlist Isabella's sympathies on the same side. But before long her feelings, in common with those of all true Italians, underwent a complete revulsion.

The stirring events which succeeded each other that autumn at Milan and Pavia—the death of the

[1] Luzio e Renier in *Arch. St. Lomb.*, xvii. p. 391.

unhappy Duke Giangaleazzo, and the election and
proclamation of Lodovico in his stead—were fully
reported to Isabella by the Mantuan agent, Donato
de' Preti. There had of late been some coolness
between Francesco Gonzaga and Lodovico, who,
not altogether without reason, suspected his brother-
in-law of being in secret correspondence with his
enemy, King Alfonso of Naples. But cordial
congratulations were addressed by the Marquis to
the new Duke and Duchess, and in January 1495,
he allowed his wife to accept her sister's pressing
invitation to visit Milan. Here Isabella was
present at the birth of Beatrice's second son,
Francesco Sforza, on the 4th of February, and held
the child at the baptismal font. A succession of
splendid fêtes were given in her honour by Niccolo
da Correggio and other Milanese courtiers, and her
letters to Francesco and Giovanni Gonzaga dwell
with enthusiasm on the magnificent banquets and
pageants, and the wonders of painting and architecture that were displayed before her eyes in the
Castello and city of Milan. On the other hand,
her secretary, Capilupi, told his master how the
Marchesa herself had won golden opinions on all
sides. " I wish," he writes on the 28th of January,
"that Your Excellency could have been in a corner
of the room when my lady received the Venetian
Ambassador, which she did with so much grace and
gallantry, and with such alacrity in responding to
his salutation, that he confessed himself her willing
slave. In the same way she charms all who come to
visit her, but above all, the Lord Duke, who calls
her his dear daughter, and always makes her dine at
his table. In short, she does the greatest honour

both to Your Excellency and herself." And Isabella herself wrote to her sister-in-law, Chiara Gonzaga, that she was enjoying herself immensely, and was more honoured and fêted by every one than she deserved. At Lodovico's urgent entreaty, her husband allowed her to spend the carnival at Milan, although, as he wrote, "all Mantua complains of your prolonged absence." [1]

But the news of the conquest of Naples by the French threw a gloom over these gay fêtes. Carnival amusements lost their brilliancy for Isabella when she thought of the desolation at Naples, and heard how her cousin, the young King Ferrante, and her mother's kinsfolk were driven into exile; and she was heartily glad when the time came to set out on her journey home. Lodovico loaded her with parting gifts, and two fat oxen, together with several lengths of gold brocade, exquisitely embroidered with doves, were among the presents which the Marchesa took back to Mantua. Beatrice was strangely moved at parting from her sister, but neither of the two dreamt they would never meet again, and Isabella little knew the altered circumstances under which she was to see the Moro's splendid home when she next came to Milan.

On the 14th of March, she reached Mantua, and before a month was over the new League was proclaimed between the Pope, the King of the Romans, the King and Queen of Spain, Henry VII. of England, the Signory of Venice, and the Duke of Milan. Francesco Gonzaga was appointed captain of the armies of the League, and, with twenty-five

[1] Luzio e Renier in *Arch. St. Lomb.*, xvii. 620.

thousand men under his command, prepared to cut
off the retreat of the French king, who, on hearing
of the coalition against him, left Naples hastily and
marched northwards. On the Feast of St. George,
Isabella paid a visit to her father at Ferrara, and
while she was there, received an urgent summons
from her lord to lend him some of her finest jewels,
with which to adorn his person at the fêtes about to
be held at Milan, to celebrate the arrival of the
Imperial Ambassador and the investiture of Lodovico Sforza with the ducal crown. Already, a year
before, when the Marchesa was at Urbino, she had,
at Francesco's desire, pledged many of her jewels in
order to raise a sum of money with which to obtain
his brother Sigismondo's advancement to the dignity
of Cardinal. " One of the greatest wishes that I
have in the world," she wrote, " is to see Monsignore
a Cardinal, so I am much pleased to hear that this
affair is about to be arranged. I send Alberto da
Bologna with the keys of my jewel boxes, that he
may give you whatever you wish, since I would not
only give my treasure, but my blood, for your
honour and that of your house." Now, like a good
wife, she sent her most precious ornaments—her big
diamonds and large rubies, and her collar of a
hundred links—all but her golden girdle, which had
been lately seen on her person at Milan, and which
she had now lent one of her father's courtiers to
wear at a masque. All her other jewels, as she
gently reminded the Marquis, were in pawn at
Venice.[1]

On her return to Mantua she took up the
reins of government in her lord's absence, and ad-

---

[1] Luzio, *Lusso d'Isabella,* in *N. Antologia,* 1896.

ministered affairs with a prudence and sagacity
which excited the wonder of grey-headed councillors.
On the vigil of the Ascension, while a procession
was passing the house of Daniele Norsa, a Jewish
banker who had lately settled in the Via San
Simone, the attention of the crowd was attracted
by a group of images, inscribed with profane verses,
which some evil-disposed person had placed on a wall
formerly decorated with a fresco of the Madonna.
The cry of blasphemy was raised, stones were thrown
by the mob, and the house was only saved from
destruction by the prompt interference of a city
magistrate. The poor Jew, who had previously
obtained the Bishop's leave to remove the painting of
the Madonna and had paid all the fees required, now
wrote to implore the protection of the Marquis, and
Francesco sent peremptory orders that he was not
to be molested. But this small disturbance was so
grossly exaggerated that Isabella felt it necessary to
write to her lord on the subject, and assure him that
no serious tumult had taken place in his absence.
" The inventors of these malicious tales," she wrote
on the 30th of June, " who have not scrupled to
disturb your peace of mind when you are occupied
with the defence of Italy, showed little regard for
my honour, or for those of my councillors. Let
Your Highness, I beg of you, keep a tranquil mind,
and attend wholly to military affairs, for I intend to
govern the State, with the help of these magnificent
gentlemen and officials, in such a manner that you
will suffer no wrong, and all that is possible will be
done for the good of your subjects. And if any one
should write or tell you of disorders of which you
have not heard from me, you may be certain that it

is a lie, because, since I not only give audience to officials, but allow all your subjects to speak to me whenever they choose, no disturbance can arise without my knowledge." Three days afterwards the news of the first skirmish between the two armies reached Mantua, and Isabella hastened to congratulate her husband on his success:—

"Most illustrious Lord,—I did not write before to-day, because I had nothing to say, but now that I hear of your success against the enemy, I will not delay one moment to congratulate Your Highness on this good news, which has given me the greatest pleasure, and I hope in God that you will gain further victories. I thank you more than I can say for your letter, and I beg of you to take care of yourself, because I am always very anxious when I remember you are in the camp, even although this is where you have always wished to be. I commend myself to Your Highness a thousand, thousand times.—From her who loves and longs to see Your Highness, ISABELLA, with her own hand."[1] Mantua, July 2.

With this letter Isabella sent her husband a little gold cross and Agnus Dei containing a fragment of the wood of the Cross, begging him to wear it round his neck in order that the virtue of this relic and his own devotions to the Virgin might keep him safe in the hour of danger. "All the clergy in Mantua," she adds, "are praying for Your Excellency, moved thereto by my anxious affection." On the 5th of July, the eve of the battle, the Marquis sent a short note thanking his dearest wife for her letter and the little cross, which he will cherish with singular devotion,

[1] Luzio in *Archivio Storico Italiano*, 1890.

but saying that he is so busy he has time neither to eat nor sleep.

On the 7th, he wrote again from the victorious camp of the League in the valley of the Taro, telling his wife of the battle which had been fought the day before, and of the heavy loss he had sustained in the death of his uncle Rodolfo, and his cousin Giovanni Maria, whom he loved as his own self.[1]

"Yesterday's battle, as you will have heard from the herald, was very fiercely contested, and we lost many of our men, amongst others, Signor Rodolfo and Messer Giovanni Maria; but certainly many more of the enemy were slain. And what we ourselves did is known to all, so that I need not speak of it here, and will only tell you that we found ourselves in a position of such peril that only God could deliver us. The chief cause of the disorder was the disobedience of the Stradiots, who gave themselves up to plunder, and in the hour of danger not one of them appeared. By the grace of God we and this army have been saved, but many fled without being pursued by any one, and most of the foot-soldiers, so that few of these remain. These things have caused me the greatest sorrow which I have ever known, and if by ill chance our enemies had turned upon us, we must have been utterly destroyed. Some French nobles were made prisoners by our company, amongst others the Comte de Pigliano and Monsieur le Bâtard de Bourbon. The enemies departed this morning, and are gone over the hill towards Borgo San Domino and Piacenza. We will watch their course and see what we have to do. If others had fought as we did, the victory would have

[1] Luzio, *op. cit.*

been complete, and not a single Frenchman would have escaped. Farewell."

A sense of bitter disappointment breathes in every line of this letter which the Marquis addressed to his wife. In spite of their heavy losses the French army had succeeded in crossing the Taro that night, and early the next morning continued their retreat across the Lombard plains. But, as the royal camp and baggage were abandoned, the advantage remained with the allies, and, before long, Francesco persuaded himself that he had won a glorious victory. Of his personal prowess on this occasion there could be no doubt. After three horses had been killed under him, he fought on foot in the thick of the mêlée till his sword broke in his hands. " Since the days of Hector of Troy," wrote the Marchesa's faithful seneschal, Alessandro da Baesso, who himself risked his life to save his master, " no one ever fought as he did. I believe he killed ten men with his own hand. And I think you must have said some psalm for him, for indeed it is a miracle that he is alive and unhurt." The French king narrowly escaped being made prisoner, and was only rescued by his chamberlain, the Bastard of Bourbon, who rushed to his help. This prince, a son of Jean, Duc de Bourbon, was himself taken prisoner, and sent to Mantua, where Isabella gave him lodgings in the Castello, and treated him with the greatest courtesy until he was exchanged two months later. " Madama lets the French Count want for nothing," wrote Capilupi to the Marquis, and when he was released, he told the Marchesa that he could not sufficiently thank her for all the kindness which he had received. This very kindness, Marino Sanuto tells us, was afterwards reckoned by the jealous Signory of Venice as a sign of Francesco's dangerous leanings towards France.[1]

Among the spoils found in the king's tent were his own sword and helmet, a silver casket containing the seals of state, and a precious reliquary with the wood of the true Cross and a limb of St. Denis, on which he set especial store. Many of these were courteously returned to Charles by the Marquis, but he sent one magnificent set of hangings to Mantua, together with a book containing the portraits of Italian beauties which had been specially executed for the king, and the shattered sword with which he himself had fought on the battle-field. Isabella received these trophies joyfully, and gave her husband's sword to Monsignore Sigismondo, who told his brother that it was as sacred in his eyes as the spear of Longinus, since the blood with which it was stained had been shed for the deliverance of Italy.[2]

Great were the rejoicings at Venice, where Francesco was compared to Hannibal and Scipio, and the Signory not only gave him the high-sounding title of Captain-general of the armies of the Republic, but increased his yearly salary by 2000 ducats and bestowed a pension of another 1000 ducats on his wife. The money was very acceptable to Isabella, whose funds were at a low ebb, and on the 29th of July she wrote to Zorzo Brognolo, begging him to pay her debts to the jeweller Pagano and spend the rest in buying four pieces of the finest *tabì* which he could find in Venice. This precious Oriental fabric, which the Italian ladies of the Renaissance valued so highly,

[1] *Spedizione di Carlo*, viii. p. 482.
[2] Luzio in *Emporium*, vol. x. 366.

was a species of watered silk, manufactured in a quarter of Damascus, which, Mr. Guy le Strange tells us, originally took its name from a Governor of Mecca called Attabiyeh. The word in its different forms of *attabì* and *tabì* passed into the English, French, and Spanish languages. *Taby* silks are often mentioned in English records of the sixteenth and seventeenth centuries. Queen Elizabeth appeared on state occasions in a dress of silver and white taby, Pepys wore a false taby waistcoat, and Fanny Burney affected a gown of lilac taby. Probably few of us are aware that the word tabby cat is derived from the name of a man who was a companion of Mahommed, and Governor of Mecca in the seventh century.[1]

But while poets and sonnet-writers were extolling Francesco as the deliverer of Italy, Isabella herself could not conceal her anxiety for her husband's safety, and she wrote to him in the camp before Novara, where he was besieging the Duke of Orleans, begging him to be less reckless of his life. " It does not please me that you should always run such terrible risks, and I pray and entreat you to be very careful and not to expose yourself to these dangers, as I am sure you discharge your office best and most efficiently by giving orders to others rather than by fighting yourself." In the same letter she enclosed the following little note, supposed to be written by her two-year-old daughter Leonora to the Marquis, and signed with the words, *Filia obsequentiss: adhuc lactans*: " To my dearest and victorious father. Most illustrious and excellent Prince, in my cradle where I am now lying, and when I am sucking in the arms of my most illustrious and sweetest mother,

---

[1] "Baghdad during the Abassieh Caliphate," p. 138.

or wherever I may be, I hear continually songs and praises of the great deeds and splendid victory of Your Highness, in defeating and driving out the French, and delivering all Italy from their barbarous hands. I also hear of the great glory and honours which are justly paid you by all the powers of Italy."[1]

Francesco himself had little time to spare, and in a short letter of the 28th of August he tells his wife that he is continually on horseback day and night, and wonders that his strength holds out, but asks her to send him some playing-cards, that he may occasionally distract his thoughts with a game of *scartino*. Besides the task of directing military operations, he had great difficulty in keeping peace between the Italians and Germans, who were continually quarrelling, and in a sudden brawl which he describes to Isabella, as many as one hundred and twenty men were slain.

When at length Novara surrendered and a treaty of peace was concluded between the Duke of Milan and the French king, Francesco Gonzaga paid a visit to Charles VIII. at Vercelli, and came away much pleased with the courtesy shown him and the splendid horses with which the king presented him. The Mantuan singers who were sent to serenade His Majesty told the Marchesa how eagerly the king had questioned them about her appearance and the gems she wore, and how anxious he was to make the acquaintance of this brilliant and fascinating lady of whom he had heard so much. This exchange of courtesies between the French monarch and the Marquis did not altogether please the Venetian

[1] Luzio in *Arch. St. It.*, 1890.

Signory, who were indignant with the Duke of Milan
for concluding a separate peace with France, and who
already looked with suspicion on his brother-in-law.
But once the French army had crossed the Alps
they were not sorry to disband their army, and on the
1st of November the Marquis made his triumphal
entry into Mantua, where he was joyfully welcomed
by his wife and both his sisters, Chiara of Montpensier and Elisabetta of Urbino, who came to spend
Christmas with her family. Great were the rejoicings
in honour of the victor's return. Sperandio, that
aged artist who, after a long residence at the court of
the Estes, had lately returned to spend his last days
in his native city, designed a fine medal representing
Francesco on horseback at Fornovo, with the proud
inscription: *Ob. Restitutam Italiæ Libertatem.*[1] But
a grander and more imposing memorial of Francesco
Gonzaga's victory had already been planned by his
wife and brother. In the thick of the mêlée at
Fornovo, the Marquis had implored the Blessed
Virgin's help, and, after the battle, he resolved to commemorate his deliverance by some noble monument.
Then he remembered the poor Jew, Daniele Norsa,
whose house in the Via San Simone had been nearly
wrecked by the fanaticism of the mob at Ascension-
tide, and in a letter addressed to his brother Sigismondo on the last day of July, he proposed that the
Jew should be made to restore the figure of Our
Lady which he had removed from the wall, in a
finer and more splendid form, as an act of reparation
to the glorious Mother. The idea was quickly taken
up by the Protonotary, who suggested that an altar-
piece of the Madonna should be painted by Andrea

---

[1] Armand, *Les Médailleurs italiens.*

Mantegna, and that the Marquis should be represented kneeling in armour, with his brothers and his illustrious lady at the Virgin's feet. The Marquis highly approved of this proposal, and fixed the price of Mantegna's painting at 110 ducats, which the Jew was required to pay down, within three days. Isabella's own portrait, however, was not eventually introduced in the picture. Perhaps she had no wish to sit to Mantegna again, and preferred that her patron, St. Elizabeth, should appear in her stead. But if, as seems most probable, in the venerable saint who kneels opposite the figure of the Marquis, we see the Beata Osanna, that revered nun whose prayers were offered day and night for the success of Francesco's arms, the suggestion may well have come from the Marchesa.[1] In the same way, the figures of the heavenly warriors St. George and St. Michael, and of the patron saints of Mantua, Andrew and Longinus, were substituted for the Gonzaga brothers. A certain Fra Girolamo Redini, a friar of the Eremitani order who was fond of meddling in political affairs, now proposed that the Jew's house should be pulled down, and that a church, dedicated to the Madonna della Vittoria, should be erected in its place. This scheme was finally adopted. The sum of 110 ducats was paid by the Jew on the 25th of August, and part of the money was handed over by the Protonotary to Mantegna, who was promised the remainder when the work was partly executed.[2]

The architect Bernardo Ghisolfo, whose name appears frequently in the Gonzaga archives, set to work at once, and by the following June the new

---

[1] Cf. "Life of Mantegna," by Miss Cruttwell, p. 93.
[2] Luzio in *Emporium*, vol. x. 360.

chapel was ready to receive Messer Andrea's altar-piece. The painter on this part worked more rapidly than usual, taking pleasure in his subject and incited by the prospect of the large reward that was awaiting him, and on the anniversary of the battle of the Taro, the great Madonna was borne in triumph from Mantegna's house near San Sebastiano to the new shrine on the site of the Jew's house, at the other end of the town. Francesco himself was absent in the kingdom of Naples at the time, but the Marchesa and Sigismondo resolved to make the ceremony as imposing as possible, and their letters to the Marquis show that their efforts were attended with complete success. On the 10th of July, Isabella wrote: "The figure of Our Lady, which Andrea Mantegna has painted, was carried from his house in procession last Wednesday, being the 6th of this month, to the new chapel of S. Maria della Vittoria, in commemoration of last year's battle and of your gallant deeds, and greater crowds assembled than I have ever seen at any procession in this town. My confessor, Fra Pietro, made a fine oration at high mass, and spoke in a manner appropriate to the occasion, begging the glorious Virgin Mary to keep Your Excellency safe and bring you home victorious. Owing to my present condition, I could not walk on foot in the procession, but I went to the Borgo to see it pass, and returned to the Castello by the new chapel, which is well adorned, and the road was thronged with people." [1]

Sigismondo adds a few particulars of interest.

[1] *Archivio Gonzaga,* quoted by Portioli, *La Chiesa e la Madonna della Vittoria in Mantova,* p. 21.

Andrea Mantegna. Pinx.   Walker & Cockerell. Ph. Sc.

The Madonna della Vittoria.

He describes the youths dressed up as angels and apostles who sang lauds on the tribunal erected for the altar-piece outside Mantegna's house, where the altar-piece was first placed, and dilates on the love and enthusiasm which the preacher's references to the Marquis evoked, as well as on the number of wax lights, torches and other votive offerings which had been already brought to the new shrine. Another correspondent, the chancellor Antimaco, describes the painting as a most excellent work, and says that it was truly amazing to see the eagerness of the crowds which pressed round to see this noble picture, and that, next to the Madonna's image, the portrait of their absent lord excited the greatest interest.[1]

The little shrine of Our Lady of Victory is standing still in a deserted byway of Mantua, but Messer Andrea's Madonna, as we all know, was carried off a hundred years ago, by the French conquerors, and hangs to-day in the Louvre among the proudest possessions of the nation whose supposed defeat it was intended to commemorate.

[1] Braghirolli, *Giorn. di Erud. Art.*, i. 206.

CHAPTER VIII

1496—1497

Campaign of Naples—Ferrante recovers his kingdom—Francesco Gonzaga commands the Venetian army—Isabella governs Mantua—Her correspondence and friendship with Lorenzo da Pavia—Birth of her second daughter—Illness of the Marquis—His return to Mantua, and visit to Venice—Death of Ferrante of Naples, of Gilbert de Montpensier, and Beatrice d'Este—Francesco Gonzaga deprived of the office of captain-general of the Venetian armies—Death of Anna Sforza.

EARLY in January, the Marquis of Mantua left home again to take the command of a new Venetian army which the Signory sent to assist Ferrante, the young king of Naples, in recovering his dominions. After the retreat of Charles VIII. this gallant prince had crossed over from Ischia, and entered Naples on the day after the battle of Fornovo. The people welcomed him with shouts of joy and the nobles flocked to his banner, and soon Montpensier, who had been left at the head of the French troops, was compelled to retire into the mountains of Calabria. There he carried on a war of petty skirmishes and depredations against the Venetian forces under the command of his brother-in-law, Francesco Gonzaga. While their husbands were fighting on opposite sides, Chiara Gonzaga remained at Mantua with her sister-in-law, to whom she was fondly attached, and whose company consoled Isabella in some measure for the departure of Elisabetta, who returned to Urbino in

February.   It was a dull year for the Marchesa, and, with the exception of a short visit to Ferrara in January, she was too much occupied with public affairs to leave home.   But, as usual, she made good use of her time.   She returned to her classical studies, applied herself to master the rules of Latin grammar, and consulted the great Ferrara humanist, Ercole Strozzi, as to the choice of a new tutor. Much of her leisure time was devoted to music. She took lessons on the lute from a new master, Angelo Testagrossa, a Milanese youth who sang like a seraph, and played the lyre and clavichord.   On her last visit to Milan she had seen and greatly admired an instrument which Lorenzo Gusnasco of Pavia, the famous master of organs, had made for her sister Beatrice.   Now she was seized with an ardent desire to possess a similar one, and on the 12th of March 1496, she addressed the following letter to Lorenzo da Pavia, whom she had often met at the court of Milan, but who had lately moved to Venice for the greater convenience of his trade :—

"M. Lorenzo da Pavia, most excellent master,— We remember that you made a most beautiful and perfect clavichord for that illustrious Madonna, the Duchess of Milan, our sister, when we were last at Pavia, and since we ourselves now wish to have an instrument of the same kind, which cannot be surpassed, we are sure that there is no one in all Italy who can satisfy our wish better than you can.   We therefore pray you to make us a clavichord of such beauty and excellence as shall be worthy of your high reputation and of the trust that we repose in you.   The only difference that we wish to see in this instrument is that it should be easier to play, because our hand is so light that we cannot play well if we have to press heavily on the notes. But you, I have no doubt, will understand our wishes and requirements. For the rest, make the instrument exactly as you choose. And the more quickly you can serve us the better shall we be pleased, and we will take care that you shall be well rewarded, and place ourselves at your service." [1]

Lorenzo hastened to reply that he would gladly serve the Marchesa, but that he feared some time must elapse before he was able to execute her commands, since he had unfortunately promised to make a viol for the Duchess of Milan and a clavichord for one of her courtiers, Messer Antonio Visconti. Isabella, however, was not to be so easily put off, and on the 19th, she wrote to the Milanese nobleman, begging him to allow Lorenzo to make her instrument first.

" Most honoured friend, and dear to us as a brother,—We have desired M. Lorenzo da Pavia, in Venice, to make us a clavichord, but hear from him that he cannot undertake this until he has finished a viol for our honoured sister, the Duchess of Milan, and a clavichord for Your Magnificence. But as we are very anxious to have our new instrument, we beg you to be as good as to yield us the next place after the Duchess, which would give us the greatest pleasure, and if you are willing, will you kindly write to Messer Lorenzo, giving him leave to make our clavichord first ? And we shall be ever ready to consult the pleasure of Your Magnificence."

[1] Lorenzo Gusnasco, *Dott. Carlo dell'Acqua*, p. 20.

On the same day she wrote to Zorzo Brognolo as follows :—

" You may tell M. Lorenzo da Pavia that we have written to M. Antonio Visconti in terms that leave us no doubt but that he will allow us to have our clavichord made first, and that he can set to work at once, and if he can finish it in less than the three months which he named, we shall be the better pleased. But if this is impossible, we are content to wait, as long as he makes a most excellent instrument." [1]

But Lorenzo was too fine an artist to allow himself to be hurried, and he sent back word by Zorzo, a month later, that he had begun the instrument, but could not possibly finish it before three months. Once more Isabella returned to the charge, and at the end of May desired Brognolo to go and see how Lorenzo was getting on, and find out if her instrument seemed to be a fine one, and how soon it would be ready. In reply, Zorzo wrote that the clavichord would be most beautiful, and would be finished by August. But, as usual, the finishing touches took longer than the master had expected, and it was not till Christmas Day that Messer Lorenzo arrived at Mantua, bringing with him the Marchesa's clavichord, which, she wrote to Zorzo, was so perfect and beautiful a thing, it could not please her better ! Lorenzo was not allowed to return to Venice without promising to undertake another commission for the insatiable Marchesa. This was a lute, which he proposed to make of inlaid ebony and ivory, " because," he writes, " these two materials go well together and are beautiful companions." On the 3rd of February 1497, he

[1] Luzio in *Arch. St. Lomb*, xvii. 637.

wrote that the lute would soon be finished, and entered readily into Isabella's suggestion that a star should be let into the woodwork of the instrument, since this was a favourite device of the Marchesa, and appears on the reverse of her medal. A few months later the Marchesa wrote to ask about a certain lute which the singer Serafino had seen in Lorenzo's shop at Venice, and begged that the instrument which he was making should be strung in such a manner as to suit her voice.

Lorenzo had, it appears, met with unexpected difficulties in completing his task, but, as before, he entered warmly into the Marchesa's idea, and took infinite pains to meet her wishes. " I cannot," he wrote, " find any ebony that is black enough and fine enough to suit me, and am much disappointed, because I hoped to make this lute the most beautiful thing in Italy and the best, both from my great desire to give you pleasure, and from my natural wish to make an instrument of the highest excellence." Accordingly he sent to Munich for the strings of the lute, as he had heard of a German master who supplied the best quality, and promised to pay especial attention to the shape of the instrument, "because beauty of form is everything," a sentiment which must have found an echo in Isabella's heart. *Perchè nella forma sta el tuto.*[1]

This, then, was the beginning of Isabella's correspondence with this remarkable man, who was closely connected with the most cultured members of the Milanese court, and belonged to a small circle of highly gifted men, which included the painter, Leonardo da Vinci ; the sculptor, Cristoforo Romano ;

[1] Aldo Manuzio, *Lettres et documents ;* A. Baschet.

the writer and collector, Sabba da Castiglione; and the great printer, Aldo Manuzio. Lorenzo da Pavia was intimate with all these distinguished men. He shared their love of music and of painting, their enthusiasm for the antique, their passion for all that was beautiful in art and letters. His fine taste and critical eye commended him in an especial manner to Isabella d'Este, who found in him a kindred spirit, not easily satisfied either with his own work or with that of others, and aiming at nothing short of perfection. During the next twenty years she corresponded with him constantly, and employed him not only to manufacture those wonderful organs, lutes, and viols, of ebony and ivory, which were as perfect in shape as in sound, but to buy pictures and antiques, amber rosaries and ivory crucifixes, enamels, cameos and Murano glass, and Eastern stuffs, crystal mirrors and inlaid cabinets, and all the rare and lovely things with which she adorned her studio. And in all the delicate and difficult negotiations which he conducted on her behalf with Venetian merchants and artists, with the painter, Giovanni Bellini, or the printer, Aldo, she found Lorenzo's knowledge and advice, his tact and patience, of the greatest value.

Books and music, as usual, were the chief occupations which filled Isabella's spare time. But she had more frivolous amusements as well. Her letters abound with allusions to the tricks and jests of the favourite dwarfs and clowns with whom she loved to be surrounded. A whole suite of apartments, with low rooms and passages suited to their size, was built for the court dwarfs at Mantua during her lifetime, and may still be seen in a wing of the Castello.

In March 1496, just when Isabella was corresponding with Lorenzo da Pavia about the clavichord, she wrote to beg her father to allow the French clown, Galasso, and Fritello, the wonderful dwarf who danced and sang, and turned somersaults in the air, to the delight of all the Este family, to come and amuse her, saying that she was as cold as ice and as dull as ditch water in her husband's absence! Her only pleasure, she declared in another letter, was to make Mattello dictate letters to the Marquis. One day she nearly died of laughing at the sight of Mattello imitating a tipsy man; another time he appeared in a friar's habit, and was announced as the venerable Padre Bernardino Mattello.[1] When Alfonso d'Este was ill and sad, in 1498, after his wife's death, the Marchesa sent Mattello to amuse him, and her brother wrote in return that he could not express the delight which the buffoon had afforded him, and that he esteemed his presence a greater boon than the gift of a fine castle. Great was Isabella's dismay when soon after his return to Mantua, this pet dwarf fell ill and died, to the grief of the whole court. She visited him repeatedly during his last illness, and told her husband the jokes which the poor fool made on his death-bed. "Most people," wrote Francesco in reply, "can be easily replaced, but Nature will never produce another Mattello." *Il primo matto nel mondo,* "the foremost fool in the world," as Isabella called him, was interred in S. Francesco, the favourite burial-place of the Gonzaga princes. Tebaldeo wrote his epitaph, and Bonsignori painted his portrait, while the bard Pistoia composed an elegy, in which he says: "If

[1] Luzio, *Buffoni,* &c., in *Nuova Antologia,* 1891.

Mattello is in Paradise, he is making all the saints and angels laugh ; if he is in hell, Cerberus will forget to bark."

The same wits and poets were called upon to write Latin epigrams and sonnets on Isabella's pet animals, on the Persian cat Martino or the *Cagnolino Aura*. The novelist Bandello tells us how the Marchesa's presence was heralded by the barking of her little dogs, and on one occasion she desired Brognolo to send to all the convents in Venice for Syrian and Thibet cats,[1] in order that she might choose the finest for herself. These pet animals were buried with great solemnity in the terraced gardens of the Castello opposite the Corte Vecchia, and cypresses and tombstones inscribed with their names marked their graves. All the ladies and gentlemen of Isabella's household were present on these occasions, and her favourite dogs and cats joined in the funeral procession. And it was characteristic of the age that every incident, from the birth of a prince or the fall of an empire, to the death of a fool or pet dog, became an occasion for producing Latin epitaphs and sonnets and elegies in the vulgar tongue.

But more serious subjects now claimed Isabella's attention. On the 6th of July, when Mantegna's Madonna was borne through the streets of Mantua, we have seen that the Marchesa's state of health did not allow her to walk in the procession, and that she witnessed the ceremony from Giovanni Gonzaga's house in the Borgo. A week later she gave birth to a second daughter. The babe was named Margherita after Francesco's mother, but her sex was a cause of bitter disappointment to Isabella, who looked with

---

[1] Luzio in *Giorn. St. d. Lett. It.*, vol. xxxiii. 45.

envy on her sister Beatrice's two fine boys. The Marquis was more philosophical in this instance, especially when he heard that the child was much prettier than little Leonora and strongly resembled him. He told his wife not to look so coldly on the poor babe, since no doubt God would send them sons all in good time, and if ever a father had reason to be satisfied with his daughters, it was he. His affection for Leonora never changed, and nothing pleased him better than to hear that his little daughter asked after her father and sent him messages. "Madonna Leonora," wrote a secretary to him in Calabria, "commends herself to Your Highness, and would like to have a fine new doll in a silk frock to play with in bed, as her old one is quite worn out." And often, on his hunting expeditions nearer home, he would send her a hare which his dogs had caught, and tell her to eat it for dinner![1] But Francesco never saw the babe whose birth he had been the first to welcome, and poor little Margherita died before her father's return on the 23rd of September.

The war in Calabria, as Isabella had foreseen, proved a tedious and difficult enterprise, and by the end of the summer both parties were heartily sick of the struggle. On the 29th of July, Montpensier was forced to surrender the strong city of Atella after a long blockade and fell dangerously ill of fever. Francesco Gonzaga, ever courteous towards his foes, sent his doctor to the French camp with presents of fruit and game for his brother-in-law, but the Venetian Signory, Marino Sanuto tells us, did not approve of their general's action, and were dissatisfied with his conduct on other grounds. However, they

[1] Luzio e Renier, *Mantova e Urbino,* pp. 75, 87.

declined to allow him to come home on leave, and
supported his application when he asked the Pope to
make his brother a Cardinal.   On his way to Naples,
Francesco had spent a few days in Rome, to pay his
respects to Alexander VI., who received him with
marked favour and presented him with the golden
rose.   This had encouraged him to renew his old
suit on behalf of Sigismondo, and the better to press
his claim, he wrote in August to ask his wife to
raise seven thousand ducats on the spot, and if
necessary to pledge her jewels for this purpose.
Isabella, who had already pawned the greater part
of her jewels for the same object two years before,
and had lately been seeking her father's help to
enable her to redeem them, replied in the following
letter :—

"I am of course always ready to obey Your
Excellency's commands, but perhaps you have forgotten that most of my jewels are at present in pawn
at Venice, not only those which you have given me,
but those which I brought when I came as a bride to
Mantua or have bought myself since my marriage.
I say this, not because I wish to make any difference
between yours and mine, but to show you that I
have parted from everything and have only four
jewels left in the house—the large balass ruby which
you gave me when my first child was born, my
favourite big diamond, and the last ones which you
gave me.   If I pledge these, I shall be left entirely
without jewels and shall be obliged to wear black,
because to appear in coloured silks and brocades
without jewels would be ridiculous.   Your Excellency
will understand that I only say this out of regard for
your honour and mine, and for this cause I pray and

entreat you not to rob me of these few things, since I would rather give you my *camora* embroidered with gems than be left without jewels. On this account I will not send away my jewels until I have received Your Excellency's reply."[1] Mantua, August 27, 1496.

As before, however, the negotiations regarding the Cardinal's hat proved fruitless, and Isabella was allowed to keep her jewels. When she wrote this letter her husband was seriously ill of fever at Fondi. He had been carried there on a litter, fearing to remain at Naples on account of an old prophecy that he should die in that city. Here he became so dangerously ill that he sent for the Venetian senator Paolo Capello and begged him in case of his death to commend his wife and little daughter to the protection of the Signory — "a sure sign," remarks Sanuto, "that he puts greater trust in Venice than in his brother-in-law of Milan, or his father-in-law of Ferrara."[2] Meanwhile Montpensier was still lying ill at Pozzuoli, and an armistice had been signed between France and Venice, so that there was nothing to keep the Marquis in the South, and as soon as he was fit to move, he started on the journey home. A few days after her infant daughter's death, Isabella set out to meet her husband, accompanied by the Protonotary Sigismondo. Early in October, the Duchess of Urbino came to meet her at Fano, and on the following day Isabella joined Francesco at Ancona, and brought him home by slow stages to Ravenna, and thence up the Po by water to Ferrara and afterwards to Mantua.

[1] Luzio, *Il Lusso d'Isabella d'Este*, in *Nuova Antologia*, 1896.
[2] *Diarii*, i. 294.

The Marquis's first duty was to report himself to the Doge and Signory, and as soon as his health was sufficiently restored, he went to Venice on the 21st of November. Here a grand reception awaited him. At Chioggia he was welcomed by the Senate and representatives; at Malamocco the Signory and foreign Ambassadors came out to meet him in state. The great doors of St. Mark were thrown open in his honour, and after mass he was conducted up the Canal Grande on the bucentaur to his own house at San Trovaso. On the following day he appeared before the Signory, to give an account of his proceedings, and in the evening he attended the wedding of Zuan Soranzo's daughter to Giorgio Cornaro, brother of the Queen of Cyprus. Marino Sanuto, who saw the Marquis on this occasion, describes him as wearing a Spanish suit and short black beard, as he appears in Mantegna's altar-piece, and remarks that his face bore evident traces of his recent sickness.

But the sad news from Naples threw a gloom over these festivities both at Venice and Mantua. On their journey home the travellers heard that the young King Ferrante had died after a short illness, brought on by the hardships and fatigue which he had undergone in his victorious campaign against the French. Both Francesco and Isabella were much attached to their brave young cousin, who had fought so gallantly to recover his father's dominions. Solemn funeral services were held in his house at Mantua, and the Carmelite Vicar-General, Fra Pietro da Novellara, preached a Latin oration in his honour. When, a year afterwards, the dead king's sister, the widowed Duchess Isabella of Milan, wrote to ask Francesco Gonzaga for a portrait of her brother which she

heard was in his possession, the Marchesa sent her
word that her lord could not part with the picture,
which was dear to him for the love which he bore
to Ferrante's memory, but would have it copied for
her by Francesco Bonsignori.

This sad event was soon followed by the death of
Gilbert de Montpensier, who breathed his last at
Pozzuoli on the 11th of November, and Isabella was
called upon to console his widow, Chiara Gonzaga,
while at the same time she had to condole with
Antonia del Balzo, on the loss of her husband Gianfrancesco of Bozzolo. A still more tragic event
darkened the Christmas festival. This was the
sudden death of the Marchesa's own sister, Beatrice
d'Este, Duchess of Milan, and wife of Lodovico
Sforza. The poor young princess, who was only
twenty-one, gave birth to a still-born son on the night
of the 2nd of January in the Castello of Milan, and
died herself an hour afterwards. The sad news, which
Francesco had to break to his wife, came as a terrible
shock to Isabella, who had lately seen her sister in
the bloom of youth and fulness of prosperity. At
first she was overwhelmed with grief, and her husband said that he had never seen his wife so utterly
broken down. "I know not," she wrote to her
father, "how I can ever find comfort." Fortunately
Elisabetta of Urbino had arrived at Mantua a week
before, and the companionship of this beloved sister-
in-law was Isabella's best consolation. When the
Duchess returned to Urbino at the end of April,
both Isabella and her husband accompanied her to
Ferrara and spent some weeks with her father and
brothers. That year the Feast of St. George was
shorn of its usual splendour. There were no races

and no banquets or comedies. The people shared
in their prince's sorrow, and Duke Ercole presented
the pallium which would have been the prize of the
races to the church of S. Francesco.[1]

On the 24th of June, the Marquis went to Venice,
having received orders from the Signory to prepare
for war. But when he reached his house in San
Trovaso, Zorzo Brognolo met him with the unexpected announcement of his dismissal from the post
of captain-general. For some time past the Signory
had entertained grave suspicions of Francesco's fidelity,
and on the day before his arrival in Venice the
Council of Ten finally issued a decree by which he
was removed from office. At first the Marquis could
hardly believe in the truth of Brognolo's announcement. He rode along the Canal Grande, Marino
Sanuto tells us, "with great arrogance," and meeting
the Procurator of the Republic in the church of San
Giorgio Maggiore, haughtily demanded an audience
from the Signory. "Every one," adds the chronicler,
"murmured at his audacity; but although he was
dismissed from his post, he was suffered to remain in
the city, because he was a *zentiluomo* of Venice, and
had inherited the privilege of citizenship from his
ancestors. And from the age of twenty-eight he had
been captain-general, and being also related to the
King of Naples and the Dukes of Milan, Ferrara,
and Urbino, he enjoyed the best time of any lord in
Italy. He had held this office for the space of eight
years, one month, and twenty-four days, and now he
says that from being the first man in Italy he has
ruined himself, and this is no doubt true. But the
Signory will save his salary." [2]

[1] Muratori, xxiv. 340.   [2] *Diarii*, i. 667.

Meanwhile Isabella, unconscious of her husband's disgrace, was spending Midsummer's day at Verona, where, by Francesco's wish, she had accepted an invitation from the Podestà to witness the jousts in honour of San Giovanni's day. The Venetian Signory were aware of her presence, and had sent orders that the Marchesa was to be honourably entertained, and was to receive 25 ducats a day for her expenses as long as she remained in Verona. After her prolonged period of mourning and seclusion, the young princess appeared once more in public with fresh brightness and charm, and rode along the lists and greeted all her friends in the most gracious manner. Not a word was breathed in her presence as to the Marquis's disgrace, and it was only when she reached Mantua and met her husband that she heard the story from his own lips. Already the bad news had reached Ferrara.[1] Alfonso d'Este galloped to Mantua to see his sister, and Isabella went back with him to take counsel with her father, while the disconsolate Marquis remained at his villa of Gonzaga, declaring loudly that his disgrace was due to the Duke of Milan's intrigues and Galeazzo Sanseverino's jealousy. " I hear," wrote Sanuto, " that he is very gloomy and goes clad in black, and wears an iron ring on his collar, which he has vowed not to lay aside until he has been on a pilgrimage to Loreto. And there is sorrow throughout the Mantovano, and the people, who had been happy and smiling before, are now sad and out of heart." [2] It was then, in token of his grief and remorse, that Francesco adopted the device of gold faggots in a fiery crucible, with the motto, *Domine probasti me et cognovisti*, which figures

---

[1] Muratori, *Diario Ferrarese*, xxiv. 345.   [2] *Diarii*, i. 697.

in the pavement of Isabella's Grotta and in the frieze of her *camerini*, and still adorns one of the vaulted ceilings in his favourite palace of San Sebastiano.[1]

All through the summer the Marquis made repeated efforts to recover the Signory's good graces. He offered to place his wife and child as hostages in their hands, and even to surrender some of his fortresses. And when he reviewed his troops on the Feast of the Assumption, he told them that they were kept for the use of the Signory, and threw them gold when they shouted *Marco!* But the Signory refused to see him or even accept a present from him, and were persuaded that he was secretly in league with the French king. There seems no doubt that Francesco had lately held secret communications with the French court, and in November Lodovico Sforza addressed an indignant remonstrance on the subject to Isabella, telling her that he held proofs of her husband's dealings with the French and the Florentines in his hands, and only refrained from sending them to Venice out of love and regard for her. Isabella was deeply distressed at this breach between her husband and brother-in-law, and did her best to effect a reconciliation between them, but her position was a difficult one and her path was by no means strewn with roses. To add to her family sorrows in this year of misfortunes, her brother Alfonso's wife, Anna Sforza, died on the 30th of November, after giving birth to a dead child, who was buried with her in the same grave. Alfonso was left a childless widower, and the sudden death of this gentle young princess was a fresh cause of grief to Duke Ercole and his people. A fortnight later another Este princess, the once brilliant and beautiful

[1] Paolo Giovio, *Imprese*, p. 33.

Beatrice, died in a fit of apoplexy at Milan, and Isabella addressed heart-felt condolences to her aunt's son, Niccolo da Correggio, remarking sadly that at least his mother had died in the natural order, and that her life had not been cut short by a cruel and untimely end.

Certainly Isabella had her full share of anxieties at this time. For, as she and all the world knew, her husband was consoling himself for his reverses in the company of a mistress named Teodora, who bore him two daughters, and shocked public feeling by appearing in splendid attire at a tournament held at Brescia in honour of the Queen of Cyprus. The Marquis himself was present on this occasion with his brother-in-law, the young Cardinal Ippolito, while his rival, the Moro's son-in-law, Galeazzo Sanseverino, appeared in the lists and was not sorry to cross swords with him.[1]

But Isabella held her peace like a wise woman, and won general admiration by her patient and dignified bearing. "You are blessed beyond most men," wrote the Bologna humanist Floriano Dolfo to the Marquis Francesco soon after his victory at Fornovo, "in having a fair, wise, and noble wife, who is altogether discreet and virtuous, and has shown herself a true mother of concord, ever anxious to gratify your wishes, while she prudently feigns neither to see nor hear those actions of yours which must be hateful and injurious to her."[2] This was plain speaking, but the writer had been long intimately acquainted with the Marquis and his wife, and the tribute of praise which he paid Isabella was well deserved.

[1] Marino Sanuto, *Diarii*, i. 697.
[2] Luzio e Renier in *Arch. St. Lomb.*, xvii. 646.

CHAPTER IX

1498—1499

Intrigues of Francesco Gonzaga with Venice and Milan—Isabella
seeks to reconcile him with Lodovico Sforza—The Marquis
goes to Milan and is appointed captain-general of the League
—Visit of the Duke of Milan to Mantua—Correspondence of
Isabella with Lodovico—Conquest of Milan by the French,
and flight of the Duke—Louis XII. enters Milan—Isabella
pays court to the French—Receives the Milanese exiles—The
Moro's return and his final surrender at Novara.

IT is a difficult task to unravel the tangled web of
Italian politics at the close of the fifteenth century
and to follow the Marquis Francesco's course of
action during the two years that elapsed between
his dismissal by the Signory of Venice and the fall
of his brother-in-law, Lodovico Sforza. His tortuous
policy and frequent changes of front are fully discussed in a learned treatise by M. Louis Pelissier,[1]
while Dr. Luzio has recently brought several fresh
documents on the subject to light.[2] But one thing
seems clear. While Francesco and his brother
Giovanni were inclined to join with Venice, Isabella
d'Este's sympathies were wholly on the side of
Lodovico, until it became plain that his cause was
irrevocably ruined. Then, like the true "cinque-
centist" that she was — to borrow M. Pelissier's

[1] L. Pelissier, *Louis XII. et L. Sforza ; Documents pour l'histoire
de la domination française dans le Milanais.*

[2] Luzio, *Arch. St. Lomb.*, 1901.

phrase—the Marchesa applied all her energies to win the French king's favour and make Louis XII. her friend.[1]

During the winter and spring of 1498, her confidential agent, Capilupi, was repeatedly sent to Milan to negotiate with the Duke, and when in April a new league was formed between him and the Emperor Maximilian, the command of the allied forces was offered to Francesco, with a yearly salary of 30,000 ducats. The Marquis went to Milan, where he was splendidly entertained, and agreed to all Lodovico's proposals, but he was secretly dissatisfied because the Duke would not give him the title of captain-general of the Milanese army, which was borne by his son-in-law Galeazzo, and sent word by his brother Giovanni to the Signory that he would greatly prefer to return to his old allegiance.[2] Isabella, however, strongly advised him to accept the post, saying that the salary was the important thing, although the refusal of the title might be vexatious. Lodovico now announced his intention of coming to Mantua himself, both to show the world the confidence which he placed in the Marquis, and to thank Isabella personally for her good offices. Great preparations were made for his reception, and the Marchesa borrowed plate and tapestries from Niccolo da Correggio, consulted Capilupi as to the Duke's favourite dishes and wines, and was greatly exercised in mind as to whether she ought to wear black and drape her rooms with sable hangings, since Lodovico had never laid aside his mourning since the death of Beatrice. And we learn, from the following letter to

[1] *Les Amies de Ludovic Sforza* (*Revue historique,* 1891).
[2] Marino Sanuto, *Diarii,* i. 1112.

Capilupi, that she gave up her own rooms in the
Castello for the use of her guest.

"Benedetto: We intend to lodge the Duke here,
in our rooms in the Castello, giving him the *Camera
dipinta*, with the ante-chamber, the Camerino of the
Sun"—Lodovico Gonzaga's device—"the Camera
of the Cassone, our own Camerino and dining-room.
And we mean His Excellency to occupy the Camera
of the Cassone himself, which we will drape with
black and violet hangings, as, although we hear that
he still wears mourning, we think this will look
rather less melancholy, and show that here at least we
have good reason for rejoicing on this occasion. But
I hope you will consult M. Antonio di Costabili"—
the Ferrarese envoy—"and Messer Visconti as to the
hangings of the other rooms, if you do not think it
well to mention this to the Duke himself, and let me
know their opinion, as it does not seem to me convenient that our rooms should be bare even if His
Excellency brings his own hangings. Please also let
me know what wines the Duke usually drinks, and
what kind of clothes I had better wear, as I said
before." [1] Mantua, June 8, 1498.

The Duke however begged the Marchesa to please
herself, and expressed himself highly gratified with
her thoughtfulness, and when he heard that Isabella
had a slight attack of fever, he sent his jester Barone
on beforehand to amuse her with his merry tricks.
On the 27th of June he arrived himself, bringing
Isabella's brother, Cardinal Ippolito, and several
foreign ambassadors in his train, and accompanied
by a suite of a thousand persons. He spent three
days at Mantua, visited the principal churches and

---

[1] Luzio e Renier in *Arch. St. Lomb.*, xvii. 656.

palaces, and admired Mantegna's glorious frescoes,
and the treasures of art which Isabella had collected
in her studio.   The Marquis gave a series of tourna-
ments and comedies in honour of his illustrious guest,
but the Venetians watched these proceedings jealously
and Sanuto remarked that the Marchesana was evidently anxious to draw her husband to the Duke of
Milan's side, and, like her father Ercole of Ferrara, was
all against Venice.

Still Francesco wavered, and sent messages to the
Signory through his brother Giovanni, who was
known to be attached to Venice, and whose wife,
Laura Bentivoglio, paid frequent visits to the convent of S. Giorgio.   On the 20th of October, he
came to Venice and threw himself at the Doge's feet,
placing his services and those of his family at his
disposal.   But, although the Signory was ready to
pay him the same salary as before, they would not
agree to give him the title of captain-general, and he
left Venice in disgust.   The next day news came from
Milan that the Marchesa had concluded an agreement with Lodovico, and that her little daughter
Leonora was to be affianced to her cousin, Maximilian, the young Count of Pavia.   " Every one
agreed," wrote Sanuto, " that the Marquis had treated
our Signory very scurvily, and the Pope is said to
have remarked that we are well rid of a great fool."

On this occasion Isabella certainly seems to have
urged her husband to come to terms with Lodovico,
and herself took an active part in the negotiations.
When, early in November, the Marchesino Stanga
and Gaspare San Severino came to Mantua and the
agreement with Francesco was finally concluded, they
visited Isabella in the Castello, and told the Duke

that she could hardly contain her joy at seeing them. Lodovico himself wrote to express his thanks for her assistance, saying that the Marchesino had told him how diligently she had laboured to bring about this happy result. On the 1st of January 1499, the imperial envoy, Erasmo Brasca, solemnly delivered the bâton and standard of the King of the Romans to the Marquis, in front of the church of S. Pietro. Isabella witnessed the investiture from a platform erected on the Piazza, and afterwards entertained the ambassador at a banquet in the Castello. The banner was solemnly blessed in the Cathedral and borne through the city in procession, after which the Marquis rode out with the ambassador to sup at his villa of Goïto. But it was reported at Venice that the children in the street cried *Marco! Marco!* at the sight of the lion on the banner, upon which the German envoy looked puzzled, and the Marquis only smiled and kept silence.[1]

All through this last year of his reign, when Lodovico's enemies were busy plotting his destruction, Isabella was in constant communication with her brother-in-law. He wrote regularly, giving her the latest political and court news, such, for instance, as that of King Charles the Eighth's sudden death in April 1498, and sent her baskets of peaches and barrels of sweet wine, with charming little notes calling her his dearest sister and signing himself "your most affectionate brother." And she in return sent him the finest trout from Garda and swans from the Mantuan lakes to sail in the moat of the Castello, and thanked him cordially for his gracious remembrance, while Evangelista, Francesco's famous

---

[1] Sanuto, *Diarii,* ii. 256.

stud groom, tamed the Duke's horses and sent them back in three days' time, fit for His Excellency to ride.

One of the last letters which Isabella addressed to Lodovico was a request for his permission to present Giangaleazzo's widow, her cousin Isabella of Aragon, with her portrait in colours. The Marchesa had always shown the greatest kindness to this unfortunate princess in the days of her rivalry with Beatrice, and still corresponded with her frequently. In 1498, she sent her a fine marble bust from Mantegna's collection, which the Duchess was anxious to possess, as it was supposed to resemble her, and allowed Leonardo's pupil Beltraffio to copy a portrait of her late brother King Ferrante II., that belonged to the Marquis. Now Isabella of Aragon expressed a great wish for her cousin's own portrait, and the Marchesa had it painted by a Parma master, Gianfrancesco Maineri, and sent to Milan by her master of the horse, Negro, but prudently asked the Duke's leave before she presented the picture to his nephew's widow.[1] " I am afraid," she wrote pleasantly, " I shall weary, not only Your Highness, but all Italy with the sight of my portraits, but I could not refuse Duchess Isabella's urgent entreaties. I send this one, which is not really very good and makes me look fatter than I am, and have desired Negro to show it to Your Highness, and if you approve, give it to the Duchess from me." The Duke replied courteously that he admired the portrait

---

[1] Luzio, *Emporium*, 1900, p. 352. This portrait may possibly be the same as that in Mrs. Alfred Morrison's collection, which was exhibited at the Burlington Fine Arts Club in 1894. Whether it is the work of the Parma artist or of Beltraffio, who was at Mantua at the time, the portrait bears a marked likeness to Leonardo's drawing of Isabella.

and thought it very good, even if it made his sister-in-law fatter than she was when he saw her last. Isabella, we know, was inclined to *embonpoint*, and lived in constant terror of growing stout, as she did in her later years. When she was at Pavia with Beatrice in 1492, she informed her husband with great satisfaction that her sister the Duchess had not grown any taller than herself, but was distinctly stouter and seemed inclined to resemble her mother in this respect. And in after years we find frequent allusions to this tendency in her letters. The portrait was sent to Milan in March 1499, when Lodovico's affairs were already in a critical state. A few weeks earlier, in February 1499, the treaty between Venice and France was signed, and the destruction of Lodovico and partition of his State was finally determined. Isabella was spending carnival at Ferrara, where her father was giving a series of Latin comedies in her honour. She wrote off without a moment's delay to her husband, telling him that news of a treaty between the Signory and King Louis of France had just reached Ferrara, and was of such great importance that she must send to him at once.

This seems to have decided Francesco's course of action. His salary was in arrears ; the old grievance against the Moro and Galeazzo rankled in his heart, although he nominally retained his command, and in May he made secret overtures to Louis XII., placing his sword at his service. The King replied graciously, and soon afterwards sent him the Order of St. Michael, at the same time recommending him cordially to his Venetian allies. The prospect of an alliance between the Pope and Louis XII. was still

more alarming. The Pope's son Cæsar Borgia had
been received with great favour at the French court
and created Duke of Valentinois, and his marriage to
Charlotte d'Albret took place at Blois on the 16th of
May. Both Francesco Gonzaga and Duke Ercole
began to tremble for their own safety, and instead of
taking up arms for the Moro, felt that the time had
come to defend their own States.

Meanwhile Isabella watched the course of affairs
with growing anxiety. She was sincerely grieved at
the downfall of Lodovico, who had been her true and
loyal friend, and thought with concern of her sister's
helpless children, whom she saw driven into exile.
But she was none the less eager to conciliate the
victor and save her husband and his State from ruin.
She sent gifts of falcons and trout to Louis XII.
when he was at Milan, a couple of dogs to Count
Egmont, and a horse to the Maréchal de Giers, and
invited Monseigneur de Ligny, who was a connection of her family, to visit Mantua. And when, in
November 1499, she heard that Cardinal d'Amboise
expressed a great wish to have a devotional picture by
Mantegna, whom he held to be the first painter in
the world, she promptly ordered Messer Andrea to
paint a St. John the Baptist with the portrait and
arms of the French prelate, and sent the picture to
the Cardinal, who declared that he valued it more
than a gift of 2000 ducats.[1] Both Duke Ercole and
the Marquis of Mantua hastened to meet the French
king when he reached Pavia, and accompanied him
on his triumphal entry into Milan. Young Baldassarre
Castiglione, the future writer of the *Cortigiano*, who

---

[1] Pelissier, *Les Amies de Ludovic Sforza* (*Revue historique*,
1891).

was in attendance on his master Francesco Gonzaga, wrote home to tell his friends at Mantua how the Marquis and the king had attended mass at San Ambrogio, and had afterwards been out hunting together, and laid stress on the great friendliness and evident conformity of tastes between His Most Christian Majesty and the Marquis. "So I hope," he adds, not without significance, "that all will go well now."[1]

Yet Isabella's heart must have ached when she heard of the havoc which the French invaders had wrought in the fair halls of the Castello; of the foulness and dirt, the confusion and disorder which reigned in that once beautiful palace. She must have thought with a pang of the gorgeous tapestries and priceless gems, antique marbles and cameos, the pictures by Leonardo and the instruments by Lorenzo da Pavia, of the rare manuscripts which Lodovico had collected at infinite pains and cost, and of poor Beatrice's rich embroideries and jewelled *camoras*, which were now the spoil of the treacherous subjects who had betrayed their prince. But she hid her grief from other eyes, and showed a smiling face to the world. And, with characteristic alacrity, she wrote on the 13th of December 1499 to Antonio Pallavicino, who had been one of the chief traitors, begging him to let her have the wonderful clavichord which Lorenzo da Pavia had made for Beatrice four years before. Antonio wrote back from Lodi, that he would gladly execute her errand on his return to Milan, and inquire what had become of the precious instrument. More than a year elapsed before he was able to gratify the Marchesa's desire, but Isabella's perseverance eventually triumphed over all difficulties, and

[1] Serassi, *Lettere di B. Castiglione.*

on the 31st of July 1501, she wrote joyfully to tell her
friend Messer Lorenzo that the beautiful clavichord
which he had made for her sister, the Duchess of
blessed memory, had been given her by Messer
Galeazzo Pallavicino, the husband of her cousin,
Elisabetta Sforza. "And I felt," she adds, "that
I must let you know this, feeling sure you will be
glad to hear it was in my hands, being as it is your
work, and so excellent an instrument that it must
always be very dear to me." [1]

At the same time, she showed the real warmth
of her heart by the tenderness with which she treated
the unfortunate Milanese exiles who came to seek
refuge at Mantua. Many of these were kinsfolk of
the Sforzas, or high-born ladies whom she had known
intimately at the Moro's court. Among them, strange
to say, were Lodovico's two mistresses, the accomplished Cecilia Gallerani and Lucrezia Crivelli. Isabella entertained Cecilia courteously, and afterwards
recommended her to the favour of the French king,
as a lady of rare gifts and charm, while Lucrezia and
her two little sons found an asylum in the Rocca of
Canneto, and lived there many years under the protection of the Gonzagas. [2] Another distinguished
visitor who spent some weeks at Mantua that
winter was the Marchesa's unfortunate cousin, Isabella of Aragon, whose only son had been carried off
to France by Louis XII., and who, with her two
young daughters, was now on her way to Bari.

The two Sanseverino brothers, Antonio Maria,
with his wife Margherita Pia—an intimate friend
of Isabella—and the brave Captain Fracassa, also

[1] Lorenzo Gusnasco, *Carlo dell'Acqua*, p. 20.
[2] Luzio in *Arch. St. Lomb.*, 1901, p. 154.

sought shelter at the Gonzagas' court ; and through
these refugees, who were in constant correspondence
with the exiled Duke at Innsbrück, Isabella heard
of the plots that were secretly made for his restoration. And she heard from her friends Leonardo da
Vinci and Luca Pacioli, the great mathematician,
who visited Mantua on their way to Venice, how
cordially the people of Milan hated the French
invaders, and how confidently they looked for
Lodovico's return. When, in the first days of
February, the Moro crossed the Valtelline Alps
and entered Milan, amidst the acclamations of his
subjects, it was to Isabella that his first letter from
his old capital was addressed. He felt confident
of her sympathy in his triumph, as he had been in
his reverses, and he fondly imagined that he could
depend on the support of his brother-in-law. We
can imagine the breathless excitement, mingled with
anxious fears for those she loved best, with which
Isabella watched the course of events during those
thrilling days. Her own impulse was to throw
herself heart and soul into the Moro's cause, and
she wrote not only to her brother-in-law, but to
Cardinal Ascanio Sforza, saying that she longed to
fly to Milan, and fight against the French herself.
The Cardinal replied, not without meaning, that her
husband's presence would be more useful. But
Francesco was too cautious a man to commit himself to so desperate a venture. He returned evasive
answers to his brother-in-law's passionate entreaties
for help, and all he did was to send his brother
Giovanni with a troop of horse to join Lodovico
before Novara.[1] By this time the Moro's doom was

[1] Prato, *Cronaca Milanese ; Arch. St. It.*, iii. 244.

already sealed, and when, on the 10th of April, he was given up to the French general Trivulzio, it was Giovanni Gonzaga who rode alone, as fast as his horse could bear him, to bring the news to Mantua.[1] Then Isabella knew that Lodovico's ruin was complete and irrevocable. All her efforts were now directed to conciliate the French victors, and to recover the favour of King Louis, who complained of Francesco's disloyalty to his ally in sending his brother to fight against him, and in receiving the Sforza partisans at Mantua. She herself was openly denounced by the French circles at Milan as an inveterate *Sforzesca,* and it needed all the influence of her father and brothers to prevent an open breach. By the exercise of her wonted tact and diplomacy the Marchesa, however, succeeded in averting the threatened rupture, and both she and her husband eventually regained the good graces of the French monarch.

[1] Muratori, xxiv. 386.

CHAPTER X

1497—1500

Isabella's literary and artistic interests—Foundation of the Studio of the Grotta in the Corte Vecchia—Mantegna's paintings for the Grotta—Cristoforo Romano comes to Mantua—Works for the studio—His medal of Isabella—Correspondence with Niccolo da Correggio—Leonardo da Vinci visits Mantua—Draws Isabella's portrait—Shows it to Lorenzo da Pavia at Venice—Isabella intends to raise a monument to Virgil—Her letter to Jacopo d'Atri.

DURING these troubled years at the close of the fifteenth century, when political affairs occupied so large a share of Isabella's time and thoughts, and private sorrows and public calamities both fell heavily upon her, she lost none of her interest in art and letters. On the contrary, it was just in these anxious days that she was most actively engaged in corresponding with painters and sculptors, and in securing works of art for her *camerini*. From the first day that she came to Mantua the decoration of her rooms, as we have already seen, had been one of her favourite amusements, and she had employed her agents in Venice and Milan and Ferrara to collect those rare and precious objects with which she loved to surround herself. Before long she found the little studio of the Castello was unable to contain all her treasures, and about the year 1496 she obtained her husband's leave to remove some of her most valued possessions to another suite of rooms on the ground floor of the

Corte Vecchia. Since the erection of the Castello the halls in this part of the old palace, which had formerly belonged to the Bonacolsi, had been partly used as public offices, while others contained Francesco's fine collection of armour. But the ground floor remained unoccupied and afforded Isabella an excellent opportunity for carrying out her plans. Here then, in a hall looking out on the Piazza del Pallone, she now founded her famous Studio of the Grotta. An inventory, taken three years after her death, gives a full list of the paintings, statues, bronzes, and medals which it contained,[1] while a poem, written by Raffaelle Toscana in 1586, supplies some interesting details regarding the place itself. *Quel loco che'l mondo la Grotta appella.* "Here," sings the poet, "are hidden the rarest treasures of Italy. Here is the suite of fine rooms which the magnanimous Isabella d'Este built and richly adorned. Two of these contain works of art which fill mortals with joy and wonder. They are decorated with rich gilding, with exquisite designs and intricate carving. Here Mantegna and other masters display their genius in sublime painting." The five pictures by Mantegna, Costa, and Perugino were still in the Grotta in 1627, and Duke Vincenzo refused to sell them to Charles I. with the rest of the Mantuan collection; but they were bought by Cardinal Richelieu immediately after the sack of the town in 1630, and are now in the Louvre. The beautiful fittings of the rooms, the richly carved and gilded wood-work, the delicate *intarsiatura*, and the majolica pavement were destroyed by the Austrian soldiers, who occupied the palace during 150 years, and only the outer court

---

[1] D'Arco, *Arte e Artefici*, ii. 134.

Parnassus

by Andrea Mantegna. (Louvre)

and the room known as the Scalcheria or Cancelleria
retain any of the original decorations. But fragments of the pavement, of coloured Pesaro tiles,
bearing the Gonzaga devices, the crucible and faggots,
which Francesco adopted, the sun which decorated
his father's Camera del Sole, the dove bearing the
motto, *Semper*, the black eagles and golden lion
granted to his ancestors by the Emperor Sigismondo,
and many other favourite emblems, may still be seen
in public and private galleries, at South Kensington
Museum, and Berlin, in the André and Rothschild
collection.[1]

According to Abbot Bettinelli, who described the
palace of the Gonzagas in the eighteenth century,
the studio took its name from the outer court leading
to the gardens, which was decorated in the *grottesca*
style, with stuccoed vaults and niches, and marble
columns, and adorned with statues and bas-reliefs.
The inscription on the walls of the *Cortile* bears the
date of 1522, and shows that it was enlarged and improved when, at her son's request, Isabella gave up her
old rooms in the Castello to inhabit the Corte Vecchia.
But the new studio already went by the name of the
Grotta at the close of the fifteenth century, and contained the Marchesa's finest pictures and choicest
books, as well as an infinite number of other beautiful
objects which she had collected from all parts of
Italy. In May 1498, she dates a letter to her husband from the Grotta,[2] and from that time we find
frequent allusions to this favourite spot in her
correspondence.

It was Isabella's dream to make this Grotta a

[1] Yriarte, *Gazette d. B. Arts*, 1895.
[2] Luzio e Renier in *Arch. St. Lomb.*, xvii. 654.

place of retreat from the world, where she could enjoy the pleasures of solitude or the company of a few chosen friends, surrounded by beautiful paintings and exquisite works of art.   Here she would read her favourite authors or sing Virgil and Petrarch's verses to her lute.   Here she would play the clavichord with the Greek and Latin mottoes which had once adorned Beatrice's *camerino* in the stately Castello of Milan, and listen to the strains of Jacopo de San Secondo's viol or the recitations of the wonderful improvisatore Serafino.   Here she would spend delicious hours with Duchess Elisabetta and her sister-in-law, Emilia Pia, and give herself up to the joys of intimate converse with the best and closest of friends.   In this sanctuary, from which the cares and noise of the outer world were banished, it was Isabella's dream that the walls should be adorned with paintings giving expression to her ideals of culture and disposing the mind to pure and noble thoughts. The subjects of these pictures were to be classic myths with allegorical meanings, chosen by herself with the help of some favourite humanist of her circle, and painted by the foremost masters of the day.

During the next seven or eight years Isabella applied herself to attain this object with all the perseverance and tenacity of her character.   No stone was left unturned, no chance of enriching her collection was ever thrown away.   Again and again in her letters she begged her chosen agents, Zorzo Brognolo in Venice, Ziliolo or Capilupi at Ferrara, to send her "some beautiful thing for the studio." Greek and Roman antiques, marble heads and reliefs newly discovered in ruins of the Eternal City or

among the temples of the Ionian Isles, reached Mantua
in response to her urgent request. She did not scruple
to ask Cæsar Borgia, who drove out Duke Guidobaldo,
or the Pallavicini, who betrayed her brother-in-law,
to give her the spoils of Milan and Urbino. The
greatest painters, the most distinguished sculptors
and goldsmiths of the day, Mantegna, Bellini,
Perugino, Costa, Michel Angelo, Cristoforo Romano,
Raphael himself, were all in turn desired to contrib-
ute some picture or statue to the decoration of the
Grotta. Often she met with refusals, oftener still
with delays and disappointments, but still she persevered with the unwearied ardour, the indomitable
passion of the true collector. First of all she began
with Mantegna. Of all living masters, none shared
Isabella's enthusiasm for antiquity or was more truly
inspired with classic feeling than this old servant of
the Gonzagas. Since his return from Rome he had
been too busily engaged on the Triumphs, and the
decoration of Francesco's villas at Marmirolo and
Gonzaga, to work for the Marchesa, and the one
portrait which he had painted, had failed to satisfy
her critical taste. But the task which she gave him
now appealed in a peculiar manner to his imagination,
and in the two magnificent tempera paintings which
he executed for the Marchesa's new studio, the aged
master rose to new heights of creative power and
romantic invention. In the one, Venus the Queen
of Love is throned on the green slopes of Parnassus
by the side of Mars, the God of War, and at the
foot of the sacred mount, Apollo and the Muses
celebrate her triumph in joyous songs and dances.
A drawing of the central figure in the lower group
by Mantegna's pen has been preserved at Munich,

and in this Muse, who leads the dance, we recognise
the fair face and radiant smile of the young Marchesa
herself, whom the painter has here introduced as the
presiding genius of the studio.[1]   In the other picture,
Minerva is seen armed with spear and helmet rushing
out of a thicket and chasing the Vices of Ignorance,
Ingratitude, Sloth, and Lust from the green bowers
and cypress arbours of a sheltered garden.   There
can be little doubt that the idea of this new series
of Triumphs, in which the victory of moral force and
of that supreme excellence which under the name of
virtù was so often on the lips of Isabella and her
contemporaries, originated with Mantegna, and that
the Marchesa afterwards adapted it with the help of
the humanist Paride da Ceresara to the other pictures
of the cycle.[2]

The Parnassus or Triumph of Love, which is by
far the finest of the two paintings, was completed by
Andrea in the summer of 1497.   The Marchesa,
in a letter written that spring, thanked her friend
Lorenzo da Pavia for some new varnish which he
had sent from Venice, and which was so excellent
that Messer Andrea would like to have twice as
much, and on the 3rd of July Alberto da Bologna
wrote to Isabella, who was absent at Ferrara:
"Nothing is now wanting to the studio of Your
Highness, and you will find Messer Andrea's picture
has been hung and its pedestal and frame gilded."[3]
The companion picture of the Triumph of Virtue
was probably finished by the end of the century, but
even before this Isabella was doing her utmost to

[1] B. Berenson, "The Drawings of Mantegna," p. 4.
[2] *Cf.* Dr. Paul Kristeller, "A. Mantegna," pp. 348, 349.
[3] Yriarte, *Gazette d. B. Arts*, 1895.

obtain works from other masters. When the Marquis visited Venice on his return from Naples, Isabella desired him to tell Giovanni Bellini how anxious she was that he should paint a picture for her studio, and on the 26th of November 1496, Alberto da Bologna, who was in attendance on his master, wrote to say that the painter had promised to satisfy her as soon as possible. In the same letter, the faithful servant, who may have felt it necessary to assure his mistress of her husband's loyalty, adds: "Not a day passes but His Excellency speaks of Your Highness in the most affectionate terms. Your image is graven on his heart, and he always speaks of you as of a dear and sweet daughter." On the 3rd of April 1497, Isabella asked Lorenzo da Pavia, with whom she was in constant correspondence, if his friend the painter Perugino were alive or dead. A report of the Umbrian master's death had, it appears, reached her ears, but if he were alive and in Venice she begged Lorenzo to ask him to paint a picture for her studio.[1] Perugino was alive, but had left Venice some months before, and Lorenzo no doubt told Isabella how full of work the painter was, and how long the Duke of Milan and the Prior of the Certosa had waited in vain for their altar-piece. But many more years were to pass before either Giovanni Bellini or Perugino could be prevailed upon to satisfy the Marchesa's wishes. As she wrote to her friend Ceresara: "We only wish that we could be as well served by painters as we are by men of letters. But we know that the wish is vain. We must be content to take what they choose or are able to give us."[2]

---

[1] Yriarte, *op. cit.*
[2] *Ibid.*, 1896.

Meanwhile, the Marchesa had been fortunate in securing the services of a master whose rare excellence she had long admired—the sculptor Giovanni Cristoforo Romano. This accomplished artist, who was born in Rome about 1465, and sent to Milan by Cardinal Ascania Sforza, was employed on the works of the Certosa of Pavia, and became one of Beatrice d'Este's favourite singers. In this capacity he accompanied her on all her journeys, "and was with her," as Marchesino Stanga wrote, "now in one place, now in another." From his boyhood Cristoforo had devoted himself to the study of antique art in Rome, and did his utmost to prevent the Eternal City from being stripped of its precious marbles. Sabbà da Castiglione tells us that he was as fine a connoisseur as Mantegna, and in the *Cortigiano* he is ranked with Michel Angelo among the foremost sculptors of the age, and would have rivalled him in greatness if he had not suffered from constant ill-health. Since Isabella had seen his charming bust of Beatrice, on her first visit to Milan, she had been very anxious to obtain a similar effigy of herself, and had begged Lodovico to allow the sculptor to come to Mantua. But although the Duke and Duchess had readily granted her request, Cristoforo had excused himself from accepting the Marchesa's invitation until he had finished his work at the Certosa, and it was not till after Beatrice's death that he consented to leave Milan. In April 1497, Isabella again begged Lodovico to allow Messer Zoan Cristoforo to come to Mantua, as she wished for his advice on certain works, and in September she wrote to Benedetto Tosabezzi, her agent at Venice, enclosing a letter from "our

sculptor and servant, M. Zoan Cristoforo Romano,"
desiring the Venetian engineer, Antonio Riccio, to
send him certain Carrara marbles, with which she
wished him to adorn her studio.[1] From this letter it
is plain that Cristoforo was already in her service, and
that he was about to design the beautiful doorway
which may still be seen in her apartment of the
Paradiso, on the upper floor of the Corte Vecchia.
Since these rooms were only built in 1520, when the
Marchesa gave up her old apartments in the Castello,
there can be little doubt that this white marble
portal, richly encrusted with porphyry and other
coloured stones, and adorned with classical bas-reliefs,
was originally destined for the Studio of the Grotta.
The subjects of these medallions agree exactly with
Mantegna's pictures and with the general scheme of
decoration. Minerva appears in one *tondo*, armed
with spear and olive; in another, Apollo hangs up
his lyre on the trunk of a tree; and on a third we
see the Muse of Poetry and Eloquence represented
with a book and cornucopia; while the whole is
framed in a frieze of Greek vases, griffins, and doves,
and carved with exquisite delicacy.

We recognise this gifted sculptor's hand in two
sepulchral monuments, bearing the date of 1498, in
the Gonzagas' favourite sanctuary of S. Maria della
Grazie, near Mantua, and Dr. Luzio has lately
discovered two sketches of the Marquis Francesco's
device of the *crogiolo* or crucible, which he designed
in the same year. We learn from a letter, which
Isabella sent to the sculptor in Rome in March 1506,
that soon after his arrival at Mantua he had carved
her bust in marble for her faithful servant, Ales-

---

[1] Luzio e Renier, *Arch. St. Lomb.*, xvii. 51.

sandro da Baesso, and afterwards repeated the work on a smaller scale, for her friend, the Marchesa di Cotrone. Unfortunately both these busts have perished. But one memorable work which Cristoforo executed at this period has fortunately survived. This is the famous portrait-medal of Isabella, with a winged figure driving away a serpent on the reverse, and the sign of the Archer and her favourite device of a star above. The latter group was probably intended as a symbolic representation of the Marchesa's virtues and wisdom; while the motto, *Benemerentium ergo*, is an evident allusion to her protection of art and letters. But the great value of Cristoforo's medal consists in the authentic portrait which it gives us of Isabella, as she was at the age of twenty-four. The beautiful face with its regular features is seen in profile, the waving locks are loosely caught up in a knot at the back of the head, and a single string of pearls adorns the bare throat. And, in order to leave no room for doubt, the words " Isabella Esten, March, Man.," are inscribed round the head. Fortunately we possess documents which fix the date of this medal with absolute certainty. The one is a letter of September 1498, in which a Ferrara poet, Giacomo Faella, tells the Marchesa that his friend Tebaldeo, with whom he has been spending the summer in the hills near Brescia, has shown him the medal of Her Excellency, and that the sight of her fair face has inspired him with a sonnet.[1] The other is a letter from Niccolo da Correggio, regarding the Latin motto which the Marchesa had desired him to choose for her medal.[2]

---

[1] D'Arco, *Arch. St. It.*, App. ii.
[2] Luzio e Renier, *Giorn. St. d. Lett.*, v., xxi., 243.

After the death of the Duchess Beatrice this brilliant cavalier left Milan to visit his old home at Correggio, but feared to accept a pressing invitation from Isabella to bring his daughter, Leonora, to see her, lest he should bring the plague to Mantua. On the 8th of June he wrote from the heart of Petrarch's country :—

"To-morrow, my dear lady, I am going to dine at Selvapiena, two miles from Rosena, where the most celebrated Messer Francesco Petrarca composed so many works. It is a pleasant spot, fit for such exercises, and if you read the life which is printed with his sonnets and triumphs, you will see it mentioned. So I go there joyfully, in spite of the long journey to Rosena, which is twenty-five miles from Correggio and a very remote place. I shall remain there some days and await the commands of Your Excellency, whose slave I am for ever."

In July he came to Mantua, and falling ill soon after his departure, wrote gallantly to his lady: "I parted with Your Excellency and with my own health at the same moment." The following May found him again at Correggio, from which place he wrote to tell Isabella that he hoped soon to be allowed to visit the "retreat of the Grotta," to which his secretary, the accomplished soldier and poet who went by the name of "Il prete di Correggio," had been lately admitted. "If I am allowed this favour I shall count myself honoured indeed, and if you do not let me in, I must reluctantly confess my inferiority and seek to learn of my more fortunate servant." A few days afterwards, Isabella wrote begging him to send her a suitable motto for Cristoforo's medal. In reply, Niccolo suggested the Latin words, *Benemerentium causa*, which, however, did not please her, as she had seen this motto before and desired something entirely new and original, upon which Niccolo replied, on the 18th of May :—

"It certainly would not do for a lady of so rare a merit to adopt a motto which had ever been used by another, although I must own that I had never seen it before. Nevertheless to please my sovereign lady I will say *Benemerentium ergo*, which has the same meaning as *Benemerentium causa*. This will show you how blindly I obey Your Excellency ! I send back your cavalier as quickly as possible, only grieving that I cannot be with you myself for another week, as I must go to Milan.—Your servant, NICCOLO DA CORREGGIO.

"*P.S.*—I have thought of two more lines which I will add, although they are of little worth.

> Naturæ officium
> Gratitudinis studio."

Niccolo met the Marchesa again in the following spring at Ferrara, where she entertained her father's guests and presided at the carnival balls and fêtes. After the Moro's fall he fixed his residence once more at Duke Ercole's court, where he was much beloved by all the princes of Este and became a devoted admirer of Alfonso's second wife, Lucrezia Borgia. But he still owned allegiance to Isabella, and sent her *canzoni* and *capitoli* on the pattern of his favourite Petrarch's compositions. One sonnet of his which especially pleased her was composed in memory of a beautiful youth in Rome, who had lately died in the arms of his mistress. Isabella on her part sent him presents of fish from Garda, and when, in 1506, his son Galeazzo married the fair and accomplished Ginevra Rangoni she presented the bride with a splendid clavichord. "Your Excellency," wrote Niccolo from Correggio, "has sent a most beautiful clavichord to my daughter-in-law, and has very kindly ordered Domino Philippi to put it in order. Besides the thanks which my daughter herself is sending you, I felt that I must thank you personally for these favours, for which we cannot be too grateful. As for the song which you ask me to select from Petrarch, I have chosen one of those which I like best, beginning: *Si è debole il filo a cui s'atiene*, which seems to me well suited for your purpose, containing verses which must be sung by turn *crescendo* and *diminuendo*. With it I send one of my own songs, composed in a similar metre, which you can sing to the same tune as the Petrarca *canzone*, and also a poem in imitation of Petrarch's *Chiare, dolci e fresche acque*. Once more I commend myself to your good graces, and am keeping Domino Philippi till to-morrow."[1]

But Isabella was never satisfied, and a few months later wrote in great distress because her favourite maid of honour had lately died, and no one could find the last *capitoli* and sonnets which Niccolo had sent her. Fortunately Niccolo, who, as a rule, never transcribed his verses, was able to supply another copy of the poem beginning with the words: *Non si è ardito il cor*, which the Marchesa especially wished to read, and with his old gallantry wrote that, old as he was growing, he was still young enough to dance with her, and to ride at the ring, and break a lance, for her sake, in the coming jousts.

[1] Luzio e Renier, *op. cit.*, p. 244.

Many other poets and artists there were who, like Cristoforo Romano and Niccolo da Correggio, found their way to Mantua or Ferrara, when Beatrice's tragic death had, in Calmeta's words, turned that brilliant court "from a joyous paradise into the blackest hell." Calmeta himself, "*l'elegantissimo* Calmeta," as he was called by his contemporaries, who had been her sister's secretary, spent some time that summer at Mantua and dedicated his commentary on Petrarch's *canzone, Mai non vo cantar*, to the Marchesa, and Serafino, the famous singer and actor, who was so great a favourite with all the Este and Gonzaga princes, also accepted Isabella's invitation. During the year which he spent at Mantua, after Beatrice's death, the Duke and Duchess of Urbino begged him in vain to come and amuse them for a little while, and both Cardinal d'Este and his brother Ferrante asked Isabella for copies of his *strambotti* and *capitoli*. The Marchesa, however, was very jealous of these poems which Serafino composed for her benefit, and when Bishop Louis Gonzaga of Gazzuolo asked her for a certain *capitolo* "On Sleep," which the poet had lately written, begged him to keep it under lock and key and not allow any one to see it, as she particularly wished these charming verses not to become public property. "This, however," she adds, "you will, I fear, find to be a very difficult thing."[1]

But the greatest of all the Milanese artists who came to Mantua after Lodovico Sforza's exile was the Florentine master, Leonardo da Vinci. Isabella had often met the distinguished artist who stood so high in the Moro's favour, and had seen and admired his masterpieces in painting and sculpture.

[1] Luzio e Renier, *Mantova e Urbino*, p. 93.

Isabella d'Este

Portrait. Medal by Christoforo Romano
(Imperial Museum, Vienna)

A year after Beatrice's death, on the 26th of April 1498, she sent to beg Cecilia Gallerani, Lodovico's former mistress, to lend her the portrait which Leonardo had painted some years before, in order that she might compare it with some fine portraits by Giovanni Bellini which she had just seen. Cecilia hastened to gratify the Marchesa's wish, and sent back Leonardo's picture by Isabella's messenger, saying that she only wished it were a better likeness ; not that this was the master's fault, for there was no painter in the world who could equal him, but because, when he painted it, she was of "youthful and imperfect age." [1] Leonardo himself seems to have paid a flying visit to Mantua in the following December, for in a letter from his villa of Goïto, the Marquis desires his treasurer to pay Leonardo the Florentine eleven ducats for certain strings of lute and viol which he had brought from Milan, and begs him to do this at once, in order that the master may be able to continue his journey.[2] But we know that he and his friend Luca Pacioli, who dedicated his "Book of Games" to the Marchesa, visited Mantua on their way to Venice at the close of 1499. It was on this occasion that Leonardo drew the beautiful portrait of Isabella, in pastels, which is now in the Louvre. The late M. Yriarte was the first to recognise Isabella's features in this drawing of the Vallardi collection, and although Dr. Luzio has lately expressed doubt on the subject, there seems little reason to question the fact. Leonardo has drawn the brilliant Marchesa's portrait in his own fashion—

---

[1] "Beatrice d'Este," pp. 53, 54.
[2] Luzio, *Emporium*, 1900, p. 352.

wearing a simple striped bodice, with the waves of
rippling hair falling low on her bare neck, without
ornament or jewel of any description. But the fine
and delicate features are the same as those in the
medal which Cristoforo designed two years before;
the eyes have the same bright and keen expression,
and the whole face is radiant with life and intellect.
Time has dealt hardly with Isabella's portraits, and
of all those countless pictures which were scattered
over Italy, this of Leonardo's is the only one which
brings her before us in the bloom of youth and
beauty. As it happens, we have a testimony to
the truth of Leonardo's portrait from no less an
authority than the great connoisseur Lorenzo da
Pavia. For the Florentine master went on from
Mantua to Venice, there to await the issue of Duke
Lodovico's descent on Milan, and to watch with
anxious eyes the result of that forlorn hope, on
which his whole future was staked. There he met
his old friend, the wise man of Pavia, and as they
talked together of their great patron and the old
life at Milan, the painter brought out his drawing
of the Marchesa and showed it to her loyal servant.
And on the 13th of March 1500, while they were
rejoicing over the wonderful news from Milan,
Messer Lorenzo wrote to the Marchesa about a
lute which he was sending to Mantua.

" Most illustrious Lady,—I send you by this
courier an excellent lute of walnut wood, made in
the Spanish fashion, which seems to me to have the
finest tone that I ever heard. I have been ill,
and as yet unable to finish the black and white
lute, which I will do, like this one, in the Spanish
style. Leonardo Vinci is in Venice, and has shown

me a portrait of Your Highness, which is exactly like you, and is so well done that it is not possible for it to be better." [1]

Leonardo, it appears, took a copy of his cartoon to Venice, and left the other at Mantua, for, a year afterwards, the Marchesa sent a message to him in Florence, begging him to send her a replica of his drawing, since the Marquis had given away the copy which she had kept. But he never painted her portrait in colours, as he had promised on that brief and memorable visit, and not all Isabella's efforts and entreaties were able to obtain a picture by his hand for her studio.

In this same year, when Leonardo came to Mantua, Isabella was intent on a new scheme, the erection of a statue to Virgil in the square in front of the Castello. Early in the century, Carlo Malatesta, acting as regent for his nephew, the young Gianfrancesco Gonzaga, had, in a fit of misguided piety, thrown a statue of Virgil which adorned the Piazza di S. Pietro into the Mincio, saying that the people of Mantua paid the Roman poet a homage only due to a saint. The Marquis Lodovico, who had learnt from his great teacher, Vittorino da Feltre, how to reverence Virgil, had been very anxious to restore this statue, but had never been able to carry out his pious intention. Now the discovery of an antique bust which Battista Fiera, a learned Mantuan physician, pronounced to be the true effigy of Virgil, fired Isabella with ambition to raise a monument to the Mantuan poet. She naturally proposed to entrust the work to the artist of all others best fitted for the task, Andrea Mantegna. A letter which her hus-

[1] A. Baschet, *Alde Manuce.*

band's secretary, Jacopo d'Atri, wrote to her from Naples, shows the enthusiasm which her intention excited among classical scholars.

"Most illustrious and excellent Madonna,—Your Excellency has doubtless heard of the great merits and talents of Pontanus,[1] of whom we may truly say that not only in our own time, but since the days of Virgil, there has never been a man of greater learning or more real merit. Yesterday, after having a long conversation with him in the name of your illustrious lord, I remembered Your Highness's desire to raise a statue to Virgil, and thought I would consult him on the subject and hear his advice. I told him I did this by your order, and explained the object which animated Your Highness and inspired your magnanimous soul with the wish to carry out this idea. As soon as Pontanus heard this, he called two learned gentlemen and said to them: 'If Paolo Vergerio, who wrote De Educando Liberis, were present, the pleasure that he would have in recognising the generous soul of this illustrious Madonna would exceed the sadness which he felt on hearing that Carlo Malatesta had thrown the statue of Virgil into the river.' Then, laying stress on these words, he added: 'Only consider, gentlemen, the magnanimity of this lady of tender years and without classical learning, who determines to revive the fame of this great man, and to render honour and glory to Mantua, where the same lord, Carlo, a man of ex-

---

[1] Pontanus, to whom he here alludes, was not only an elegant Latin poet, whose verses were afterwards published by Aldus, but held high office under King Alfonso of Naples and his son Ferrante, and enjoyed the confidence of the reigning monarch, Federico.

perience and learning, outraged the poet's memory
and the fame of that noble city.   Here, indeed, is a
royal lady, worthy of all praise and commendation,
and had I heard of this before, I would certainly have
given her a place in my book *De Magnanimitate.*'
We then proceeded to discuss the question whether
the poet's statue should be made of bronze or marble,
and agreed that although bronze is certainly the
nobler material, yet, since there is always a risk that
it may be melted down to make guns or bells, we
should prefer a fine marble statue, placed on a noble
pedestal in some honourable place.   The work should
be given to some good sculptor, who would take the
poet's portrait from nature, for I had just told Pontanus of the effigy lately discovered by Messer
Battista della Fiera.   And in order not to depart
from the antique style, the statue should stand by
itself, with a laurel crown on the head, and the
drapery, either an antique toga caught upon the
shoulder or a senator's robe, such as Messer Andrea
Mantegna may think best.   The hands should hold
nothing, and the statue should be perfectly plain, without a book or anything else, but with antique sandals
on the feet, and the attitude would be such as Messer
Andrea shall decide.   At the base there should only
be a few words, such as—*Publius Virgilius Mantuanus,*
and also—*Isabella Marchionissa Mantuæ restituit*—as
may please Your Excellency.   These gentlemen
agreed that Pontanus must consider what would be
the best words to be engraved on the base, and he
agreed to do this willingly.   What I did will, I
hope, be agreeable to Your Excellency, since it was
prompted by true affection, and by one who desires
your glory and feels that this will bring you immortal

fame.—Your slave and servant, JACOPO D'ATRI."[1]
Naples, 17th March 1499.

A drawing, now in the His de la Salle collection
in the Louvre, of a statue of Virgil, covered with
laurel and holding the Æneid, in the style, although
not by the hand, of Mantegna, was probably executed
by Isabella's order, but her project was never carried
out, and Mantua was left without a monument of her
greatest son. The only memorial erected in Isabella's
lifetime was the fine terra-cotta bust of Virgil, which,
in 1511, the doctor Battista Fiera placed on an arch
in front of the church of S. Francesco, together with
a bust of the Marquis, and of the Carmelite poet
Battista Spagnuoli. The arch was destroyed by the
Austrians in 1852, but the three busts are still
preserved in the Museum of Mantua.

[1] A. Baschet, *Gazette d. B. Arts,* 1866.

CHAPTER XI

1500—1502

Birth of Isabella's son Federico—Cæsar Borgia his godfather—
Relations of the Gonzagas with him—Elisabetta of Urbino
goes to Rome—Letters of Sigismondo Cantelmo—Comedies at
Ferrara and Mantua—Treaty of Granada and partition of
Naples—Cæsar Borgia conquers Romagna—Abdication and
exile of Federico, King of Naples—Betrothal of Alfonso d'Este
to Lucrezia Borgia—Preparations for the marriage in Rome—
Il Prete's letters to Isabella—Wedding of Lucrezia and her
journey to Ferrara.

THE year 1500, which saw the final ruin of Lodovico
Sforza and the rise of Cæsar Borgia, was a memorable one for Isabella d'Este, both in her public
and private life. On the 17th of May, within a
month of the catastrophe of Novara, she gave birth,
in the Castello of Mantua, to the long-wished-
for son and heir. Some time before, Suor Osanna
foretold this event, and bade the Marchesa be of
good cheer, since her prayers were heard and she
would soon bear a son.[1] Now the joyful news
was hailed with acclamation, not only throughout
Mantuan territory, but at Ferrara and Urbino. The
sumptuous cradle which Duke Ercole had sent for
his first grandchild's birth, and which Isabella had
refused to let her daughters use, was at length
brought out; and the happy mother borrowed Spanish
leather hangings and tapestries from Ferrara for the

[1] Donesmondi, *Storia Eccles. di Mantova.*

decoration of her infant son's nurseries at his christening. This ceremony took place on the 16th of
July, but was not marked by any public rejoicings.
As Isabella wrote to her sister-in-law, "the troubled
state of Italy has deprived him of a more honourable
baptism."[1] The choice of the godfathers was signifi-
cant. The first was the Emperor Maximilian, whose
friendship the Marquis was anxious to secure without
breaking with Louis XII., and who was himself
rejoicing over the birth of his grandson, the future
Emperor Charles V. Little did Isabella know how
great an influence the babe, who first saw the
light at Ghent, on that auspicious Feast of St.
Matthias, was destined to wield over the fate
of Italy and the fortunes of her new-born son.
The second of Federico's sponsors was Cardinal
Sanseverino, the warlike prelate, who, like all his
brothers, had been a devoted partisan of the Sforzas,
and had entered Milan at the head of the Moro's
followers. None the less, he had, a few months
before, succeeded in making his peace with France,
through the friendship of Cardinal d'Amboise, and
soon afterwards returned to Milan. The third august
personage whom the Marquis chose to hold his son
at the font was Cæsar Borgia. The Pope's son, as
young Castiglione wrote home, was the tallest and most
splendid-looking man among all the princes and nobles
who escorted Louis XII. on his entry into Milan.
Now he was rapidly becoming the most prominent
figure in Italian politics. His energy of will and
powers of mind were as great as his strength of
body ; his ambition was as boundless as his courage.
His influence over the Pope was absolute. He was

[1] Luzio e Renier, *Mantova e Urbino*, p. 106.

already master of Rome and aspired to reign over all
Italy.   The Pope's son, wrote the Ferrarese envoy,
Pandolfo Collenuccio, " has a great soul and seeks
fame and grandeur, but cares more to conquer States
than to govern and defend them.   He is fierce in his
revenge and never forgives a wrong, so I hear on all
sides."   The truth of this report was confirmed by the
Pope himself, who remarked, in conversation with
another Ferrara agent, Costabili : " The Duke is a
good-natured man, but he cannot forgive an insult.
The other day I told him that Rome was a free city,
where every one had a right to say what he pleased.
' That may be all very well for Rome,' replied
Cæsar, ' but I will teach people to be sorry for what
they say.' " [1]

From the first, Francesco Gonzaga and his wife
realised the growing power of Duke Valentino, as he
was popularly called in Italy, and lost no opportunity
of conciliating this dangerous personage.   A few days
after his son's birth, the Marquis wrote to ask him to
stand sponsor to the little Federico, an honour which
Cæsar accepted with alacrity, as we learn from a note
written on the 24th of May :—

" I heard of the fortunate and much-desired birth
of Your Excellency's little son with exultation as
great as if it had been my own, and gladly accept
the honour you propose to do me, begging that you
will depute one of your councillors to represent me
at the font and will give my congratulations to your
most illustrious consort, hoping this babe may be the
first of a numerous race of sons destined to perpetuate
the name of two such noble and glorious parents." [2]

---

[1] Pastor, " History of the Popes," vi. 113.
[2] F. Gregorovius, " Lucrezia Borgia," p. 66.

But enough was known of Cæsar Borgia's designs at Mantua to excite the worst fears, and the suspicion which the Marquis Francesco entertained of his new ally is evident from a letter which he addressed to Elisabetta of Urbino, in March 1500, begging his sister to abandon her intended visit to Rome.

Already in the summer of 1499, the Duchess had invited Isabella to accompany her on a pilgrimage to Rome in this year of Jubilee, but the critical state of public affairs in Lombardy and the approaching birth of her child compelled the Marchesa reluctantly to decline the proposal. As the time of Elisabetta's journey drew near, the Marquis became seriously alarmed for his sister's safety, and urged her by their mutual love to consider the present state of things and the risks to which she would be exposed. If she is in need of change, let her come to Mantua and give his wife the pleasure of her company. "The year is long," he adds, "and later on we will all three go to Rome and visit the holy places together in a more convenient season." But when this letter reached the Duchess, she was already on her way to the Colonnas at Marino, and wrote to the Marquis from Assisi, full of concern at the objections which he raised to her plans.

"Most illustrious Prince and dearest Brother,— A few days ago I left Urbino on my way to Rome to keep the Jubilee, as I told you some time ago, and this morning reached Assisi, where I received your letter begging me to give up my journey. This has caused me the greatest possible grief and vexation. On the one hand, my sole desire is now, as it has ever been, to comply with your wishes, and pay you the obedience due to a father. On the other, as you see, I have already started and am beyond the borders of the State, and Signor Fabrizio Colonna and Madonna Agnesina, my honoured sister-in-law, have engaged a house and made all the necessary arrangements for me. And since I have promised to be at Marino in four days, and Signor Fabrizio is on his way to meet me, I do not see how I can give up the journey with honour to my lord and myself, more especially since everything has been considered and arranged beforehand by my good lord. Neither will Your Excellency have any fear for my safety when you hear that I go to Marino first, and on with Madonna Agnesina *incognito* to Rome, there to visit the churches chosen for this Holy Jubilee, without making myself known or speaking to any one. In Rome, we shall be lodged in the house of Cardinal Savelli, which is conveniently situated in the midst of the Colonna quarter, but I intend to return to Marino as soon as possible and spend most of my time there. So Your Highness need have no doubts or fears for my safety, although I confess that, if I had not already started, I would have given up my intention, not from any fear of danger or disturbance, but in order to satisfy Your Excellency. But since I have already got as far as this on my journey, I am sure this letter will satisfy you, and I beg and pray you to write to me in Rome so that I may know that you are satisfied and may keep the Jubilee with greater content and peace of mind. Otherwise I shall be in continual distress and anxiety. I commend myself heartily to your good graces, and remain your younger sister, ELISABETTA."[1]

[1] F. Gregorovius, *op. cit.*, p. 134.

The next day Elisabetta continued her journey, and after spending Holy Week in Rome and visiting St. Peter's and the Tombs of the Apostles, in strictest *incognito*, she returned with her sister-in-law to the Colonnas' castle of Marino in the Alban hills, and enjoyed the company of Madonna Agnesina and her seven-year-old daughter, the little Vittoria, who was already betrothed to the young Marquis of Pescara. A fresh sorrow awaited her at Urbino in the death of her husband's half-brother, Antonio, a valiant soldier who had fought at Fornovo with Francesco, and whose wife, Emilia Pia, was her devoted friend and companion. The Duchess's tender heart was full of sympathy for the heart-broken widow, and she wrote to Isabella saying that both she and the Duke were doing their best to comfort poor Madonna Emilia, whose grief was enough to move the stones to pity. Isabella herself wrote in the most affectionate terms to Emilia Pia, begging her to take comfort, " since this is a journey on which we all must go," and telling her that, as she had proved herself the best of wives in the past, it was now her duty to try and conform herself to the divine will, in order that her prayers for her husband's soul might be the more acceptable in the sight of God.[1] Before long Emilia dried her tears and recovered her old gaiety, but in spite of her charms and popularity, she never consented to marry again, and remained faithful to the memory of her lamented husband.

Early in the following year Isabella visited Ferrara and spent some time at her father's court, where several Latin comedies were acted, including the "Mercadanti," the "Asinaria," and the "Eunucho."

[1] Luzio e Renier, *Mantova e Urbino*, p. 107.

" These plays," she remarks in a letter to Mantua, "are certainly full of vain words, and are not without doubtful passages to which some persons might take objection. All the same, they are very amusing, and excite much laughter, chiefly owing to the frequent changes of voice and excellent performance of these actors." At her urgent entreaty the Duke agreed to return with her to Mantua, where the Marquis made great preparations for some dramatic representations to be given in his honour. But, at the last moment, the arrival of papal envoys with important proposals from the Borgias detained Ercole at Ferrara, and the carnival fêtes at Mantua took place without him. One of his favourite courtiers, however, Sigismondo Cantelmo, the husband of Isabella's intimate friend, Margherita Maroscello, accompanied the Marchesa home, and sent the Duke full accounts of the performances in the magnificent theatre prepared for the occasion in the Castello. His elaborate descriptions of this building and allusions to the Triumphs of Mantegna, with which the stage was decorated, lend especial interest to the following letter :—

" Most excellent Prince, my dear Lord,—The arrangements made by this illustrious Lord Marquis have been most splendid, and deserve to be studied by all who wish to erect appropriate theatres for the performance of ancient and modern plays. I do not doubt that Your Excellency has already heard of the representations which have been given. None the less, I should fail in my duty if I did not write to tell you what, indeed, requires a better scribe than I am— all the magnificence, grandeur, and excellence of the said representations, the beauty of which I will try to describe as briefly as possible. The stage itself is quadrangular in form, but somewhat extended in length. Each side has eight arcades, with columns well proportioned to the size and height of the arches. The base and capitals of each pillar are richly painted with the finest colours and adorned with foliage, and the arches, with their reliefs of flowers, offer an admirable perspective, each being about four *braccia* wide and proportionately high, the whole representing an ancient and eternal temple of rare beauty. The back of the stage was hung with cloth of gold and foliage, as required for the recitations, and the sides were adorned by six paintings of the Triumphs of Cæsar by the famous Mantegna. On the two other and smaller sides of the stage there were similar arcades, but only six in number. Two sides of the stage were given up to the actors and reciters; on the two others were steps occupied on the one hand by women, on the other by strangers, trumpeters, and musicians. At one angle were four very lofty columns with rounded bases, and between them a grotto designed with great art, but in the most natural manner. The roof overhead blazed with hundreds of lights like shining stars, with an artificial circle, showing the signs of the zodiac, and in the centre, the sun and moon moving in their accustomed orbits. Within the recess was a Wheel of Fortune inscribed with the words, *Regno, regnam, regnabo*, and in the midst, the golden goddess, seated on her throne, bearing a sceptre adorned with a dolphin. The lowest tier of the stage was hung with the Triumphs of Petrarch, also painted by Mantegna, and large golden candelabra hung from the centre of the roof, each holding three double rows of torches and a shield with the arms of His

Cæsarean Majesty, the black eagle with the royal and imperial diadem. At the sides of the stage were two large banners with the arms of His Holiness the Pope and the Emperor, and smaller ensigns with those of the Most Christian King and illustrious Signory of Venice. Between the arches were banners with the arms of Your Excellency and of the German prince Duke Albert of Bavaria, and the devices of this Signor Marchese and the Signora Marchesana. Higher up on the walls were busts and statues of gold, silver, and other metals, which added greatly to the decorative effect of the whole. Last of all the roof was hung with sky-blue cloth to imitate the blue vault of heaven, studded over with the constellations of our hemisphere.

" The recitations were exceedingly fine and enjoyable. On Friday 'Philonico' was given, on Saturday 'Il Penulo' of Plautus, on Sunday the 'Ippolita' of Seneca, on Monday the 'Adelphi' of Terence. All of these were admirably recited by skilled actors, and received the greatest applause from the spectators. As Monsignore Louis d'Ars, the son of the illustrious M. de Ligny, is now here, and had not seen the first play, I hear the 'Philonico' will probably be given again. If I have forgotten anything, I hope soon to supply the omission by word of mouth, when I see Your Excellency, to whose good graces I commend myself. — Your Excellency's servant and slave, SIGISMONDO CANTELMO." [1] From Mantua, Feb. 13, 1501.

This minute description, obscure as it is in some places, at least enables us to form some idea of the

---

[1] Campori, *Lettere artistiche*, 1866, and D'Ancona, *Origini del Teatro*, vol. ii.

construction of the new theatre and of its splendid
and elaborate decorations, while the presence of the
French visitors, whom the Gonzagas were especially
anxious to conciliate, showed that the event was not
without political significance.

That autumn Isabella gave birth to a third
daughter, who received the name of Livia, but
died at the age of six. Neither this child nor
Leonora, who was already seven years old, appears
to have interested her mother much, and she seldom
mentions their names in her letters. She was, however, careful to give them an excellent education,
and first Sigismondo Golfo, then Francesco Vigilio,
taught Leonora Latin and grammar. The Marchesa
chose these teachers herself, and would allow no
carelessness or irregularity. On one occasion, when
Golfo absented himself for some weeks, she sent
him an order to return at once, if he did not wish
to lose his situation. But all her fondest hopes
centred round her little son, Federico. She watched
the growth of this precious infant with the ten-
derest affection, and when the Marquis was absent
from Mantua sent him daily reports of his little
son. "I am quite well," she writes on the 3rd of
July 1501, "and so is our beautiful boy, who is
always asking for his *Pà*." Again, on the 7th of
August, the proud mother writes : "To-day our
little boy began to walk, and took four steps
without any help ; although, of course, he was carefully watched, much to our delight and his own.
His steps were a little uncertain, and he looked
rather like a tipsy man! When I asked him afterwards if he had any message to send his father, he

said, ' *Ti Pà!*' so I must commend him to you as well as myself."[1]

Meanwhile political events of grave importance were taking place in other parts of Italy. The Pope's daughter, Lucrezia Borgia, after the dissolution of her first marriage with Giovanni Sforza, the widower of Maddalena Gonzaga, became the wife of Alfonso, Duke of Bisceglia, an illegitimate son of Isabella's uncle, the late King Alfonso of Naples, and nephew of the reigning king, Federico. The union proved a happy one, but the unfortunate prince was so foolish as to quarrel with Cæsar Borgia, and in July 1500 he was attacked by five masked assassins as he left the Pope's rooms, and seriously wounded. "Every one here," wrote Calmeta from Rome to Elisabetta Gonzaga, "knows that this is Duke Valentino's doing." A few weeks later the wounded man was strangled in his bed in the Vatican by Cæsar's guards before the eyes of his wife. "The Pope," wrote the Mantuan envoy, Cattaneo, "is very much displeased at this event, both on account of the King of Naples, and for the sake of his daughter, who is in despair."[2]

Immediately after this deed, which excited general horror, Cæsar Borgia set out to conquer Romagna at the head of an army of 7000 men. First Pesaro, then Rimini, surrendered without a blow, and Giovanni Sforza fled to Mantua, and sought refuge in his first wife's home. Francesco received his brother-in-law kindly, but told him plainly that he could do nothing against Borgia. In spite, however, of Isabella's professions of friendship

---

[1] Luzio, *Precettori*, &c., p. 37.

[2] Pastor, "History of the Popes," vi. 613.

for her son's sponsor, she could not conceal her
admiration for the gallant little town of Faenza,
which remained loyal to its prince, Astorre Manfredi,
and alone among the cities of Romagna offered a
determined resistance to the conqueror. On the
20th of April 1501 she wrote to her husband: " I
rejoice to hear that the citizens of Faenza are so
loyal and constant in their lord's defence, and feel
that they have redeemed the honour of Italy.
May God give them grace to persevere ; not that
I wish Duke Valentino any ill, but because neither
this poor Signor nor his faithful subjects deserve
such ruin. I thank Your Excellency for giving me
news of the first battle, of which Messer Carlo da
Sesso also informs you in the enclosed letter, which
I opened in your absence." [1] But five days after
this Faenza was forced to surrender, and the brave
young Manfredi was taken captive to Rome, and
strangled in Castell' Sant' Angelo by Cæsar's orders.
At the same time Isabella had to lament the ruin
of her mother's family and the downfall of the last
king of the house of Aragon. Federico's doom was
already sealed. In November 1500 a secret treaty
was concluded between Louis XII. of France and
Ferdinand the Catholic, who agreed to divide the
kingdom of Naples between them. In June a large
French army crossed the Alps and marched against
Naples, and a month later Gonsalvo di Cordova
landed in Calabria with a Spanish force. The Pope
ratified the treaty publicly, and Cæsar Borgia left his
army in Romagna to join the French before Naples.
After a fiercely contested battle, Gaeta and Naples
opened their gates to the victors, and on the 4th

[1] D'Arco, *Arch. St. It.*, App. ii.

Federico fled to Ischia, and abdicated his throne in favour of the French king. He retired to France, where a pension and the Duchy of Anjou were granted him, and where he spent the remaining three years of his life.

Everywhere Cæsar Borgia and his French allies were triumphant, and no one knew in which direction their arms would next be turned. The situation was an anxious one, and Isabella was greatly alarmed to hear from her father's envoy at Milan that her husband had incurred the suspicion of the French Viceroy, Cardinal d'Amboise, by his supposed intrigues with the Emperor. One day, when the Ferrarese ambassador was dining with the Viceroy, his host suddenly asked him what he thought of the Marquis of Mantua's plot to drive the French out of Italy. Then, turning to Trivulzio, the Cardinal said: " M. le Maréchal, what would you do if you knew that the Signor Marchese kept a spy here to report all our actions ? " " I should dismiss his ambassador at once," replied Trivulzio. And that same evening the Mantuan representative, Tosabezzi, received notice to leave Milan.[1]

Under these circumstances Francesco Gonzaga saw that his best policy was to cultivate the friendship of Cæsar Borgia, and he took care to offer no opposition to Duke Valentino's latest scheme. This was the proposal of a marriage between his sister Lucrezia and the Duke of Ferrara's eldest son, Alfonso d'Este. A few weeks after the murder of her second husband, the report of this intended alliance was already the common talk of Rome. " The Pope's daughter," wrote a German pilgrim

[1] D'Arco, *Arch. St. It.*, App. ii.

who visited Rome in this year of Jubilee, and was grievously shocked at these scandals, "lives here in great state, and is about to marry a third husband, the first being yet alive. If one does not please her, she asks for another." In February 1501, when Isabella was spending the carnival at Ferrara, formal proposals to this effect were made to her father by the Pope's envoy. At first the proud spirit of the Este princes recoiled with horror from the thought. Not only was Lucrezia the Pope's bastard, but her own character was by no means free from stain. There might be no grounds for the horrible crimes which were freely imputed to her in Rome, but the Ferrarese ambassador reported that she had been engaged in an intrigue with a papal chamberlain named Peroto, and had given birth to a child a year after the dissolution of her first marriage. The bare idea that a woman against whom such charges could be brought, should reign in the place of the good Duchess Leonora, seemed intolerable to the Duke and his children. At first Alfonso quite declined to entertain the proposal, and Isabella regarded it with unqualified disgust, although she was too prudent to give vent to her feelings in public. But by degrees this natural repugnance melted away before the solid advantages of the proposed marriage. The Pope not only offered to give his daughter the enormous dowry of 300,000 ducats, but to reduce the yearly tribute paid by Ferrara as a fief of the Church from 400,000 ducats to a nominal sum of 60 ducats, and to surrender several important fortresses and valuable benefices to the Duke. Louis XII. warmly supported the Pope's proposals, and Ercole began to realise the substantial benefits which he and his State would derive from the marriage.   When the Emperor, moved by his invincible hatred for the Borgias, commanded him as his liege lord to break off the negotiations, the Duke only returned a civil answer, and made use of Maximilian's despatch to secure better terms from the Pope.

At length, after prolonged conferences, the marriage contract was finally signed on the 26th of August, and Ercole wrote to inform his daughter Isabella of the fact.   On the same day the marriage was publicly proclaimed in Rome.   Both the Pope and Cæsar were exultant, and Lucrezia, who, in spite of her troubled past, was of a singularly child-like and light-hearted nature, gave vent to her delight by dancing all night with so much energy that she was laid up with an attack of fever the next morning.   The Mantuan agent, Cattaneo, supplied Isabella with abundant details of the preparations that were made for the wedding during the next few weeks.

"The dowry," he wrote on the 13th of December, "will consist of 300,000 ducats, counting the value of the presents which this Madonna will receive. First of all, 100,000 ducats will be paid down in gold at Ferrara ; then she will have clothes, plate, jewels, fine linen, costly hangings and trappings for horses and mules representing another 200,000 ducats.   Her trousseau will contain no less than 200 *camoras*, each of which will be worth 100 ducats, with sleeves and gold fringes valued at 30 ducats apiece.   One robe alone is valued at 20,000 ducats, and a jewelled hat is said to have cost 10,000 ducats, while in Rome and Naples more gold has been employed in preparing her outfit during the last few weeks than is generally required in two years."

On the 23rd of December, Alfonso d'Este's brothers, Don Ferrante and Cardinal Ippolito, arrived in Rome with a brilliant suite to solemnise the marriage, and escort the bride to Ferrara. Lucrezia, clad in white and gold brocade, with pearls and rubies in her hair, received the two princes on the steps of the Vatican, and Cæsar led them into the palace, while the Pope looked on from a balcony, and greeted his guests with effusion. He conversed freely with the Ferrarese envoys, saying that he meant Lucrezia to have more beautiful pearls than any other princess, and praised her beauty and goodness, comparing her to the Marchesana of Mantua and the Duchess of Urbino. But in spite of these assurances we see how deep was the distrust which the Borgias inspired and how anxious Duke Ercole felt with regard to Lucrezia's own character by the following letter which his confidential agent, Gian Luca Pozzi, wrote on the evening of his arrival in Rome :—

"To-day, after supper, Girardo and I waited on the most illustrious Madonna Lucrezia, in the name of Your Excellency and Don Alfonso. We conversed together on many subjects, and in all she said we found her very sensible, discreet, of good and loving nature, and sincerely attached both to Your Excellency and Don Alfonso, so that I confidently believe Don Alfonso will find real comfort in her society. Besides which, she is singularly graceful in all her actions, and her manners are full of modesty and decorum. She is a good Christian, filled with the fear of God, and is going to confess to-morrow, and to communicate on the Feast of the Nativity of Our Lord. She has a sufficient share of good looks, and her pleasing expression and graceful manners make her seem more beautiful than she really is. In short, her qualities are such that I am sure there is nothing to fear from her, but rather everything to hope for. Your Highness may rest assured that, bound as I feel to speak the truth without prejudice, I tell you this with great joy and consolation."[1]

The bride made the same excellent impression on *Il Prete*, that faithful servant of Niccolo da Correggio, whom Isabella, in her anxiety to receive full particulars of the marriage, had sent to Rome in her brother's suite. This admirable chronicler described the wedding ceremony and fêtes, the dresses and jewels of the chief personages, and the bride's dowry and trousseau, with a fulness and exactness which, as Gregorovius remarked, are worthy of a *Times* reporter. He was especially careful to obey the Marchesa's wishes, by giving a minute description of Lucrezia's appearance and character. "She is a charming and very graceful lady," he wrote after the first interview. "I can tell you that our Cardinal's eyes sparkled at the sight of her."

On the 29th of December, he wrote again to Isabella: "This noble Madonna is seldom seen in public, being occupied in preparation for her departure. But on Sunday, the Feast of St. Stephen, I went to see her later in the evening, and found her sitting near the bed with ten maids-of-honour, and twenty other ladies wearing handkerchiefs on their heads after the Roman fashion. They soon began to dance, and Madonna danced very gracefully and well with Don Ferrante. She wore a *camora* of black velvet trimmed with gold fringe, with narrow sleeves slashed to show her white linen chemise, a

[1] F. Gregorovius, "Lucrezia Borgia," p. 189.

vest of black velvet richly embroidered in colours, a gold-striped veil and a green silk cap with a ruby clasp on her head. Her maids-of-honour have not yet got their wedding dresses. Our own ladies are quite their equals in looks and in everything else. But two or three of them are decidedly graceful. One from Valencia dances well; another, called Angela, is very charming. Without her knowledge I have chosen her for my mistress! Yesterday the Cardinal and Don Ferrante rode through the town with the Duke, all wearing masks."[1]

The wedding was celebrated on the 30th of December, in the Aula Paolina, before the Pope, who sat on his throne, attended by thirteen Cardinals and the foreign Ambassadors, only the Emperor's representative being conspicuous by his absence. The bride was magnificently attired in a robe of gold brocade, with flowing sleeves that trailed on the floor. Her train of crimson velvet, trimmed with ermine, was borne by ten maids-of-honour. Her golden hair was tied back with a black ribbon, and she wore a gold net over her hair, and a string of pearls with a pendant of large emeralds, pearls, and rubies round her neck. The Duke of Ferrara's mandate was read aloud, the Bishop of Adria delivered an address which was shortened by the Pope's orders, Ferrante placed the ring on the bride's finger in his brother's name, and she replied in a clear voice that she received it of her own free choice. Then Cardinal Ippolito presented her with Duke Ercole's present, a gorgeous casket of jewels, valued at 70,000 ducats, filled with precious gems, rings, necklaces, and the famous pearl necklace which, Isabella re-

---

[1] F. Gregorovius, *op. cit.*, p. 194, &c.

membered with a sigh, had belonged to her dearly
loved mother. The Pope was delighted, and exclaimed as he took the jewels in his hands that the
young Cardinal's charm of manner doubled the value
of the jewels. But Duke Ercole had been careful
to insert a proviso in the contract stipulating that the
jewels were to be returned, and only the wedding
ring kept by Lucrezia if the marriage were afterwards
dissolved.

Cardinal Ippolito then presented the bride with
his own gift of four jewelled crucifixes, and the other
Cardinals followed with their gifts, after which the
whole company witnessed a succession of races and
jousts on the Piazza before the Vatican. Steel
weapons were used, and as many as six noble youths
were wounded, reports *Il Prete*. " Then Cæsar,"
he goes on, "took the Madonna's hand and danced
before the Pope with rare grace, and the maids-of-
honour followed and danced very well in couples.
His Holiness was in high spirits, and laughed all the
time. This lasted over an hour. Then the comedies
began. One was in Latin verse, and a shepherd and
children were introduced, and looked very fine, but I
could not understand its meaning. After that the
company dispersed, and only His Holiness, the bride,
and her brother and brothers-in-law sat down to the
wedding feast at the Pope's table."

Isabella's correspondent gave her detailed accounts
of the week's festivities that followed, of the comedies
and ballets, the masquerades and dancing, the recita-
tion of epithalamiums and marriage hymns, the bull-
fights organised by Cæsar Borgia, and the torchlight
processions in which Lucrezia took part.[1] At length,

---

[1] Gregorovius, *op. cit.*, pp. 200–217.

on the 6th of January, the wedding party set out for
Ferrara, escorted by a cavalcade of Roman horsemen.
The bride was attended by a suite of 180 persons, and
Angela Borgia, that *damigella elegantissima* who had
fascinated *Il Prete* at first sight, was her chief lady-
in-waiting.   By the Pope's command the bride was
received with royal honours at Terni, Spoleto, Foligno,
and each place where a halt was made.   At Gubbio
Duchess Elisabetta herself came to meet her, and
Duke Guidobaldo, who had strong reason to distrust
Cæsar Borgia, no doubt felt it prudent to give his
sister a splendid reception at Urbino.   Elisabetta herself accompanied the bride over the mountain passes
to Pesaro, where Lucrezia was lodged in the very
palace which she had occupied for some years as the
wife of Giovanni Sforza.   At Imola, the party rested
for a whole day in order that the bride might set her
jewels and clothes in order for her entry into Ferrara,
and wash her head.   This, Ferrante d'Este explained
in a letter to his father, she had been unable to do for
ten days, owing to which she suffered severely from
headaches.   Some days were spent at Bologna, where
a banquet was given by the Bentivoglios in her
honour, after which the party embarked on bucentaurs, and travelled by water first along a canal, and
then up the river Po as far as Castell Bentivoglio, a
town about twenty miles from Ferrara.   Here the
bride was surprised to see Don Alfonso, who had
ridden out in disguise to meet her, and spent two
hours in her company to her great delight.   She
wrote that night to tell her father of the prince's
courtesy, which gratified the old Pope highly.   The
next day he sent for the Ferrarese envoy to express
his satisfaction, and spoke with genuine affection of

Lucrezia, saying repeatedly : "I have done great things for her, and I mean to do more." As the Venetian ambassador, Paolo Capello, remarked : "The advancement of his children is the only thing that he seems to care about."[1]

[1] M. Sanuto, *Diarii*, iii. 847.

CHAPTER XII

1502

Isabella presides at Lucrezia Borgia's marriage festivities—Reception of the bride at Ferrara—Isabella's letters to her husband —Comedies, balls, and fêtes—The ambassadors' gifts—Isabella entertains the French ambassador—Her interview with the Venetian envoys—Return to Mantua—Lucrezia Borgia's life at Ferrara—Her relations with Isabella and the Marquis.

WHILE Elisabetta Gonzaga was escorting Lucrezia Borgia on her journey through Central Italy, Isabella d'Este came to Ferrara at her father's request, to receive her brother's bride. Her own letters to Francesco give full descriptions of the wedding festivities, which were on a splendid scale and are said to have cost Duke Ercole 25,000 ducats. On the 29th of January, two days after her arrival, Isabella wrote :—

" My dearest Lord,—My father came to my room after dinner to-day and arranged the order of the bride's entry, which is to be as follows. On Tuesday, I shall accompany Don Alfonso with only a few ladies in a barge as far as Malalbergo to meet her, after which she will sleep at my lord Alberto d'Este's house at Casale, and I shall return home with the Duchess of Urbino, who however must go back on Wednesday to keep the bride company. Madonna Lucrezia Bentivoglio with half of these ladies will go to meet her and follow her in the procession, while I remain here with the other half to receive her at the steps of the Palace. It is true that I mean to go and see the entry from the Custom-house, but as soon as the procession has passed by, I shall return to the Palace. After making these arrangements, my father took me to see the hall where the comedies are to be acted, which is 146 feet long by 46 wide. Steps have been made from the Piazza with a partition to divide the men from the women, who will be in the centre, with the men on either side; the ceiling and steps are hung with green, red, and white draperies. On the opposite side of the hall is a wooden stage about the height of a man, with battlements, and the scenery for the comedies, which are to be six in number. About 5000 persons are expected, but the seats will be reserved for strangers, and any that remain will be given to Ferrarese gentlemen. Five shields with coats of arms hang from the roof—those of the Church, of France, Este, and Borgia, and the black and white eagle which was our old coat of arms. I saw nothing else worthy of note. The wooden beams of the roof are left bare, but perhaps these are to be draped later. I will tell you what more is to be seen on the day itself. All these gentlemen are busy preparing sumptuous dresses and gold chains, but the attire of the women will be splendid beyond words! I have not left the house these two days, owing to the number of visitors which I have had. To-night we go to the house of M. Ercole Strozzi. I am sending 500 oysters by the sailors who take back the barge, and I hope Your Excellency will enjoy them for love of me. Kiss my darling boy a thousand times over!—Your wife, Isabella." [1]   Ferrara, Jan. 29, 1502.

[1] This and the following letters from Ferrara were published by D'Arco in *Arch. St. It.*, App. ii. See also F. Gregorovius, " Lucrezia Borgia."

On the 1st of February, the Marchesa described
her first meeting with the bride: "Soon after eight
o'clock I entered Don Alfonso's barge together with
Don Giulio (her half-brother) and my own gentlemen
and ladies. At Torre della Fossa I changed boats
and went on to Malalbergo, where we met the bride
in a ship with Don Ferrante and Don Sigismondo and
a few others, and here I found the Duchess of Urbino
with them. The boat came alongside, and one bark
having curtsied to the other with joyous haste, I
entered the bride's with Madonna Laura (Giovanni
Gonzaga's wife), and after exchanging salutes we went
on our way and she did not enter the small bucentaur
for fear of losing time. About four o'clock we
reached Torre della Fossa, where my father was
standing on the shore awaiting us. The archers in
their red and white liveries, seventy-five in number,
were drawn up in a row, and the whole court gathered
round the Duke, who took Madonna Lucrezia by
the hand and kissed her, after she had insisted on
first kissing his hand. Then we entered the large
bucentaur, where all the ambassadors shook hands
with us, and we sat down in the following order:
the bride between the French and Venetian, myself
between the Venetian and Florentine, and the Duchess
of Urbino between the Florentine and Sienese, the
Lucchese envoy being close by. My father and
Don Alfonso sat on deck above, talking and joking
together, and were much amused by the Spanish
clowns, who paid the bride all manner of compliments, and so, amid great cheering and shouting
and the sound of trumpets and guns, we reached
Casale about five. After accompanying the bride
to her rooms we all left, and I took the Duchess of

Urbino in my *carretta* to her lodgings, which are those of Ventimiglia above the *loggia*. I will not describe Madonna Lucrezia's appearance, as you have seen her. She wore a vest of wrought gold trimmed with crimson satin, with slashed sleeves in Castilian fashion, a crimson satin mantle, turned back on one side and lined with sable, open at the throat to show a frilled chemise, in the usual fashion. On her neck she wore a string of big pearls, with a pendant of ruby and a pear-shaped pearl, and a gold coif on her head, but no band. Madonna Lucrezia Bentivoglio received her on the shores of the Po with a great company of ladies. Madonna Teodora was presented to her by Don Alfonso's seneschal as chief lady-in-waiting, together with twelve Ferrarese maidens wearing *camoras* of crimson satin, and black velvet mantles lined with black lamb. The gentlemen of her household have not yet been chosen. Five carriages were sent to meet her—one hung with gold brocade, and led by four white horses, each worth fifty ducats apiece; one covered with red velvet, led by roan horses, all very fine; and three hung with purple satin, with horses of different colours. I have not mentioned Don Alfonso, because, as I told Your Excellency before, he went last night to Bentivoglio, returned to Ferrara this morning, and joined my father at Torre della Fossa. The Duchess of Urbino is very well and lively, and commends herself to Your Excellency with me, and I beg you to kiss the dear child of our love. —Your wife, ISABELLA."

On this occasion the Duchess of Urbino wore black velvet embroidered with a gold pattern, while Isabella herself was attired in a black velvet robe trimmed with lynx fur, with a green velvet vest studded over with gold plaques—a gift from Francesco—a gold circlet on her head, and a gold collar set with diamonds round her neck. Her beauty and distinguished air attracted general admiration, as the Marchesa di Cotrone, who accompanied her to Ferrara, wrote that evening to the Marquis.

" The bride is not beautiful, but sweet and attractive in appearance, and although she had many ladies with her, and among them that illustrious Madonna, the Duchess of Urbino, who is very handsome and a worthy sister of Your Excellency, yet my illustrious lady was universally pronounced, both by our people and by those who came with the Duchess, to be by far the most beautiful, so much so that if the bride had foreseen this, she would have made her entry by torchlight! There can be no doubt of this, since others are as nothing at my lady's side. So we shall bear the prize back to the home of my own Madonna." [1]

On the following day the Duke and his son rode out to meet the bride at Casale, and escorted her across the bridge of Castel Tedaldo, and through the town to the ducal palace. The pageant is described by contemporaries as the grandest ever seen in Ferrara.

" I will tell you the order of this illustrious bride's entry," writes Isabella, " and whatever else is worth noting, as best I can. First of all came my father's seventy-five archers in white and red liveries, with three captains in different costumes, then eighty trumpeters, among them six of the Duke of Romagna's, wearing cloth of gold, and purple and

[1] D'Arco, *op. cit.*

white satin uniforms, and twenty-four pipers and trumpeters. Behind them came the nobles and gentlemen of Ferrara, of whom seventy wore golden chains, none of which cost less than 500 ducats, while many were worth 800, 1000, and even 1200 ducats. Then followed the Duchess of Urbino's suite, all in black velvet and satin, and after them Signor Don Alfonso and M. Annibale Bentivoglio. His Highness rode a big bay horse with purple velvet trappings embossed with gold. He wore a suit of grey velvet covered with scales of beaten gold, worth at least 6000 ducats, a black velvet cap trimmed with gold lace and white feathers, and grey leather gaiters. Eight squires walked behind him, four men and four boys, in French suits of gold brocade and purple velvet, with hose of red and purple cloth. Then came the bride's suite, twenty of whom were Spaniards clad in black and gold, but only twelve of the whole company wore gold chains, and these not at all large ones or equal to those worn by my gentlemen. These were followed by the Bishops of Adria, Comachio, Cervia, and two others sent by the Pope. Then came the ambassadors, walking two abreast—a Lucchese and a Sienese together, the other Sienese with a Florentine, and so on, the two Venetians wearing long crimson satin mantles; last of all the four Roman ambassadors in long cloth-of-gold mantles lined with crimson satin. Behind them were six drummers and two Spanish jesters in brocade of variegated colours. Then the bride, under a crimson baldacchino carried by the doctors. In front of her was a big dapple-grey horse, given her by the Duke, with crimson trappings embroidered with gold, led by eight grooms in purple and yellow vests and hose."

The Venetian chronicler[1] informs us that, as the bride rode over the bridge of Castel Tedaldo, her horse took fright at the guns, and would have thrown her if her groom had not rushed to her help, and placed her on a mule. Isabella continues: "The bride was mounted on a roan mule with velvet trappings covered with gold lace, and fastened with nails of beaten gold. She wore a cloth of gold *camora* with purple satin stripes and flowing sleeves after the French fashion, and a *sbernia* of wrought gold, open on one side, and lined with ermine, as were her sleeves. Round her throat was the necklace of rubies and diamonds which belonged to Madonna of Ferrara, of blessed memory! On her head was the jewelled cap which my lord father sent together with the necklace to her in Rome, without any band. Six of Don Alfonso's chamberlains, all wearing fine gold chains, held the reins. The French ambassador rode at her side, outside the baldacchino."

The bride, according to another account, sent for the French envoy, Philippo Bert, when the procession started, and made him ride at her side, as a token of the Pope's gratitude to the King of France for bringing about the marriage.

"Behind the bride, the Duchess of Urbino and my lord father; the Duchess on the right on a roan mule, with black and gold velvet trappings, wearing a black velvet robe adorned with certain triangles of beaten gold which are astrological signs, a string of pearls at her throat, and a gold coif on her head. My Lord Duke rode a roan horse, with black velvet and a suit of purple velvet, and was followed by two ladies, Donna Hieronima Borgia and the wife of

[1] Marino Sanuto, *Diarii*, iv. 222-230.

Fabio Orsini, both in black velvet; and behind them, Madonna Adriana, a widowed relative of the Pope. These were the only women on horseback. Madonna Lucrezia Bentivoglio rode in a chariot hung with gold brocade, followed by twelve other chariots, bearing the bride's ladies and her own Ferrarese and Bolognese ladies. Behind them came two sumpter-mules, with black and silver trappings, elaborately worked, and fifty-six more with red and yellow clothing, and twelve with purple and yellow. A few arches, as I told Your Excellency, were erected at certain points along the route, and there were some representations which are not worth mentioning, and no one paid much attention to them."

At five o'clock the procession reached the Piazza, where two rope-dancers descended simultaneously from opposite towers, and at the same moment the doors of the dungeons were thrown open and all the prisoners released. On the steps of the ducal palace, the Marchesa, magnificently arrayed in a *camora* of cloth of gold, embroidered with her favourite device of musical notes and rests, received the bride, and conducted her to the Sala Grande, followed by the Duke and the whole company. In this noble hall, hung with Leonora's priceless tapestries, two Ferrara poets, Celio Calcagnini, the friend of Raphael and Erasmus, and Ariosto, recited a Latin Epithalamium in the bride's honour, and hailed Lucrezia as *pulcherrima Virgo*—a title which may well have sounded ironical in the ears of the bystanders, when applied to one whom the Romans had derisively called "the Pope's daughter, wife, and daughter-in-law."

The following day was spent in dancing and acting, and in the evening Isabella took up her pen and wrote: "To give Your Excellency an account of to-day's doings: After dinner we brought the bride out of her rooms, and led her into the Sala Grande, which was so crowded with people that there was no room to dance. However, we got through two dances as best we could." Cagnolo, who had come to Ferrara in the French ambassador's suite, tells us that Lucrezia came down from the tribunal, where she was seated between Isabella and Elisabetta, and danced Roman and Spanish dances, to the sound of tambourines, with rare grace. He adds that although she is not regularly beautiful, her golden hair and the dazzling whiteness of her skin, together with her gentleness and winning manners, render her most attractive. "She is very gay and light-hearted, and is always laughing."[1]

Then the acting began. "My father," continues Isabella, "brought in all the actors, and showed us the costumes which have been prepared for the five comedies, to show us that the dresses had been made on purpose, and that those which were worn in one comedy would not have to be used again. There are in all one hundred and ten actors, men and women, and their clothes are of *cendale* (a fine silk) and camlet. The leader of the troop appeared in the character of Plautus, and explained the argument of the five plays, the 'Epidico,' the 'Bacchidæ,' the 'Miles gloriosus,' the 'Asinaria,' and 'Cassaria.' After this we passed into another hall, and about six o'clock the first play began. Neither the verses nor the voices struck me as very good, but the *Moresche* dances between the acts were very well danced, with great spirit. . . . The

[1] Zambotto, *Cronaca.*

last was danced by Moors with lighted torches in their hands, and was a fine sight. It was not over till past ten, and then every one went home to supper." The Marchesa evidently found these prolonged festivities very tedious, and at the end of this letter she adds a postscript in which her real feelings are expressed.

"I will not deny that Your Excellency, in my eyes, enjoys far greater pleasure in being able to see my little son every day, than I find in these fêtes. If they were the finest in the world, they would not please me without Your Excellency and our little boy. But I will not believe that he has forgotten me already. If he does not remember me out of affection, he must remember me if only because he is kissed so often! So I hope Your Excellency will be sure to kiss him a few more times for love of me! Don Alfonso and the bride slept together last night, but we did not pay them the usual morning visit, because, to say the truth, this is a very cold wedding! I hope that my person and suite compare favourably with those of others who are here, and we shall at least carry off the prize of the card-playing, since Spagnoli has already robbed the Jew of 500 gold pieces. To-day we are to dance till four o'clock, and then see another comedy.—Your wife, ISABELLA." Feb. 3.

On the 4th, the bride did not leave her room till late in the day, and the Duke took his chief guests to see the sights of Ferrara—the treasures of art contained in the Castello and the Schifanoia palaces, the guns in which his son Alfonso took especial interest, and the holy Dominican nun, Sister Lucia of Viterbo, who had received the stigmata, and whose wounds were said to bleed afresh every Friday.

"Yesterday," wrote Isabella on Saturday the 5th, "we all stayed in our rooms till five o'clock, because Madonna Lucrezia chooses to spend all these hours in dressing, so that she may outshine the Duchess of Urbino and myself in the eyes of the world, and being Friday, there was no dancing. At half-past five the 'Bacchidæ' began, and was so long and tiresome, with so few dances, that I wished myself many times at Mantua. It seems a thousand years till my return, both because of my longing to see Your Excellency and my little son, and of my wish to escape from here, where I do not find the least enjoyment. Your Excellency need not envy me for being at this wedding, which is a cold and dull affair! I only wish I had stayed at home. If I had time to write to you more fully, I should be less bored. But, as soon as I am out of bed, my brothers come in and do not leave my side all day. Besides which all the ladies come and visit me, since Donna Lucrezia is not to be seen until she appears in the Sala. We sup about eleven o'clock and go to bed at one or two. You may imagine how little I enjoy all this. Pity me! Last night only two dances were introduced in the play, and at the end we heard nothing but groans and complaints from the spectators, who had already sat there more than four and a half hours. Nothing else is worth saying, only I beg you not to forget to kiss Federico for me.— Your wife, ISABELLA.

"P.S.—I must tell you that to my credit I am always the first to be up and dressed!" February 5, 1502.

Lucrezia spent that day in her room, washing her head and writing letters to tell her father of the splendid fêtes which had been given in her honour. And Sanuto informs us that she privately presented Duke Ercole with the pontifical bull releasing the fief of Ferrara from the payment of tribute. In the evening Isabella invited Monseigneur Bert, the French ambassador, to supper in her rooms, and placed him between the Duchess of Urbino and herself at table. The conversation, Cagnolo tells us, was witty and brilliant. The Marchesa looked her loveliest in a robe of white and silver *tabì*, and at the urgent entreaty of her guests, consented to sing to them after supper, accompanying herself on the lute, to the delight of all who were present. Afterwards she took the ambassador into her private rooms and discussed political affairs confidentially with him for nearly an hour, in the presence of two of her ladies. Finally she took off her own perfumed gloves and presented them to Monseigneur Bert, who received them with the deepest reverence and gratitude, saying that he counted them even more precious than the sacred linen bestowed on him by Suor Lucia, and would keep them in a reliquary to the end of his days.

On Sunday the whole court attended high mass in the Duomo, and Don Alfonso was solemnly invested with a consecrated cap and sword, presented by the Pope to his dear son. Another ball was given in the Sala Grande, at which Isabella looked radiant in a gown of crimson satin and black velvet, trimmed with massive gold cord, and ruby and pearl buttons; and the bride, who appeared in a violet robe patterned over with gold fish-scales, and a jewelled coronet on her head, danced French country dances with great charm and spirit. After this came a performance of the "Miles gloriosus," ending with a true mummers' dance of the rudest description, in which shepherds, wearing rams' heads, fought and butted each other with their horns to the infinite amusement of the spectators.

On Monday a new diversion was provided for the guests, in the form of a single combat which took place on the Piazza in front of the ducal palace, between Vincenzo da Imola, a soldier in the Marquis of Mantua's service, and a Bolognese gentleman of Annibale Bentivoglio's suite. After a desperate encounter with lances and clubs, Vincenzo succeeded in unhorsing his adversary, and would have slain him if the Duke had not divided the combatants. "Vincenzo remained on horseback," writes Isabella, "and rode round the enclosure amidst infinite shouting, all the people crying *Turco!* while the poor Bolognese showed his broken staff! So we bore off the palm."

In the evening the "Asinaria" was performed with a marvellous interlude of satyrs, who danced to the tune of a musical clock, and chased wild beasts and birds over the stage. Then a Mantuan musician played three lutes at once, and the whole performance ended with a ballet of the harvest, in which the different operations of digging, ploughing, sowing, reaping and thrashing the corn were represented to the rustic music of bagpipes. Isabella appeared in a gown of crimson velvet, striped with gold bands, and a tiara of immense diamonds on her head, while the bride wore a robe of woven gold, and a long chain of priceless gems round her neck.

On Shrove-Tuesday, which was the last day of

the carnival, the ambassadors visited the bride's chamber, and presented her with costly gifts. First of all, Duke Ercole gave his daughter-in-law his own magnificent jewels. Then the French ambassador presented the bride with a rosary of golden beads, perfumed with musk, and her chief maid-of-honour, Angela Borgia, with a precious chain. At the same time he gave the Duke a golden shield with an enamelled figure of St. Francis, made in Paris, and Don Alfonso a similar shield, bearing an image of the Magdalene, no doubt, remarks Cagnolo, because he had taken to himself a bride who in virtues and charms resembled this saintly maiden, and of whom it might be said, as it was of Mary Magdalene, " to her much is forgiven, because she loved much ! "

The other ambassadors followed with gifts of rich brocades and bronze and silver ewers and bowls, but the most remarkable presentation was made by the Venetian envoys, who took off the magnificent crimson velvet and ermine mantles which they had worn all the week, and laid them at the feet of the bride—" upon which," wrote the Marchesa di Cotrone to Francesco Gonzaga, "every one who was present burst out laughing."

A ball took place afterwards, at which the royal ladies appeared in their most gorgeous costumes, and Isabella wore a violet velvet robe embroidered with gold acorns, and a magnificent jewelled tiara. The last comedy, the " Cassaria," was performed with a series of elaborate musical interludes and recitations in honour of the happy pair. Don Alfonso, who was an accomplished musician, played the viol, and took part in a concerto for six instruments, and at the close of the last ballet — a war-dance of Swiss

soldiers—a golden ball melted away in the air and revealed the forms of four Virtues, who sang a delicious
quartette.   But the musical part of the entertainment
was decidedly superior to the comedy, which Isabella
declared to be " lascivious and immoral beyond words,"
so much so that she refused to allow any of her ladies
to be present.

The next morning, being Ash Wednesday, was
spent by Isabella in religious exercises with her
family.   But in the afternoon, by way of relaxation,
she was present with the whole court at a performance
given by a youth named Cingano, who anticipated
Blondin by walking on a rope from the roof of the
bishop's palace to the Sala Grande in the ducal palace.
The Duke's son and the royal ladies, as well as all the
foreign envoys, came out to witness the feats of this
performer, who danced with his eyes blindfolded,
walked backwards in a steel cuirass, and was seen
hanging by his feet to the rope suspended in mid-air
above the square, to the infinite amusement of the
august company.[1]   That evening the Marchesa received farewell visits from the foreign ambassadors,
and made use of this opportunity to ingratiate herself
and her husband with the Signory of Venice, as we
learn from the following letter, which her secretary
Capilupi addressed to the Marquis :—

" My dear Lord,—To-day my Madonna and the
Duchess were in the bride's room when the Venetian
ambassador came to take leave of her, and at the
same time pay their respects to Her Excellency and
the Duchess of Urbino.   But they first of all addressed my Madonna, in a long speech, saying that
the Signory had charged them to call upon Your

[1] Muratori, *Diario Ferrarese,* vol. xxiv. 404

Highness if you had been at the wedding, and that since you were not present, they wished to pay the same honour to the Marchesa, because of the services rendered by Your Excellency to their State, whose loyal son they count you to be, and on whose good offices you may always depend. Madonna then took up her speech and answered them in a clear voice, with as much elegance and prudence as if she had been a consummate orator. I am quite unable to write down all that she said, but I must tell you one thing which every one thought very wise and admirable. 'If this illustrious Signory,' she remarked, 'had made trial of Your Excellency in your youth, and had employed you in the defence of Italy at that time, now that you are older and more experienced, they might avail themselves of your services with more advantage.' These and other appropriate words amazed the ambassadors and others present so much that they all confessed themselves her slaves. The ambassadors then turned to the Duchess of Urbino, and in their words plainly showed that they honoured her in the first place as Your Excellency's sister, and in the second as the Duke of Urbino's wife, and she also replied discreetly. Last of all Donna Lucrezia spoke, but although she has had more husbands than either your wife or sister, she could not attain by a long way to the wisdom of their answers. Your Excellency will rejoice to learn what an excellent impression Madonna your wife has made on all these lords and ambassadors. Her disgust and displeasure at the foul comedy of yesterday was evident to all, so that the Duke had good cause to be ashamed; her conduct was only praised, since, as Your Highness knows, she would not allow any of her maidens to be present.—Your faithful servant, BENEDICTUS CAPILUPUS." [1] Ferrara, Feb. 9, 1502.

The next day Isabella took leave of her relatives, and, accompanied by the Duchess of Urbino, returned to Mantua, where she arrived on Monday the 14th, and joyfully embraced her little Federico once more. A few days afterwards she addressed a courteous note to Lucrezia, announcing her safe arrival and signing herself " Your loving sister." [2]

Lucrezia on her part was unfeignedly anxious to cultivate Isabella's friendship. In a letter which Laura Bentivoglio addressed to the Marchesa a few months afterwards, from Ferrara, she described a visit which she had paid to Alfonso's wife, in the following terms :—

" She made me sit down, and asked with charming sweetness after Your Excellency, begging to hear about your clothes, and especially about your head-dresses. Afterwards, in speaking of her Spanish robes, she said if she had anything that you would care to see or possess, she would gladly oblige you, being most anxious to please Your Excellency. And she expressed a wish that you would write to her sometimes and be more familiar in your intercourse with her, and asked repeatedly if the betrothal of Duke Valentino's daughter with your son had been arranged. To-day she wore a *camora* of black satin and gold foliage, with a hem that looked like a flame of pure gold, and flowing sleeves, such as Your Excellency wears, and a necklace of the finest pearls. Her head was dressed in her usual fashion,

---

[1] Luzio, *Precettori*, p. 36.

[2] F. Gregorovius, " Lucrezia Borgia," App.

with a very bright emerald on her forehead and a green velvet cap wrought with beaten gold. Her manners and gestures were most natural and quite charming, and she looked very pretty, but has grown rather thinner, although she is not ill."

Lucrezia always showed great curiosity about the Marchesa's clothes, and on one occasion, Lucrezia d'Este, who visited her while she was undergoing a cure, wrote as follows to Isabella: "I found her lying on the bed wearing a black silk robe with tight sleeves and frills at the wrist, and after many caresses and affectionate greetings, she inquired what were the latest Mantuan fashions and praised my head-dress. I promised to make some caps in our style, and send them to her. Certain rosettes which I wore on my forehead also pleased her, and she begged me to show them to a jeweller and have them copied for her." [1]

But, in spite of mutual compliments and fine speeches, the two ladies were never on intimate terms, and Dr. Luzio points out that most of the letters from the Gonzaga archives quoted by Lucrezia's biographer Gregorovius were in reality addressed to the Marquis and not to Isabella.[2] In later years some rivalry arose between the two princesses, and Isabella could not forgive her old friends, Niccolo da Correggio and Ercole Strozzi, for transferring their devotion and dedicating their poems to her sister-in-law. Lucrezia, however, proved an excellent wife to Alfonso, by whom she was fondly beloved, and who sincerely lamented her early death in 1519. She bore him four children, the eldest of whom,

---

[1] Luzio in *N. Antologia*, 1896.
[2] Luzio, *Precettori*, p. 37.

Ercole, was born in 1508, and succeeded his father as Duke in 1534. Her conduct during the latter years of her life was exemplary, and she edified the people of Ferrara by the charitable institutions which she founded, and spent much of her time in Duchess Leonora's favourite convent of Corpus Domini.

CHAPTER XIII

1502

Isabella's visit to Venice—Her letters to the Marquis—Courtesy of the Doge and Signory—Her income and expenditure—Proposed marriage between Federico Gonzaga and Cæsar Borgia's daughter—Elisabetta of Urbino goes with Isabella to Porto—Cæsar Borgia seizes Urbino—Flight of Duke Guidobaldo to Mantua—Isabella asks for the Venus and Cupid of Urbino—Cæsar Borgia sends them to Mantua—Michel Angelo's Cupid sold to Charles I. and brought to England.

As soon as Isabella had recovered from the fatigues of the wedding festivities at Ferrara she began to make plans for a new expedition. The Duchess of Urbino had never seen Venice, and a vow which Isabella had made to the Santo at Padua afforded a good excuse for paying a second visit to the famous city. This time the two princesses decided to go in the strictest *incognito*, in order that they might be able to dispense with tedious ceremonies, and devote themselves wholly to sight-seeing and their own amusement. So they set out one morning in March, taking only two ladies with them—the Marchesa di Cotrone and the faithful Emilia Pia—and escorted by the Protonotario Sigismondo Gonzaga and two of Isabella's most trusted servants, her seneschal Alessandro da Baesso and her secretary Benedetto Capilupi. The Marquis accompanied his wife and sister as far as Sermide, where they took boat to the mouth of the Po, and spent the night at a wretched hostelry at Stellata. As usual, Isabella gave her husband a full account of her doings in a letter from Venice, where she arrived on the 14th of March.[1]

"My dear Lord,—Yesterday morning we left 'la Stellata' so early that we reached Chiozza an hour after dark, but since the hostelries were all full we had to send Benedetto Capilupi to inform the Podestà of our arrival, which we did the more readily, hearing that he was M. Alvise Capello, brother to M. Paolo, and a great friend of Your Excellency; and although we begged him to direct us to some private lodging near the inns, he insisted on receiving us in his own house in the kindest manner possible, and, above all, allowed us to remain strictly *incognito*. So we accepted his invitation, and were honourably lodged and entertained at supper in the palace. That night we were too tired and travel-stained to see His Magnificence, but this morning he visited us and regretted that he had not been aware of our coming, so as to pay us greater honour, as the Signory would have wished, and begged us to dine with him. We replied that we were on our way to discharge a vow at Padua, but had come through Venice, as the Duchess had never seen this city, and that since we were in travelling dress we should not have made ourselves known to him, only that he was a friend of Your Excellency, and, we felt sure, could be trusted to keep our secret; to which he replied that we had done well, and that the moment he heard of our arrival he had

---

[1] This and the five following letters in the *Archivio Gonzaga* were published by Dr. Luzio, *Mantova e Urbino*, 307–315.

sent word to the Signory, but we begged that on no
account should we be received and publicly entertained by them. So we came on here quietly this
evening, and are lodged in the house of M. Niccolo
Trevisano, which is occupied by the Duke of Urbino's
ambassador. We found Franceschino Trevisano
in the house, and hear from him that all Venice
knows of our arrival, and that Your Excellency's
friends are delighted. We all three commend ourselves to you, and I beg you to kiss my boy.
To-morrow I will send some fish and oysters. I
thank Your Excellency for allowing me to come
here, and am enjoying Venice much more than I did
last time, and think the city far more beautiful.
The Duchess owns that it is more marvellous than
Rome, and wonders at the sight, and is lost in
admiration, and kisses Your Excellency's hand.—
With the right hand of your wife, ISABELLA."
Venice, March 14, 1502.

The next day she resumed her tale :—

" I was sure Your Excellency would be vexed to
hear of the discomforts that we endured at the
Stellata, but I hope you will understand that mine
were not serious, and that I have spirit enough to
put up with such trifling inconvenience, although, of
course, we should have been more comfortable if we
had stayed with Your Excellency at Sermide. The
only disadvantage would have been that we could not
have reached Chiozza that evening, where, although
we arrived unexpectedly, we were very honourably
entertained by M. Alvise Capello at his expense, as I
told you before. Yesterday we stopped at Ponia to
see those big ships, and went on board a very large
one which is being built and is said to be three thou-

sand tons and more. This morning we went to hear mass at Sta. Maria dei Miracoli, and then to S. Giovanni e Paolo and the Scuola di S. Marco, and returned home by another way. Directly after dinner we went to S. Marco, hoping to find very few people at that hour, but we were mistaken, as there were a good many, and then, so as not to leave anything undone and to see this marvellous city well, we climbed the Campanile of S. Marco, where we greatly enjoyed the beautiful view and examined the noble buildings on all sides. When we descended, we returned by boat and went to S. Giorgio and to the Misericordia, and came home by the Grand Canal. As yet I have seen none of our friends, except Genua, who shook hands with me in the Campanile, and this evening he called at our lodgings to see if we required anything. Monsignore and I spoke to Francesco directly about the jewels. Monsignore pretended that he had found a friend who would lend him 3000 ducats before Your Excellency heard of this, in order to conduct the transaction the more secretly with regard to the 2000 ducats which the Albani will pay. We have sent for the Jew, and Monsignore and I will do our utmost to settle this business. The Duchess is anxious to see the Doge and Signory, who will not appear till the procession of Olives on Sunday, so we have settled to stay here over that day, although I, having seen them already, do not care about it, but I must do this for her sake. On Monday we shall be at Padua, Tuesday at Vicenza, Wednesday at Verona, and so as not to travel on Holy Thursday or Friday, we will spend these two days there and make our communions. On Saturday we shall be at Mantua, and I pray you to give a hundred kisses to my darling boy, so that when I am there he will not think it strange to be kissed." Since the Doge had invited the Marchesa to visit the Collegio, as she had done before, Isabella sent Capilupi and Baesso to make her excuses and those of the Duchess to the Prince and Signory, and explain that they were travelling *incognito*, and had no clothes in which they could appear. The Doge returned a courteous answer, and gave orders that the Treasury of S. Marco and the Arsenal should both be shown to the distinguished visitors.

"Meanwhile," writes Isabella, "we went to hear mass at Ca' Grande, and afterwards landed at the Rialto and walked through the Fish-market and the Merceria to the columns of S. Marco. There were such crowds of people that it was difficult to make our way, but we enjoyed it so much that we did not mind the walk, and Monsignore was the most tired of the party. The Duchess is as well as possible. At the columns we took a boat and came home, where we found a secretary from the Signoria waiting to tell us that four gentlemen were coming to visit us on the part of the Doge and Senate. We begged him to dispense with this ceremony, but we had hardly finished dinner before they were here. The Duchess and Monsignore and I met them on the stairs and led them into the room, and I replied to their compliments, laying stress on the love and devotion of Your Excellency for this illustrious Signory. When they were gone M. Alvise Marcello appeared, having cleverly delayed his visit till theirs was over, and spent some time in friendly conversation. He seems as much devoted to you as ever.

M. Filippo Capello also called and talked in the same familiar way with Monsignore and me. Then we went to the 'Vergine,' where we enjoyed seeing the nuns' rooms and hearing two of them sing, but owing to the new regulations lately introduced by Frate Raphael da Varese, who is preaching in S. Marco this Lent, no men are allowed to enter the convent. On our return home we found Alvise Marcello, who told Monsignore that he had got the order to view the Treasury to-morrow morning and the Arsenal after dinner. We commend ourselves to you, and so does M. Alvise a thousand times. I enclose the names of the gentlemen, begging you to kiss our little son for me: M. Alvise Moncenigo, M. Zoanne Gabriele, M. Pietro Justiniano, M. Alvise Molino." Venice, March 16.

The next day Messer Alvise called early with a present of fish and confectionery from the Signory,[1] valued, Sanuto tells us, at twenty-five ducats. This gift included four large chests of fish of different kinds, eight large gilt marzipane cakes, twenty-nine boxes of sweetmeats, four pots of ginger and four of syrup of violets, as well as twenty pounds of wax candles. Isabella sent these presents by messenger to Mantua that evening, begging the Marquis to accept them for her sake. She added a postscript to the effect that the Pope's ambassador had informed the Duchess how warmly the Doge had spoken of their august visitors in the College, saying that the Duke and Marquis could give no better proof of their confidence in the Signory than by sending those persons who were dearest to them to Venice. "And all our friends here say the same thing."

[1] Sanuto, *Diarii*, iv. 234.

After this the Marchesa proceeded to give her husband the following account of their day :—

" We went to mass at the Carità, and on to S. Marco, where the Pala and Treasury were shown us by Messer Paolo Barbo, the procurator. Then we were taken to the Great Hall of the Council, and to the Armoury of the Doge's Palace, after which we went on foot by the Merceria, which were prepared for us, as far as the Rialto, where we took boat and came home to dinner. Afterwards we went to the Arsenal, which our friend Messer Alvise Marcello showed us with the greatest care and kindness, and Messer Carlo Valerio and Paolo Capello came to shake hands. When we had seen all, M. Alvise took us into the house which he occupies close by, as Treasurer, and entertained us in the usual manner. M. Alvise and M. Paolo Capello came with us in the boat to S. Antonio, where we saw the Sepulchre, and on our way home we called on our neighbour, the Queen of Cyprus, who had invited us to visit her. These gentlemen escorted us home, and so the day ends, and if Your Excellency considers the length of the journey, and all we have seen and done, you will count us to be the most gallant ladies in the world !" Venice, March 17, 1502.

The two princesses had certainly made good use of their short visit, and Isabella was delighted with all that she had seen and done. We do not hear if she saw her friends Lorenzo da Pavia and Aldo Manuzio, or the painter Giovanni Bellini, who had excited her displeasure by his long delays in executing the picture for her Grotta. But it was Alvise Marcello to whom she applied two years later to help her in the matter, and the other patricians are fre-

quently mentioned in her correspondence. Queen
Caterina Cornaro was an old friend of the Este princesses, whom Isabella had already visited in her
mountain home of Asolo, and to whom she wrote
after her return to Mantua, thanking her for the
affection and kindness which she had shown her.
On the morning of the 21st, the ladies left Venice,
and by evening reached Padua, where they were
entertained by Count Achilles Borromeo, and Isabella found time to inform her husband that the
French ambassadors were expected at Padua on their
way to Venice, having been abruptly dismissed by
the Emperor. Maximilian had refused to grant
Louis XII. the investiture of Milan and the incor-
poration of the duchy in the kingdom of France,
while the French monarch on his part declined either
to release Lodovico Sforza or to allow the exiled
partisans of the Sforzas to return to Milan. "Until
the present time," she adds, "the King of France has
taken little count of the Venetians, but now he is
most anxious to secure their friendship." And she
ends with expressing her delight in the good news
which her husband gives her of Federico, whose
company she longs to share, but hopes to make up
for lost time on her return. After spending the last
days of Holy Week in the house of Count Canossa
at Verona, and receiving a gift of fish from the
cavalier Giorgio Cornaro, in the name of the Signory
of Venice, Isabella and her sister-in-law reached
Mantua on Easter Eve, and the happy mother once
more clasped her precious boy in her arms.

A week afterwards, Francesco left home to attend
some races in the neighbourhood, and Isabella's letters
as usual were full of fond allusions to the child's

cleverness and charms. "The boy always seemed
intelligent," she writes on the 4th April, "but since
Your Excellency's departure, he surprises me every
hour with his pretty ways, and seems determined to
keep me amused in your absence. He sits in your
place at meals, and plays a thousand other tricks,
which I do not tell Your Excellency lest I should
excite your envy." Again, two days later, she wrote:
"Yesterday, when I was saying my office, he came
in and said he wanted to find his papa, and turned
over all the cards till he found a figure with a beard,
upon which he was delighted, and kissed it six times
over, saying, ' *Papa bello!* ' with the greatest joy
possible." [1]

Another and less pleasant task to which Isabella
now turned her attention was the settlement of her
accounts. The expenses of her visit to Ferrara had
been heavy; besides the cost of her own sumptuous
toilette, and those of her ladies, presents of costly
brocade and chains had to be given to the actors
and buffoons, the trumpeters and musicians. Marino
Sanuto tells us that on this occasion the Marchesa
had shown remarkable liberality to all of these, but
especially to the Spanish jesters in the bride's train. [2]
At Venice, as we have seen, she had been engaged
in raising fresh loans to pay the Albani and redeem her
jewels; and soon after her return to Mantua she addressed a letter to her father, Duke Ercole, to whom she
had more than once applied for help in her difficulties.
This time, however, she gave him a full statement of
her income and expenditure, which is of great interest, and shows that if this brilliant lady occasionally

[1] Luzio, *Precettori*, p. 38.
[2] *Diarii*, iv. 230.

erred on the side of extravagance, she was a prudent and clever manager, who made the most of her money, and had a shrewd eye to business.

"My honoured Lord and Father,—When I first entered this illustrious house I was given a yearly allowance of 6000 gold ducats, to pay for my clothes and provide dowries for my maidens, and all that is necessary for my servants—including two gentlemen; the Court supplying the food of about a hundred persons. Afterwards, in order that I might be free to increase or diminish my household, my illustrious consort gladly agreed, by the advice of his stewards, to take this burden from off their shoulders, and give me another 2000 ducats for the expenses of my whole company. Of this income 6000 was charged on the toll of the mills, 1000 on an excise duty, and the other 1000 on the lands of Letopalidano, near Gonzaga. So you see that in all I have 8000 ducats a year. It is true that by my own economy, and that of my servants, the income of this estate has been increased by about 1000 ducats, with which I have been enabled to buy some neighbouring lands; so that at present the rent brings in about 2500 ducats a year. But I also have to feed about fifty more persons of my household. And it is true that my lord has given me other houses for my pleasure, such, for instance, as Sacchetta and Porto; but their income does not exceed their expenses, and sometimes I have to spend more money to keep them in repair. This is all I can tell Your Excellency for your satisfaction."

By this statement it is clear that Isabella enjoyed a yearly income of from 8000 to 9000 ducats—no inconsiderable sum, if we consider that the ducat was worth about eleven and a half francs—or, roughly

speaking, nearly ten shillings—and that money has
increased five times in value since those days.[1] But
considering the large demands upon her purse, and
her passion for pictures and antiques, as well as fine
clothes and jewels, it is decidedly to her credit that
she was able to keep out of debt, and could often raise
money to help her husband in bad times or sudden
emergencies. The question of the Cardinal's hat for
her brother-in-law, Sigismondo, was now once more
raised. But this time it was complicated with another
scheme. This was nothing less than the betrothal of
Isabella's two-year-old son, Federico, to the infant
daughter of Cæsar Borgia and Charlotte d'Albret.
The proposal was first made by Duke Valentino.
Early in June 1502 he addressed a charming letter to
Isabella, expressing his joy at the prospect of this
fresh link between them, and during the next few
months this marriage was the object of constant
negotiation. Both parties were equally wary.
Francesco stipulated that his brother should be
raised to the Cardinalate at once, while Borgia,
on his part, demanded substantial pledges for
the consummation of the marriage in future years.
But flattering as were the terms in which the Duke
expressed his delight at the prospect of the union
between his family and the Gonzagas, both the
Marquis and Isabella looked upon his proposals
with deep distrust. Their suspicions were not
removed by the events which took place in the
course of the following summer. About the 20th
of June Isabella and her sister-in-law went to Porto
with a few chosen ladies, and little Federico, because, as his mother said, she could not be happy

1 See A. Luzio in *Nuova Antologia*, 1896.

without him.   While they were enjoying the fresh
breezes and delicious gardens of this charming
country-house, the most terrible and unexpected
news reached them from Urbino.

" We were here," wrote Isabella on the 27th of
June to her sister-in-law, Chiara de Montpensier,
" very quiet and contented, enjoying the company
of the Duchess of Urbino, who has been with us
since carnival, and often wishing that you were here
to complete our happiness, when news of the unexpected and perfidious seizure of the duchy of Urbino
reached us.   The Duke himself arrived here with
only four horsemen, having been suddenly surprised
and treacherously attacked, so that he narrowly
escaped with his life.   We were quite stunned by the
blow, and are still so bewildered and unhappy that
we hardly know where we are, as Your Excellency
will understand ; and so great is my compassion for
the Duchess that I could wish I had never known
her." [1]

On the 13th of June, the day after Cæsar Borgia
addressed his affectionate letter to Isabella rejoicing
over the proposed marriage of their children, he left
Rome at the head of a large army, and marched
through the district of Spoleto, laying the whole
country waste, and spreading terror wherever he
came.   Before his departure he sent friendly messages to Duke Guidobaldo, asking him to allow
his troops to march through the territory of Urbino,
and begging for the help of some artillery in his expedition against the Varani of Camerino.   But when
he reached Spoleto, instead of marching against
Camerino as had been expected, he suddenly turned

[1] Luzio, *Mantova e Urbino,* p. 125.

up the rocky defile of the Furlo Pass, and marched along the great Flaminian Way, and through the valley of the Metaurus towards Urbino. On the 20th of June, the Duke, "supposing himself to be in perfect security,"[1] had ridden out to sup in the orange gardens of the Zoccolanti convent, a favourite sanctuary of the Dukes of Urbino, where Piero della Francesca had painted his fine altar-piece, now in the Brera. Here, in the shady groves on the outskirts of the convent garden, he was enjoying the beauty of the summer evening, when a messenger arrived in hot haste from Cagli to say that Duke Valentino was outside the city, marching on Urbino at the head of 2000 men. It was too late to think of resistance. Cæsar's mercenaries were advancing in every direction. Already the passes of the Apennines were guarded, and a price had been set upon the Duke's head. Guidobaldo's only hope of safety lay in flight, and, yielding to the entreaties of his servants, he fled for his life, taking with him his young nephew, Francesco della Rovere. After many adventures and narrow escapes, the fugitives succeeded in reaching Mantua safely. "I have saved nothing but my life, my doublet, and my shirt," wrote Guidobaldo on the 28th of June to his kinsman, Cardinal Giuliano della Rovere, in a long letter giving a vivid description of his midnight flight, and of the false promise with which Borgia had deceived him. "Such ingratitude and treachery," he adds, "were never before known."[2] Even Lucrezia was appalled at her brother's action, and told the

---

[1] Dennistoun, "Dukes of Urbino," vol. ii. p. 325, &c.

[2] Alvisi, "Cæsar Borgia"; Dennistoun, "Dukes of Urbino," vol. i. p. 391; Yriarte, "Cæsar Borgia," vol. ii.

prete of Correggio that she was miserable when she remembered how kindly the Duchess of Urbino had treated her, and would not have had this happen for all the world.

At sunrise on the 21st of June, the Duke of Romagna, as Cæsar now styled himself, entered Urbino, and, clad in a splendid suit of armour, installed himself on the ducal throne in the ancient palace of the Montefeltri. No resistance was possible, and the few loyal subjects who dared oppose the victor were stabbed or thrown into prison. During the next few weeks a long train of mules was seen descending the steep hillside, laden with the priceless tapestries and statues, the paintings and treasures of gold and silver plate, which were the pride of the ducal house. Sanuto reckons the value of the booty carried off by Duke Valentino on this occasion at 150,000 ducats, or nearly half a million of our present money.

In the general grief and consternation at Mantua, Isabella did not lose sight of her own interests. She remembered a wonderful torso of Venus, and a Cupid of almost equal beauty, which she had seen and admired in her brother-in-law's collection, and wrote off without delay to Rome, begging her brother, Cardinal Ippolito d'Este, to secure these rare statues, if possible, for her Grotta. Her letter was written on the 30th of June, only three days after Guidobaldo reached Mantua.

"Most Reverend Father in God, my dear and honoured Brother,—The Lord Duke of Urbino, my brother-in-law, had in his house a small Venus of antique marble, and also a Cupid, which were given him some time ago by His Excellency the Duke of

Romagna. I feel certain that these things must have fallen into the said Duke's hands, together with all the contents of the palace of Urbino, in the present revolution. And since I am very anxious to collect antiques for the decoration of my studio, I desire exceedingly to possess these statues, which does not seem to me impossible, since I hear that His Excellency has little taste for antiquities, and would accordingly be the more ready to oblige others. But as I am not sufficiently intimate with him to venture to ask this favour at his hands, I think it best to avail myself of your most revered Signoria's good offices, and pray you of your kindness to ask him for the said Venus and Cupid, both by messenger and letter, in so effectual a manner that both you and I may obtain satisfaction. I am quite willing, if it so please Your Reverence, that you should mention my name and say that I have asked for them very urgently, and sent an express courier, as I do now, for, believe me, I could receive no greater pleasure or favour either from His Excellency or from your most dear and reverend Signoria, to whom I commend myself affectionately.—Your sister, ISABELLA, Marchioness of Mantua."[1] Mantua, June 30, 1502.

The letter, in its frank, straightforward tone, is highly characteristic of the writer. Even at this critical moment, when her heart is wrung with sorrow for the poor Duke, who has fled to Mantua in his shirt-sleeves, and the beloved Duchess, Isabella does not hesitate to seek a favour at the hands of the treacherous prince who had caused their ruin. It is true, she will not stoop to ask this favour of Valentino

[1] Gaye, *Carteggio d'Artisti*, vol. ii. 53.

in person; she has no *domestichezza* with him, and is not on sufficiently familiar terms with him for that. But she is none the less ready to make use of his connection with her own family in order to attain her object and gratify her passion for rare antiques. The Cardinal, who was in high favour at the Vatican since Lucrezia's wedding, complied with his sister's request without delay, and Cæsar Borgia hastened to gratify the fancy of the illustrious Madonna, whose goodwill he was especially anxious to gain. Within the next few weeks, the Duke of Romagna's chamberlain, bringing with him a mule laden with marbles, arrived at Mantua; and on the 22nd of July, the Marchesa told her husband joyfully that the precious statues were safe in her Grotta.

"Yesterday, the muleteer arrived safely with the Venus and Cupid which Duke Valentino has sent here, and his chamberlain, Messer Francesco, presented them to me." And after begging Francesco, who had gone to meet the French king at Milan, to take steps for recovering the Duchess of Urbino's dowry, she adds the following postscript: "I do not write of the beauty of the Venus, because I believe Your Excellency has seen it, but for a modern thing the Cupid has no equal."[1]

This Cupid, which justly excited the accomplished Marchesa's admiration, was not, as she apparently knew, a genuine antique, but the work of a young Florentine sculptor, Michel Angelo Buonarroti, whose fame was already great in Rome. In those early days, when Savonarola's sermons were shaking the heart of Florence, the youth of twenty carved a Sleeping Cupid with quiver and torch at his side, which was

[1] Alvisi, "Cæsar Borgia," p. 537.

so like a Greek marble that a dealer took it to Rome
and sold it to Cardinal Riario as an antique. The
Cardinal found out the fraud and returned the Cupid
to the dealer, but invited the sculptor to Rome.
Michel Angelo, indignant at the fraud which had been
practised in his name, sought out the dealer and
demanded him to restore his Cupid; but the agent
laughed him to scorn, and soon found another purchaser in the Pope's son, who, wishing to conciliate
the Duke of Urbino, presented him with this Cupid
and an antique torso of Venus. Guidobaldo, it seems,
set great store on this Cupid, and when, towards the
close of 1503, he had recovered his dominions, he told
Cattaneo, the Mantuan agent at the Papal court, that
he wished the Marchesa would restore his statue. But
Isabella replied with her usual readiness that, glad as
she was to hear that the Duke was recovering his scattered treasures, she must remind him that he had
given her permission to ask Borgia for the Cupid;
and, to prove her case, sent Cattaneo Guidobaldo's
own letter on the subject. After this there was
nothing left for the Duke but to beg the Marchesa
to keep the statue and to assure her that his person
and property were altogether at her disposal.[1] So the
Cupid remained in the famous Grotta, where it is
mentioned in the inventory of 1542, as the work of
Michelagnolo fiorentino.

De Thou, who visited the Castello in 1573,
praised the statue highly, and in June 1630, Charles
the First's agent, Daniel Nys, mentions it together
with the Cupids of Praxiteles and Sansovino as the
rarest objects in the ducal collection. There seems little
doubt that this Cupid, which Michel Angelo carved,

[1] Luzio in *Arch. St. Lomb.*, 1886.

and which had so strange a story, and both Guidobaldo and Isabella valued so highly, came to England
in 1632, with the rest of the Mantuan art-treasures,
and for a while adorned the palace of Whitehall or
the halls of Hampton Court.   But nothing is known
of its fate in after years, and it probably disappeared
with so many other rare and precious things at the
sale of Charles the First's collections.

CHAPTER XIV

1502—1503

Louis XII. at Milan—He receives the exiled princes and the
Marquis of Mantua—Cæsar Borgia arrives at Milan and concludes an agreement with the king—Isabella's warnings to
her husband—The Duke and Duchess of Urbino forced to
leave Mantua and take shelter at Venice—Francesco Gonzaga goes to France—Isabella governs Mantua—Her negotiations with Borgia regarding her son's marriage—Cæsar's
campaign in Romagna—Treacherous murder of Vitellozzo and
his companions—Isabella sends Valentino a present of masks
—Death of the Pope and sudden revolution in Rome—
Return of Duke Guidobaldo to Urbino—Election of Pope
Pius III.

ALL the victims of Cæsar Borgia's high-handed policy,
and all those who looked with alarm at his rapid
success, now turned to the French king for help.
Early in July, Louis XII. crossed the Alps to make
preparations for war against the Spanish forces, who,
under Gonsalvo di Cordova, had attacked his troops
in Naples. On the 28th he entered Milan, bringing
with him Federico of Aragon, the ex-king of Naples,
and attended by the Duke of Ferrara and the Marquis of Mantua, who had joined him a week before
at Vigevano. Here, too, came the unfortunate Duke
of Urbino and Giovanni Sforza to plead their cause
against Valentino. Louis received the exiled princes
with fair promises, and Francesco Gonzaga was beginning to talk loudly of avenging their wrongs,
when Cæsar Borgia himself appeared suddenly on

the scene. "This inscrutable Duke," as Machiavelli calls him, "who hardly ever speaks, but always acts," left his victorious army in Umbria, and after paying a flying visit to his sister Lucrezia, who had given birth to a dead child and was lying dangerously ill at Ferrara, reached Milan on the 7th of August. His coming changed the face of affairs and destroyed Elisabetta Gonzaga's last hopes. He accompanied the king to Genoa on the 26th, and did not take leave of him until Louis had promised him his support in completing the conquest of Central Italy in return for his help against the Spaniards in Naples.

All this while Isabella was going through agonies of fear and suspense. The imprudent words which her husband had spoken in public against Valentino had filled her with alarm for his safety, and she implored him repeatedly in her letters to be more careful in future, and, above all, to take every precaution against poison, knowing the unscrupulous nature of the Duke and the crimes which he had already committed.

"I cannot conceal my fears for your person and State," she writes on the 23rd of July, only the day after she had received Borgia's gift of the Venus and Cupid. "It is generally believed that His Most Christian Majesty has some understanding with Valentino, so I beg of you to be careful not to use words which may be repeated to him, because in these days we do not know who is to be trusted.[1] . . . There is a report here—whether it has come from Milan by letter or word of mouth, I do not know—that Your Excellency has spoken angry words against Valentino before the Most Christian King

[1] D'Arco, *Notizie d'Isabella,* p. 59.

and the Pope's servants, and whether this is true or not, they will doubtless reach the ears of Valentino, who, having already shown that he does not scruple to conspire against those of his own blood, will, I am certain, not hesitate to plot against your person. And being jealous for your life, which I count dearer than my own, and knowing how your natural goodness leads you to take no precautions for your safety, I have made inquiries of Antonio da Bologna and others, and hear from them that you allow all manner of persons to serve you at table, and that Alessandro da Baesso eats with you, leaving grooms and pages to do the offices of carvers and cupbearers. So that I see it would be perfectly easy for any one to poison Your Excellency, since you have neither guards nor proper servants. I pray and implore you therefore, if you will not take care for your own sake, to be more careful for my sake and that of our little son, and I hope that you will in future order Alessandro to discharge his office of carver with the greatest caution. If he cannot do this, I will send Antonio or some other trustworthy servant, because I had rather run the risk of making you angry than that both I and our little one should be left to weep for you."

She added the following postscript in her own writing: " My dearest lord, do not laugh at my fears and say that women are cowards and always afraid, because *their* malignity is far greater than my fears and your own courage. I would have written all this letter with my own hand, but the heat is so great we are nearly dead. The boy is very well and sends you a kiss.—ISABELLA, who longs to see Your Highness."[1]

[1] Luzio e Renier, *Mantova e Urbino,* p. 137.

At the same time Isabella wrote to her old friend, Niccolo da Correggio, who had also gone to meet King Louis, begging him to acquaint her with all that was happening at Milan.

On the 8th of August, Niccolo, ever loyal to her wishes, wrote to tell her of Cæsar Borgia's unexpected arrival, and of the affectionate way in which the King had welcomed him :—

"To obey your orders I must tell you that last night Duke Valentino arrived here on horseback. I cannot tell you with what warm demonstrations of friendship His Christian Majesty welcomed him. He was returning from the house of Messer Trivulzio, when he met the Lord Duke arriving from the Porta Romana, and, embracing him with great joy, he led him to the Castello, and lodged him in the room nearest to his own. He himself ordered the Duke's supper, choosing certain favourite dishes, and he visited him three or four times in the course of the evening, even when he had put on his night-shirt and was about to go to bed! He ordered seneschals and servants for the said Duke, and begged him to wear his own shirts and clothes, saying that he is not to ask any one else for what he needs, but make use of the king's wardrobe, carriages and horses, as if they were his own. Only think, His Majesty went so far as to propose that a litter for the camp, to suit the Duke's taste, should be provided. In fact, he could not do more for a son or brother. Yesterday, being Sunday, His Christian Majesty went to mass at San Stefano, where Duke Galeazzo was murdered, and afterwards dined in the house of your illustrious father, the Duke of Ferrara, which is now occupied by Messer Teodoro di Trivulzio, and

went to a dance at the house of Francesco Bernardino Visconti, and after supper he went to see
some more dancing in the house of Bishop Pallavicini
outside the Porta Lenza, and the Lord Duke accompanied His Majesty on horseback, and did not return
to the Castello until past nine.   I did not go to the
festa, but hear that Ippolito was at the Bishop's
house.   This morning the king is gone to dine at
Binasco, where he remains to-night, and goes on to
supper at Pavia to-morrow.   The illustrious Lord
Duke, your father, will also go to Pavia, starting
three or four hours earlier.   His Christian Majesty
goes on to Genoa, not, as was said at first, to Parma,
since he is returning to France sooner than was
expected.   I do not know what else to tell Your
Highness of public matters, for it is rash to pronounce any judgment in these times.   But the
Signor Marchese will soon return, and will tell you
more of these caresses between the Duke and the
king." [1]

This letter confirmed Isabella's worst fears.   She
used all her influence to induce her husband to pay
court to the dreaded Valentino.   As a further precaution, she induced him to write a letter expressing
his friendly sentiments for the Duke, which she could
show to the chamberlain who had just presented her
with the two antiques.   Her fears, as it turned out,
were not unfounded, for Sanuto reports that Francesco
publicly denounced Cæsar Borgia as a bastard and a
priest's son, and that Valentino, on arriving at Milan,
openly challenged him to fight.   During mass the
next day the Marquis told the Venetian envoy that
he would fight the Duke single-handed with sword

---

[1] Luzio, " Niccolo da Correggio," in *Giorn. St. d. Lett.*, xxi. p. 240.

and dagger, and boasted that he would deliver Italy.
King Louis, however, succeeded in reconciling the
two princes, and when he returned to France they
parted good friends. In a conversation which Borgia
had at Genoa with the Mantuan treasurer, Ghivizzano,
he laid stress on his friendly feelings for his lord, and
on the Pope's esteem for both Francesco and his
wife, but insisted that if the Marquis wished to
remain his ally, he must not keep the exiled Duke
at his court. Accordingly, on the 9th of September,
both the Duke and Duchess of Urbino left Mantua,
Elisabetta declaring that her husband would be
exposed to greater peril without her, and that she
would never leave him, were they to die in an
hospital. Fortunately they found shelter at Venice,
which, Sanuto remarks, became the refuge and resort
of all the princes whom Duke Valentino had expelled,
and were hospitably received by the Signory, who
gave them a pension and a house at Canareggio.[1]
But poor Elisabetta was reduced to the greatest
straits for want of money. At one time she even
entertained the idea of entering the service of the
Queen of France, Anne de Bretagne, who, in the
kindness of her heart, had sent the unhappy Duchess
generous offers of help. But she could not make up
her mind to leave her husband, while no power on
earth would induce her to accept Valentino's offer of
a liberal pension if she would consent to the dissolution of her marriage, and Guidobaldo would agree to
renounce his patrimony and become a priest.

In these melancholy circumstances Isabella showed
the same tender affection and sympathy for her unfortunate relatives. She ventured to ask Duke

[1] *Diarii*, iv. 329, 701.

Valentino for the recovery of Emilia Pia's property, and sent her trusted seneschal Alessandro da Baesso and other members of her household constantly to and fro with letters and presents to Elisabetta. On the 5th of October she wrote as follows :—

" My dear and honoured Sister,—The good news of your safe arrival at Venice, and of the kind reception which you have had both in public and private, rejoiced my heart, and I thank you warmly for your letters. I could not answer before, because I had no messenger to send, but now that Alessandro is going to you, I would not put off writing any longer. You will hear from him that my lord and all of us are well, excepting Leonora, who still has fever. We have weaned Federico, who after the first night and day has got over it easily. My lord starts to-morrow for France as arranged. Your Highness may think how sad I am without your conversation, but I hope you will console me by writing constantly, and I will do the same, and commend myself to you as well as to the illustrious Lord Duke and Madonna Emilia." [1]

But when, a few days after this, Guidobaldo, responding to the call of his old subjects, made a desperate attempt to recover his throne, the Marquis turned a deaf ear to his sister's entreaties, and refused to lift a hand against his ally, Duke Valentino. As might have been expected, his gallant effort proved fruitless, and the love of his people availed little against the might of Borgia. Guidobaldo was forced to fly from Urbino a second time, but fell dangerously ill at Città di Castello. It was not until the end of January that he succeeded in escaping to Venice. During some weeks Elisabetta remained

[1] Luzio, *Mantova e Urbino*, p. 145.

ignorant of his fate, and Sigismondo Gonzaga, who hastened to Venice and tried to comfort her, gave Isabella a piteous account of her sorrow and anxiety.

Meanwhile, Francesco Gonzaga had started for France on the 6th of October, as Isabella informed the Duchess, on the invitation of King Louis, who wished to consult him on Italian affairs and hoped to secure his help against the Spaniards. He had promised his wife that he would be at home for Christmas, and Isabella's letters show how eagerly his return was expected.

"After I sent my last letter," she writes on the 2nd of December, "Federico wished to have supper with me, which he did with the most charming grace in the world, and afterwards, as he was at play with ten gold ducats before him, I made some one knock at the door and pretend that a poor beggar was asking for alms. Upon which he took up a ducat at once, and without any prompting, desired the money to be given him, saying: 'Tell him to pray to God for me and also for my *Pà*.' This delighted all who were present. I hope this childish inspiration will have the effect of soon bringing you home, where your presence is eagerly desired."[1]

But Louis XII. insisted on taking the Marquis to spend Christmas in his château at Loches, and eventually kept him at his court until the end of January. Both the King and Queen treated Francesco with marked courtesy, and Anne of Brittany renewed an offer which she had formerly made to educate his daughter Leonora at her court and marry her to a prince of the blood-royal. This plan was eventually abandoned, but at one time it seems to

[1] Luzio, *Precettori*, p. 38.

have been seriously entertained, as we learn from a curious autograph letter addressed by the Queen to Isabella, which is still preserved in the Gonzaga archives :—

" A ma Cousine la Marquise de Mantove.

" Ma cousine, mon cousin votre mari m'a dit que lui et vous me veuliez bailler votre fille pour estre avec mey et vous la m'envoyerez, mais que eussiez sceu mon vouloir. Ma cousine, envoiez la moi quant vais voudrez, car je la traieteray tout ainsi que si elle estoit myenne, et pouvez estre seure, ma cousine, que tout ce que je pourriez faire pour vous, toujours my employereay de bon cœur. Priant Dieu, ma cousine, qu'il vous ait en sa garde.—Votre bonne cousine, ANNE.

" Escript à Loches, le 15 jour Decembre." [1]

During her husband's absence, Isabella administered public affairs with her usual tact and ability, and managed to keep Duke Valentino in good humour. The negotiations regarding Federico's marriage and Sigismondo's Cardinalate still dragged on, and the Duke sent an envoy to Mantua to discuss the terms of the contract with the Marchesa. But both parties regarded each other with mutual suspicion, and in her letter to Francesco, Isabella complained that the Pope returned equivocal answers as to the Cardinal's hat, while the Duke refused to fix the amount of his daughter's dowry. Cæsar's object, it is clear, was to gain time, and to keep in touch with the Gonzagas and with France, until the dream of his life was successfully accomplished, and he had established one great kingdom of Central Italy. All through the autumn of 1502, he continued

---

[1] L. Pelissier, *Revue historique*, 1891.

his career of conquest. After quelling the rebellion in Urbino, he marched against Sinigaglia, which was held by Guidobaldo's sister Giovanna for her young son Francesco della Rovere, and captured and sacked the town. Then he seized Perugia and Città di Castello and proceeded to attack Siena. The conquest of Tuscany was his next object, and he entered into negotiations with the Emperor for the investiture of Pisa, Siena and Lucca. On the 1st of January 1503, he informed the Marchesa Isabella, who had repeatedly sent him congratulations on his victories, of his latest success at Sinigaglia, and of the cold-blooded murder of his old colleagues, Vitellozzo, Oliverotto, and their companions. This treacherous act, which Machiavelli describes as the " *bellissimo inganno* di Sinigaglia," forms the subject of a long letter which Isabella wrote to her husband on the 10th of January, and which throws considerable light on the political situation.

" My dear Lord,—Much as I desire Your Highness's return, and impatiently as I long to see you again, I quite understand from your letter of the 16th of December, which the muleteer has brought me, that the cause of your delay is honourable and useful to Your Excellency as well as agreeable to His Most Christian Majesty. This being the case, I am content with your explanations, and take no little pleasure and comfort in hearing how much favour and attention is paid you by His Majesty. The fact that he supplies you with money from his own purse, over and above the pension which you receive, is in itself, as you say, a great sign of affection. I thank you warmly for telling me this, and have communicated the good news to the most revered Protonotary, the Magnifico Giovanni Gonzaga, and other of our gentlemen, who feel no small pleasure in hearing that you are so highly honoured. After my last letter of the 3rd, I should not have written again if I had not received your letter, from which I gather that this one will reach you before you leave Lyons. Although you have doubtless heard of the capture and death of the confederates of La Marca, I will tell you the account which I have received from our mutual brother, Signor Giovanni. On the 3rd he wrote to say that the illustrious Lord Duke of Romagna was congratulating himself with Signor Giovanni Bentivoglio on the capture at Sinigaglia of Paolo Orsini, Vitellozzo, the Duke of Gravina and Oliverotto de Fermo. He justifies his action because, in spite of the pardon which they had received from His Holiness and His Excellency after their former rebellion, they came to Sinigaglia as soon as the French troops were gone, with the intention of seizing his person. Fortunately he heard of this and was able to forestall their action and treat them as they would have treated him. The said captains went to Sinigaglia by order of the Duke, with his safe conduct, and took possession of the town in his name and then rode out to meet him. The Duke shook hands with them and embraced them, re-entered the town riding between Vitellozzo and the Duke of Gravina, and talking with them. But as soon as they entered the house where he took up his abode, he made them prisoners with his own hands, and they were led away bound and condemned to die the next morning. Both Vitellozzo and Oliverotto had their heads cut off. By the same letter I hear that the Prefetessa, hearing of the

Duke's advance, abandoned the town, leaving the
Rocca well defended, and went by Florence to
Genoa, to join S. Pietro in Vincula (her brother-in-
law, Cardinal Giuliano), which Francesco Malatesta
also confirms. Signor Giovanni wrote on the 5th,
to say that the Lord Duke had informed his brother-
in-law (Annibale Bentivoglio) of the death of
Vitellozzo and Oliverotto, and that the Duke of
Gravina and Paolo Orsini are prisoners, and will
shortly be put to death in their turn. From Rome
we hear of the imprisonment of Cardinal Orsini,
and M. Giovanni Lucido (Cattaneo), writing from
Rome on the 3rd, tells me that the Pope threw
Rinaldo Orsini, Cardinal Archbishop of Florence,
and Giacomo Sante Croce into prison on the same
day, and that all Rome has taken up arms in self-
defence. But the Pope is well prepared and there
will not be any revolt. Signor Giovanni tells me
that the Duke left Sinigaglia after the town had been
sacked by his troops, and hastened against Perugia,
where Giovanni Baglioni and his men-at-arms surrendered. I hear that a plot has been made in
Siena against Pandolfo Petrucci, who has imprisoned
twenty-two citizens, and put three of the chief
among them to death. The Lord Duke has written
a very courteous letter to Signor Giovanni Bentivoglio, begging him to conclude an alliance with
him, and asking for 100 light horse and 30 men-
at-arms, whom he is sending under the Cavaliere
della Volta. I also hear that Signor Giovanni
Maria da Camerino has fled and that his women
are gone to Florence, and the people of Ancona
have sent envoys to the Duke promising to pay
him obedience. No one knows where the Duke

of Urbino is, but, from what we hear, we think that he escaped from Citta di Castello through the Casentino, and Modesto, who has just arrived from Venice, tells me it is reported there that he has reached a place of safety and will soon be in Venice; but of this I have not heard either from the Duchess or from any one else. Francesco Malatesta writes from Florence that the devoted friends of Your Excellency there are alarmed at the extraordinary good fortune and exaltation of the Duke of Romagna, and wish that you were at home, feeling that they could better decide on their course of action if they knew they could depend on you and your forces. It is said that the Pope has renewed negotiations with the Florentines, and I hear this also from Rome, but it is not likely that they will trust him. All the same, if Your Excellency has not already concluded this alliance, I beg you to make haste and to settle matters, while you are with the Most Christian King, as long as you can do this with profit and honour, for there is no knowing what may happen. As to the affairs of Naples, I hear so many different reports that I do not know what to believe, and leave Your Excellency to learn the truth at court. There is nothing more to say, excepting that I and Federico and our other children Leonora and Livia are well and commend ourselves to your good graces. —Your obedient wife, ISABELLA."[1]

A few days after writing this letter, which gives so graphic a picture of Cæsar Borgia's treacherous and vindictive acts, the Marchesa thought it well to conciliate the all-powerful Duke by offering him a present of a hundred masks, which she sent him

[1] D'Arco, *Notizie d'Isabella,* p. 265.

together with the following letter congratulating him on his " glorious victories."

" Most illustrious Lord,—Your kind letter informing us of Your Excellency's fortunate progress has filled us with that joy and delight which is the natural result of that friendship and affection which exists between you and ourselves, and in our illustrious lord's name and our own we congratulate you on your safety and prosperity, and thank you for informing us of this, and also for your offer to keep us informed of your future successes. This we beg you of your courtesy to continue, since, loving you as we do, we are anxious to hear often of your movements, in order that we may rejoice in your welfare and share your triumphs. And because we think that you should take some rest and recreation after the fatigues and exertions of these glorious undertakings, we send you a hundred masks by our servant Giovanni, being well aware that so poor a gift is unworthy of your acceptance, but as a token that if in our land we could find an offering more worthy of your greatness, we would gladly send it to you. If these masks are not as fine as they should be, Your Excellency must blame the masters of Ferrara, since owing to the law against wearing masks in public, which has only lately been revoked, the art of making them has been in a great measure lost. We beg you to accept them as a token of our sincere goodwill and affection for Your Excellency. As for our alliance, we have no more to say until we hear the decision of His Holiness regarding the securities required for the payment of the dowry, which we await in order finally to conclude the agreement." [1]

[1] Gregorovius, " Lucrezia Borgia," App.

The Duke, who not only followed the practice of
other noble youths in riding out in disguise in search
of adventures, but always wore a mask on his face
in the streets of Rome,[1] was highly gratified by the
Marchesa's present, and wrote to express his thanks,
from Aquapendente, on the 1st of February:—

"Most illustrious and excellent Madonna, honoured *Comatre*,[2] dearest Sister,—We have received
Your Excellency's gift of a hundred masks, which
are most acceptable to us not only on account of
their remarkable beauty and variety, but because of
the time and place of their arrival, which could not
possibly be more opportune. It seems, indeed, as
if Your Excellency must have foreseen the order of
our plan of campaign and our present journey to
Rome. After having taken the city and province
of Sinigaglia with all its fortresses, in a single
day, and justly punished the perfidious treachery of
our foes, we released the cities of Castello, Fermo,
Cisterna, Montone, and Perugia from the yoke of
tyrants, and brought them back to their old obedience to His Holiness. Last of all, we deposed
the tyrant Pandolfo Petrucci from the dominion of
Siena, where he had shown such atrocious cruelty.
And these masks are above all precious to us because they afford a fresh proof of the singular affection which we know that you and your illustrious
lord cherish for us, and have already shown in other
ways, and now testify again by the long letter which
accompanies them. For all this we thank you in-

---

[1] A. Giustinian, *Dispacci*, i. 412.

[2] *Comatre*, Fr. *commère*, gossip. Cæsar Borgia habitually addresses Isabella by this title because he had stood godfather to
her son.

finitely, although the greatness of your merit and of
your goodness towards us is beyond words, and
claims recognition by deed. We shall wear the masks
with pleasure, and their perfect beauty will need no
other ornament. As for our mutual relationship, we
are doing our utmost to bring this about, and when
we reach Rome will see that His Holiness gives his
consent to the contract. The prisoners for whom
Your Excellency intercedes shall be set free, and as
soon as we have information to this effect, we will
let Your Highness hear from us without delay.—Of
Your Excellency the *compare* and younger brother,
CÆSAR, Duke of Romagna. From the pontifical
camp at Aquapendente." [1]

When Cæsar Borgia wrote this letter, he was
hurrying back to Rome to quell the rising of the
Orsini, who, in revenge for the Pope's violent acts,
had entrenched themselves in their fortresses of Ceri
and Bracciano, and were ravaging the Campagna up
to the gates of Rome. While he was engaged in this
fresh warfare, news reached him of the reverses which
the French troops had suffered in Naples. On the
28th of April, Gonsalvo de Cordova gained a decisive
victory over the French general, Louis d'Ars, at
Cerignola, and soon afterwards entered Naples in
triumph. Louis XII. lost no time in raising a new
army, and in July the Marquis of Mantua, who had
only lately returned from France, started for the
South with La Trémouille, at the head of a considerable force.

Isabella was once more left to hold the reins of
state in these critical times. Since her visit to Venice
after Lucrezia Borgia's wedding, she had not left

[1] Gregorovius, "Lucrezia Borgia," App.

Mantua for a single day, but in April 1503, she paid a short visit to her father, and spent St. George's day at Ferrara, where, as usual, she received a warm welcome. On the 24th, she wrote to her husband :—

" Yesterday, besides receiving visits from a large number of ladies and gentlemen, these Signors, my brothers, remained continually with me, and about four o'clock my sister-in-law (Lucrezia) came to my room, and after conversing very pleasantly for some time, took me in her chariot for a drive through Ferrara till late, when the said Signors returned with me to my lodgings. To-day the representation of the Annunciation has been given. I went to the Castello to fetch this lady, who continues to show me great honour and affection, and we went together to the Archbishop's house, where I found my lord father, and saw the wooden stage which had been erected and sumptuously adorned for the occasion. A young Angel spoke the argument of the play, quoting the words of the Prophets who foretold the Advent of Christ, and the said Prophets appeared, speaking their prophecies translated into Italian verse. Then Mary appeared, under a portico supported by eight pillars, and began to repeat some verses from the Prophets, and while she spoke, the sky opened, revealing a figure of God the Father, surrounded by a choir of angels. No support could be seen either for His feet or for those of the angels, and six other seraphs hovered in the air, suspended by chains. In the centre of the group was the Archangel Gabriel, to whom God the Father addressed His word, and after receiving his orders, Gabriel descended with admirable artifice, and stood, half-way in the air, at the same height as the organ. Then, all of a sudden, an infinite number of lights broke out at the foot of the angel-choir, and hid them in a blaze of glory—which really was a thing worth seeing, and flooded all the sky with radiance. At that moment the Angel Gabriel alighted on the ground, and the iron chain which he held was not seen, so that he seemed to float down on a cloud, until his feet rested on the floor. After delivering his message he returned with the other angels to heaven, to the sound of singing and music and melody, and there were verses recited by spirits, holding lighted torches in their hands and waving them to and fro as they stood supported in the air, so that it frightened me to see them. When they had ascended into heaven, some scenes of the Visitation of St. Elizabeth and St. Joseph were given, in which the heavens opened again and an angel descended, with the same admirable contrivance, to manifest the Incarnation of Jesus to Joseph, and set his doubts at rest regarding the Conception of the Holy Virgin. So the *festà* ended. It lasted two and a half hours, and was very delightful to see, because of the fine machinery which I have described, as well as other things of the kind which I have left out. But the heat was great, because of the immense crowd of people. On Thursday I think we are to have a representation of the Magi and of the Innocents, of which I will inform Your Excellency, to whom I send by this courier a basket of fresh honeycomb.—You most devoted wife, ISABELLA." [1]

On the following day the spectacle of the Magi offering their gifts at the cradle of Bethlehem, with the guiding star in the sky above, and a fine display of opened heaven and angelic choirs, excited great

[1] D'Arco, *Notizie d'Isabella.*

admiration, while the Massacre of the Innocents moved the spectators to tears, and many women and children who were present cried aloud.[1]

A fresh sorrow awaited Isabella on her return home. This was the death of her sister-in-law, Chiara de Montpensier, whose troubled life ended at Mantua on the 2nd of June. The poor Duchess of Urbino, living as she was in penury and exile at Venice, felt this fresh blow keenly, and wrote to Isabella saying that after losing state, home, and fortune, she was now deprived of the sister who had been to her as a mother. Suddenly an unexpected event turned the tide of affairs and changed the whole political situation.

On the 18th of August, Pope Alexander VI. died in the Vatican. His illness had been very short. On the 5th of August, he and his son Cæsar, who was on the point of starting to join his army at Perugia, and embark on a fresh series of conquests, dined with Cardinal Adriano da Corneto at his villa. The following day Cæsar wrote a letter to Isabella d'Este, gratefully accepting an offer of a couple of her dogs, which belonged to a breed that he admired especially. A week afterwards both he and his father fell seriously ill of malarial fever, which attacked all the guests who had dined at the Cardinal's villa. The old Pope, who was seventy-three years of age, became rapidly worse, and on the afternoon of the 18th Costabili wrote to Duke Ercole,[2] and Cattaneo sent word to the Marquis of Mantua, that His Holiness was sinking. He died that night, but Cattaneo, who informed the Marquis of the event

---

[1] D'Ancona, *Origini*, vol. ii.
[2] *Archivio di Stato, Modena.*

early the next morning, says expressly that there was
no suspicion of poison, although both father and son
were taken ill at the same time.[1]

The news spread like wildfire through the whole
of Italy. It reached Francesco Gonzaga as he was
marching south with the French army at Parma,
and he sent it on by express courier to Mantua. It
rejoiced the heart of Giovanni Sforza, who was ill in
bed himself, but told his brother-in-law that the good
news had nearly cured his malady, and that he only
hoped soon to hear that Valentino was also dead! It
reached the exiled Duke and Duchess in their sad
retreat at Venice, and Guidobaldo started without
delay for Urbino, where the people rose in arms and
welcomed him with acclamation. Never was an
exiled prince greeted with such passionate delight.
The children poured out to meet him with olive-
branches in their hands, and hailed his return with
triumphal songs. Old men wept tears of joy,
women and children thronged the streets, and
mothers held up their little ones to see the Duke, and
told them never to forget that day. " The very
stones," wrote Castiglione, " seemed to rejoice, and
to sing for gladness." [2] Emilia Pia's secretary, who
described the scene to the Marchesa Isabella, told
how high-born women danced with glee in the
streets, and old blind men of eighty were led up to
the Duke, and asked leave to touch him with their
hands that they might be sure he was there again.
" Some brought their children in arms to see him ;
others uttered words which would have moved the

----

[1] *Archivio Gonzaga*, quoted in Pastor, " History of the Popes,"
vi., App.

[2] Serassi, *Lettere di Castiglione.*

stones to tears."[1] Elisabetta herself wrote to tell Isabella the welcome which the Duke had received from his faithful people. She remembered how, in the darkest days of her distress at Mantua, the good Sister Osanna bade her dry her tears, since Borgia's dominion would prove as transitory as a blaze of straw, and thanked God that her words had proved true.[2]

Meanwhile all Rome was in a ferment. "The confusion," wrote Cardinal Egidio of Viterbo, "was such that it seemed as if everything were going to pieces." Cæsar Borgia, after vainly trying to take possession of Castell' Sant' Angelo, was borne in a litter to Nepi, and placed himself under the protection of the French army, which had advanced to Viterbo. On the 16th of September, thirty-seven Cardinals met in conclave. At first the French candidate, George d'Amboise, was thought certain of success, but Giuliano della Rovere strongly opposed his election; and before the conclave met, the Mantuan agent, Ghivizzano, wrote to the Marquis, saying: "The Cardinals are buzzing about us like bees, and intriguing in all directions, but neither D'Amboise nor Giuliano will be Pope: it will be Siena or S. Prassede." The issue proved that he was right. On the 22nd the aged Cardinal Piccolomini of Siena was elected. "A good man," says Ghivizzano, "whose previous life and acts of charity make the people hope that as a Pope he will be the very reverse of Alexander VI. And so they are beside themselves with joy."[3] On the same day Francesco

---

[1] Luzio e Renier, *Mantova e Urbino*, p. 149.

[2] Donesmondi, *Storia Eccl. di Mantova*, ii.

[3] *Archivio Gonzaga;* Pastor, "History of the Popes," vol. vi. p. 619.

Gonzaga wrote a remarkable letter to his wife from the French camp outside the walls of Rome, telling her of the Pope's election, and repeating the legend which had already sprung up in the popular mind, that the devil himself had come to fetch the soul of the hated Borgia.

"Most illustrious and beloved Wife,—In order that you may hear the latest details which have reached us of the Pope's death, we write to inform you how, in his last illness, he began to speak and act in a way which made those about him think that he was wandering, although he retained perfect possession of his faculties. His words were: 'I will come, you are right, only wait a little longer,' and those who were in his secrets afterwards revealed that in the conclave held after the death of Innocent III. he had made a compact with the devil and had bought the papal tiara at the price of his soul. One article of the compact was that he should sit in the papal chair for twelve years, which he actually did, as well as four more days. There are others who say that seven devils were in the room at the moment when he gave up the ghost. And when he was dead, his blood began to boil, and his mouth foamed as if he were a burning caldron, and this lasted as long as he was above ground. His corpse swelled to such a size that it lost the very shape of a human body, and there was no difference between its breadth and length. He was carried to the grave with little honour, his body being dragged from the bed to the sepulchre by a *facchino*, who fastened a cord to his feet, because no one would touch him, and his funeral was so miserable that the wife of the lame dwarf at Mantua had a more honourable burial than this Pope. And every day the most shameful inscriptions are written over his grave for his last epitaph. To-day we hear that Siena is elected Pope. He is said to be a neutral person, without passions or party. We are altogether at the service of Your Highness, and beg you to kiss Federico many times. We have sent to ask for victuals and a passage through Rome for our army, as had been already promised, but since the new Pope had not yet been elected, we do not know what answer to expect. We hear that the enemy are at Genazzano and are advancing against us. Monseigneur Tremoglia is ill and has been forced to retire, so we are left in command of the camp. *Bene valeat. Conjux Marchio Mantuæ. Ex Insula.* 22 Sept. 1503. *Xmo Regis Locum tenentis Generalis.*"[1]

[1] Gregorovius, "Lucrezia Borgia," App. p. 123.

CHAPTER XV

1503—1505

Death of Pius III.—Election of Julius II.—Return of Elisabetta to Urbino—Cæsar Borgia sent to Spain, and his capture—Birth of Isabella's daughter Ippolita—Francesco Gonzaga resigns his command of the French armies—Returns to Mantua—The French lose Naples — Comedies at Urbino, Mantua, and Ferrara—Death of Duke Ercole—Quarrels and plots of the Este brothers—Marriage of Francesco Maria della Rovere and Leonora Gonzaga—Sigismondo Gonzaga raised to the Cardinalate—Letters of Emilia Pia—Castiglione and Bembo—Death of Suor Osanna—A Dominican vicar-general—Birth of Isabella's son Ercole.

THE election of Pope Pius III. proved to be only a temporary measure. The new Pontiff was already worn out with age and infirmities, and the fatigues of his coronation, added to the anxieties of his office, brought on a fatal illness of which he died on the 17th of October, only a month after his elevation to the papal see. This time all parties agreed to choose Giuliano della Rovere, and on the 1st of November, after the shortest conclave ever known in the long history of the Papacy,[1] he was proclaimed Pope under the title of Julius II. His election produced a complete revolution in the policy of the Holy See. The Duke of Urbino, whose sister was the wife of Giovanni della Rovere, Prefect of Rome, was appointed Captain - general of the Church, with Giovanni Gonzaga as his lieutenant, and his nephew

[1] Pastor, "History of the Popes," vi. 210.

Francesco della Rovere, the son of Julius the
Second's brother, was publicly recognised as heir to
the duchy. Elisabetta, who had remained in Venice
until peace and order were restored in her lord's
dominions, now took leave of the Doge and Senate,
and after thanking them publicly for the hospitality
which she had received at their hands, returned to
Urbino the first week in December. On the 11th,
her seneschal, Alexander Picenardi, gave Isabella the
following account of the rejoicings which hailed her
entry :—

"Most illustrious Mistress,—I venture to give
Your Highness an account of the entry of Her
Excellency the Madonna into Urbino, but could not
describe the disasters and discomfort that we suffered
from bad weather, bad roads and bad hostelries
between Venice and Urbino. When at length we
were four miles from Urbino, the whole population
poured out to meet her, chanting Te Deums, with
olive-boughs in their hands and crying 'Gonzaga
and Feltro!' And when we reached Urbino, a
great number of gentlemen and citizens were
at the gates, and came out to greet her with the
greatest joy, kissing and clasping her hand with tears
of tenderness, so that it was three hours before Her
Excellency could reach the Piazza. Then she
alighted from her horse in front of the Vescovado
and entered the church, where all the ladies of Urbino
were assembled, bringing her an olive-branch with
golden leaves, and all with one voice called out Her
Excellency's name and embraced her with great joy.
Then Monsignore the Bishop, robed in his vestments,
took Madonna the Duchess by the hand and led her to
kneel down before the high altar, where all the clergy

were assembled, and they began to sing *Te Deum laudamus* and other devout prayers. When the blessing had been given, they came out of church and entered the palace, accompanied by the Bishop and all the clergy and a great multitude of people, and they remained in the palace till past midnight, and every day and every night Her Excellency has been fêted in this manner. She is very well and commends herself to Your Illustrious Highness, and, poor as I am, I venture to throw myself at your feet, and hope Your Excellency with forgive my presumption. —Your most faithful servant, ALEXANDER, Seneschal." [1]

Thus the good Duchess came back to reign over this people who adored her, and charm the hearts of men by her gentleness and sweetness. For the next few years the court of Urbino shone with more than its old lustre, and the most brilliant cavaliers and most accomplished scholars and artists—Castiglione and Bembo, Cristoforo Romano and l'Unico Aretino— sought a home in this palace, where Guidobaldo and Elisabetta held up before the world a noble example of the purest virtue and the most refined culture.

By degrees the home of the Montefeltri regained its former splendour. It is true that the priceless tapestries of the Trojan war were never recovered, but the famous library, and many of the treasures of art which the palace had formerly contained, were restored by Cæsar Borgia, who, in his anxiety to conciliate the new Pope, was abject in his professions of friendship for the Duke, whom he had wronged so cruelly. But the election of Julius II. had sealed his doom. He was too dangerous a rival to be allowed to

---

[1] Luzio e Renier, *op. cit.*, p. 150.

remain in Rome, and after surrendering the chief fortresses of Romagna to the Pope, he went to Naples.
Here Gonsalvo de Cordova arrested him by order of
King Ferdinand of Aragon, in spite of a safe conduct
which had been given him.   He was sent to Spain in
August 1504, and after languishing for two years in
prison, succeeded in making his escape from the
Tower of Medina del Campo, and fell in March 1507,
at Viana, fighting for his brother-in-law, the King of
Navarre, against Castile.   So this hero of great
powers and greater audacity, whose extraordinary
career had filled Italy with amazement, and whose
name struck terror into every heart, died at the early
age of thirty-one, and the meteor which had flashed
upon the world with sudden brilliancy, vanished into
night.   Six months after his father's death he was
already forgotten in Rome.   "Of Valentino," wrote
the Mantuan envoy, Giovanni Lucido, "one hears
no more."   To the last he remained on friendly
terms with the Gonzagas, and when he reached
Pampeluna, he wrote a long account of his escape
to the Marquis, signing himself, "Your *Compare et
minore fratello*," and telling him that now, after all
his labour and efforts, he was at length a free man.
And Lucrezia, in her letters to Francesco, thanks
him repeatedly for "the singular and truly fraternal
love that you have ever shown to my brother the
Duke."

While these strange events were thrilling the
heart of Italy, and one Pope was succeeding the
other at the Vatican, Isabella remained at Mantua,
directing the government in her husband's absence,
and much occupied with her little son.   On the
12th of November, she took the three-year-old child

to see an Italian comedy, the "Formicone," adapted from Apuleius, acted by some pupils of Francesco Vigilio, who held a public school in Mantua, and whom she had already determined in her own mind to choose for Federico's tutor. The performance was admirable, and Isabella, in writing to her lord, tells him that " a son of our steward distinguished himself in the part of a servant, and will be of great use in our comedies, while Federico was surrounded by a fine troop of children." But the Marquis disapproved alike of Messer Francesco and of his comedies, and wrote back rudely that Isabella need not take Federico to those plays and encourage Vigilio's hopes of having the child for a pupil, since he meant the boy to have little book-learning, and acquire that little from other teachers, and hoped soon to take him out to fight at his side and make a man of him.[1]

The day on which Isabella attended the representation of Messer Vigilio's comedy was marked by another event, as we learn from her brother-in-law the Protonotary's letter to the Marquis.

" Yesterday I went with this illustrious Madonna and Signor Federico to the school of Messer Franceso, whose scholars recited a fine comedy exceedingly well. It was a very pretty sight, and pleased us all highly. Afterwards we drove as usual to take the air in the town, and returned to the Castello about five o'clock; and Madonna sat down to cards to spend the evening after her usual custom, and played till after eight. Then she rose from the table and told me that she would not come to supper as she felt pains, and went to her room, and we sat down

D'Ancona, *Origini*, ii. 389, and Luzio, *Federico Ostaggio*, p. 62.

to table, and I supped in the Castello. And before we had finished, the said Madonna gave birth to a little girl, and although we greatly desired a boy, yet we must be content with what is given us." [1]

This fourth daughter who was born to Isabella received the name of Ippolita, and became a nun in the Dominican convent of S. Vincenzo.

Meanwhile Francesco Gonzaga was conducting the campaign in the kingdom of Naples under great difficulties. The French troops under his command were turbulent and undisciplined, his movements were impeded by heavy floods, and his plans were foiled by the superior generalship of the Great Captain, although he succeeded in crossing the river Garigliano and relieving Gaeta. At length, heartily sick of the task, and being unable, in the words of the Venetian diarist, "any longer to endure the pride, quarrels, and disobedience of the French," he resigned his command on the plea of illness, and returned to Mantua. [2] A few weeks after his departure, on the 28th of December, the French were completely defeated in a battle on the banks of the Garigliano, and Piero dei Medici, who fought on the French side, was drowned in the river. The fortress of Gaeta, which Gonsalvo had long blockaded in vain, now surrendered, and Naples was lost to France. On the 11th of February a treaty was signed at Lyons by which Louis XII. gave up all claim to the kingdom, and Ferdinand of Aragon remained in undisputed possession of Southern Italy.

Francesco's return and the restoration of Duke Guidobaldo to his duchy were celebrated with bril-

[1] Luzio e Renier in *Giorn. St. d. Lett. It.*, vol. xxxiv. p. 27.
[2] M. Sanuto, vol. xxiv.

liant fêtes both at Mantua and Urbino. Among the dramatic performances given at the Duke's court, was the so-called Comedy of Pope Alexander VI. and Valentino, a representation which included Lucrezia's wedding, Cæsar Borgia's conquest of Urbino, the death of the Pope, and the triumphant return of Guidobaldo and Elisabetta.[1]

Duke Ercole came to Mantua at Isabella's urgent entreaty, and highly commended the series of comedies that were given in his honour. After he had returned home, a dramatic version of the history of Joseph, by a Ferrara poet, was given in the ducal theatre, and Isabella's old friend, the chamberlain Bernardo dei Prosperi, sent her full accounts of the performance. "Yesterday," he writes, "this Signor had the first part of the story of Joseph represented, up to his imprisonment in Egypt. It was very touching, and admirably acted in perfect silence, because we have adopted the good customs learnt at Mantua, and no longer allow every rogue to come in and interrupt the performance. There was no music but that of the organ and some flutes, which were very soft and pleasant to hear."[2] The Duke's health had lately given much cause for anxiety, and he was no longer able to ride; but in July he travelled in a litter to Florence to pay his vows at the shrine of the Annunziata. After his return he fell seriously ill, and Isabella hurried to Ferrara to nurse him. But he rallied again, and retained his keen interest in literary subjects. On the 27th of October Isabella sent him one of the satirical productions known as *prediche d'amore*, which had been

---

[1] D'Ancona, *Origini*, ii. 21 ; Ugolini, *Storia di Urbino*, ii. 128.
[2] D'Ancona, *op. cit.*

lately composed at Milan by a witty friar named Fra Stoppino.[1] He lingered on through the winter months, and died on the 25th of January 1505.[2]

Alfonso, who had been absent on a long journey to France, England, and Spain, hurried home on hearing of his father's illness, and the day after his death, rode through Ferrara clad in white, during a heavy fall of snow. A bold soldier and mighty hunter, the new Duke was a man of extraordinary physical strength, and would spend whole nights in the marshes of Comacchio, tracking wild boars, in the roughest weather, to the despair of his courtiers and attendants. He inherited the artistic traditions of the house of Este, built the sumptuous marble villa of Belvedere on an island in the Po, and employed Giovanni Bellini and Titian to decorate the Castello. But his fierce and vindictive temper was the cause of great family dissensions, and the first year of his reign was marked by a terrible domestic tragedy which cost Isabella many tears. First of all, in November 1505, a quarrel arose between Cardinal Ippolito d'Este and his half-brother Giulio, an illegitimate son of the late Duke, who were both in love with their sister-in-law Lucrezia's fair maid-of-honour, Angela Borgia. One day Angela laughingly told the Cardinal that his brother Giulio's eyes were worth more than his whole person, upon which Ippolito, in a fit of jealous rage, hired a band of assassins to attack Don Giulio on his return from a hunting expedition at Belriguardo. The ruffians tried to put out his eyes and partially blinded him. Don Alfonso reprimanded the Cardinal severely, and when Don Giulio

[1] Luzio e Renier, *Mantova e Urbino*, p. 169.
[2] Frizzi, *Storia di Ferrara*, iv. 250.

had recovered his sight, Niccolo da Correggio succeeded in effecting an apparent reconciliation between the brothers. But a few months afterwards Giulio entered into a conspiracy with his younger brother Ferrante to murder both the Duke and Cardinal and seize the duchy. The plot was discovered, and Ferrante was thrown into prison. Giulio fled to Mantua, where Isabella not only gave him shelter, but did her utmost to save him from Alfonso's wrath, and wrote long letters to her old friend Niccolo on the subject. But the Duke was implacable, and Niccolo visited Isabella, in July 1506, at her villa of Sacchetta, and laid proofs of Giulio's guilt before her eyes. After this the unfortunate prince was given up, and imprisoned together with Ferrante in the dungeon of the Castello of Ferrara. Here the unhappy brothers were left to languish in captivity during the whole of Alfonso's reign. Ferrante died in prison in 1540, and Giulio was only released in 1559, two years before his death. By this time he was eighty-three years of age, and the Ferrarese chroniclers relate that when the old man came out of his cell he still wore the clothes which had been in fashion when he was first imprisoned more than half a century before.[1]

This tragic incident threw a gloom over Isabella's family life, and after 1506, her visits to Ferrara became less frequent than of old. But her strong family instincts made her cling to her father's house, and in the long struggle which Alfonso maintained against three successive Popes, he found a loyal friend and supporter in his sister.

While these dark shadows saddened Isabella's old home, happier events were taking place at Mantua.

[1] Frizzi, *op. cit.*, p. 255.

The month of her father's death was also that of her daughter Leonora's betrothal to Francesco Maria della Rovere, the nephew and heir of her brother-in-law, Duke Guidobaldo. This marriage had long been desired by Elisabetta, and was equally agreeable to the Marquis of Mantua, as a means of obtaining the Cardinalate, which he had been striving to obtain for his brother during the last fifteen years. The Venetian ambassador, Giustiniani, mentions a report as to the proposed marriage in his despatches from Rome as early as 1503;[1] and Emilia Pia, in writing to Isabella at the close of 1504, remarks that "the new Cardinals are to be made at Easter, and it is held certain that Our Reverend Monsignore, the Protonotary, will be one." The official proclamation actually took place in the Consistory held in the following November, when Sigismondo Gonzaga was proclaimed Cardinal, together with eight other prelates nominated by the Pope. In January 1505, Lodovico Canossa was sent to Mantua with formal proposals by the Duke of Urbino, and on the 2nd of March, the marriage was celebrated in the Vatican, Giovanni Gonzaga acting as his niece's representative. The Pope insisted that the bride should bring her husband a dowry of 30,000 ducats, but only 20,000 ducats were to be paid at once, and the remainder of this sum at a period to be fixed by the Duchess Elisabetta. Leonora's portrait was sent to Rome, at the request of the Pope, and in a letter of April 30, Isabella expressed her regret to the Prefettessa Giovanna della Rovere that it was only a black and white drawing, since there was no painter at present in Mantua who could handle colours well,

[1] *Dispacci*, ii. 359.

but said that she hoped to be able to send a better
picture soon. It was a strange excuse for Isabella
to advance, but Mantegna's health, we know, was
failing, and his son Francesco and Bonsignori were
probably engaged elsewhere. This proposed marriage led to an active renewal of correspondence
between the courts of Mantua and Urbino, and since
Elisabetta's time was fully occupied, she often
employed Emilia to write to Isabella in her stead.
The letters of this witty and accomplished lady
abound in information of the most varied description.
She thanks the Marchesa for an account of the
Queen of France's coronation, which Mario Equicola
has sent from Blois, and gives her in return all the
latest gossip from Rome and Urbino.[1] She describes
the funeral services in honour of Queen Isabella of
Spain, the banquets and representations given by Cardinal Sanseverino, and the wedding of Julius the
Second's daughter, Madonna Felice, to Giovanni
Orsini, the eccentric lord of Bracciano, whom Leonora's
husband, Francesco Maria, denounced as a madman.
She tells Isabella the marriages which are expected to
take place, and those which have ended in smoke,
and discourses in the same witty fashion of carnival
plays and Lent sermons. She has a great deal to
say of the eloquent friar, whose preaching is converting every one at court, and rejoices to hear
that Isabella is attending the sermons of two of
her own friends, who are giving Lent courses at
Mantua, although they can hardly rival the Urbino
monk. In the same letter she informs the Marchesa
of the alarm which had been excited in Rome by
a report, brought from Spain by the merchants of

[1] Luzio e Renier, *Mantova e Urbino*, pp. 158–168.

Valencia, that Cæsar Borgia had escaped from prison.
In reality, as Emilia explains, Valentino had tried to
let himself down from his prison window by a
rope made of his bedclothes. But his attempt
failed. The rope gave way, and he fell and dis-
located his shoulder. The Marchesa's lively correspondent ends by telling Her Excellency that she is
sending her a certain kind of wood that is said to
have a marvellous property for polishing the nails
and the hands, as well as a recipe for washing the
teeth, which is used by the Queens at Naples. And,
in return, Isabella sends Emilia some of the silver
boxes containing perfumes of her own manufacture,
which were eagerly sought after by persons of quality,
and were so highly appreciated by Pietro Bembo in
the days when he was secretary to Pope Leo X.[1]

In the summer of 1504, Elisabetta invited
Isabella to accompany her to Rome. The Marchesa,
who had never seen the Eternal City, was enchanted
at the prospect, and declared that she would either
come *incognito*, clad in black, or else as a maid in the
Duchess's train. This journey, however, was ultimately abandoned, partly from fear of the plague in
Rome, of which there were several cases; partly
because of the wish of the Pope to cut down
expenses and restore order in the disordered finances
of the Vatican. "This Pope," writes Emilia, "is
so niggardly that I know not if our plan will succeed."
But she rejoices to hear that the standards of the
Church, which are said to be very gorgeous, and the
bâton of Captain-general, are on their way to
Urbino.

That summer a distinguished Mantuan gentle-

---

[1] V. Cian in *Giorn. St. d. Lett. It.*, ix. 120.

man, Baldassarre Castiglione, entered the Duke's
service and settled at Urbino, much to the displeasure
of his own liege lord. The Marquis Francesco's
consent had indeed been formally asked, but he was
naturally reluctant to lose so brilliant and accomplished a figure from his court. When, a year
afterwards, Guidobaldo sent him as envoy to Ferrara,
he was forbidden to cross the Mantuan frontier; and
when, in 1506, he went to England to receive the
Order of the Garter, which Henry VII. conferred on
the Duke of Urbino, Francesco refused to allow him
to visit Mantua and embrace his mother before he
started on this long journey. Neither Elisabetta's
intervention nor a humble request which Castiglione
himself addressed to the Marquis could induce him
to relent, and it was not till his return from England,
in the spring of 1507, that he was allowed to set foot
on his native soil. Isabella, however, proved a good
friend to Castiglione, and earned his undying gratitude by her constant efforts to appease her husband's
resentment.

Another Mantuan subject and kinsman of Francesco, Cesare Gonzaga, also settled at Urbino in
these days, but always remained on friendly terms
with the Marchesa, and was one of her constant correspondents. A devoted friend and companion of
Castiglione, he assisted him in the composition of
the pastoral play, " Tirsi," which the two authors
recited at the carnival of 1506, and is one of the chief
speakers who figure in the " Cortigiano." Cesare
was the brother of Luigi Gonzaga, who lives in
Ariosto's verse, and whose splendid palace of Borgo-
forte, near Mantua, was often honoured by Isabella's
presence, and his gay letters were much appreciated

by the Marchesa. In the summer of 1504, he writes that he hears she has been reading Esop, and is so much devoted to Latin literature as to despise all poetry in the vulgar tongue, and ends by begging her not to tire out all her teachers !

Again, at the close of 1510, when Cesare is on duty in the papal camp at Modena, he snatches a moment to beg Her Excellency to allow Marchetto to set a madrigal of his composition to music, and send him the melody of her favourite sonnet " Cantai." " If you will do me this kindness," he adds, " I shall be grateful to you till the Day of Judgment, and do not think it strange if in these troublous times I make such a request, for, after all, *Marte ha solo la scorza, e il resto Amore*' (Mars only has the bark of the tree, and Love holds the rest)." [1]

Yet another member of this brilliant group, whose name lives in Castiglione's immortal pages, and who, like him, sang the praises of the gentle Duchess, was also intimately connected with Isabella d'Este. This was the Venetian Pietro Bembo, who came to Rome in the spring of 1505, on a mission from the Doge and Signory, and was sumptuously entertained by the Duke and Duchess, in their anxiety to make some return for the hospitality which they had received at Venice during their sad days of exile. Isabella was already well acquainted with Pietro's father, the old Podestà of Verona, and with his brother Carlo, whose palace she had visited in Venice, and who had lent her some portraits of Petrarch, Dante, and Boccaccio, which she wished to have copied at Mantua. In January 1503, Isabella begged Pietro to accompany

[1] D'Arco, *Documenti,* 81 ; *Arch. St. It.,* App. ii.

his friend Ercole Strozzi to Mantua, but at that time
he had been unable to accept her invitation, which
thus, in his courtly phrase, rendered him at once the
happiest and most miserable man in the world.
Again, in October 1504, Bembo was on his way to
visit Mantua, when he heard, on arriving at Verona,
that Isabella had been summoned to her dying father's
bedside.   The Marchesa renewed the invitation early
in April, and Pietro wrote from Venice, saying that to
visit Mantua was one of the greatest wishes of his
heart, but regretting that as yet he is unable to wait
upon her.   "Since, however," he adds, " I cannot come
myself, I send Your Highness, by Zuan Valerio, part
of my family, that is to say, three youths who have
not yet left the house, and commend them humbly
to Your Excellency's good offices." [1]   The three
sonnets of his composition, which Bembo enclosed,
were highly appreciated by Isabella.   She was still
better pleased when, two months later, their author
presented himself at Mantua on his way back to
Venice, with letters from Elisabetta and Emilia Pia,
who availed herself of this opportunity to send the
Marchesa a flask of myrtle scent.   On this occasion
Isabella showed her cultured guest the treasures which
she had collected in the little room in the old Castello,
with their delicately inlaid woodwork, and frieze of
music notes and playing cards, and the new studio of
the Grotta in the Corte Vecchia, where her choicest
pictures and marbles were arranged.   There Bembo
saw Michel Angelo's sleeping Cupids and Mantegna's
two priceless paintings, the Triumphs of Venus and
of Pallas, as well as Perugino's Triumph of Chastity,
which had lately arrived from Florence, and promised

[1] D'Arco, *Notizie d'Isabella*, p. 312.

to try and induce his friend Giovanni Bellini to
paint a similar fantasia for the Marchesa's *camerino*.
He saw Isabella's rare books and manuscripts, the
dainty Aldine editions of Virgil and Petrarch, in the
production of which he had helped the great Venetian
printer ; Messer Lorenzo's wonderful organ and viols
and ebony and ivory lutes, and all the rich stores
of antique cameos and medals which were Isabella's
proudest possession.   Isabella herself, as she wrote to
tell Bembo's friend Tebaldeo, was delighted to see
how much her illustrious guest appreciated all her
treasures, and charmed him by singing some of his own
songs to the music of her lute.   After his departure
Bembo sent her the following letter, beginning, after
his usual custom, with the words *Jesus Christus :*—

" I send Your Excellency, my dear Madonna and
most honoured mistress, ten sonnets and two somewhat irregular *tramotti*, not because they are worthy
to come into your hands, but because I wish that
some of these verses may be recited and sung by Your
Signory, remembering with what surpassing charm
and sweetness you sang the others, on that happy
evening which we spent together, and knowing that
my poor compositions can never attain to greater
honour.   Most of the sonnets and both the *tramotti*
are quite new, and have not yet been seen by any one.
I must confess that they will not, I fear, answer Your
Signory's expectations, any more than they satisfy my
wishes.   But I know that, if they are sung by Your
Signory, they will be most fortunate, and nothing
will be needed to delight the listeners except the
beautiful and charming hand and the pure, sweet
voice of Your Most Illustrious Highness, to whose
good grace I never cease to commend myself.   Your

Signory will deign to commend me to my Lady Alda Boiarda.—Of Your Illustrious Signory the servant, PIETRO BEMBO." [1]   Venice, July 1, 1505.

About the same time, Isabella received a still more famous visitor in the person of the great Florentine, Niccolo Machiavelli, who came to Mantua in May, to bring Francesco Gonzaga the formal intimation of his appointment to the post of Captain - general of the Republic.   His name had been first suggested by Louis XII. to the Gonfaloniere Piero Soderini, and negotiations had been in progress during some weeks, as we learn from a letter which Isabella wrote to her husband from Ferrara in April.

"My dear and most illustrious Lord,—The artichokes which Your Excellency sent me were especially acceptable, both as coming from you and as being the first which I had seen this year. My brothers and sister-in-law enjoyed them with me, for love of you, and I thank you warmly for taking the trouble to send them.   Yesterday morning I received yours of the 17th, containing much good news.   Truly, as Your Excellency remarks, nothing can be better for us than the establishment of peace between the most powerful King of the Romans and France and our other allies.   We shall be able to judge of this better when we hear particulars of the treaty, but the idea that the Florentines wish to secure you for their captain seems to me to promise well and to be likely to lead to great honour.   You will no doubt consider this offer with your wonted prudence, and I will keep my counsel, for it is not a thing to be discussed with other persons, until it is finally arranged.   I think of coming to Revere

[1] D'Arco, *Notizie d'Isabella*, p. 312.

on Saturday, and on Sunday to Mantua. Here we
have no further news since the last which I gave
you. Please kiss Federico for me.—Your wife,
ISABELLA."[1]   Ferrara, April 19, 1505.

This was the errand which brought Machiavelli
to Mantua early in May. Unfortunately we have
no further information as to his visit, interesting as
it would have been to learn the impression which so
brilliant a lady and skilled a diplomatist as the
Marchesa made upon the author of the "Prince."
His mission proved unsuccessful, for the salary
which the Florentines offered was far inferior to
that which the Marquis had received from the
Venetians, and after some prolonged negotiations,
Francesco finally declined the post.

The death of Suor Osanna, who breathed her last
in Isabella's arms one day in June 1505, was a
great sorrow to the Marchesa. She had shared all
her joys and griefs with this saintly friend, and
the good Sister is said to have loved her exceedingly. To Osanna's prayers Isabella confidently
believed that she owed the gift of the long-desired
son, whose birth the holy nun prophesied some
months before the event, while in all private and
public calamities the Gonzagas always turned to her
for help and consolation. Now the Marchesa placed
a silver head on the Sister's grave, and employed her
favourite sculptor, Cristoforo Romano, to raise a noble
monument to her memory in the Dominican church.
During the next few years Isabella endeavoured by
every possible means to obtain the beatification
of her sainted friend, an honour which was finally
bestowed upon Suor Osanna by Pope Leo in 1515.

[1] D'Arco, *op. cit.* 277.

Her efforts on behalf of "this our dear mother," as she calls her, were warmly supported by Frate Francesco Silvestri, the distinguished Dominican friar who filled the chair of theology at Bologna during many years, and was afterwards appointed General of the Order by Pope Clement VII. This learned and accomplished ecclesiastic, to whom Bandello dedicates one of his novels and whom he praises as a most rare and singular man, endowed by nature with every gift of body and mind, was one of Isabella's most constant friends and correspondents. He shared her love of music and pictures, and encouraged her to persevere in her own studies, and above all to train her children in the love of learning and in the fear of God. In March 1504, when Isabella, released by her husband's return from the cares of government, once more returned to her classical studies, Frate Francesco writes to her from Milan: "I hear that you are still studying grammar. I hope that, when I visit you next, I shall find you studying rhetoric." And, in a Latin letter of July, he exhorts her to attend to her son's education, and warmly approves the choice of Vigilio as his preceptor. "See that Federico receives a liberal education," he writes when the boy is barely four years old, "and applies himself in these tender years to letters, so that he may grow up worthy of his wise and excellent mother." When her father died, Francesco's letter was the most beautiful and consoling among all the infinite number of condolences which Isabella received, and when Suor Osanna died, six months later, it fell to the friar to pronounce her funeral oration. In later years, Francesco's arduous duties as Vicar-General and General

LA BEATA OSANNA

By F. BONSIGNORI

(Mantua)

of the Order compelled him to travel through France and Italy to inspect Dominican convents, but his interest in the Marchesa and her family never failed, and he remained a true and faithful friend until he died at Rennes in 1528.

In the autumn of 1505, Isabella fell seriously ill of fever, and could not shake off the attack for several weeks. Her friends in all parts of the world wrote to express their anxiety, and combined to beguile the dulness of her convalescence. Bembo made anxious inquiries after her health from Venice. Cristoforo Romano called on all the Dominican friars of *Le Grazie* at Milan to pray for her recovery, and promised to visit the Seven Churches in Rome, and say a prayer at each altar for his dear lady. Mario Equicola sent the latest literary curiosities from Blois for Isabella's amusement, confessing, however, that he could find nothing in France that would be new to her! Elisabetta despatched her favourite jester, Fra Serafino, to Mantua without delay, and Emilia Pia wrote lively letters to cheer the invalid. But Isabella forgot all her troubles when, towards the end of November, she gave birth to a fine boy.

"I rejoice," wrote Cristoforo from Rome, "to hear of this fortunate event, and thank God that your illness has had so happy an ending. Be of good cheer, dear lady, and may God give you much joy in your children!" This second son, the future Cardinal who was one day to preside over the Council of Trent, received the name of Louis or Alvise in honour of the King of France. But Isabella preferred to call him Ercole, after his grandfather, and when the boy grew up to manhood, he became known by this second name.

CHAPTER XVI

1505—1507

Isabella's visit to Florence—Mario Equicola's treatise, *Nec spe nec metu*—Ravages of the plague at Mantua—Isabella retires to Sacchetta with her family—Francesco Gonzaga joins Pope Julius II. at Perugia—Conducts the papal army against Bologna —Flight of the Bentivogli—Entry of the Pope—Letters of Isabella—Frisio sends her antiques from Bologna—Birth of Isabella's son Ferrante—Visit of Ariosto to Mantua—Favour shown him by Isabella—Ariosto pays her a splendid tribute in his *Orlando Furioso*.

In March 1506, Isabella took a journey to Florence to discharge a vow which she had made during her illness, to Santa Maria dell' Annunziata, and spent the Feast of the Annunciation in that city. It was the first and, as far as we know, the only visit that she paid to this town, where were living so many friends, and which must have had many attractions for her. Great, indeed, must have been the interest with which she saw the Duomo and the Campanile of Giotto, the churches and palaces on the banks of Arno, and above all, the frescoes and pictures of her artist-friends. Perugino, it is true, had failed to satisfy her, and young Raphael had lately left for Urbino; but Isabella probably met the Florentine master Lorenzo di Credi, since he soon afterwards painted a Magdalene by her order. And she looked with wonder and admiration at the great cartoons which Leonardo and Michel Angelo — the sculptor of her Cupid—had designed for the decoration of the Council Hall, in the Palazzo Pubblico.

The Marchesa paid several visits to Madonna Argentina, the wife of the Gonfaloniere Piero Soderini, and met Leonardo's uncle, but did not succeed in seeing the painter, who had retired to Fiesole in disgust at the failure of his experiments in wall-painting, and was buried in the absorbing study of hydraulics.

Before she left Florence, she desired a sculptor named Filippo Benintendi to model a silver effigy of herself, to be placed by that of her husband in the chapel which Alberti had built for Lodovico Gonzaga, in the Annunziata church. But the plague broke out after her return to Mantua, and for some time to come, money was very scarce in the Gonzaga treasury. So the poor sculptor never received the 25 ducats which the Marchesa had promised him, and nearly two years afterwards, he ventured to remind her of this omission, telling her at the same time how beautiful her image appeared, standing as it did in the finest part of the church, and how much admiration it excited from every Mantuan who came to Florence. Unfortunately this silver head shared the fate of all Isabella's busts, and perished in a fire which destroyed all the ornaments and works of art in the Gonzaga chapel.[1]

On the Marchesa's return home, the alarming increase of the plague compelled her to leave Mantua and take her children to the villa of Sacchetta, where they spent the summer months. Here, on her birthday, the 16th of May, she received a present of exceptional interest in the shape of a treatise,

[1] Luzio in *Emporium*, 1900, p. 355.

composed by Mario Equicola, on her favourite motto, *Nec spe nec metu.*

The Marchesa, as we have already seen, in common with most Italian lords and ladies of the age, was in the habit of adopting special devices and mottoes. The musical notes which gave expression to her love of music, the candelabra bearing the motto *Sufficit unum in tenebris* which Paolo Giovio suggested, and which were embroidered in gold on her festal robes, may still be seen among the decorations of her *camerini* at Mantua. There too, inscribed in quaint characters, we may read the words of her favourite motto, *Nec spe nec metu,* by which she expressed that serene equanimity and philosophic frame of mind to which she aspired, neither elated by hope nor cast down by fear. She chose this motto for her own as early as 1504, when, at the request of her friend Margherita Cantelma, she gave one of the Imperial ambassadors who visited Mantua and Ferrara gracious permission to use the words in writing and in his armorial bearings and on the liveries of his servants, " we ourselves," she wrote at the time, " being the inventor of this motto, and having adopted it as our peculiar device." [1] In the following autumn Mario Equicola, the Calabrian secretary of Margherita Cantelma, who had followed her and Sigismondo to Ferrara, and was often employed by the Este princes, wrote from Blois to inform Isabella that he had written a book on this device, and only awaited her permission to publish the work.

" Most illustrious Lady,—It was the custom of ancient authors to seek for noble and excellent subjects in order to render their works immortal.

---

[1] Luzio e Renier, *Giorn. St. d. Lett. It.,* xxxiii. 49.

Signora mia, although I am only a poor man of letters, I thank God, who has allowed me to serve Your Excellency, from whose rare talents and lively wit I hope some of my writings may acquire fame and authority. In this firm hope, I have composed a book of some forty sheets, in interpretation of *Nec spe nec metu,* making mention of the words on every page. In the said book I introduce discussions on the meaning of this motto, which will show Your Signory the methods of ancient poetry, philosophy, and theology, connecting *Nec spe nec metu* with each in turn, and praising this motto above all others ever composed. I beg you to give me leave to publish and print this little work, and if you wish, will send it to you before it is published. I await your pleasure, certifying that the twenty-seven chapters on this inscription are nearly finished, after which I will illustrate the musical signs." [1]

Mario had apparently divided his book into twenty-seven paragraphs, in allusion to the mystic number XXVII., *vinte sette,* another device adopted by Isabella, which, we learn from Paolo Giovio,[2] signified that all the sects (*sette*) of her enemies were conquered (*vinte*). Isabella readily gave the desired permission, and the book, printed and bound in elegant covers, was presented to her by Margherita Cantelma on her next birthday. "Your letter and the book which Madonna Margherita sent us," wrote Isabella in reply, "are a more delightful birthday present than any gift of gold or other precious things, since you have thereby exalted our little device to sublime heights." But, with her usual candour, she

[1] D'Arco, *Notizie d'Isabella,* p. 313.
[2] *Delle Imprese,* p. 59.

remarks to her friend Margherita, in a letter written on the same day: "I certainly never imagined all these mysteries when I made the little motto!"

Mario, however, succeeded in ingratiating himself with the Marchesa, who invited him to Mantua on his return from France, and whom he describes, in a letter to Cardinal d'Este, as one of the Trinity whom he served on earth. "The first," he explains, "is Your Highness; the second, Signor Sigismondo Cantelma; the third, the Signora Marchesana." When Mario left Mantua in the following September, Isabella sent a bust of herself as a gift to his mistress, Margherita Cantelma, in return for the pains which this beloved friend had taken with her birthday present. A year afterwards, he accompanied Margherita again to Mantua, and assisted at some dramatic performances given by Bishop Lodovico Gonzaga and Antonia del Balzo at Gazzuolo. "You must blame Madonna Antonia," wrote Margherita, on the 15th of November, "who insists on keeping me here a night to see the Most Reverend Monsignore's comedy. I will not describe the amusements to which these lords and ladies devote themselves until we meet; they really are so many and varied that I am convinced time does not fly for them, and they are more youthful, more joyous and blooming than ever. None the less I am longing to be in the sacred Grotta, with her who is the true goddess of my adoration." Bishop Lodovico was the last survivor of Lodovico and Barbara Gonzaga's sons, and only died in 1511, while his sister-in-law, Antonia, lived till she was close upon a hundred, and, as we learn from Bandello's writings, preserved her joyous nature and love of letters to the last. In

March 1508, we find Equicola again reading Latin
poetry at Mantua with Isabella, and in the autumn he
finally obtained leave from Cantelma and his wife to
enter the Marchesa's service, and eventually succeeded
Capilupi as secretary of his "most illustrious and
learned pupil."

When Mario's *libretto* reached Isabella, she had,
as we have said, left Mantua to escape from the
plague, and was spending the summer at Sacchetta.
It was a dreary year in the chronicles of the house of
Gonzaga. The chronicler Schivenoglia records that
the plague broke out at carnival, and lasted so long
that the gates of Mantua remained closed until the
day of the Blessed Virgin's Nativity in September.
More than 2000 persons died in the city and suburbs,
and the expenses of the epidemic cost the Government 140,000 ducats. Trade suffered severely, and
the people were reduced to the greatest misery.
The taxes were not paid, the revenue was in arrear,
and Isabella was once more compelled to pledge her
jewels. But she battled bravely with this new
calamity, and exerted herself with her wonted energy
to found charitable institutions and to relieve the
distress of her husband's subjects.

When the plague was beginning to abate, the
Marquis received a summons from Pope Julius II.,
who was starting an expedition against Perugia and
Bologna, and invited Francesco to meet him at
Urbino. By a bull issued on the 10th of January,
this warlike Pope had proclaimed his intention of
recovering all those territories of which the Holy
See had been unjustly robbed, and the Baglioni and
Bentivogli were the first usurpers against whom he
directed his arms. Duke Guidobaldo recommended

his brother-in-law to His Holiness as the most valiant
and expert captain in Italy, and Julius, acting on
his suggestion, summoned Francesco to his help.
When he left Rome towards the end of August, so
promptly did the Marquis respond, that he reached
Perugia at the head of 200 horse on the 17th of
September, a few days after the Pope had entered
that city in triumph. "The faith which His Holiness places in us," he wrote to Isabella, "leaves us
no choice in the matter, yet we cannot but feel compassion for that noble family of Bentivoglio, which
has always been so friendly to us."[1] On the 25th
Julius II. reached Urbino, where great preparations
had been made for his reception, and Elisabetta had
borrowed Isabella's biggest pearls and finest tapestries
to do honour to His Holiness. So numerous were
the guests that Elisabetta wrote to tell her brother
that to her regret she was unable to give him lodgings in the palace, which, "being neither Mantua
nor Ferrara," could with difficulty accommodate the
Pope and his seventy-eight Cardinals. After a
rough journey by bridle-path over the mountain-
passes, in torrents of rain, the Pope reached Imola,
and here, on the 25th of October, the Marquis of
Mantua was appointed lieutenant-general of the
army in the place of Guidobaldo, who was laid up
with gout. At the same time news was received of
the flight of Giovanni Bentivoglio and his family,
who had left for Milan, with a safe conduct from
Charles d'Amboise, the French general. A fortnight later, on the 11th of November, the Pope
entered Bologna in triumph.

The weather was lovely and the roses were still

[1] Luzio e Renier, *Mantova e Urbino*, p. 174.

in bloom when, on the Feast of St. Martin, the victorious Pope, wearing his purple cape and richly jewelled mitre, borne aloft on the Sedia Gestatoria, made his way through the crowded streets to the Cathedral of S. Petronio. Before him marched the pontifical standard-bearers, and, immediately behind him, ten white palfreys with golden bridles, closely followed by the Duke of Urbino, the Marquis of Mantua, Francesco Maria, Prefect of Rome, and a suite of nobles. Last of all, borne aloft in the air, came the Papal Cross and the Host, under a silken baldacchino, accompanied by the Sistine choir and forty priests with lighted tapers in their hands. Thirteen triumphal arches were erected along the route, and gold and silver medals, struck in honour of the occasion, were thrown to the crowds of spectators who came to witness the stately pageant and receive the Pope's blessing from the steps of S. Petronio.

Francesco Gonzaga wrote glowing accounts of the great ceremony, and of the marked favour with which the Pope treated him. "It is even possible that we may bring him with us to Mantua," he wrote to his wife, and forthwith he desired her to see that the Castello was made ready, and gave orders that the frescoes of the *Camera Dipinta* should be carefully restored, where they had suffered damage, by Andrea Mantegna and his sons, "or, if they cannot or will not do the work, by M. Francesco Bonsignori." But when this letter was written the great master was already dead. A brief mention of his death appears in one of Isabella's letters to her husband, but she was too full of joy and triumph at the thought of Francesco's triumphant success to dwell on this irreparable loss.

On the 21st of September she wrote:

"I received Your Excellency's letter, describing your entrance into Perugia, and all the honours and favours and promises which you have received from His Holiness. May God in the highest be praised! And I thank Your Excellency for informing me of this, since nothing can give me greater joy and satisfaction than to hear of your prosperity and exaltation. Let Your Signory boldly ask the Pope to come to Mantua, and we shall contrive to do him honour. I will have the corridor arranged, and the *Camera Dipinta* restored by Mæstro Francesco, because, as you will have heard, Messer Andrea died immediately after your departure. Federico's cure has been pronounced complete by the doctor this morning. He dressed, and dined with good appetite, and is playing merrily in his room, so he is making a good recovery. I will not write more now, as Monsignore is sending this courier in great haste. Ercole and the girls are well."

Three days later she wrote again:—

"I ordered Ghisolfo to have the corridor leading to the *Camera Dipinta* covered in, but we cannot find the key of the armoury, and have not liked to force the door open, because of all the things which it contains, and it ought not to be left open all day, while men are going to and fro, and are at work in the corridor. Your Excellency must tell me what you wish about this, as there will be plenty of time. The son of M. Andrea Mantegna will repair the *Camera*, as Mæstro Francesco (Bonsignori) cannot leave his Cenacolo (in the convent of the Zoccolanti Friars). I have been to see the new rooms at S. Sebastiano, which are very fine, and the pictures seem to me admirable, Federico and the other children are well, and so am I."[1]

The pictures to which Isabella here alludes were in all probability Mantegna's Triumphs of Cæsar, for which a new hall had been lately prepared in Francesco's newly-built palace, S. Sebastiano, near the Porta Pusterla. In a letter of April 17, 1506,[2] Corradi had already informed the Marquis that he has ordered the carved pilasters for Messer Andrea's canvases, and it is these pillars, as Dr. Kristeller points out,[3] that we see reproduced in Andrea's well-known wood-cuts. But the Triumphs were still employed as stage decorations, we learn from a letter of Francesco Gonzaga, who, in giving Vigilio orders for the representations of a comedy in December 1501, desired him not to move the Triumphs from Marmirolo, as those which are in Mantua will be sufficient to adorn the theatre.[4]

We find another allusion to the new rooms in the Palazzo della Pusterla in a long letter which was addressed by Isabella to her husband on the 5th of October, and which, although written in her most lively strain, shows that her relations with him were none of the happiest.[5]

" Your letter apologising for not having written before has filled me with confusion, for it is I who ought rather to have begged your pardon for my

[1] D'Arco, *Arte e Artefici*, ii. 68.

[2] *Ibid.*, 69.

[3] "Andrea Mantegna," p. 279.

[4] D'Ancona, *Origini*, ii.

[5] This interesting letter escaped the notice of D'Arco and other historians, and is only to be found in a rare pamphlet published in 1870 by P. Ferrato and entitled *Lettere di Principesse di Casa Gonzaga.*

delay, not you, when I know you have hardly time
to eat! but, since you are so kind as to make excuses
to me, you will also be so good as to forgive my
delays, which were caused by Federico's illness and
my reluctance to give you any news which would
make you anxious. Now, thank God, he is perfectly
well, and I can the more gladly discharge my duty.
The hat for which you ask shall be made as soon as
the master arrives, and shall be as fine and gallant
as possible. If you will say how soon you require it,
I will try and have a coat made to match, if there is
time; but pray tell me this at once. Thank you for
wishing me to see your entry into Bologna. It will
no doubt be a magnificent sight. I am very well,
and, if you desire it, will come gladly. I think even a
bomb would have some trouble to make me miscarry.
Your Highness must not say that it is my fault if I
quarrel with you, because, as long as you show any
love for me, no one else can make me believe the
contrary. But no interpreter is needed to make me
aware that Your Excellency has loved me little for
some time past. Since this, however, is a disagree-
able subject, I will cut it short, and say no more. I
am sorry Your Highness objects to my calling our
boy Ercole. I would not have done this if I had
thought you would dislike it. But Your Highness
knows that when you were at Sacchetta you said
he was very like my father, of blessed memory; and
I said that, this being the case, you were wrong not
to call him Ercole. You laughed, and said no more;
but if you had told me your mind, then I should
not have made this mistake. But only let me have
another boy, and you may call him Alvise, or whatever you like, and leave the other to be Ercole for me.

But I am sure that, if I had a thousand sons, I shall never care as much for any of them as I do for Federico. All the same, let Your Highness please yourself, and I will do as you wish. A few days ago I was in Your Excellency's new house, and, as I wrote before, thought it most beautiful. You write that I am making fun of you, which is not true, because, if the rooms were not fine, I should keep silence; but, as the effect seemed strikingly fine to me, I wrote this to you, and I repeat that they are beautiful, and all the more so in my eyes because Your Highness has followed the example of my room, although, I must confess, you have improved upon it. I will not weary you any more with words of little importance, but commend myself a thousand times over to Your Highness.—By the hand of ISABELLA, who longs to see you." Mantua, Oct. 5, 1506.

On the 20th of October, Isabella wrote again as follows:—

"Your letter, giving me an account of your fortunate progress, has given me great pleasure, both as showing me that you are in good health, and telling me of all the honour and glory you are gaining. I thank you exceedingly, and must tell you in return that I and Federico, Alvise, and all the girls are well. Alvise's nurse has had an attack of fever, so I have given him Livia's nurse, until she has recovered, which will not, I hope, be long now. As soon as the felt hat, which is being made after Bernardus del Armaria's directions, is finished, I will have it covered with velvet and embroidered with such taste that it shall be the finest and most gallant thing in the world! Please see that the pearls which I

lent to the Duchess of Urbino are soon restored to you.
Francesco Mantegna has begun to repair the frescoes
in the *Camera Dipinta*, and Ghisolfo is having the
corridor covered. The painters are gone to Venice
to copy the Italia. The Vicar of Serravalle writes to
say that part of the Castle wall towards the Po has
fallen down, of which danger he says he warned
Your Excellency and the Masters of Revenue some
time ago. I sent orders to the said officers to provide
for its repair. Owing to this accident Federico's
nurse lost 70 measures of wheat and 200 of millet."

In her next letter Isabella told her husband of
the unexpected difficulties experienced by Girolamo
Corradi and Bonsignori, the two artists whom she had
sent by his orders to copy a fresco with a figure of
Italia in the ducal palace at Venice, which was to be
reproduced in his palace of S. Sebastiano. At the
same time she informed him of the jealousy with
which the Signory evidently regarded his close
relations with the Pope and the King of France.[1]

"When Messer Hieronimo the painter and his
companion went to Venice to copy the Italia, I
wrote to Carlo Valerio begging him to assist them,
and he, being anxious to serve Your Excellency,
asked His Serenity the Prince for his permission,
because without this they could not obtain entrance
into his ante-chamber, and those artists who formerly
ventured to copy the painting without his leave, went
there at their own peril. Messer Hieronimo now
informs me, on Messer Carlo's part, that the Prince
refused to give his consent, saying : ' Look at those
letters which we have received, informing us that the
Marquis of Mantua every day speaks against this

[1] D'Arco, *Arte e Artefici*, ii. 71.   Gaye, *Carteggio*, ii. 90.

Signory, not in public, where he uses honourable expressions, but in private, and not only does he himself act thus, but his servants follow his example, which is most injurious to the State.' It is plain they nourish hatred against Your Excellency, and every day they say that they receive similar information. Messer Carlo promised to behave with great circumspection, and advises Your Excellency to say some good words to the Signory's ambassador now in attendance on His Holiness, so that he may report them, and not leave the Senate under so unfavourable an impression. Whatever turn affairs may take, he begs you to be careful not to let any one know that this warning has come from him. As to the copy of the Italia, he says it will be best to wait a month or two, and after that he will try to obtain the necessary permission. It has seemed to me right, both for your sake and for that of Messer Carlo, to give Your Excellency this information, while you are with the said ambassador. Federico continues to gain strength.—Your wife, ISABELLA, with her own hand."[1] Nov. 1, 1506.

A fortnight later the Marchesa wrote again, on receiving Francesco's account of the Pope's triumphal entry into Bologna.

" I was filled with joy on hearing the account of the solemn entry into Bologna, which Your Excellency described so fully in your two letters of the 11th, but this evening I am still more delighted to hear that you soon hope to return home. Here I expect you eagerly, since my present condition will not permit of my coming to join you at Bologna. I have received four ducats of the Pope's new coinage,

---

[1] D'Arco, *Arte e Artefici*, ii. 72.

which I distributed as you desired, thanking you very much for letting me have them. As soon as I received your first letter, saying that His Holiness has removed the interdict from Bologna, all the priests in this city began to celebrate mass in thanksgiving. I told Messer Annibale Bentivoglio, who is at Revere, of the permission which you informed me has been granted him, at your request, to keep his house and all its contents. He has replied that he is well aware how much he owes to Your Excellency, and begs me to thank you in his name, hoping that you will continue to give him your good protection, since his only hope is placed in Your Highness."

The Bentivogli, as we saw, had fled from Bologna before the papal army, and their splendid palace, newly decorated with frescoes by Francia's hand, had been razed to the ground. In this general ruin, Annibale, the eldest son of the ruling prince, and his wife, Lucrezia d'Este, Isabella's half-sister, gratefully availed themselves of the Gonzagas' help and protection. They came to Mantua, where both the Marquis and his wife treated them with the greatest kindness, and braved the wrath of the fiery old Pope, who was furious with Francesco for giving shelter to his enemies. "His Holiness," wrote the Mantuan envoy, "began to bellow like a bull with rage, and not only threatened Your Excellency, but Heaven itself." At the same time Isabella did not neglect this opportunity of enriching her own collection with the spoils of her vanquished friends. A certain Niccolo Frisio, who, according to Bembo, was German by birth, but thoroughly Italian in all else, and had earned Castiglione's gratitude by nursing him during a serious illness in Rome, wrote

on the 27th of November to inform the Marchesa
that he had recovered two alabaster heads which had
belonged to the Protonotary,Antonio Bentivoglio, and
had been stolen.   One was a head of Antonia ; the
other, which had pearls in the hair, a bust of
Faustina.   " I only regret," he added, " that I am
not in Rome, where I might have secured a couple
of paintings on the Labours of Hercules, which
would, I am sure, have pleased you better ; but, if I
return to Rome, I hope to be able to do you this
service.—From him who would have desired to see
Your Excellency reigning in the capitol, in the great
days of triumphant Rome, your servant, NICCOLO
FRISIO." The busts were duly sent to Mantua,
and found a place in the Grotta, by the side of that
famous bust of Faustina which had been Mantegna's
greatest treasure.[1]

Francesco's return was celebrated with great
rejoicings at Mantua, and the performance of the
" Formicone " was once more given in the Castello
at the New Year, under Messer Vigilio's direction.
Soon afterwards Isabella gave birth to a third son,
who received the name of Ferrante, and became a
valiant soldier, as well as a prime favourite of the
Emperor Charles V.

Isabella herself was dangerously ill for some days,
and narrowly escaped with her life.   On her recovery,
her brother, Cardinal d'Este, sent the poet Ariosto
to convey his affectionate congratulations to the
Marchesa on this happy event, an attention which
Isabella greatly appreciated.   During the few days
which he spent at Mantua, Ariosto read to the
Marchesa the greater part of his *Orlando Furioso*,

[1] D'Arco, *Arte e Artefici*, ii. p. 73.

and this, she wrote to the Cardinal, "made these hours in bed pass not only without weariness, but with the greatest possible pleasure." From the first Isabella showed the keenest interest in the Ferrara poet's verses, and encouraged him to continue his *Orlando*, and weave the scattered fragments into one great poem. He often came to visit her at Mantua, and listened attentively to her advice and criticism. When his poem was published in 1516, her husband allowed the paper on which it was printed to be sent from Venice to Ferrara free of duty, a privilege to which great importance was attached, and which was only granted to a few highly favoured scholars. As soon as the book appeared Ariosto came himself to Mantua, and presented a copy to Isabella herself, and another to her husband, while, in a later edition, he paid a magnificent tribute to her charms and virtues.

CHAPTER XVII

1507—1508

Louis XII. invites Francesco Gonzaga to help him in the siege of Genoa—Visit of Isabella to Milan—Fêtes in the Castello—Isabella's correspondence with Elisabetta Gonzaga—Her intended journey to France—Death and funeral of the Duke of Urbino—Visit of Duke Francesco Maria to Mantua—Birth of Isabella's youngest daughter—Murder of Ercole Strozzi, and death of Niccolo da Correggio—Rivalry of Isabella and Lucrezia Borgia.

EARLY in April 1507, Louis XII. entered Italy with a large army, and invited the Marquis of Mantua to help him in quelling a rebellion which had broken out in Genoa, and was secretly supported by Machiavelli and the Florentines. Francesco gladly accepted the king's proposal, and distinguished himself greatly in the siege of Genoa. After the surrender of that city he entered Milan in triumph with Louis, who appointed him Grand Master of the Order of St. Michel, and expressed so earnest a wish to make the Marchesa's acquaintance that Francesco sent an express courier to beg his wife to come to Milan at once. Isabella set out immediately with her little son Federico, now a child of seven, and travelled by Lodi to Milan. Once more she saw the beautiful city which she had known so well in the reign of her brother-in-law, the unhappy Duke who languished in the dungeon of Loches, and with that strange forgetfulness of the past which marked the

men and women of her age, danced and supped with
King Louis in these same halls of the Rocchetta
where Beatrice had died. Great as were the changes
and melancholy the scenes of destruction which met
her eyes in this once splendid palace of the Sforzas,
Isabella found many old friends and familiar faces
in the brilliant crowd of courtiers. Galeazzo di San
Severino was there, in close attendance on the king
as Grand Écuyer de France, and distinguished
himself in the tournament given in the Marchesa's
honour on the piazza in front of the Castello, which
had been the scene of his prowess in old days. So,
too, was the Moro's favourite painter, Leonardo the
Florentine, who came to Milan at the French king's
urgent entreaty to erect triumphal arches and arrange
the court pageants held in honour of his victory.
And before Isabella left, another old friend appeared
on the scene in the person of Antonio Pallavicini,
now Cardinal di S. Prassede, who arrived in great
haste on the 7th of June as papal legate, and was
received with the stately ceremonial due to the Pope's
representative. But, melancholy as were the associa-
tions which these old scenes and well-known faces
must have recalled, Isabella seems to have enjoyed
herself exceedingly. Her brilliant charms made a
profound impression on King Louis and all his
courtiers, and the monkish chronicler, Jean d'Auton,
singled her out among all the fair and high-born
ladies who were present at the royal ball in the
Castello as *une belle dame qui danse à merveilles*.[1]
On her return to Mantua the Marchesa wrote in high
spirits to tell her sister-in-law at Urbino all that she
had seen and done in Milan. Her letter, breathing

---

[1] *Chronique de Louis XII.*, publiée par R. de Maulde La Clavière.

as it does a gay spirit of fun and rivalry eminently characteristic of the writer, must be given in full:—

"Since Your Excellency went to Rome and Rome came to Urbino, I have never ventured to rival the grandeur of your court, nor to pretend that I have seen as many rare and excellent things as you have done, but have looked on in silence and not without hidden envy at Your Highness. But now that I have been to the first and noblest court in Christendom, I can boldly not only challenge you, but compel you to envy me. A few weeks ago, I was summoned by my illustrious lord to Milan to pay homage to His Most Christian Majesty, and arrived there on the vigil of Corpus Christi. After dinner, as I was about to go and pay my respects, I received a message from him, desiring me to go to the lists on the Piazza where the Giostra was being held. So I went there at the stated hour and found His Majesty, who came to meet me on the steps and received me with the greatest courtesy possible. All the Milanese ladies were present and the Princess of Bisignano, as well as all the barony and nobility of France and the great lords of Italy, the Duke of Savoy, the Marquises of Mantua and Montferrat, and all the castellans of the Milanese towns, and the ambassadors of every power in Italy. The French lords are so numerous that it would be impossible to name them all. But I must mention the Duc de Bourbon, our nephew, a tall youth of handsome and majestic appearance, who closely resembles his mother (Chiara de Montpensier) in complexion, eyes, and features. If the Roman Court is marvellous for its ceremonial and order, that of France is no less amazing and extraordinary for confusion and disorder—so much so that it is quite impossible to distinguish one man from another! It is also certainly remarkable for its freedom and absence of etiquette. In this court, for instance, cardinals are not treated with any greater honour than chaplains are in Rome. No one gives place to them or pays them any respect, from the king downwards. His Majesty, however, is always most courteous and respectful to all who presume to approach him, and above all to ladies, always rising from his seat and lifting his cap to show them honour. Thrice over he came to visit me in my lodgings. The first time, when I happened to be dining with Signor Zoanne Giacomo Trivulzio, he waited more than half-an-hour for my return, and each time he remained no less than two or three hours, conversing on different subjects with the greatest friendliness in the world, neither did he fail to speak honourably of Your Highness in the course of conversation. Madonna Margherita di San Severino (sister of Emilia Pia), the Contessa di Musocho, and sometimes the Princess of Bisignano, who are well versed in the French language, were our interpreters. In spite of repeated efforts, I never succeeded in finding His Majesty in the Castello, saving one day when he invited me to a public banquet in the Rocchetta, where the Princess of Bisignano and I had the honour of sitting at his table. We danced in an informal manner both before and after supper. His Majesty danced with me, and the Cardinals Narbonne, San Severino, Ferrara, and Finale, who were present at the banquet, were constrained by him to dance, much to our amusement and diversion. I will not write about

the public spectacles held on the Piazza, because I
know that they will have been fully described by
your ambassador. Certainly I have seen better-
managed jousts, but .I never saw, and do not think
that, in all Christendom, it would be possible to see,
a greater number and variety of people! Most of
them were nobles—not only those of Milan, which
must be the first or second largest city in the world,
but the whole court of France and most of the
courts of Italy were here assembled, so that Your
Excellency will understand how proud and glorious
a sight it was! The assembly was a much larger
one than we could have seen at the king's own
palace in France, because the lords who followed
him to Italy do not reside at court, and if they are
occasionally present at some solemn ceremony, we
should not have seen all the people and nobles of
Milan, and indeed we may say of Italy, since the
gentlemen and citizens of many different cities
came to witness these spectacles. O how great was
my happiness! and how it makes me rejoice every
time that I remember it! Only think what it
would be if Your Signory were here and we could
communicate by word of mouth! I have written
all this to deliver myself from the sin of envy, and
also to describe a thing which is excellent in spite
of its disorder! I am sure that the Roman court
is not to be compared with the French court, where
the temporal and spiritual are united. If Your
Excellency could have seen the procession of Corpus
Christi set out from the Duomo with little enough
order—first the clergy, then an infinite number of
Swiss guards with halberds on their shoulders,
behind them the Gentlemen of the Guard, battle-

axes in hand, and after them under a baldacchino borne by the chief lords came the Legate of France bearing the Body of Christ, followed by the king, with seven Cardinals and all the barony of France and Italy, and people of Milan and the neighbouring towns—it would have seemed to you the finest spectacle which you had ever witnessed! It is true that Your Signory may say, 'I have seen Rome'; still you must confess that you saw it undone and in ruins. But I have seen Genoa, Florence, and Milan, which in our age are no less worthy of admiration, in their most triumphant days. I will not deny that I have a great wish to see Rome, not for the sake of the court and the different nations who are represented there, for I could not look upon anything finer than what I have seen here, but in order to visit the antiquities and famous ruins of Rome and to realise what the triumph of a victorious Emperor must have been. But this occasion has not been entirely without Roman ceremonies, since at the entrance of my friend, the Most Reverend Cardinal and Legate of S. Prassede, he was received by the Legate of France and eight Cardinals, all the orders of clergy, and singers, with great magnificence, because His Most Reverend Signory holds the rank of the Pope whom he represents, so that I may say I have seen both the Pope and the Roman court. Afterwards I paid His Signory two visits at his lodgings, where I was most lovingly received, embraced, and honoured, and was able to realise the splendid state of the Cardinals who live in Rome. This impression was confirmed by the visit which I received from Cardinal de Rouen and all the other Cardinals attached to this court, who came in a body, not to pay me honour, which would not have been suitable on their part, but merely to show me courtesy. I might go on and describe all the separate visits which I received from Italian and French lords and Milanese ladies, as well as from the King and the Cardinals, but this and all the rest I will leave to Your Signory's imagination, lest I give you too much reason to envy me!" Mantua, July 7, 1507.

Elisabetta, however, declined to own herself vanquished, although, owing to Duke Guidobaldo's illness, it was two months before she sent the following rejoinder :—

" It is already over a month since I received Your Signory's letter, which was delightful and acceptable beyond words. If I could, my dear lady, express in words or writing the pleasure and satisfaction which I take in reading your eagerly expected and much - prized letters, it would take me all eternity! And I am sure that if you realised a small part of the happiness they give me, you would more often employ your secretary. On the other hand, if I complain, I do not wonder that they are few and far between, knowing that all dear and precious things are rare. . . . Although Your Excellency thinks that you have delivered yourself from the sin of envy in order to excite my jealousy by telling me all the great and magnificent things which you have seen at Milan, I must reply that I feel no envy whatever. What sight can be greater than that of Rome ? I saw that city, which is and has ever been acknowledged to be the head of the world, with all the marvellous ancient and modern treasures which it contains, to my great and endless wonder and delight.

I saw, above all, the Pope, who represents God
upon earth, surrounded by the whole Roman court,
which is second to none. I confess that these things
which Your Signory has seen with so much pleasure,
are also splendid, but if you had seen these other
great sights, you would, I do not doubt, hold them
to be very inferior. But of one thing I can boast
with far greater reason than Your Excellency, which
is that, although I have only once visited. Rome,
Rome and the Roman court has been, not once, but
twice to visit me at Urbino. Now Your Excellency
will see if I cannot challenge you to a glorious duel
and carry off an honourable victory! And further,
I will tell you of other things, which will, I am
certain, cause Your Signory voluntarily to retire
from the fray, and perhaps make you regret that
you ever entered the lists, seeing that you are entirely vanquished. The Most Serene Catholic King,
being at Gaeta, desired to imitate the example of the
Pope and Sacred College, and himself proposed to
come to visit me at Urbino, which he would have
done had he not been afterwards obliged to change
his plans and take another voyage elsewhere." This
was Ferdinand the Catholic, who came to visit his
newly conquered kingdom of Naples with his new
wife, Germaine de Foix, in October 1506, and remained there until the following June, when he met
Louis XII. at Savona, before that monarch returned
to France. "And the great King of the Romans,
after holding many Diets, was unable to obtain the
Electors' consent to his journey into Italy, so that
till now it has been impossible for him to visit
Urbino in person and keep his promise of showing
me His Majesty. All this will help Your Highness

to understand that I do not in the least envy the sights which you have seen, nor do I need to go elsewhere to see nobler and more wonderful things, since, without leaving home, Heaven has granted me these rare favours. Nor do I intend to take any more journeys, unless it is to see and enjoy the company of Your Signory, which I shall always count the greatest of all pleasures, and which I desire above all things, both for the sake of embracing you and enjoying your presence, and because I have so many things to discuss with you that, without the help of Madonna Emilia, five days of uninterrupted talking would hardly satisfy me. I hear that Your Signory has made a vow to visit Loreto and exhort you to fulfil this vow soon, after which I intend to lay such snares for you that, whether willingly or by force, you will find yourself in my power! My lord Duke has recovered from his indisposition. I am well and hope to hear the same of you, &c.—Your sister, ELISABETTA, Duchess of Urbino." Urbino, Sept. 7, 1507.

When Elisabetta's letter reached Isabella she had just received an unexpected invitation from Louis XII. and Anne of Brittany to visit the French court, and accept the office of godmother to the babe whose birth was hourly expected, and who, it was confidently hoped, would this time prove a Dauphin. The Marchesa was overjoyed at the prospect, and wrote triumphantly to tell the Duchess of this new and unexpected honour, and to express her delight at the prospect of a journey beside which the glories of her pilgrimages to Rome, and papal and royal visits, grew pale.

"I made the sign of the Cross at the sight of a

letter of Your Signory's which was more than six
lines in length, and felt so much pleasure at the
sight that I read it with greater care and attention
than the short ones which I usually receive. Your
Excellency, I feel, here tacitly confesses that she
prefers the style which I have acquired on my
journeys to that which she has learnt by going only
to Rome! And since you are under this obligation
to me, I will not this time thank you for your long
and affectionate letter. Neither will I promise to
write more often, as you ask, because, if you look,
you will find that you have many more of my
letters in your file than you can register of your
own. But, in accusing me of neglect, Your Highness was evidently anxious to forestall my charges,
knowing well that neither the pleasures and good time
which I enjoy here, nor the pressure of overwhelming
business, ever prevent me remembering one whom I
love as my own soul. In reply, I must say that
you have indeed beheld great things in Rome and at
Urbino, and that you hoped to have seen more if the
Catholic King had come to visit you or if the Most
Serene King of the Romans had been able to undertake his journey to Italy, and the Diets had not
determined otherwise. But how can these things
in any way compare with my prospects in the near
future, putting aside all that I have seen and done
in the past, as is well known to Your Signory? The
Most Christian King thinks that the Queen cannot
bear a son unless I am present, and he has therefore
begged me earnestly to stay with her for this event,
in order that I may both honour the birth with my
presence, and hold the infant at the sacred font.
What greater honour could there be in this world

than to be gossip and sponsor to a King of France! O what splendour, pomp, and glory will be mine! I shall not only visit Paris, the most flourishing University and populous city of the universe, but the whole of France, Burgundy and Flanders, and may perhaps reach Sant' Iago of Galicia. O how many new lands and royal sights I shall see on this journey! Your Signory and Madonna Emilia, who know so much of the country and its customs, will be able to imagine these. But what if my journey to France takes place, and the coming of the Emperor to Italy, which had been overruled by so many Diets, should be abandoned? In this case, the glory which you love will return to me, and the Germans, I think, may give up Diets in future, and eat and drink to their hearts' desire! I do not know if after this you can claim to be my equal, and if it will be possible for me to accept your invitation to Urbino so easily! When I return to Italy I begin to wonder if this earth will be worthy to bear me, if carpets will not have to be spread under my feet, and a baldacchino sent to meet me wherever I go! But, joking apart, I really hope to start for France in a few days, and am busy making preparations. When I return we must think of meeting, for I am as anxious about this as Your Highness can be."[1] Mantua, 25th September 1507.

Whatever her moods may be—grave or gay, impatient or gentle, stern or gracious—Isabella always interests and attracts us; but Isabella in high spirits, intent on some new departure and gaily challenging

---

[1] This and the three preceding letters in the *Archivio Gonzaga* were first published by Dr. Luzio in a pamphlet entitled *Gara dei Viaggi.*

the world in her buoyant fancy, is altogether irresist-
ible. Unfortunately she was doomed to disappointment, and this journey to France, to which she looked
forward with so much delight, never took place.
There were many difficulties in the way. Money, as
usual, was scarce at Mantua, and the Marquis was
reluctant to let his wife undertake so long and
expensive a journey. Her presence was urgently
required at home during his frequent excursions, and
the negotiations that were being secretly carried on
between the Pope and his allies might, at any moment,
as Francesco well knew, involve him in war with
Venice. So Isabella was compelled to put off her
expedition, and devote herself to her husband and
children. She could not even visit Ferrara, and
assist at the splendid fêtes that were held at her
brother's court, during the carnival of 1508, when
an Eclogue composed for the occasion by Ercole
Pio was represented, in which the shepherds of
Arcadia paid a glowing tribute to three nymphs
who dwell on the banks of the Po, the Mincio, and
the Metauro, and Lucrezia, Isabella, and Elisabetta,
who were there extolled as the most famous ladies
of the age. For in January her little girl Livia died,
and Francesco himself fell seriously ill, and showed
the first symptoms of that incurable disease which
eventually ended his life. At the same time, sad
news came from Urbino. The unusual severity of
the winter brought on a fresh attack of the gout,
from which Guidobaldo had suffered all his life, and
on the 11th of April 1508 he died.

The good Duke was only thirty-five years of age,
but his sufferings had been intense during the last
weeks of his life, and death came as a welcome

release. " Why do you envy me so great a blessing ? "
he said, with a smile, to his heart-broken wife and
weeping friends ; " is it not a great good to be freed
from this terrible burden of pain ? " And a few hours
later he passed away, repeating a favourite passage
from Virgil, to Castiglione, who stood at his bedside.

Elisabetta was inconsolable. She nursed her
beloved husband with the greatest devotion, and won
general admiration by the wisdom with which she
conducted affairs of state, and secured the peaceful
succession of Guidobaldo's young nephew, Francesco
Maria della Rovere. " Never was there so prudent
and wise a Madonna," exclaimed her brother Giovanni
Gonzaga, who hastened to Urbino to comfort his
sister ; " she is indeed to be commended in all that
she does." [1] Three days after his death, Guidobaldo
was buried by his father's side, in the little church of
the Zoccolanti friars, in the shady gardens which he
had loved so well, and where, on that fatal night, six
years before, he had first received the news of Cæsar
Borgia's invasion. On the 2nd of May, a solemn
requiem mass was held in the Duomo, and was
attended by many princes and foreign ambassadors.
A huge catafalque was erected in the nave, decorated
with the late Duke's arms and banners, and his robes
as Knight of the Most Noble Order of the Garter
were laid on the bier, while his old tutor Odasio
pronounced a touching and eloquent oration, which,
Giovanni Gonzaga informed his brother, " was said
to be very beautiful by persons who understand
these things better than I do." [2] Four days later,
Isabella's faithful secretary, Capilupi, whom she had

---

[1] Luzio e Renier, *Mantova e Urbino*, p. 182.
[2] Dennistoun, " Memoirs of the Dukes of Urbino," ii. 79.

sent to express her grief and sympathy with the
widowed Duchess, reached Urbino, and thus describes the gloom and mourning which now reigned
in the once gay and brilliant palace :—

" I found this illustrious Madonna surrounded by
her women in a room hung with black, with the
windows all closed, and only one candle on the floor.
She was sitting on a mattress spread on the floor, with
a black veil over her face and a black vest up to her
throat, and it was so dark I could hardly see, and had
to be led up to her like a blind man by my cloak.
She took my hand, and we both began to weep, and
it was some time before her sobs and my own allowed
me to speak. I gave her Your Excellency's letter,
and expressed my sympathy in as few words as possible. . . . We spoke of Your Excellencies and your
children, and of different subjects, and she told me
the great kindness which His Holiness has shown
at this time, and I stayed with her more than two
hours. The new Duke was sitting among the women,
but when the Duchess called him he rose, and I
gave him your messages. He replied briefly, but in
a prudent and sensible manner. He looks to me
taller and slighter than I expected, but it was too
dark to judge fairly. The Duchess speaks of him
very warmly, and he treats her with the reverence of
a son and a servant. To-day we spent more than
three hours together, and I induced her to talk of
other subjects, and even made her laugh, which no
one had as yet succeeded in doing. I begged her to
open the shutters, which no one had dared suggest,
and I think that in two days' time she will consent
to do this. She still eats her food on the floor. I
complained of the black veil which displeased Your

Highness; she excused herself for wearing it, but had not thought of this before Signor Giovanni arrived, and could not remove it now with decency, but says that when Donna Leonora comes here as a bride, she will change it joyfully, and says that if this marriage proves as prosperous as she desires, she will no longer feel widowed, and that this will be the greatest joy that she can ever hope to know on earth. . . . The funeral ceremonies, as Signor Giovanni has told you, were sumptuous. There were 825 mourners, wearing long cloaks with trains and hoods. All the friars and priests of the state and five bishops were present, and stood round the catafalque, with an infinite number of lighted torches, but they were hardly as numerous or as fine as those at Mantua. The universal grief and lamentation here is beyond description."[1]

The young Duke, Francesco Maria, now expressed a great wish to visit his promised bride. For some time past he had been anxious to come to Mantua, and his natural eagerness to see his future wife was further stimulated by Leonora's uncle, Giovanni Gonzaga, who told him that, when he had seen Donna Leonora and the Marchese's famous breed of horses, he would have seen the two finest things in the world! For, he assured him, there was no fairer and sweeter maiden in the whole of Italy, while no Christian king or prince had a stud to equal that of Mantua. Accordingly, on the 25th of August, Francesco Maria made his appearance at Mantua, and spent two days with the Marquis and his daughter. Isabella herself was absent, having lately given birth to another daughter at her summer villa on the heights

---

[1] Luzio e Renier, *Mantova e Urbino,* p. 185.

of Cavriana, and Federico Cattaneo sent her the
following account of the young suitor's visit: "Yesterday evening about seven, the Duke of Urbino
arrived at the Castello, travelling *incognito* with only
four persons, and remained upstairs with our illustrious
lord for about half-an-hour.   As soon as he arrived,
our Signor sent for Madonna Laura (the wife of Giovanni Gonzaga), whose little girl died two days ago.
She came at once, and with her Madonna Violante,
Madonna Costanza, Madonna Orsini degli Uberti,
and as soon as they were in the Castello they dressed
Madonna Leonora in white tabby.   If Your Highness could have seen the confusion there was at that
moment!   As for me, I very much wished you could
have been there for many reasons, and many others of
your servants did the same.   The Cardinal then came
in, took Madonna Leonora by the hand, and led her
down the little staircase near the *Camera Dipinta*.
They entered the Camera of the Sun, and found the
Duke with our illustrious Signor and many other
gentlemen.   The Duke came to meet Madonna
Leonora and kissed her.   But he did not seem to
have succeeded very well, and our Cardinal pushed
him towards her again, and then he threw his arm
round her head, and kissed her on the mouth.   After
this they sat down together and talked of many
things, and more especially of pictures.   Presently
my lord called me and bade me fetch the portrait
of Your Highness by Lorenzo Costa, the Ferrara
painter, which I had lately placed in its frame.   I
brought it directly, and every one admired it.   Then
we all took our leave.   The Duke went to St.
Sebastian, and every one else to his own house.   Of
Madonna Leonora's modesty and bearing I can only

tell Your Signory that she behaved not as a child, but as a very prudent lady. The Duke leaves here on Monday, and goes to Viterbo." Mantua, 26th August 1508.

The young Duke was eighteen years of age and had already distinguished himself as a gallant soldier, but gave signs of that violent temper for which he was famous in after days. Only a few months before, he had stabbed one of Duke Guidobaldo's favourite cavaliers with his own hand, because the unfortunate young man aspired to the hand of his widowed sister, Maria Varana.[1] But he always behaved with the greatest deference to his widowed aunt, and was anxious to acquire the good graces of his bride's parents. He sent the Marquis a scimitar which had belonged to the lamented King Ferrante II. of Naples, and presented Isabella with a set of costly trappings for a horse which had been the property of Cæsar Borgia, saying he knew that she was not only fond of driving in a chariot and riding mules, but was an excellent horsewoman, and thought that she might relish a share "in the spoils of one who knew not how to make use of his good fortune."[2] Leonora was by this time a lovely maiden of fourteen summers, whose beauty was already the theme of courtiers and poets, and whose riper charms Titian's brush was to render immortal in years to come. The little daughter who was born to her mother that August received the name of Livia Osanna, after her lamented friend the Beata Osanna. The body of this holy nun had been taken up a few weeks before, in the Marchesa's presence, and after being exposed to the

---

[1] Dennistoun, *op. cit.*, ii. 305.
[2] Luzio e Renier, *Mantova e Urbino*, pp. 186, 187.

veneration of the public for a whole day, had been
solemnly interred in the beautiful Arca designed by
Cristoforo Romano, in San Domenico. This second
Livia was vowed to the cloister from her infancy,
and became a Poor Clare in the convent of Santa
Paola, or Corpus Domenico. Here the Emperor
Charles V. himself came to see her, and the fame
of her sanctity attracted many illustrious visitors.
Sister Paola, which name the princess adopted on
taking the veil, is mentioned more than once in her
mother's correspondence, and several letters which
she herself addressed to her cousin Duke Ercole of
Ferrara and his wife Renée are preserved in the
Gonzaga archives, and were published by Ferrato.

In November Isabella went to Ferrara, where she
still found a warm welcome from her brother Alfonso,
in spite of the family quarrels which saddened her
home, and the coolness between her and *la Diva
Borgia*, as Lucrezia was styled by flattering poets
and courtiers. But two of her oldest friends were
missing. Ercole Strozzi, the accomplished Latin poet
and intimate friend of Bembo, whose house was often
honoured by Isabella's presence, and who himself
frequently came to Mantua, had been foully murdered in cold blood one summer day when he left his
house to take an early walk and enjoy the morning
air. His wife, the beautiful Barbara Torelli, had
only given birth to her first child a fortnight before,
and now wrote " with streaming tears and broken
heart " to tell her friends at Mantua the sad news.
The murdered man was buried with great pomp, and
the learned humanist, Celio Calcagneni, pronounced an
eloquent oration over the corpse of his gifted friend.
" Great is the sorrow we all feel here," wrote Bernardo

dei Prosperi to Isabella—"most of all, because he was so rare and excellent a man of letters." Not a word was said as to the murderer, but it was generally known in Ferrara that Alfonso d'Este had long been jealous of Barbara Torelli's preference for Ercole, and had secretly planned his destruction. Before Strozzi's death, the Marquis of Mantua had promised to stand godfather to his new - born daughter, and now sent the poet Tebaldeo to represent him at the christening.

Something of the same mystery overshadowed the fate of Isabella's brilliant kinsman, Niccolo da Correggio, who died in January 1508, at Ferrara, away from his own house—to the bitter grief of his wife, Cassandra Colleoni. In her letter of condolence, Isabella expressed her pity for this poor Madonna, and alluded covertly to some love intrigues in which her old friend had been unhappily entangled. Only a year before, Alfonso had presented Niccolo with a fine palace in the Via degli Angeli, which had formerly belonged to his unhappy brother Giulio, in recognition of his services in discovering that prince's plot against the Duke's life. And in February 1507, he wrote to the Marchesa in his old strain, telling her how eagerly her coming was awaited at Ferrara, and how busy he was preparing masquerades for her amusement. The Duke, he added, was longing to see his sister, and confidently expected her to spend the next two months at his court. But soon after this the old courtier incurred his lord's displeasure, and Bernardo dei Prosperi, in a letter informing Isabella that Signor Niccolo was at the point of death, ascribes his melancholy condition to grief at his disgrace. "His case," adds Bernardo, "has been pronounced hopeless by seven doctors, and in this miserable end we must plainly see the judgment of a just God."[1]

No sooner did Isabella hear of her old friend's death than she wrote to his son Giangaleazzo, desiring him to send her the MS. volume of poems which his father had dedicated to her many years ago. Giangaleazzo replied courteously, begging for time to make certain corrections which his father had been unable to finish. Upon this, the Marchesa sent him a long letter, couched in her most imperious tones,[2] telling him that she could bring witnesses to prove how, at the time of Alfonso's wedding to his first wife, Anna Sforza, his father Niccolo, being in the room above the court chapel, showed her his book in three parts, containing sonnets, *capituli*, and *canzoni*, with an epistle dedicating each in turn to herself. "This," she goes on to say, "he confirmed again when he was with me in my villa of Sacchetta, at the time of Don Giulio's affair, saying that, in asking me to be the patroness of his book, he resembled those persons who, in order to keep their house clean, paint a saint upon the outer walls." Then, lapsing into a gentler and more pathetic strain, Isabella recalled the long familiarity and friendship which she had enjoyed with his father long before he was born, and which dated back to her earliest childhood, and ended by desiring him to send the precious MS. without delay by the present courier.[3]

Giangaleazzo now sent a servant to Mantua with fresh excuses and explanations. The MS. which his

---

[1] Luzio e Renier in *Giorn. St. d. Lett. It.*, xxiii. 77.
[2] D'Arco, *Notizie d'Isabella*, p. 315.
[3] Luzio e Renier, *op. cit.* 79.

father had shown her was, he explained, not worthy
of her acceptance, being marked in certain places,
and not as elegantly bound as Niccolo himself would
have desired, so that he must beg her to wait a
little longer.   To these excuses the Marchesa paid
little heed, beyond sending the writer a curt note,
saying that, no doubt, his father being the most
generous of men, would have wished to adorn the
book before he presented it to her.   Since he was
unfortunately no more, she must request Giangaleazzo
to forward the volume, which, as he ·is evidently
aware, had been promised to her.

But the book never came, and in August, Mario
Equicola, Isabella's confidential servant, wrote from
Ferrara, telling her that Duchess Lucrezia was going
to Correggio to obtain Messer Niccolo's *canzoniere*, a
piece of information which roused Isabella's ire to
the highest pitch.   However, Giangaleazzo managed
to evade Lucrezia's request with equal success, and, as
the best way out of the difficulty, kept his father's
canzoniere in his own hands.   We have another
proof of the rivalry which existed between Isabella
and her sister-in-law in a letter,[1] written by Mario
in August 1508, telling her that, in looking over the
MSS. of his friend Ercole Strozzi, he had discovered
a Latin epigram, originally written for the Sleeping
Cupid of Isabella's Grotta, which had been altered
and adapted to fit a marble Cupid belonging to
Duchess Lucrezia.   " This," he adds, " is in reality
a very inferior modern work, but her flatterers
pretend that it is a genuine antique ! "   In conclusion,
the excellent secretary proposes his readiness to go
to the stake, if need be, in order to maintain the

[1] A. Luzio, *I Precettori*, p. 43.

truth, and prove to all the world that Ercole Strozzi's verses were originally written in honour of the Sleeping Cupid in the Isabellian Grotta, and inscribed to his own Madonna Marchesana. So keen was the competition of these great ladies for the tribute paid them by scholars and poets, so highly did they prize the honour of seeing their own names linked with these Latin verses which were to perpetuate their fame for all time. *Tantum possunt camœnœ.* "Such power have the Muses!"

CHAPTER XVIII

1500—1506

Isabella's relations with painters during the early years of the
sixteenth century—Her letters to Leonardo da Vinci—Correspondence with Fra Pietro da Novellara, Angelo del Tovaglia,
Manfredi, and Amadori—She asks Perugino for a painting for
her studio—Description of the Triumph of Chastity composed
by Paride da Ceresara—Perugino's delays—Correspondence
with Malatesta, Tovaglia, &c.

WE have seen how, in the closing years of the fifteenth
century, Isabella founded her famous studio of the
Grotta, in the ancient portion of the Castello known
as the Corte Vecchia, and began to collect works of
art for its adornment.   In spite of the many distractions which occupied her time and thoughts, in spite
of her husband's absence, and the active part which
she took in public affairs, she pursued this object
with unremitting energy and perseverance.

Never at any period of her life were her relations
with artists more frequent and more full of interest
than in these first ten years of the new century.
Andrea Mantegna, the court painter of the Gonzagas,
as we have already said, executed the first pictures for
the decoration of her new studio.   And naturally
enough the great Florentine master who had visited
Mantua at the close of 1499, and drawn her portrait,
was one of the next artists to whom she applied.
After Leonardo's return to Florence in April 1500,
he sent the Marquis a sketch of the house of Angelo

del Tovaglia, a wealthy merchant whom Francesco often employed on business matters, and which he had greatly admired on a visit which he paid to Florence that spring.

" I send you," wrote the Mantuan agent, Francesco Malatesta, in August, " a drawing of the house of Angelo Tovaglia, by the hand of your servant Leonardo Vinci, who desires to be commended both to you and to Madonna. But he said that to make the house perfect, and satisfy your idea, you would have to transport the site of Messer Angelo's house to the spot where you intend to build. The drawing has not been coloured, nor have I thought it necessary to put in the evergreens, ivy, box, cypresses and laurels of the garden, but if you wish it, the said Leonardo offers to send you a painting as well as a model of the villa." [1]

The birth of Isabella's son, and the political troubles of that anxious year, prevented her from availing herself of Leonardo's offers of service at the time, but in the following March she wrote the following letter to the cultured ecclesiastic, Fra Pietro da Novellara, who was at the time preaching a course of Lent sermons in Santa Croce of Florence:—

"Most Reverend Father in God,—If Leonardo, the Florentine painter, is now in Florence, we beg you will inform us what kind of life he is leading, that is to say if he has begun any work, as we have been told, and what this work is, and if you think that he will remain for the present in Florence. Your Reverence might find out if he would undertake to paint a picture for our studio. If he consents, we would leave the subject and the time to him ; but

[1] Luzio in *Emporium,* 1900, p. 353.

if he declines, you might at least induce him to paint us a little picture of the Madonna, as sweet and holy as his own nature. Will you also beg him to send us another drawing of our portrait, since our illustrious lord has given away the one which he left here ? For all of which we shall be no less grateful to you than to Leonardo." Mantua, March 27, 1501.

The Carmelite Vicar-General replied without delay:

"Most illustrious and excellent Lady,—I have just received Your Excellency's letter, and will obey your orders with the utmost speed and diligence. But, from what I hear, Leonardo's manner of life is very changeable and uncertain, so that he seems to live for the day only. Since he has been in Florence, he has only made one sketch—a cartoon of a child Christ, about a year old, almost jumping out of his mother's arms to seize hold of a lamb. The mother is in the act of rising from S. Anna's lap, and holds back the child from the lamb, an innocent creature, which is a symbol of the Passion, while S. Anna, partly rising from her seat, seems anxious to restrain her daughter, which may be a type of the Church, who would not hinder the Passion of Christ. These figures are as large as life, but are drawn on a small cartoon, because they are represented either seated or bending down, and one stands a little in front of the other, towards the left. And this sketch is not yet finished. He has done nothing else, excepting that two of his apprentices are painting portraits to which he some-times adds a few touches. He is working hard at geometry, and is quite tired of painting. I only write this that Your Excellency may know I have re-ceived your letters. I will do your commission, and let you know the result very soon, and may God keep you in His grace.—Your obedient servant, FR. PETRUS NOVELLARA, Carm. Vic.-Gen."[1]   Florence, April 3, 1501.

The letter is of great importance, both as showing Leonardo's absorption in geometrical studies, and giving a description of the famous cartoon which he drew for the Servi friars, and which not only filled all the artists with admiration, but brought crowds of men and women to the convent hall, where this masterpiece was exhibited during two days.   "The whole city was stirred," wrote Vasari, "and you might have fancied that you saw a procession on some solemn feast day."   And Girolamo da Casio, the Bologna poet, with whom Isabella was in constant correspondence, wrote a sonnet on the cartoon which had moved all Florence to wonder.

Ten days later the Carmelite friar wrote again to tell Isabella the result of his efforts:—

"This Holy Week I have succeeded in learning the painter Leonardo's intentions by means of his pupil, Salaï, and some of his other friends, who, to make them more fully known to me, took me to see him on Wednesday in Holy Week.   In truth, his mathematical experiments have absorbed his thoughts so entirely that he cannot bear the sight of a paint-brush.   But I endeavoured as skilfully as I could to inform him of Your Excellency's wish. Then, finding him well disposed to gratify you, I spoke frankly to him on the subject, and we came to this conclusion: if he can, as he hopes, end his engagement with the King of France without displeasing him by the end of a month at latest, he would rather serve Your Excellency than any other

---

[1] Luzio, *I Precettori*, App.

person in the world. But, in any case, as soon as
he has finished a little picture which he is painting
for a certain Robertet, a favourite of the King of
France, he will do your portrait immediately and
send it to you. I left two good petitioners with him.
The little picture which he is painting is a Madonna,
seated as if at work with her spindle, while the Child,
with His foot on the basket of spindles, has taken up
the winder, and looks attentively on the four rays
in the shape of a cross, as if wishing for the cross,
and holds it tight, laughing, and refusing to give
it to His mother, who tries in vain to take it from
Him. This is all I have been able to settle with the
master. I preached my sermon yesterday. God grant
it may bring forth much fruit, for the hearers were
numerous. I commend myself to Your Excellency.
—FRATER PETRUS DE NOVELLARA." Florence, April
14, 1501.[1]

Leonardo's promises, however, remained as usual
unfulfilled, and hearing no more of her Madonna, or
portrait, in July Isabella wrote to Manfredo de
Manfredi, her father's envoy at Florence, begging
him to deliver a letter which she had written into
the master's own hands.

On the 30th, Manfredi replied:—

" I have given Your Excellency's letter to Leonardo, the Florentine. I delivered it myself into his
own hands, telling him that I would take charge of

[1] This letter is quoted by M. Muntz, " Leonardo da Vinci," ii.
121; but the date of April 10, 1503, which he borrows from Calvi's
life of the master, is clearly wrong. D. Richter and Signor Solmi
give April 4, 1501, as the correct date; but since Easter Day fell
on the 11th of April in that year, Wednesday in Holy Week
must have been the 7th, and the letter was probably written on
the 14th.

any letter which he might wish to send in answer, and would see that it was faithfully delivered to you. Leonardo replied that he would send an answer shortly, and hoped to be able to oblige Your Excellency. But, since no letter came, I sent again to ask his intentions, and he replied that all he could say for the moment was that I might send you word that he had begun to do what Your Highness desired. This is all that I have been able to obtain from the said Leonardo."

A few months later, on the 3rd of May 1502, Isabella, hearing that certain vases which had belonged to Lorenzo dei Medici were for sale, wrote to her agent, Francesco Malatesta, desiring him to show these vases to some competent person, "such, for instance, as Leonardo, the painter, who used to live at Milan, and is a friend of ours, if he is in Florence, and consult him as to their beauty and quality." This was a task quite to Leonardo's taste, and he did not hesitate to give the Marchesa the benefit of his opinion on the precious vases.

"I have shown them to Leonardo Vinci, the painter," wrote Malatesta on the 12th of May, "as Your Highness desired. He praises all of them, but especially the crystal vase, which is all of one piece and very fine, and has a silver-gilt stand and cover; and Leonardo says that he never saw a finer thing. The agate one also pleases him, because it is a rare thing and of large size, and is all in one piece, excepting the stand and cover, which are silver-gilt; but it is cracked. That of amethyst, or, as Leonardo calls it, of jasper, is transparent and of variegated colours, and has a massive gold stand, studded with so many pearls and rubies that they

are valued at 150 ducats. This greatly pleased Leonardo, as being something quite new, and exquisite
in colour. All four have Lorenzo Medici's name
engraved in Roman letters on the body of the vase,
and are valued at a very high price: the crystal
vase, at 350 ducats; the jasper vase, set with gems,
at 240 ducats; the agate vase, at 200 ducats; and the
jasper vase, on a plain silver stand, at 150 ducats."[1]

At the same time Malatesta enclosed coloured
drawings of the four vases, in order that Isabella
might make her choice, only regretting that it was
impossible for any painter to reproduce the beautiful
lustre which charmed the eyes of Leonardo.

The prices of those rare works of art were
probably beyond the Marchesa's means in this expensive year, when Lucrezia Borgia's wedding and
her visit to Venice had exhausted her treasury, but
Leonardo's praises must have filled her with longing
to add them to her collection. She had not yet
given up all hope of obtaining a picture from the
Florentine master, and two years afterwards, when
Leonardo was at work on the cartoon of the Battle
of Anghiari for the Council Hall in the Palazzo
Pubblico, this indefatigable princess once more returned to the charge. This time she wrote a
charming letter to Leonardo, which she sent to the
merchant Angelo del Tovaglia, whose villa had
excited the envy of the Marquis some years before,
and who was now engaged in conducting negotiations
on her part with Perugino.

"Since we desire exceedingly," she wrote to
Angelo on the 14th of May 1504, "to have some
work by the hand of Leonardo Vinci, whom we

1 Luzio, *Arch. Stor. dell' Arte*, i. 181.

know both by reputation and by personal experience to be a most excellent painter, we have asked him, in the enclosed letter, to paint us a youthful Christ of about twelve years old. Do not scruple to present this letter to him, adding whatever words may seem to you most suitable, so as to persuade him to serve us ; and let him know that he shall be well rewarded. If he excuses himself and says that he has not time, owing to the work which he has begun for that most excellent Signory, you can tell him that this will be a means of recreation and pleasure when he is tired of historical painting, and that for the rest he can take his own time, and work at leisure."

The letter which Isabella sent to Leonardo was as follows :—

"To Master Leonardo Vinci, the painter. M. Leonardo,—Hearing that you are settled at Florence, we have begun to hope that our cherished desire to obtain a work by your hand may be at length realised. When you were in this city, and drew our portrait in carbon, you promised us that you would some day paint it in colours. But because this would be almost impossible, since you are unable to come here, we beg you to keep your promise by converting our portrait into another figure, which would be still more acceptable to us; that is to say, a youthful Christ of about twelve years, which would be the age He had attained when He disputed with the doctors in the temple, executed with all that sweetness and charm of atmosphere which is the peculiar excellence of your art. If you will consent to gratify this our great desire, remember that apart from the payment, which you shall fix yourself, we shall remain so deeply obliged to you that our sole desire will be to do what you wish, and from this time forth we are ready to do your service and pleasure, hoping to receive an answer in the affirmative." Mantua, May 14, 1504.

On the 27th of May, Angelo del Tovaglia replied :—

" I received the letter of Your Highness, together with the one for Leonardo da Vinci, to whom I presented it, and at the same time tried to persuade and induce him, with powerful reasons, to oblige Your Excellency by painting the little figure of Christ, according to your request. He has promised me without fail to paint it in such times and hours as he can snatch from the work on which he is engaged for this Signory. I will not fail to entreat Leonardo, and also Perugino, as to the other subject. Both make liberal promises, and seem to have the greatest wish to serve Your Highness. Nevertheless, I think it will be a race between them which is the slower! I hardly know which of the two is likely to win, but expect Leonardo will be the conqueror. All the same, I will do my utmost."

Angelo's prophecy was destined to be fulfilled to the letter. More than a year passed away before Perugino's picture found its way to Mantua, while neither the honest merchant's entreaties nor the charming Marchesa's honeyed words were able to move Leonardo to action. Once more, on the 30th of October, Isabella wrote to Angelo, with a second letter to Leonardo, gently reminding him of his promise.

" You sent me word by Messer Angelo some time ago that you would gladly satisfy my great desire. But the large number of orders which you receive make me fear lest you have forgotten mine. I have, therefore, thought it well to write these few words, begging you to paint this little figure by way of recreation when you are tired of Florentine history."

Still the master, intent as he was on painting his great picture on the wall of the Council Hall, gave no sign of life. But in January his favourite pupil, Salaï, offered his services to the Marchesa, and professed his readiness to paint some *cosa galante* for Her Excellency. His offer was not accepted, but a few months later Isabella desired Angelo del Tovaglia to send Salaï to judge of the merits of the picture which Perugino had at length finished for her studio, and, if necessary, suggest alterations.

In March 1506, Isabella herself came to Florence, as we have seen, and spent the Feast of the Annunciation in the city of flowers. She did not see her friend Leonardo, who was studying the cause of rivers and the flight of birds in his country retreat at Fiesole. But she met his uncle, Alessandro Amadori, the Canon of Fiesole, with whom so much of his time was spent, and for whom he cherished a deep and lasting affection. To this courteous ecclesiastic the Marchesa confided her great wish to obtain a little picture from the hand of the famous master, and he promised to use all his influence to induce his nephew to satisfy her ardent desire. On the 3rd of May, a week or two after she had returned to Mantua, Alessandro wrote to her as follows:—

"Here, in Florence, I act at all hours as the representative of Your Excellency, with Leonardo da Vinci, my nephew, and I do not cease to urge him by every argument in my power to satisfy the desire of Your Excellency, and paint the figure for which you asked him, and which he promised you several months ago, in the letter that I showed Your Excellency. This time he has really promised me that he will soon begin the work and satisfy your wish, and desires me to commend him to your favour. And if, before I leave Florence, you will tell me whether you prefer any especial figure, I will take care that Leonardo satisfies Your Highness, whom it is my greatest wish to oblige. I visited Madonna Argentina Soderini this afternoon, and she was glad to hear from me that Your Highness had reached Mantua safely. I gave her Your Highness's messages, and she sends the enclosed note in return. May God prosper Your Excellency."[1]

The Marchesa wrote back gratefully on the 12th of May from Sacchetta, where she had been driven by the sudden outbreak of the plague in Mantua:—

" We were very grateful for your letter of the 3rd, telling us that you had conveyed our inquiries to the Signora Gonfalionera, as we learn by a letter from Her Highness ; neither are we less pleased with the dexterity which you have shown in dealing with Leonardo Vinci, in order to induce him to satisfy us and paint that figure for which we asked. We thank you for all your trouble, and beg you to persevere in your kind efforts on our behalf."[2]

But before the end of May, Leonardo left Florence to enter the service of Charles d'Amboise, the French Governor of Milan, and spent over a year in that city, at the express request of King Louis,

[1] Luzio in *Arch. Stor. dell' Arte,* i. 181–184.
[2] Yriarte, *Gazette d. B. Arts,* 1888 ; Muntz, " Leonardo da Vinci," ii. 113 ; Solmi, " Leonardo," p. 159.

who himself came to Milan for six weeks in 1508, and begged that *notre chier et bien amé Léonard de Vinces* should be allowed to remain at his court. There Isabella probably met him when she spent that joyous fortnight at Milan, and renewed her acquaintance with so many of her old friends. But he never painted her picture, and the only work by Leonardo's hand in the Gonzaga collection was a small painting afterwards given to her son Federico by Count Niccolo Maffei, after his return from France. This work is described in the inventory of 1627 as " a woman's head, with dishevelled hair," valued at 180 ducats, and hung in a passage leading to the Studio of the Grotta.[1]

Isabella was more fortunate in her dealings with other painters, and ultimately succeeded in obtaining a picture for her studio from Perugino, although this artist's delays and prevarications provoked her sorely. The Umbrian master enjoyed a great reputation in North Italy at the close of the fifteenth century. He had painted noble altarpieces at Cremona and the Certosa of Pavia, and Duke Lodovico Sforza had repeatedly invited him to enter his service, and decorate his rooms in the Castello of Milan. Perugino was well known at the court of Mantua, since his young wife, Chiara, was a daughter of Luca Fancelli, the well-known architect, who had spent forty years in the service of the Gonzagas. When the painter was at Venice in 1496, Isabella asked him, through his friend, Lorenzo da Pavia, to paint a picture for her studio. But her request came too late, for by this time Perugino had left Venice, and was busily

[1] D'Arco, *Arte e Artefici,* ii. 161.

engaged in painting his great altar-pieces at Florence
and Perugia. Accordingly, in 1500, Isabella wrote
to Giovanna della Rovere, the sister of Duke Guidobaldo of Urbino, and mother of her future son-in-
law, Francesco Maria, saying how much she desired
to obtain a *poesia* for her studio from Perugino, and
begging this lady to use her influence with the painter.
The Prefettessa, however, was not encouraging.
Perugino, it was true, had lately painted a series of
frescoes at Sinigaglia, but was reluctant to accept
orders, and very slow in executing them. Moreover,
he would be sure to raise difficulties as to the subject
of the picture, and did not care to paint compositions
of this kind. The issue proved Giovanna to have
been right, but Isabella was not easily discouraged,
and two years and a half later she wrote to Francesco
Malatesta, desiring him to approach Perugino on the
subject.[1]

" Since we desire," she wrote in September 1502,
"to have in our *camerino* paintings of allegorical
subjects by the best painters in Italy, among whom
Il Perugino is famous, we beg you to see him and
find out, through the intervention of some friend, if
he is willing to accept the task of painting a picture
on a *storia* or invention which we will give him, with
small-sized figures, such as those which you have
seen in our *camerino*. You will find out what
payment he requires, and if he can set to work soon,
in which case we will send him the measurements of
the picture with our *fantasia*. And be sure to send
me a prompt answer."

[1] W. Braghirolli, *Notizie e documenti inediti intorno a P. Vannucchi,* from the *Archivio Gonzaga ;* and C. Yriarte, *Gazette des Beaux
Arts,* 1895.

At first Malatesta gave the Marchesa little hope of success. Perugino, he told her, was a man fertile in excuses and difficult to deal with, and he advised her to employ Filippino Lippi or Sandro Botticelli in his stead. But Isabella insisted that he should begin by approaching Perugino. The first interview proved satisfactory, and Perugino, tempted by the Marchesa's liberal offer of 100 ducats, promised to paint a *fantasia* for her studio, within the next few months, on any subject that she liked to choose. Two months afterwards Capilupi sent a letter to another agent in Florence, Vincenzo Bolzano, desiring him to give Perugino a paper with full details of the subject, drawn up by Isabella's favourite humanist, Paride da Ceresara, and at the same time obtain his formal agreement to the contract. If the painter agreed to Isabella's conditions, the size of the picture and a sketch of the composition were to be given him, and 20 ducats were to be paid in advance. "The Marchesa," adds the secretary, "desires that the picture should be painted on canvas, like Mantegna's compositions, and recommends the master to use the greatest care and diligence, but this, no doubt, will be superfluous, since Her Excellency feels certain that Perugino will not wish his work to be unworthy of his fame, especially as it will have to bear comparison with Mantegna's paintings."

The contract was duly signed, the money paid down, and the Marchesa's programme handed to the painter. This curious document, which both M. Muntz[1] and M. Yriarte[2] reproduce in full, shows how minute were the directions which painters received

[1] *Histoire de l'Art pendant la Renaissance,* ii. 62.
[2] *Gazette d. B. Arts,* 1895.

from the poets and humanists of the day, and how little freedom in the choice of subject was allowed them by their patrons. Isabella, no doubt, went too far in this direction, and the best painters felt their imagination cramped by her minute instructions. Mantegna, whose genius overcame all difficulties, probably moulded the material to suit his fancy, and certainly succeeded best in the paintings which he executed for her studio. Giovanni Bellini, as we shall see, quite refused to paint the subject assigned to him, and Perugino found the theme little suited to his art, and failed to satisfy her. Nor is his failure surprising when we read her directions.

" My poetic invention, which I wish to see you paint, is the Battle of Love and Chastity—that is to say, Pallas and Diana fighting against Venus and Love. Pallas must appear to have almost vanquished Love. After breaking his golden arrow and silver bow, and flinging them at her feet, she holds the blindfold boy with one hand by the handkerchief which he wears over his eyes, and lifts her lance to strike him with the other. The issue of the conflict between Diana and Venus must appear more doubtful. Venus's crown, garland and veil will only have been slightly damaged, while Diana's raiment will have been singed by the torch of Venus, but neither of the goddesses will have received any wound. Behind these four divinities, the chaste nymphs in the train of Pallas and Diana will be seen engaged in a fierce conflict— in such ways as you can best imagine—with the lascivious troop of fauns, satyrs, and thousands of little loves. These last will be smaller than the god Cupid, and will carry neither gold bows nor silver arrows, but darts of some baser material—

either wood or iron, as you please. In order to give full expression to the fable and adorn the scene, the olive tree sacred to Pallas will rise out of the ground at her side, with a shield bearing the head of Medusa, and the owl, which is her emblem, will be seen in the branches of the tree. At the side of Venus, her favourite myrtle tree will flower, and to heighten the beauty of the picture, a landscape should be introduced with a river or the sea in the distance. Fauns, satyrs, and loves will be seen hastening to the help of Cupid—some flying through the air, others swimming on the waves or borne on the wings of white swans, but all alike eager to take part in the Battle of Love. On the banks of the river, or on the shore of the sea, Jupiter will be seen in his character as the enemy of Chastity, changed into the bull that carries off the fair Europa. Among the gods attending on him, Mercury will appear flying like an eagle over Glaucera, the nymph of Pallas, who will bear a small cistus engraved with the attributes of the goddess; Polyphemus, the one-eyed Cyclops, will be seen chasing Galatea, Phœbus in pursuit of Daphne, who is already changing into a laurel; Pluto carrying off Persephone to the infernal realm, and Neptune about to seize Coronis at the moment she is metamorphosed into a raven. I send you all these incidents, in a small drawing, which may help you to understand my explanations. If you think there are too many figures, you can reduce the number, as long as the chief ones remain—I mean Pallas, Diana, Venus, and Love—but you are forbidden to introduce anything of your own invention."

This was the elaborate and intricate composition which Perugino, the painter of Madonnas and Saints with angelic faces and seraphic expression, was now required to paint. Anything less suited to his genius it would have been hard to find. The subjects which he generally represented were of the simplest kind; the figures were few and for the most part in repose. He could paint a sweet-faced Madonna looking down on her Babe, a Saint with upturned eyes and rapt expression standing at the foot of the Cross, even a nude Apollo serenely confident of victory, but this crowded canvas, with its multitude of figures, fighting and chasing each other, was altogether beyond his powers. We can hardly wonder that he showed considerable reluctance to attack the subject. First one excuse was suggested, then another, to account for his protracted delays. But every letter which Isabella received from her different agents in Florence told the same tale. Perugino had not even attempted to begin a sketch of the composition. At length even the Marchesa's patience became exhausted, and she sent Angelo del Tovaglia to demand an explanation from the painter. Upon which Perugino declared that he was doubtful as to the size of the figures, and begged for exact measurements of the personages in the foreground of Mantegna's picture. These Isabella sent him, with the following note, on the 12th of January 1504 :—

"Excellent Friend,—The enclosed paper, with the thread wound round it, gives the length of the biggest figure on M. Andrea Mantegna's pictures, close to which your own will hang. The other figures behind can be of any size that you like. You will know now how to act. Above all, we beg you to be quick with the work, for the sooner we can have it, the better we shall be pleased."

Five weeks later, some alterations having been made in the lighting and arrangement of the studio, Isabella sent fresh directions for the painter's benefit. Still Angelo was unable to report progress, and in April, Isabella wrote indignantly, demanding Perugino to restore her twenty ducats, if his picture were not ready in a month's time, and telling Tovaglia to appeal to the Gonfaloniere in case of the master's refusal to refund the money. After writing this angry letter, the Marchesa apparently thought better of it, and sent a young Mantuan painter, Lorenzo Leombruno, to Florence, with a letter of recommendation to Perugino, desiring him to report on the state of the picture, and, if it were not yet begun, to claim her ducats. But when Leombruno reached Florence, at the end of April, Perugino had gone to Umbria, and did not return till the following autumn. Then, however, he professed the greatest anxiety to fulfil his obligations to the Marchesa, and Isabella sent him the following letter on the 31st of October, the same day on which she wrote to Leonardo asking him to paint a Christ :—

"*Perusino*,—We have seen, by two letters which you wrote to M. Angelo Tovaglia, that you hope soon to finish our *Storia*, which gives us great pleasure. But, as we feel the greatest impatience in the world to see it, we beg that you will finish it and let us have it as soon as possible. Farewell."

In point of fact, the picture had only just been sketched out on the canvas, as we learn from Agostino Strozza, the cultured Abbot of Fiesole, who, at Tovaglia's suggestion, visited Perugino's shop, and sent his report to Isabella early in November. Yet another agent was employed by the impatient

Marchesa, in the person of Luigi Ciocca, who promised Isabella to pay the patriarch, as he called him, frequent visits, and accepted the commission the more readily because of the lovely maidens whom he found sitting as models to the painter. Perugino now pleaded poverty in excuse for his delays, saying that he lived from hand to mouth, and was compelled to do work which brought him ready money, and put off other commissions, but promised to finish the Marchesa's picture by Easter. When, however, Ciocca ventured to criticise the drawing of certain fauns in the picture, Perugino replied with so much arrogance that Ciocca's anger was roused, and he would have given him a rude answer if it had not been for the presence of the maidens. This remark alarmed Isabella, who wrote at once to Abbot Strozza, upon whose judgment in artistic matters she could rely, begging him to inspect Perugino's drawing, as she would rather give up the picture than have one which neither did her nor the painter honour. Leonardo's pupil, Salaï, was now called in to give his opinion, as Ciocca explains in the following letter :—

"Most illustrious Madonna,—To-day the Reverend Abbot of Fiesole and I spent some time with Perugino, and told him our opinion of the work, and succeeded in persuading him to carry it swiftly to perfection, so much so that he has promised to use the greatest art, diligence, and attention to satisfy his honour and duty, and meet your wishes. I am also glad to tell you that a pupil of Leonardo Vinci, Salaï by name, young in years but very talented, whom I sent to Perugino, praises the *fantasia* greatly, and has corrected some of the small defects which the abbot and I had pointed out.   We will continue to do our utmost, in order that Your Excellency may be satisfied.   This Salaï has a great wish to do some gallant thing for Your Excellency himself, so if you desire a little picture, or anything else from him, you have only to tell me the price you are ready to give, and I will see that you are pleased.—Your servant, ALOISIUS CIOCCA."[1]   Florence, Jan. 22, 1505.

At Salaï's suggestion the artist rectified certain errors of drawing which satisfied Ciocca, who told the abbot that he thought the picture was as good as could be expected from Perugino, who excelled in the treatment of larger forms, but had little experience in handling small-sized figures and crowded compositions.   Another point which disturbed Isabella considerably was that she heard Perugino had represented Venus as a nude figure, contrary to her express directions.   This, she told the abbot, must not be allowed, since, if one single figure were altered, the whole meaning of the fable would be ruined.[2]

When the Marchesa's letter reached Fiesole, the abbot hastened to Perugino's shop, but it was only to find that the painter had left Florence.   " I cannot understand the man's behaviour," he wrote to Isabella on the 22nd of February 1505, "and begin to fear he will prove me to be a liar.   I find it is already a fortnight since he left Florence, and I cannot discover where he has hidden himself, and when he is likely to return.   His wife and friends either do not know where he is or else they are hiding it from me, probably because, contrary to all his promises, he has undertaken some other work.

---

[1] Braghirolli, *op. cit.*   [2] Yriarte, *op. cit.*

Not a day passes without my sending to inquire of
him, and as long as he was working at the picture
I called at least once a week. Perhaps a fresh advance of money might fire his zeal; but he is an
unaccountable fellow, who does not seem to see any
difference between one person and another. I never
met a man in whom art can accomplish such great
things, where nature has done so little." This con-
trast between the ideal beauty of Perugino's creations
and the baseness of his conduct, his unscrupulous
behaviour and greed for money, seems to have been
felt by all who came in contact with the great Umbrian master, and agrees with Vasari's unfavourable
estimate of his character.

A month later the abbot told Isabella that Perugino was still absent, but that, as he now discovered,
he had gone to Perugia, and was detained there by a
lawsuit on behalf of a friend. In reality the master
had accepted a commission to paint a fresco at his
native town of Citta della Pieve, which, after much
bargaining, he executed in March 1505 (O.S. 1504).
He went on to paint a S. Sebastian at the neighbouring town of Panicale, and did not return to
Florence until the beginning of May, when Ciocca
upbraided him with the shameful way in which he
had treated the Marchesa. " Upon which," writes
Ciocca, " he declared, as usual, that he was sorely
pressed for money, and muttered between his teeth
that he knew he should be left with the picture on
his back, and have to wait for his ducats. I told
him to remember that he was not dealing with men
of Spoleto or the March, but with a Marchioness
of Mantua, a generous lady, who showed the highest
appreciation of all that was good and beautiful, and,

above all, of works of art. Let him only finish his picture, and make it as perfect as possible, and Her Highness will show him that she keeps her engagements in a very different manner!" Once more the painter promised, for the hundredth time, to finish the picture in a fortnight, and, "strange as it seems," wrote Ciocca, "this time he has really kept his word!"

On the 7th of June, Isabella wrote to the painter herself, addressing him as her very dear and famous friend, and sending him the eighty ducats that were still due to him. Before her letter reached Florence the picture had been sent to Mantua, and on the 14th Perugino composed a letter, with the help of a less illiterate friend, thanking the Marchesa for the money, and saying that he hopes his work will satisfy her wishes and his reputation, since he, as is well known, has never failed to prefer honour to gain. He further explained that he had painted the picture in *tempera*, because Leombruno had told him that Messer Andrea Mantegna's pictures in the Marchesa's studio were executed in this medium.

On the 30th of June, Isabella wrote: "The picture has reached me safely, and pleases me, as it is well drawn and coloured; but, if it had been more carefully finished, it would have been more to your honour and to our satisfaction, since it is to hang near those of Mantegna, which are painted with rare delicacy. I am sorry that the painter Lorenzo of Mantua advised you not to employ oils, for I should have preferred this method, as it is more effective. None the less, I am, as I said before, well satisfied, and remain kindly disposed towards you."[1]

[1] Braghirolli, *op. cit.*

Perugino replied on the 10th of August, expressing his regret that he had not known the medium
employed by Mantegna, and saying that he would
have greatly preferred to use oils rather than *tempera*,
which did not suit the texture of his canvas, but hoped
some day to be allowed to paint the Marchesa another
more delicately finished picture.   Isabella, however,
was not sufficiently pleased with the Triumph of
Chastity to order a second painting for her studio,
and when, after Perugino's death, his widow, Chiara
Fancelli, offered her a picture of Mars and Venus
surprised by Vulcan, which the artist had intended
for the Marchesa, she declined to purchase the
painting.[1]   The correctness of Isabella's judgment
is confirmed by the sight of Perugino's picture, which
hangs in the Louvre to-day, side by side with the
works which Mantegna and Lorenzo Costa executed
for the Marchesa's Grotta.   The Triumph of Chastity
is the feeblest and least satisfactory of the series, and
lacks the charm of the Ferrarese artist's graceful compositions, while it sinks far below the level of the
great Paduan master's conceptions.   Both in style
and subject Isabella's *poesia* was ill-adapted to Perugino's art, and had, it is plain, inspired him with little
interest.   The composition is crowded and confused,
without life or unity ; the execution is poor and
flimsy, and the figures and trees are curiously out of
proportion.   The chief beauty of the picture lies in
the clear Umbrian sky, in the lovely landscape of
blue hills and river, and in the laughing faces and
gambols of the countless loves who are sporting on
the grass.   Venus, we note, does not wear either
the crown, veil or garland prescribed by Isabella, and

[1] Braghirolli, *op. cit.*

the Marchesa must have recognised that in this instance at least the painter was right. But, as she
said herself, the Triumph of Chastity was hardly
worthy of the place of honour which it occupied
in her studio, or of the painter's great name and
reputation.

CHAPTER XIX

1501—1507

Isabella asks Giovanni Bellini for a picture—Her correspondence
with Lorenzo da Pavia and Michele Vianello—The subject
changed to a Nativity—Delays of the painter—Isabella calls in
Alvise Marcello—Asks for her money to be returned—The
picture is completed and sent to Mantua in 1504—Isabella's
negotiations with Giovanni Bellini through Pietro Bembo for
another picture, which is never painted.

GIOVANNI BELLINI had naturally been one of the
first painters to whom Isabella d'Este applied when
she began to adorn her new studio. His father,
Jacopo, had frequently visited Ferrara and worked
for the Este princes, and Francesco Gonzaga often
met both the brothers Giovanni and Gentile during
the years that he spent in the service of the Venetian
Signory. Isabella herself admired Giovanni's paintings in the Council Hall on her first visit to Venice
in 1493, and three years afterwards asked the great
master to paint a picture for her Camerino. In 1498,
we know that she had been interested in comparing
certain paintings by Giovanni with Leonardo's portrait of the youthful Cecilia Gallerani,[1] and the excellence of his art was well known to her through his
personal friends, Lorenzo da Pavia, Aldo Manuzio, the
great printer, and other cultured Venetians, with
whom she was in constant communication. Early
in March 1501, Michele Vianello, a distinguished connoisseur, who, according to Messer Lorenzo, had the

[1] " Beatrice d'Este, Duchess of Milan," p. 53.

finest collection of works of art in Venice, and who was on intimate terms both with the painter and the master of organs, spent a few days at Mantua, and promised the Marchesa to induce Giovanni to paint a *fantasia* to match the allegories of Mantegna.[1]

"On my arrival here," he wrote, March 5, "I went to see Zuan Bellini, to execute the commission given me by Your Signory before I left, and told him your wish, and the *Storia* which you desire him to paint. Zuan Bellini replied that he was obliged to work for this Signory in the Palace, and could never get away from early morning till after dinner, but that he would manage to find or rob time in which to serve you, both for your sake and for love of me. But I must warn you that the said Zuan has many other works on hand, so that it will be impossible for you to have your picture as soon as you wish. I think it will be a year and a half before it is finished. As to the price, he asks 150 ducats, but may reduce it to 100. This is all I can do."

Isabella lost no time in clenching the bargain, and on the 1st of April, Michele wrote again: "I have seen Zuan Bellini several times, and told him Your Excellency's wishes, and he has agreed to do the work for 100 ducats in a year's time. He will set to work as soon as possible, and I hope that you may have the picture in a little over a year. He promises to take the greatest pains, and begs you to send him 25 ducats, and hopes to begin the work directly after the holidays.—Your servant, M. VIANELLO."

On the 4th of April, Isabella wrote: "Messer Michele,—I am glad to hear that you have induced

[1] W. Braghirolli, *Archivio Veneto*, vol. xiii. ; C. Yriarte, *Gazette d. B. Arts*, 1896.

Zuan Bellini to do the picture, and in order that he may set to work with the more courage after Easter, I send him the 25 ducats as agreed." The money, however, was not sent till the 25th of June, when Michele acknowledged its receipt, and promised to give it to Bellini as soon as he returned from the country, where he was spending a few days at his villa. "I have," he continued, "already spoken to him several times about your picture. He seems most anxious to serve Your Signory, but does not like the idea of the *Storia* you propose, and is unwilling to paint this, because, if this picture is to be a companion to M. Andrea's work, he would like to do his best, and is sure that he cannot make anything good out of such a subject. He seems so reluctant to undertake this *Storia* that I doubt if Your Excellency would be satisfied, and it would, I think, be better to let him do as he pleases, for in that case I am certain you would be better served. But he will do nothing without your orders."

Isabella knew Bellini too well to insist further, and on the 28th of June, she wrote to Michele as follows: "If Zuan Bellini objects so much to this *Storia*, I am content to leave the subject to his judgment, as long as he paints a story or fable of his own invention, representing something antique, which has a fine meaning. I should be very glad if he would begin the work at once, so that it may be finished within the year, or even sooner, if possible. The size of the picture has not been altered since you were here and saw the place that it was to occupy in the studio, but for greater safety I will send you the correct measurements, and will tell our sculptor, Zoanne Cristoforo, to write to you on this matter."

The next mention we find of Giovanni's picture is in a letter of the 27th of August from Lorenzo da Pavia, who, writing on the 26th of July, tells the Marchesa that Vianello is doing his best to make Giovanni Bellini paint her picture. A month later he sends her some rosaries of the finest ebony, and a Virgil and Petrarch lately issued by the Aldine press, and after expressing his joy that she has obtained possession of the clavichord which he had made for her dead sister, Duchess Beatrice, adds significantly: "Giovanni Bellini is going to paint you a beautiful *fantasia*, but he has not yet set to work. He is a slow man, and excuses himself because he is still engaged in the Palace, but promises to do both things." And he ends by advising his mistress to apply to Perugino, a recommendation which she promptly followed, to her cost.

But the months went by, and Isabella, hearing no more of her picture, wrote on the 20th of December to ask Messer Michele what the painter was about. "After we sent you the 25 ducats for Zuan Bellini, we never heard if he had begun our picture. If it is to be finished in a year, he ought already to have done a great part of the work. So please see him, and tell me the exact state of the picture, and beg him to persevere, so that we may have it at the promised time. But if he has not begun the work, and you know that he will not or cannot keep his promise, you will see that he returns our money, so that we may employ another master, since we desire, above all things, to see the decoration of our Camerino completed." [1]

Michele wrote in reply, on the 12th of January

[1] Braghirolli, *op. cit.*

1502, that the painter had been ill for some time, and had more work than he could do, but that he promised to finish the picture by the end of September, if the Marchesa would consent to wait so long. Then an interval of eight months elapsed, during which Isabella went to Ferrara for Lucrezia Borgia's wedding, and afterwards came herself to Venice, where she no doubt saw Lorenzo da Pavia and Messer Michele, and probably received Bellini's excuses and assurances of his readiness to serve her in person. But when, at the end of August, she asked Lorenzo for news of her picture, he replied :—

"Giovanni Bellini has never done anything! not indeed for want of constant entreaties both on my part and on that of Messer Michele, but I always thought, as I told Your Highness, that he would never paint this picture. He is not the man for these subjects (*historie*). He says that he will do them, but he never does! By way of helping on matters, I asked one of my friends, a poet of talent, to invent a very simple theme which could be easily painted, and which I now enclose, but even thus, I fear, he will never undertake the work, and M. Michele will therefore ask him to return the 25 ducats."

This, however, proved to be less easy than Lorenzo supposed, and on the 10th of September, he wrote: "As for the money, Your Highness must understand that it is difficult to make the painter give back the ducats. Now he pretends that he will paint you a charming *fantasia* after his own fashion, which is, it must be confessed, a rather lengthy fashion! M. Michele begs you to write him a letter which he can show the painter, and will compel him to restore the money."

Isabella now determined to give up the idea of a painting for her studio, and to ask Bellini for one of those sacred subjects in which he excelled. On the 15th of September, she wrote to Vianello: "M. Michele,—You may remember that many months ago we gave Zuan Bellini a commission to paint a picture for the decoration of our studio, and when it ought to have been finished we found that it was not yet begun. Since it seemed clear that we should never obtain what we desired, we told him to abandon the work and give you back the 25 ducats which we had sent him before, but now he begs us to leave him the work, and promises to finish it soon. As till now he has given us nothing but words, we beg you will tell him in our name that we no longer care to have the picture, but that if in its stead he would paint a Nativity (*Presepio*-manger) we should be well content, as long as he does not keep us waiting any longer, and will count the 25 ducats which he has already received as half payment. This, it appears to us, is really more than he deserves, but we are content to leave this to your judgment. We desire this Nativity should contain the Madonna and Our Lord God and St. Joseph, together with a St. John Baptist and the usual animals. If he refuses to agree to this, you will ask him to return the 25 ducats, and if he will not give back the money you will take proceedings through the *Via della Ragione*" (a Venetian Court of Justice). When this letter reached Venice the painter was absent, but as soon as he returned Vianello made him Isabella's offer, which he accepted gladly, promising to do a most excellent thing for the Marchesa, and only stipulating that the price should be 100 ducats, the same which he was to receive for the *Storia*. This, however, Isabella refused to give, saying that 50 ducats was sufficient, since the Nativity must be of a smaller size, and could not be placed in her Camerino, but should be hung in a bedroom. The exact dimensions of the new picture were sent to Venice by Francesco Gonzaga's secretary, Battista Scalona, and Vianello acknowledged the receipt of the measurements, and told Isabella that Bellini agreed to paint the *Presepio* and to introduce "the Child and St. John Baptist, with a distant landscape and other inventions, if this is agreeable to Your Highness. As to the price, he agreed to take 50 ducats, and anything more which may seem good to Your Excellency. So I ordered the canvas to be prepared with *gesso*, and he promised to begin at once."[1]

Isabella now suggested the addition of a St. Jerome to the group, but the painter demurred to this, and the Marchesa was compelled to yield. " Apparently," she wrote to Vianello on the 25th of November, " Bellini will not hear of St. Jerome being introduced in my Nativity; but I did not choose the subject, and it is he who seems to be reluctant to paint the picture at all, so let him do as he pleases. I am willing to have the *Presepio*, as long as it is worthy of his reputation. As for the medium and material, canvas or panel, he may do as he likes, as long as he keeps to the measurements supplied."[2]

A whole year went by, and, hearing no more of her picture, Isabella once more desired Lorenzo da Pavia to inquire if Giovanni Bellini were alive or dead! On the 6th of October 1503, Lorenzo wrote: " I have been to see Zuan Bellini, who declares the canvas

[1] Braghirolli, *op. cit.*   [2] Yriarte, *op. cit.*

will be ready in six weeks." But on the 3rd of January, after repeated visits to the old master's shop, he writes: "I am always seeing Zuan Bellini. He is working at the picture, but very slowly, and asks for another six weeks' respite, pretending that the colour will not dry fast enough in winter."

By this time Isabella's patience was fairly at an end, and on the 10th of April 1504, she addressed the following letter to her long-suffering agent: "Lorenzo,—We can no longer endure such villainy as Giovanni Bellini has shown us regarding this picture or panel of the Nativity which he agreed to paint for us, and we have decided to recover our money, even if the picture is finished, which we do not believe. I have written to the Magnifico Messer Alvise Marcello, our *compatre*, begging him to claim the money, and if Bellini refuses to return it, compel him to do so by the command and authority of His Most Serene Highness the Prince [the Doge, Leonardo Loredano]. You will therefore beg His Magnificence to do this office, in order that we may get out of the hands of this ungrateful man."

On the same day the indignant Princess addressed the following letter to Alvise Marcello, a patrician of high rank, who, in his capacity of Venetian ambassador at Mantua, had been godfather to one of her children, and who had paid her special attention when she had lately visited Venice: "Three years ago I gave Giovanni Bellini, the painter, 25 ducats as part payment of a subject which he had promised to do for my studio. Afterwards, since he declined to paint this *Storia*, he agreed to execute a Nativity of Our Lord for the said sum, as Michele Vianello and Lorenzo da Pavia are aware. The master has never kept any of his promises, and does not, it is plain, intend to keep them. We hardly know what steps to take next, but we see clearly how little is the respect which the painter has shown us. Bellini has never considered his obligations to us, and we are determined to have our money back. As there is no one in Venice whom we trust more than Your Magnificence, we have thought it best to ask you to desire Bellini to return our 25 ducats, without accepting either excuses or promises, for we will have no more of his work. If he refuses, I beg of you not to shrink in this extremity from saying words to the Prince, or to any magistrate who can order an execution, so that he may not be allowed to insult us in this fashion. If he refuses to give back the money, which we can hardly believe, you might appeal to Michele Vianello or Lorenzo da Pavia; and Your Magnificence may rest assured that you can do us no greater service than to recover our money, and, what is of far more importance, prevent Bellini from doing us so great an injury."[1]

Even the noble Venetian Senator, however, hesitated to take strong measures against the great master, who stood so high in the public estimation, and who was already seventy-seven years of age. All he did was to send Lorenzo da Pavia once more to try to bring the old man to reason. This time Bellini declared that he had been overwhelmed with work, and obliged to paint a picture for the Doge—probably the noble portrait of Loredano in the white peaked cap, which is now in the National Gallery. But when it came to returning the money he stoutly refused, and produced the picture, which was three-parts finished.

[1] Yriarte, *op. cit.*

" He will certainly finish it now," wrote Alvise to the Marchesa, " because of his great poverty—*per essere lui miserrimo*," a strange statement on the part of so renowned and industrious a painter, who was, moreover, in receipt of a considerable pension from the State. However, Messer Alvise's courteous phrases, and, yet more, the prospect of having her picture, produced a softening effect on the Marchesa's temper, and a humble letter which Giovanni himself sent her on the 2nd of July, satisfied her offended dignity, and induced her to overlook the past :—

" Most illustrious Excellency,—If I have been slow to satisfy the wish of Your Highness, which was no less my own, and you have found it tedious to wait so long for the promised picture, I beg your pardon on bended knees, praying you of your wonted kindness to attribute this delay to my innumerable occupations, and not to any forgetfulness of Your Excellency's orders, which are graven in my heart continually, since I am your most devoted servant ; and I pray God that if I have not satisfied Your Highness in point of time, you may at least be content with the work, and if this does not satisfy your great wisdom and experience, you will ascribe my failure to the weakness of my own poor powers.— Humbly commending myself to Your Excellency, your most humble servant, JOHANNES BELLINUS, *pictor*."[1]   Venice, July 2, 1504.

Four days afterwards, Lorenzo da Pavia was able to inform his mistress that the picture was at length completed, and, better still, that it was a beautiful work of art, fully worthy of the grand old master's fame.

[1] Braghirolli, *op. cit.*

" Most illustrious and excellent Madonna,—I have been to Zuan Bellini several times with the Magnifico Alvise Marcello to ask for the return of the money without being able to effect anything, but this morning I went back and saw the picture, which is really finished and wants nothing. And it is indeed a beautiful thing, even finer than I could have expected, and will, I am sure, please Your Excellency. The painter has made a great effort to do himself honour, chiefly out of respect to M. Andrea Mantegna, and although it is true that in point of invention it cannot compare with the work of Messer Andrea, that most excellent master, I pray Your Excellency to take the picture, both for your own honour and also because of the merit of the work. He need not lose his money, in any case, for I have found a purchaser who will give me the money for you, but I will do nothing until I hear from you, and perhaps it may not come to anything. Although the said Zuan Bellini has behaved so badly that he could not possibly have acted worse, his excuses are not altogether without reason, and Your Highness must accept his excellence and forget his ill conduct. And I say this because his works are among the finest in Italy, and all the more because he is growing old and will only become feebler. If you wish it, he will have a most beautiful frame made for the picture, and take its measurements before we send it to you.—Your LORENZO DA PAVIA."[1] Venice, July 6.

No sooner did Isabella receive Lorenzo's letter than, full of joy at the prospect of receiving her picture, she wrote off to the old painter, graciously

[1] Braghirolli, *op. cit.*

assuring him of her willingness to forgive the past and accept his work.

"Messer Zuan Bellini,—If the picture which you have painted for us agrees, as we believe and hope, with your fame, we shall be satisfied, and are ready to forgive you the wrong which your long delays have caused us. Therefore, I beg you to give the canvas to Lorenzo da Pavia, who will pay you the 25 ducats that are still owing, and we pray you to pack it in such a manner that it may be brought here conveniently, and without risk. If we can oblige you in any way we will do so gladly, when we have seen if you have served us well." Mantua, July 9, 1504.

At the same time she sent these few lines to Lorenzo: "Since Zuan Bellini has finished the picture, and it is as beautiful as you tell us, we are willing to take it and send you the 25 ducats remaining to complete the payment, by our secretary, Battista Scalona. Please have it packed so that it can travel safely, and give it to Scalona."[1]

The faithful Lorenzo sent off the picture with a deep sense of relief, but not without some feeling of alarm. "It seems to me," he wrote on the 16th of July, "that a thousand years will elapse before I hear how you like this picture. Certainly it is a beautiful work, although I confess, if I had ordered it, I should have preferred the figures to have been larger. And, as I said before, in point of invention no one can rival Andrea Mantegna, who is indeed a most excellent painter, the foremost of our age. But Zuan Bellini excels in colouring, and all who have

[1] Braghirolli, *op. cit.*

seen this little picture think it admirable; and it is very highly finished, and will bear close inspection." But his fears proved groundless, and Isabella expressed the greatest delight and admiration for the picture. "I am indeed glad," wrote Lorenzo, "that the painting pleases Your Excellency, and this news has given me the most lively pleasure. It is a very fine work, but I still think the figures are too small. The mistake lay in not asking the painter for two or three drawings or sketches from which a choice could be made. But no one ever mentioned this to me, and Bellini would never let me see his work, or I might have made some objection to the size. If the picture could speak, it might complain of being painted in so narrow a space."[1]

Isabella, however, had no fault to find, and kept Giovanni Bellini's Nativity to her dying day among her most cherished treasures. But it disappeared with so many other precious works after the sack of Mantua, and the last mention we find of it is in the inventory of 1627, where it is described as—"A picture of about three *braccia* long, by Giovanni Bellini, with a Blessed Virgin, the Child, St. John the Baptist, St. Jerome, and St. Katherine, on panel."[2]

The best proof that we have of Isabella's satisfaction with Bellini's painting is the fact that before a year was over she once more renewed her request that he would paint a *Storia* for her Camerino. This time she had recourse to a powerful ally in the person of Pietro Bembo, who, as we have already seen, paid a visit to Mantua in June 1505, and

[1] Yriarte, *op. cit.*
[2] D'Arco, *Arte e Artefici di Mantova,* ii. 188.

promised to use his influence with Bellini to induce him to paint a *Storia* to match the paintings of the Grotta, by Mantegna and Perugino. The accomplished scholar was intimate with the grand old master, who had lately painted a beautiful portrait of his mistress, and on his return to Venice lost no time in fulfilling his errand. On the 27th of August, he wrote to Isabella :—

"I send Your Illustrious Signory many thanks for your messages to me by M. Zuan Francesco Valerio, which show me—what is more precious to me than anything else in the world — that you remember I am your good servant. I have not forgotten that I promised, if possible, to induce Zuan Bellini to paint a picture for your Camerino, in which matter I have been greatly helped by M. Paolo Zoppo, a loyal servant of Your Highness, and a dear friend of Bellini. In fact, we have stormed the castle with so much vigour that I believe it will shortly surrender. All that we now require to make the victory complete is that Your Excellency should write a warm letter to the master, begging him to oblige you, and if you send it to me, you may be sure it will not have been written in vain. Since I left you, I have been so busy that I have nothing new to send, so you must pardon me if this letter is empty. I kiss your hands and commend myself to my honoured lady, Alda Boiarda.—Your servant, PIETRO BEMBO."[1]

Isabella was ill with fever when this letter reached her, but as soon as she recovered she employed Capilupi to write the following letter to Bellini :—

"Messer Joanne,—You will no doubt remember

[1] Gaye, *Carteggio,* ii. 76.

how greatly we desired to have a painted *Storia* from
your hand to hang near those of your brother-in-law,
Mantegna, and how earnestly we formerly begged
you to gratify our wish.   But since, by reason of
your numerous engagements, you were unable to
gratify us, we were content to accept, instead of the
Storia, a Nativity, which pleased us greatly, and is
as dear to us as any picture we possess.   But the
Magnifico Pietro Bembo, when he was here a few
months ago, heard of this our great desire, and gave
us hopes that it might be gratified, since he believed
that many of the works upon which you were engaged are now finished, and, knowing the sweetness
of your nature and your readiness to oblige all men,
more especially persons in authority, he assured us
that you might be willing to satisfy us.   Since then,
however, we have been constantly ill with fever, and
unable to attend to business, but now that we are in
better health we write to ask if you will paint this
picture, and choose the poetic invention yourself, if
you do not wish us to give it to you.   And, besides
giving you full and honourable payment, we shall
remain under eternal obligations to you.   When
we hear that you agree to this, we will send you
the measure of the canvas and the earnest money."
Mantua, October 19, 1505.

Bellini replied before long, expressing his readiness
to undertake the work, and on the 7th of November,
the Marchesa wrote to thank him :—

   " We are very happy to hear that you are willing
to satisfy our intense desire, and paint the picture
about which we wrote lately.   Nothing will please
us more than to have a work from your hand.   We
will have the measurements taken, and will send you

particulars of the lighting, according to the place where the picture is to hang. And since the Magnifico Pietro Bembo is soon returning to Venice, and has seen the pictures in our Grotta, he will be able to decide on the subject with you. We will then send you the earnest money, and beg you to persevere in your present kindly intention towards us. Meanwhile, farewell." [1]

On the 20th, Bembo, who had been absent from Venice for some weeks, wrote to the Marchesa: "Having just returned from the March, where I spent some time, I find Your Signory's letters on the subject of Bellini's picture, in answer to mine, which are already old. And I also hear that M. Paolo Zoppo and M. Lorenzo da Pavia, both of them good servants of Your Highness, have been diligent in my absence. But to-day I have been to see Zuan Bellini, and find that he has firmly resolved to gratify your wish, which I am sure he will do admirably. He only awaits your answer as to the size and lighting of the picture."

Lorenzo, who now appears on the scene again, had lately returned from a visit to the Court of Urbino, where the good Duchess Elisabetta had given him a warm welcome, and had shown him the beauties and treasures of the ducal palace. But the negotiations with Giovanni Bellini, far from being ended, were, as he knew by experience, only just beginning. Meanwhile, news reached Venice of Isabella's illness, and of the birth of her son Ercole, and Bembo hastened to send the illustrious lady condolences on her prolonged sickness and congratulations on her happy deliverance.

[1] Gaye, *op. cit.*, p. 80, &c.; C. Yriarte, *Gazette*, &c., 1896.

On the 2nd of December, the Marchesa dictated the following letter to her secretary, Capilupi:—

"Magnifico Messer Pietro,—We were glad to hear from the letter of Your Magnificence that you had reached Venice safely, and feel sure that, as you grieved over our sickness, so you will have rejoiced over the fortunate birth of our son, since we are persuaded that you love us with the same fraternal affection that we feel for you. We thank you sincerely for your good offices with Bellini, and beg you to keep an eye upon him until we are able to leave our bed, and send him the necessary directions for the size and lighting of the picture. At present you might remind him to finish any other works upon which he is engaged, in order that, after the Christmas festival, he may be able to attend to our affairs without distraction. I hope Your Magnificence will not object to choosing the subject of a *fantasia* which may satisfy Bellini. Since you have seen the other pictures in our Camerino, you will know what is most appropriate, and will be able to choose a graceful theme of new and different meaning. You can, we repeat, do us no greater pleasure than this, of which we shall ever remain mindful, and, as before, most ready to serve you." [1]

On the 1st of January 1506,[2] Bembo replied: "Bellini, whom I have seen several times of late, is excellently disposed towards Your Excellency, and is only awaiting the measurements of the canvas to begin work. But the invention, which you tell me I am to choose for the picture, must be adapted to

---

[1] V. Cian, *Un Decennio nella Vita di P. Bembo*, p. 218.

[2] This letter is dated 1505 in D'Arco and Gaye. It should be 1505 O.S., *i.e.* 1506.

the painter's fancy. He does not care to have his imagination fettered by innumerable instructions, but prefers to arrange his composition according to his own ideas, being confident that in this way he can produce the best effect. All the same, I will endeavour to meet your wishes as well as his own."

In return, Pietro begs this gracious lady to do him a great favour. A certain kinsman and very dear friend of his, a man of great parts and excellent learning, Messer Francesco Cornaro (or, as he chose to Latinise his name, Cornelio), " being, like all noble and gentle souls, passionately fond of rare things," had engaged Messer Andrea Mantegna to paint some canvases for him, at the price of 150 ducats, 25 of which he paid down when he sent the measurements. "Now he tells me," continued Bembo, "that M. Andrea refuses to go on with the work without asking a much larger sum, which seems to M. Francesco the strangest thing in the world, especially as he possesses letters from M. Andrea in which he himself fixed this price. I therefore beg and implore Your Signory to persuade M. Andrea to keep faith with M. Francesco, and begin his pictures, since he who is called the Mantegna of the world ought above all men to keep (*mantenere*) his promises. . . . M. Francesco does not care about one or two hundred ducats—thank God, he has them in abundance; but he does not like to be lightly esteemed and mocked at, and, if Your Excellency thinks Mantegna's work is deserving of a higher reward, is perfectly ready to accept your decision. . . . I hope also that Messer Andrea's well-known courtesy and *gentilezza* will not render Your Excellency's task difficult, and I promise you that M. Francesco will gratefully repay

all that you do for him with M. Andrea, by helping
on your business with M. Zuan Bellini, over whom
he has great influence, and will, as well as myself,
remain most deeply obliged to Your Most Illustrious Excellency."[1]

The picture in question was the noble Triumph of
Scipio, now in the National Gallery, which was still
in Mantegna's shop at the time of his death, eight
months later.

Isabella replied to this letter of Bembo on the
31st of January: "We are delighted to hear that
Bellini is going to do the picture, and recognise
that this is owing to Your Magnificence. We will
find out the particulars of the size and the lighting,
and will send them to you, together with the earnest
money. Meanwhile we beg you earnestly to settle
the subject with the painter. M. Andrea Mantegna
has been very dangerously ill these last days. He is
very near his end, and although just now he is a little
better, it is impossible to speak to him of pictures, or
of anything but his health. If he recovers we will
see that the Magnificent Francesco Cornelio receives
satisfaction."[2]

But a series of unexpected interruptions interfered
with the execution of Isabella's plans. In March, she
paid her first visit to Florence, and the sudden outbreak of plague on her return compelled her to leave
Mantua in haste and take refuge with her children
and servants in her villa of Sacchetta. On the 11th
of May,[3] she wrote to Bembo, regretting that owing
to her hurried departure from the Castello, and the
disturbance caused by this terrible visitation, she had

[1] Gaye, *op. cit.*, pp. 71–73. [2] Yriarte, *op. cit.*
[3] V. Cian in *Giorn. St. d. Lett. It.*, vol. ix.

been unable to send the measurements of Bellini's
picture, but hoped to do this as soon as the plague
abated, and begged him in the meantime to compose
the *poesia* and keep the painter in the same excellent
dispositions. Meanwhile, she had heard from Lorenzo
da Pavia of the death of his friend, the accomplished
Michele Vianello, who had served her so loyally and
well in her former negotiations with Bellini. The
cabinetto of this refined collector, with all its priceless
contents, was shortly to be sold by auction, and
Isabella was especially anxious to acquire a rare agate
vase, and a picture of the Passage of the Red Sea
and the Destruction of Pharaoh, by the Flemish
artist Van Eyck, or, as she calls him, John of Bruges.
She lost no time in acquainting Bembo with her
wishes, and once more begged his assistance. " I
have reverently received Your Most Illustrious
Excellency's letter," wrote Messer Pietro on the
13th of May, " and understand that you wish to
buy the agate vase and Destruction of Pharaoh
which belonged to Vianello. I will see Taddeo
Albano and Lorenzo da Pavia, and will endeavour
to satisfy Your Excellency, as is my bounden duty.
As for Bellini, I will not fail to obey you. I was
very sorry to hear of the plague at Mantua, which
deprived me of the pleasure of paying my respects
to Your Highness this Easter, which was, I confess,
the chief object of my journey." [1]

A prolonged correspondence on the subject of
Vianello's sale took place between the Marchesa and
Lorenzo da Pavia, and Isabella sought the help of
all her friends in Venice to attain the desired end.
On the day of the sale, Messer Michele's palace was

[1] Gaye, *op. cit.*, p. 82.

crowded with the most distinguished collectors in
Venice, and the utmost excitement prevailed when,
after a fierce struggle with Messer Andrea Loredano,
the picture by John of Bruges was knocked down to
Lorenzo da Pavia for the large sum of 115 ducats.
" I was in an agony of fear," writes the excellent
Lorenzo, " and should have felt happier if it had been
a little less." [1] Money was very scarce, as he knew,
just then at Mantua. All Isabella's jewels were
pledged, and she found it difficult to meet her
current expenses, but she managed to borrow the
money from her good friend, the banker Albano,
and wrote joyously to tell her favourite sculptor,
Cristoforo Romano, of the new treasures which she
had secured.[2]

Soon afterwards Pietro Bembo left Venice for
Urbino, and we hear no more of his *poesia* or of Zuan
Bellini's picture. Only in a letter of the 9th of
January 1507,[3] Lorenzo da Pavia remarks: " I learn
by Your Signory's letter that you are very impatient
to have the viol of ebony and sandal-wood, and feel
quite ashamed by my own delays. I seem to have
caught Messer Zuan Bellini's malady! " But, in his
defence, let it be remembered that the old painter
was over eighty years of age.

[1] A. Baschet, *Alde Manuce.*

[2] A. Venturi, *Cristoforo Romano, Archivio dell' Arte,* i. 151.

[3] C. Yriarte, *Gazette d. B. Arts,* 1896.

CHAPTER XX

1504—1512

Mantegna's last works for Isabella d'Este—His illness and debts
—He appeals to Isabella for help, and sells her his antique
bust of Faustina—Calandra's description of Comus—Death of
Mantegna and tribute of Lorenzo da Pavia—Pictures in
Andrea's workshop—The Comus finished by Lorenzo Costa—
Letters of Antonio Galeazzo Bentivoglio to Isabella—The
Triumph of Poetry or Court of Isabella—Costa's portrait of
the Marchesa—Francia paints the portrait of her son Federico
and her own—Correspondence on the subject with Casio and
Lucrezia Bentivoglio—Death of Giorgione.

THE year in which Isabella d'Este made a last attempt
to obtain a picture for her studio from the aged
Bellini was also that of Mantegna's death. His
health had long been failing, and when, in April
1505, he implored Isabella's good offices on behalf of
his son, who had incurred the Marquis's displeasure,
and been banished from Mantua, his feeble state of
mind excited the Marchesa's deepest compassion.

" M. Andrea Mantegna came to recommend his
son to me," she wrote to her lord on the 1st of April,
" looking all tearful and agitated, and with so sunken
a face that he seemed to me more dead than alive.
The sight filled me with so much compassion that I
could not refuse to beg Your Excellency to restore
his son to him with your usual goodness, for, gravely
as he has sinned against you, the long service, incomparable excellence, and rare merits of M. Andrea

CASTELLO DI MANTOVA

To face p. 362, vol. i

claim this favour on behalf of his rebellious son. If
we wish him to live and to finish our work Your
Excellency must gratify him, or else we shall soon lose
him, and he will die, rather of grief than of old age;
so I recommend him with all my heart to your good
graces.—Your wife, ISABELLA, with her own hand."[1]

The Marquis, however, absolutely refused to pardon Francesco Mantegna, saying that he had insulted
the best of his servants, and in spite of his pretences
was in reality the most irreligious man in the world!
Finally, he desired Isabella to tell M. Andrea that,
greatly as the Marquis would always honour him,
his son was unworthy of receiving any favour at
his hands.[2] More than a year passed before Francesco was allowed to return to Mantua and to resume
his labours in the palace of S. Sebastiano. Meanwhile, Andrea, as we have seen from Isabella's letter
to Bembo[3] in January 1506, fell dangerously ill, and
for some days was not expected to live. He recovered,
however, but his son's misconduct and the pecuniary
difficulties in which he found himself weighed heavily
upon his mind, and the sad words which he inscribed
on his last picture, the St. Sebastian of the Franchetti
collection, bear witness to the deep gloom which had
settled on his soul: *Nil nisi divinum stabile est ;
cœtera fumus*—"Nothing but the Divine endures;
the rest is smoke." In his distress the old master
turned to Isabella, and addressed the following letter
to the Princess, who had always proved his best and
kindest friend :—

" Dear and illustrious Lady,—Accept, I pray Your

[1] D'Arco, *op. cit.*, ii. 58.
[2] Kristeller, "Andrea Mantegna," App., Doc. 73.
[3] See p. 359.

Excellency, my humblest and most sincere recommendations to your favour. I feel myself by the grace of God somewhat better, and although I have not yet recovered the full use of my limbs, yet the little talent which God gave me is still undiminished, and is, as ever, at the command of Your Excellency. I have almost finished the drawing of the *Storia* of Comus for Your Excellency, and hope to go on with it as my fancy is able to help me. *Illustrissima Madonna mia*, I commend myself to you, because for many months past I have not been able to obtain a farthing, and am in great need, and feel myself sorely embarrassed, since, never expecting these bad times, and being desirous not to remain a vagabond on the face of the earth, I had bought a house for the price of 340 ducats, payable in three instalments. Now the first term is ended, and I am pressed on all sides by creditors, and, as Your Excellency knows, I can neither sell nor mortgage anything now, and I have many other debts ; so it has come into my mind to help myself as best I can by parting from my dearest possessions, and, since I have been often asked at different times, and by many persons of note, to sell my dear Faustina of antique marble. Necessity, which compels us to do many things, prompts me to write to Your Excellency on the subject, since, if I must part from it, I would rather you should have it than any other lord or lady in the world. The price is 100 ducats, which I might have had many times over from great masters ; and I beg of you to let me know your intentions, and commend myself infinite times to Your Excellency.—Your servant, ANDREAS MANTINIA." [1]

[1] D'Arco, *Arte e Artefici*, ii. 61.

To this piteous appeal Isabella returned no answer. Her time and thoughts were fully occupied, and she was not even able to send Bellini the measurements of the picture, which she was so anxious to obtain. Then came her visit to Florence and the sudden outbreak of the plague. After that she was reduced to dire straits for want of money, and may well have found it difficult to give Messer Andrea the hundred ducats for his beloved Faustina. But as soon as the plague began to abate she sent the son of her old Castellan, Gian Giacomo Calandra, from Sacchetta to pay the painter a visit and inquire about his antique bust, which she coveted greatly, but could not afford to buy at so high a price.

"This morning," writes Calandra, "I visited Mantegna in Your Excellency's name, and found him full of complaints on his sufferings and needs, which have compelled him to mortgage his property for 60 ducats, besides having many other debts. But he still refuses to reduce the price of his Faustina, and hopes to get it. I pointed out that this was hardly the time for any one to lay out so large a sum, and it comes to this: he would rather keep the marble than let it go for less than 100 ducats, but if great want should compel him to lower the price, he will let Your Highness know. This he promised me faithfully. But if he finds a purchaser who will give 100 ducats, since you cannot give that, he will let it go without writing to you again. I do not see that he has any hope of selling it at this price, unless it is to Monsignore the Bishop [Louis Gonzaga, Bishop of Mantua, and uncle of the Marquis], who is fond of these things and spends largely. But I think he hoped to excite the jealousy of Your Excellency by

the thought of another customer, and so I feel bound
to tell you this.   Afterwards he begged me to entreat
Your Highness to advance some money to supply his
needs, that he might be able to work better at his picture of the God Comus.   I did not fail to make ample
excuses, but promised that I would tell you this, as
I do now.   I asked to see his picture, in which he
has drawn these figures : the God Comus, two Venuses
(one draped and the other nude), two Loves, Janus
with Envy on his arm pushing her out, Mercury, and
three other figures, who are put to flight by him.
The others are still wanting, but the drawing of
these is most beautiful.   I must tell you that he is
hurt at your not having answered his letter, and he
said with a smile that perhaps it was out of shame
because you could not help him in his present
necessities.   And, indeed, it seemed to me that he
quite understood my excuses.   As to your reply to
his letter, I told him that Your Excellency did him
quite as much honour by sending her servant in
person as by writing to him, and that, if you did not
show him the courtesy and liberality which his talents
deserved, you had no reason to be ashamed, since the
state of the country was a more than sufficient excuse.
I have written this to Your Highness, because it
seems to me that a letter from you would console
him, if you would write without taking any notice of
his resentment.   If you are not satisfied with what I
have done in the matter, I beg you to forgive me,
for I have done what I could, and I kiss your hands
humbly.—Your faithful servant, Jo. Jac. CALANDRA."
Mantua, July 15, 1506.

Isabella now desired Calandra to send the bust by
boat across the lake to Sacchetta, and promised to

let Andrea know her decision as soon as she had seen it. On the 1st of August, Gian Giacomo wrote as follows :—

"Your Highness will have heard from Capilupi that I received the Faustina from M. Andrea Mantegna, who, although he gave it me into my hands without any conditions, and was very willing to gratify your wish, yet did this with great ceremony, and entrusted the marble to me with repeated injunctions, and many signs of jealous affection, so much so that if six days were to expire without his seeing it again, I am almost certain that he would die. Although I have not said a word about the price, he himself repeated that he would not take less than 100 ducats, begging your pardon for this his pertinacity, but declaring that, unless he were compelled by necessity, he would not part from it for much more. I am sorry I could not send it by to-day's boat, and perhaps six days may elapse before another boat starts, but Your Signory will let me know if you wish it to be sent by messenger."[1]

Immediately on receiving the precious bust, Isabella wrote to tell Mantegna that she would keep it, and give him the price which he asked.

"M. Andrea,—We have received your head of Faustina, which pleases us, and which we desire to have for the price which you ask, for, even if it were not worth the 100 ducats, we should be glad to give it you for your pleasure and convenience. But since, owing to the disturbance caused by the plague, we have no ready money, we are sending you our servant Cusatro to make arrangements which may meet your needs and our own, because he can tell

[1] D'Arco, op. cit., ii. 66.

you what we are able to do, and we will not fail to do whatever he promises. We beg you to be content to settle the matter with Cusatro, and shall be content to abide by whatever you and he may decide. We will keep the head until Cusatro returns, and, if you do not agree to his terms, will return it at once." Sacchetta, August 4, 1506.

The result of Cusatro's interview with the painter was that the Marchesa agreed to be responsible for 100 ducats which he owed to his chief creditor. Immediately after her servant's return to Sacchetta, Isabella hastened to set the old man's mind at rest on the subject.

"M. Andrea,—We sent for Hieronimo Bosio, your creditor, and, according to the arrangement which you made with Cusatro, we came to an agreement as to the 100 ducats, which he will be content to take from us. So you need have no further anxiety on the subject, and whenever you wish it we will pay these 100 ducats, which will be given to him, and paid by us for the Faustina. Of the remaining 27 ducats which you still owe, Hieronimo cannot dispose, because they are due to his brother Alessandro, and we have not at present the means of paying the money, which we would gladly do, as earnest money for the picture which you are painting for us, and in order to give you ease and peace of mind. But you will excuse us, because you know the extreme difficulty that we have in finding money at the present time."[1] Sacchetta, August 7.

Isabella, it is clear, was genuinely anxious to deal kindly by the old painter, whose great services she

[1] Kristeller, *op. cit.*, App., Doc. 79 and 80.

fully appreciated, although in her passion for enriching her studio she did not scruple to deprive him of his beloved Faustina. As Calandra had prophesied, he did not long survive the loss of his treasured marble. Six weeks afterwards he died, on Sunday the 13th of August, and Francesco Mantegna, the son who had caused him so much sorrow, wrote to inform his patron, the Marquis, of his death, telling him that with his dying breath his father had asked for His Excellency, lamenting his lord's absence, and had sent him a last message. "We are sure," he adds, "that Your Excellency, who always rewards his true servants generously, will not forget the fifty years' service rendered you by such a man, and will help us in our present loss and sorrow."[1]

On the following day the news of Mantegna's death reached Venice, and, in a brief note to Isabella, that true artist, Lorenzo da Pavia, paid a noble tribute to the great painter: "I am much grieved to hear of the death of our Messer Andrea Mantegna. For, indeed, we have lost a most excellent man and a second Apelles, but I believe that the Lord God will employ him to make some beautiful work. As for me, I can never hope to see again a finer draughtsman and more original artist. Farewell.—Your servant, LORENZO DA PAVIA in Venecia."[2] October 16, 1506.

The great master had no truer epitaph.

Isabella's reply was brief but sincere: "Lorenzo,— We were sure that you would grieve over the death of M. Andrea Mantegna, for, as you say, a great light has gone out."[3]

---

[1] D'Arco, *op. cit.*, ii. 67.

[2] Armand Baschet, *op. cit.*, p. 47.

[3] Kristeller, *op. cit.*, App., Doc. 84.

The Marchesa's interest in Mantegna's family did not cease with his death, and through her influence his son was allowed to retain his house in the Borgo Pradella. In November 1507, Lodovico Mantegna wrote begging her to help him to recover certain moneys, which Cardinal Sigismondo had granted the brothers on the tolls in payment of the pictures which he had kept, so that they might be able to defray the expenses of their father's funeral and of their own mourning. Two years afterwards Lodovico died, and Francesco, after trying to kill his widowed sister-in-law, and seize his nephew's patrimony, applied to Elisabetta of Urbino for redress, declaring that he had been cruelly defrauded by the corruption and malignity of legal officers. The kind Duchess wrote in touching terms to her brother, the Marquis, begging him to repair the supposed injustice which had been done to Mantegna's son—"for the sake of the more than ordinary love which I bore to Messer Andrea, who, as Your Excellency knows, was a man of rare genius and most devoted to our house. Truly," she goes on, "this love that we bore him in life, did not end with his death, but also extended to his son Francesco, for whom I am inclined to cherish the greatest devotion, because he is now Messer Andrea's only surviving son."[1] But Francesco's real character was too well known at Mantua for the Marquis to attend to his complaints, and, in spite of Elisabetta's intercession, he never recovered his patron's favour.

Among the works that remained in Mantegna's workshop at the time of his death were the so-called Triumph of Scipio, which had been ordered by

[1] D'Arco, *op. cit.*, ii. 77.

Francesco Cornaro, and the famous *Cristo in scurto,*
or foreshortened Christ, from which the painter would
never part in his life-time. Both of these were retained by Cardinal Sigismondo Gonzaga, while a
third, the imposing St. Sebastian, now belonging to
Baron Franchetti of Venice, became the property
of Bishop Louis Gonzaga. After that art-loving
prelate's death in 1511, this noble work passed into
the hands of Cardinal Bembo, in whose house at
Padua Marco Antonio Michiel saw it. But no
mention was made of the unfinished Comus, which
had evidently been ordered by Isabella for her
studio, and now passed into her hands. A few
months afterwards she employed the Ferrarese artist,
Lorenzo Costa, who settled at Mantua in November
1506, and succeeded Mantegna as court painter, to
finish this *Storia,* which in style and subject agrees
exactly with the works which Mantegna, Perugino,
and Costa himself had already painted for her Grotta.
The group of Janus and Envy and Mercury driving
out three figures of the Vices on the right, agrees
exactly with Calandra's description, while the word
Comes is inscribed on the triumphal arch which occupies a prominent place in the picture. In the inventory of 1542, this painting is described as being " by the
hand of M. Lorenzo Costa, and containing a triumphal
arch and many figures making music, together with
a fable of Leda." The real title of the *Storia,* it is
plain, was the Triumph of Music, in the person of
the mirth-loving Comus, the god of musical inspiration, who is here seen leading the joyous Bacchic
train, while Orpheus and Arion are both introduced

[1] This has been convincingly shown by Dr. Kristeller, *op. cit.,*
p. 358.

in the foreground of the picture. The subject was no doubt chosen by Paride da Ceresara, at Isabella's suggestion, to form the companion picture of the Triumph of Poetry, which Lorenzo Costa had already painted at Bologna.

During the summer of 1504, when Isabella was moving heaven and earth to obtain painted allegories for her studio from Giovanni Bellini and Perugino, she received a visit from the Protonotary, Messer Antonio Galeazzo Bentivoglio, a brother-in-law of her sister Lucrezia d'Este, and displayed the treasures of the Grotta before his admiring eyes. This courtly prelate, whose portrait Francia has introduced in a well-known Nativity, promised to ask the painter, Lorenzo Costa, who had been long settled at Bologna, to undertake a picture for the Marchesa's studio, and soon after his return, wrote to inform her that Costa would gladly execute her commission, and paint any *fantasia* which she might choose.

Isabella wrote off without a moment's delay to Paride da Ceresara, who had already supplied Perugino and Bellini with *fantasie* at her request, begging him to invent a composition similar to those which had not yet been executed by these dilatory masters.

"I really do not know," she remarks, "which of us two suffers the most from the interminable delays of these painters—I who see no end to the decoration of my Camerino, and you who are every day required to supply new compositions, which these wayward masters either refuse to execute or else render inaccurately. We have, therefore, decided to employ some new painters, so that we may be able to complete the work within a fixed period."[1]

[1] C. Yriarte, *Gazette d. B. Arts,* 1896.

Five days later, the Marchesa received the poet's composition, which seemed to her perfect of its kind. "If only," she exclaimed with a sigh, "painters were as rapid as poets!" On the 27th of November, she forwarded Paride's instructions to Bologna, together with threads, giving the length and breadth of the picture, enclosed in a sealed packet, and a sketch of the composition, "because," as she remarked, "words do not always express our whole meaning." In conclusion, she promised to send the earnest money, and begged Messer Antonio, who understood drawing well, to see that the painter began the picture at once, and did not drag on his work after the fashion of Perugino and Bellini.

The courteous Protonotary hastened to satisfy her on these points. "As soon as I received the letter by your courier," he wrote on the 1st of December, " I sent for the painter, who was greatly pleased with Your Excellency's *fantasia*, and says that he will execute it in his own way, omitting nothing, but improving the composition. I feel sure that he will satisfy you thoroughly, because he works with his whole heart. Afterwards, in speaking of the lighting, I told him that the painting was to hang in the place where Your Excellency showed me, that, as far as I could recollect, the light would fall in the opposite direction, and that I thought Messer Andrea's picture was varnished, which surprised him, as it was painted on canvas. Will you, therefore, kindly tell me if M. Andrea's picture is varnished or not, and send me the precise size of the figures, so that the painter may see that his work corresponds in all respects with the neighbouring pictures? As soon as the painter receives this information, and all things necessary are ready,

he will begin work, and I will see, as I promised, that
Your Excellency is well and promptly served, and
that you are not made to wait as interminably as you
were by your other artists. . . . When once the picture is begun, and seems to be likely to answer our
expectations, I will let you know for your own satisfaction, but not to remind you of the price, for there
must be no mention of money between us, since I
wish Your Excellency kindly to accept the painting
for my sake, and you may rest assured that it will be
well and speedily finished. I wish for nothing in
exchange, but that you would be kind to Violante,
who is always in my thoughts, so much so that I
shall be forced to come and spend ten days with you
next carnival.—Your servant and kinsman, ANT.
GAL. BENTIVOLUS."[1]   Bologna, December 1, 1504.

Violante was the Protonotary's young niece, a
daughter of Alessandro Bentivoglio and Ippolita
Sforza, whom Isabella treated with great kindness,
and who eventually married Gianpaolo Sforza, Marquis of Caravaggio, and is often mentioned in
Bandello's novels.

The Marchesa replied to this letter without delay,
and sent the painter full directions, repeating her
anxiety that Costa's painting " might not suffer from
the baneful influence of that fatal constellation which
seems to have presided over the execution of the other
pictures in my poor Camerino."[2]

Unfortunately, that winter Costa fell seriously ill,
and was at the point of death, as M. Antonio told
the Marchesa in April, so that he was quite unable
to begin the picture. By August, however, it was

[1] Luzio in *Emporium*, 1900, p. 359.
[2] Yriarte, *op. cit.*

well advanced, and Isabella's constant correspondent, the poet Casio, informed her that it would be ready before Christmas, and would, he felt sure, please her exceedingly. But early in the following January, the Protonotary wrote again to the Marchesa, apologising for the painter's delay in finishing her picture, which would have been ready before this if his father, Giovanni Bentivoglio, had not employed Costa to adorn the new mortuary chapel of St. Cecilia.[1] Lorenzo's fresco of the saint distributing her goods to the poor in this chapel bears the date of 1506, and can only have been finished a few months before the Bentivogli were driven out of Bologna by Pope Julius II. Before that time, no doubt Isabella had received her picture safely, and may indeed have taken it back with her when she passed through Bologna that spring on her return from Florence. Costa's work hung in the studio of the Grotta on the same wall as Mantegna's allegories, and is described in the inventory of 1542 as " a picture by the hand of the late Messer Lorenzo Costa, painter, with many figures and trees and a Coronation." The exact subject is not easy to determine, but there seems little doubt that the Triumph of Poetry was the theme assigned to the artist, and that Costa, being, as Mario Equicola tells us, as amiable a courtier as he was excellent a painter, dexterously contrived to pay a compliment to the Marchesa[2] by representing her as Queen of the realm of song. A winged boy seated on the lap of the Muse of Poetry is in the act of placing a laurel crown on Isabella's brow, as she presides over her court, surrounded by poets who

---

[1] A. Venturi, *Archivio St. d. Arte*, i. 249.
[2] C. Yriarte, *op. cit.*

pour out their deathless lays, and fair maidens playing the lutes under shady groves. In the foreground
young girls are seen wreathing the ox and the lamb
with flowers, while in the distance armed cavaliers
recall the exploits which live in immortal verse. The
knight in the foreground, who has slain the hydra at
his feet, has been supposed to represent Baldassarre
Castiglione, but more probably wears the features
of Isabella's brother-in-law, Annibale Bentivoglio, or
the courtly Protonotary himself. The fair landscape,
with the distant hills and blue river, winding its
way between grassy banks and woodland glades,
supplies a charming setting for these gallant knights
and lovely maidens, and the whole is conceived
and painted in Costa's most graceful and attractive
manner.

That Isabella was well satisfied with the picture
may be gathered from the fact that when the Bentivogli were expelled from Bologna she invited Costa
to come and take Mantegna's place at her court.
"Tell the painter Costa," she wrote to her friend
Casio, on the 16th of November 1506, only five
days after the Pope's triumphal entry into Bologna,
"that if he likes to come here we shall be very glad
to see him."[1]

By the end of the month, Lorenzo was settled
at Mantua, where the Marquis employed him to continue the decorations of his palace at St. Sebastian,
which Mantegna had left unfinished. He received a
yearly pension of 669 lire, 10 soldi, and in 1509 the
Marquis gave him 1200 ducats, as well as a house and
250 acres of land at Revere, and granted him the
privilege of a citizen of Mantua in a deed drawn up in

[1] Gruyer, *L'Art à la Cour de Ferrare*, ii. 209.

the most flattering terms. Costa remained at Mantua
to the end of his life, and enjoyed the favour of
Isabella's husband and son until, in 1535, he died of
fever at the age of seventy-five, after a few days' illness.[1]
Unfortunately, nothing remains of all the frescoes
with which he adorned the villas of Revere and Marmirolo and Francesco Gonzaga's favourite palace of
St. Sebastian.

In a letter of April 11, 1509, Isabella tells her
husband that Costa is decorating the halls of this
palace, and Vasari describes the portraits of the
Marquis and his three sons, Federico, Ercole, and
Ferrante, assisting at a sacrifice to Hercules, which
he painted at one end of the hall where Mantegna's
Triumphs hung. In another hall he represented
Francesco led by Hercules up the steep and thorny
ways of the mountain of Eternity, and Isabella surrounded by her ladies playing instruments of music.
These figures, Vasari tells us, were all painted from
life, and remind us of that admirable portrait of
Isabella which the Marquis showed his future son-in-
law, Francesco Maria, when he visited the Castello in
August 1508. This work pleased the Marchesa so
much that she wrote from Cavriana begging Calandra
to compose an appropriate distich which might be
inscribed on the picture, and when she went to
Ferrara in the following autumn her brothers were so
anxious to see the portrait that a courier was sent to
Mantua to bring it. The original of this portrait has
disappeared, but, as Dr. Luzio has lately pointed out,[2]
there can be little doubt that the portrait of Isabella
d'Este in the collection of Gonzaga portraits made

---

[1] Gruyer, *op. cit.*, ii. 218.

[2] Luzio in *Emporium*, 1901, p. 435.

by Archduke Ferdinand of Tyrol in 1579, and now in the Vienna Gallery, was copied from Costa's painting, which was then still preserved at Mantua. Although the work of an inferior artist, this picture is of great interest, especially as the way in which Isabella wears her hair, and the shape and striped material of her bodice, bear a marked likeness to Leonardo's drawing.

About the same time that Isabella employed Costa to paint a *Storia* for her studio she entered into correspondence with his more famous friend, the goldsmith-painter, Francia. Francia's fame as the first goldsmith in Italy had spread far beyond his native city, and his name was familiar to the Marchesa, since he had often worked for her family. In 1488, he made a beautiful gold chain of linked hearts for Duchess Leonora, and after Isabella's marriage he sent her a chain of engraved gems, while his name appears on the title-page of the Virgil issued from the Aldine press, as the maker of the famous Italic types first used by the great printer. So, when this distinguished master offered to paint a picture for her studio, she accepted his proposal readily. On the 17th of August, the poet Casio, in writing to inform her of the progress of Costa's picture, begged her to send the drawing for the canvas that Francia was to paint, since he was anxious to set to work, and had declined to accept any other commissions until he heard from the Marchesa. And the writer adds that he has brought the master some fine ultramarine blue from Florence expressly for this purpose.

Probably the frescoes upon which Francia was engaged during the next year in the Chapel of St. Cecilia, and the revolution which took place at

Bologna in 1506, delayed the execution of his work, but we certainly hear no more of Isabella's *Storia* for some time to come. At length, five years later, in December 1510, the painter himself wrote to the Marchesa, saying :—

"Hearing that Your Highness desires a canvas for her Camerino, we await your commands, and will be ready to begin the picture after Christmas, and devote ourselves to the work with all possible diligence, although we shall have to encounter a perilous competition. But Apelles and Parrhasius, we trust, will come to our help.—FRANCIA, *aurifex*." Bologna, December 12, 1510.

A month later he returned to the subject.

"I hear from Girolamo Casio that Your Highness would like me to paint the canvas for your Camerino which was ordered in past years by our mutual friend. I will gladly place my time and powers at Your Excellency's disposal, and if you will send me the canvas as well as the measure and lighting correctly, so that I may not make any mistake, I will begin it immediately, and devote myself to the work with the utmost diligence, so that I may please Your Highness and gain honour myself.—FRANCIA, *aurifex*."[1] Bologna, January 11, 1511.

After this, however, we hear no more of the *Storia*, and the idea was apparently dropped. But we know that about the same time this popular master painted a portrait of Isabella's son Federico, and another of herself, both of which pleased her greatly. The first was executed in July 1510, when the young prince, a boy of ten, was on his way to Rome, where the Venetians required him to re-

[1] C. Yriarte, *op. cit.*

main as a hostage on his father's release. Isabella, anxious to have her darling son's portrait as a consolation in his absence, sent an express to the seneschal Matteo Ippolito, begging him to engage Francia to paint Federico's picture during his short stay at Bologna.

"As soon as Your Excellency's letter reached me," wrote Matteo, on the 29th of July, " I sent for the painter Francia, who gladly undertook to draw Signor Federico's portrait, but fears that he cannot finish it as quickly as you desire. I am sure, however, that when you see the picture it will please you better than anything which you have seen for many a long day. It would be impossible for anything to be more like him than is this sketch. At first the master refused to colour it, saying that he had to make a pair of bards for His Excellency the Duke." This was Francesco Maria, Duke of Urbino, who was then in command of the papal forces at Bologna, and for whom, Vasari tells us, Francia painted a fine set of harness. "So I had to apply to His Excellency, who desired him at once to leave his commission and satisfy Your Highness. As soon as it is ready I will send it to you, and will let you know how much the painter thinks he ought to be paid for this portrait." [1]

The picture reached Mantua safely on the 10th of August, and the enchanted mother wrote to Casio, declaring that it would be impossible to have a better likeness, and expressing her wonder that so perfect and admirable a thing should have been made in so short a time. Since, however, the boy's hair was too fair, she sent the picture back to Casio in November,

[1] A. Bertolotti, *Artisti bolognesi*, p. 33.

begging him to ask Francia to correct this mistake, which he did. Unluckily, just then the Marquis Francesco came to Bologna with the Pope, and was so much delighted with his son's likeness that he insisted on showing it to His Holiness and the Cardinals, and ultimately allowed it to be taken to Rome by a certain Zoan Petro da Cremona, who quite refused to restore it.

"Francia," wrote Casio on the 7th of November, "declared that he would not paint a replica of the portrait for all the gold in the world!"

Isabella was furious at the loss of her precious picture, and wrote so indignantly to Rome on the subject that the missing portrait was returned forthwith. On the 20th of November, Casio took Francia to see Federico, who had come to join the Pope at Bologna, and compare his portrait with the original. The comparison was satisfactory, and both Francia and Casio agreed that it was impossible to improve the picture, which was accordingly sent back to Mantua. Isabella immediately sent Casio 30 ducats, which Francia acknowledged courteously, saying that the execution of Signor Federico's portrait hardly deserved such liberal payment, but that he accepted the money as a gracious present from Her Excellency, and remained her grateful servant for life.[1]

A few months later, when a fresh turn in the tide had brought back the Bentivogli under French protection to Bologna, Lucrezia d'Este begged her half-sister to allow Francia, who had succeeded so well with Federico's likeness, to paint her own portrait. The Marchesa agreed readily, and sent

[1] C. Yriarte, *op. cit.*

Lucrezia a drawing of herself, from which Francia promised to paint the picture, with Madonna Lucrezia's help. This princess declared that Isabella's face was so deeply engraved on her heart that she felt sure she could describe her features, colouring, and expression all perfectly. But the war that was raging at the gates of Bologna, and a tertian ague which attacked the painter, interfered with his good intentions, and, after two unsuccessful attempts, Lucrezia herself had to confess that his portrait was a failure.

" Dear and honoured sister," she wrote on the 7th of September, " I have lately paid constant visits to the house of the painter Francia to see how much his portrait resembled you. To speak frankly. it does not seem to bear you the least likeness, representing you as being thinner and more severe-looking, and altogether different from the picture which my imagination retains of you ; so I have begged the painter, for his honour and my satisfaction, to go to Mantua and see Your Excellency in life, so that his work may really resemble nature. This, however, he refuses to promise, saying that it is too dangerous to venture on a comparison in which chance has more to do than art, as is the case in trying to paint a life-like portrait. But he promises to try once more, and to alter anything that I wish as often as I like, and perhaps by this means he may be able to produce a better likeness, although I fear it cannot really resemble you, since he has not seen you. Meanwhile, I will do my best to persuade him to come to Mantua.—Your most devoted sister, LUCRETIA ESTENSIS."[1]

[1] Luzio in *Emporium*, 1901, pp. 427–430.

Isabella, however, had not the least wish that Francia should come to Mantua. In the first place, as she told Lodovico Sforza many years before, she was quite tired of sitting for her portrait. In the second, she was afraid of exciting the jealousy of her own court painter, Lorenzo Costa.

" I thank you," she wrote to her sister on the 26th of September, " for your kindness in trying to induce Francia to come to Mantua, so as to paint my portrait better, but hope you will not urge him to do this any more, for, to say the truth, I do not care for him to come here on this account, because the last time my portrait was taken the necessity of sitting still and without moving for a long while became so tiresome that I never mean to do it again ; but Your Highness has our image so deeply impressed on her memory that I feel sure she will be able to correct the master's mistakes. And you must also remember that, if we received Francia here, we should not know how to do this without offending Costa, and should find it difficult to retain his friendship."

On receiving this letter, Lucrezia promised not to press the matter further, and told Isabella that her sons' tutor was satisfied that Francia's latest attempt resembled the drawing which had been sent from Mantua, and that it would be still more life-like if he would let her see his picture once or twice before it was finished. On the 25th of October, she wrote triumphantly to tell Isabella that the portrait was quite ready, and met with general approval, although Francia, who evidently was more anxious to produce a fine work of art than a correct likeness of a lady whom he had never seen, had not chosen to consult Madonna Lucrezia again on the subject.

"Our Francia, the foremost goldsmith among painters, and among goldsmiths most illustrious as a painter, yesterday brought me Your Illustrious Signory's portrait, completely finished and placed in a gold frame, to hear my judgment on his work. I praised it greatly, since it seemed to me to deserve high commendation. But if Your Excellency is not wholly satisfied after inspecting it more closely, you must not impute the fault to me, since I only saw it once while he was engaged on the work, although then I certainly tried to describe Your Excellency's appearance to him. But you must blame the painter, who, seeing that his work was superior to the other, did not care to show it to me again, after promising to bring it here many times before it was finished, and to alter anything in it to which I took objection. I must, however, confess that I see little in the portrait that does not satisfy my taste. I hope Your Excellency will say the same, for certainly, if you compare it with the original sketch which was sent from Mantua, it is no less like nature than that one, while it is far more perfect in point of art. All those who know you in this city agree in saying that in Francia's portrait they seem to see your living image, and the most confidential servants of your illustrious lord the Marquis say the same—above all, Scalona, by whom I send this letter. So I conclude that you will be satisfied with our Francia in this first and difficult task, which, as he himself says, has almost more to do with chance than with art. I will send both portraits to Your Excellency as soon as possible, by way of Ferrara, and commend myself ever to you, together with my daughters, who are indeed also yours, since you have married them so much to our satisfaction." [1]

Lucrezia, it must be explained, had a large family of daughters, whom Isabella treated with great kindness during the years of their exile at Mantua, and one of whom, Camilla, married Pirro Gonzaga of Gazzuolo, the youngest son of Antonia del Balzo, and who, as well as her cousin Violante, is often mentioned in Bandello's novels.

On the 6th of November, Francia's picture was sent to Ferrara by boat, and the painter himself addressed the following letter to the Marchesa :—

"Most illustrious Madonna,—We send the portrait of Your Highness, which we have done as well as we could with the help of our M. Lucrecia Bentivoglio's counsel, and if it is not as perfect as it ought to be, you must graciously pardon the painter, who places himself at your pleasure and service. *Nec plura ; vale et vivas felix.*—FRANCIA, *aurifex.*" [2]

On the 25th of November, the portrait had reached Mantua, and Isabella lost no time in expressing her satisfaction with Francia's work.

"To the most excellent painter, Francia. Maestro Francia,—I have received your portrait, and every one who has seen it can tell that the work is by your hand, because of its great excellence. I am exceedingly obliged to you for giving me so much pleasure. You have indeed made us far more beautiful by your art

---

[1] A. Luzio, *op. cit.*, p. 429.

[2] Yriarte, *op. cit.*

than nature ever made us, so that we thank you with all our heart, and as soon as we can find a trusty messenger we will pay the debt which we owe you, without speaking of the obligation under which we shall always remain to you."

But although the beauty of Francia's picture was undeniable, the critical Marchesa was not altogether satisfied with the likeness. The eyes, she thought, were decidedly too black, and she asked Lucrezia if the painter could not make them lighter. Neither the princess nor the artist, however, approved of this suggestion, as Lucrezia explained in a letter written on the 9th of December. "Il Francia, our painter, seems to be in heaven, so full of delight is he to hear that his portrait has pleased Your Excellency— still more, to hear you say that his art has made you more beautiful than nature. It would, as he owns, be too great arrogance for the art of painting to claim superiority over nature; none the less, he is by no means displeased to receive so great a compliment from such a lady! As to changing the eyes from dark to light, the result would be doubtful, and he would reluctantly run the risk of spoiling what is good in the picture, and of exchanging a certain for an uncertain advantage. It would be necessary to alter the shadows of the picture to suit the colour of the eyes, and then it would have to be varnished over again, and if the eyes were a little damaged by this operation, the picture would lose all its charm. None the less, if you were here to sit to him, he would do his best to please Your Excellency, whom he will be ever ready to oblige; nor would I be slow to undertake whatever commands you give, great or small, saying, as Eolus did,

'Juno—Thine, O Queen, it is to command; mine it is to see that thy command is obeyed.' Farewell, therefore, and love me and my children from your heart.—Your devoted sister, LUCRETIA ESTENSIS DE BENTIVOLIS."[1]

Isabella recognised the truth of Francia's words, and contented herself with sending him 30 ducats in the following March, with renewed thanks for his admirable portrait, and many excuses for the delays caused by the war that was desolating North Italy.

The strangest part of the tale yet remains to be told. According to documents lately published by Dr. Luzio from the Gonzaga archives,[2] Francia's portrait was given away by the Marchesa that winter to a Ferrarese courtier named Zaninello. This gentleman had lately presented her with the original MS. of Pistoja's *Rime*, superbly bound and richly illuminated, with a dedication to herself. This was one of those gifts on which Isabella laid especial store, and the volume of the dead poet's works found a place among her choicest treasures. In 1531, the Ferrarese poet Berni asked her permission to borrow the book; on another occasion Alessandro Bentivoglio, to whom Isabella lent it, returned the volume adorned with a set of finely worked clasps. The Marchesa replied, half in jest, half in earnest: "It was really not necessary for Your Highness to have had these handsome clasps made for my book of Pistoia's poems, so as to play the part of a good tenant! I did not ask you to pay rent, but lent it to you solely for your pleasure, as I would lend you

---

[1] Luzio in *Emporium*, 1900, p. 429.

[2] *Op. cit.*

anything that I possess ; certainly I could do no less. But since, with your wonted *gentilezza,* you have chosen to adorn my book, I thank you warmly for your gracious courtesy." [1]

The Marchesa, it seems, hardly knew how to repay Zaninello for his splendid present, and, learning from her faithful Bernardo dei Prosperi that nothing would please the donor better than her own portrait, she sent him Francia's beautiful painting to adorn his cabinet of pictures. Still more surprising is it to find that in the following May she presented this same Ferrara gentleman with Francia's portrait of her darling Federico, so that, as Zaninello wrote, his lowly roof was glorified by the presence of both mother and son, both Venus and Cupid. Unfortunately this portrait, in which Isabella confessed the painter's art had made her more beautiful than she was in life, has shared the fate of so many others, and is only known to us by the famous picture which Titian painted from Francia's model. [2]

Many other objects of *virtù,* good pictures and rare antiques, poems and songs, came to Isabella from Bologna, sometimes through her kinsfolk the Bentivogli, more often through her friend Girolamo Casio. One letter of his, dated the 15th of April 1506, when Isabella was expected at Bologna on her return from Florence, contains a curious list of articles which he has procured for her. " There are, first of all, the olives, which you will accept for my sake ; then the Magdalen painted

---

[1] Cappelli, *Rime di A. Cammelli d. il Pistoia,* p. 58.

[2] This interesting fact has been lately proved by Dr. Luzio in his paper on Isabella's portraits (*Emporium,* 1900).

by Lorenzo da Credi"—perhaps the well-known
picture by the Florentine master now at Berlin—
"also a picture of fruit by Antonio da Crevalcore—
a master most excellent in his art—but painted
larger than life. The pupil of Francia has finished
his Madonna, which is much praised by some persons.
You will see it soon, and can have it if you like
for as many gold ducats as it weighs! Seriously,
the work is worth more than 10 ducats, but you
must pay what you choose, and I will see that he is
satisfied. Your Excellency need not trouble yourself about the money—I will settle that for your
sake—to whom I commend myself from the bottom
of my heart. *Semper felix valeat !*—Your most
affectionate servant, H. CASIUS."

In the year that Francia painted her son's portrait, Isabella, who never neglected an opportunity
of securing a work by a great master, heard of
Giorgione's death from her friends at Venice, and
wrote immediately to the banker Taddeo Albano,
begging him to inquire after a wonderful *Notte*
which the dead artist was said to have painted. The
fame of this master, whose exquisite art must
have charmed Isabella's refined and poetic nature
beyond all others, had reached Mantua long before,
and on her visits to Venice she had often seen
the noble portraits which he painted of her patrician
friends, and the frescoes which adorned the marble
palaces along the Canale Grande with their glowing
colours. Now that Zorzo da Castelfranco had died
of the plague in the flower of his age, the Marchesa
hastened to ask Messer Taddeo and her faithful
Lorenzo da Pavia to secure one of his paintings for
her Camerino.

"Dearest friend," she wrote to Albano on the 25th of October 1510, "we hear that among the possessions left by Zorzo da Castelfranco, the painter, there is a picture of a *Notte*, very beautiful and original. If this is the case, we wish to have it, and beg your Lorenzo da Pavia or any other person of taste and judgment to go and see if it is a really excellent thing. If it is, I hope you will endeavour to secure this picture for me, with the help of our dearest *compare* the Magnifico Carlo Valerio, or of any one else you may think fit. Find out the price, and let us have the exact sum; but if it is really a fine thing, and you think well to clench the bargain for fear others should carry it off, do what you think best, for we know that you will act for our advantage, with your wonted loyalty and wisdom."

Taddeo replied on the 8th of November :—

"Most illustrious and honoured *Madama mia*,— In reply to Your Excellency's letter, the said Zorzo died more of exhaustion than of the plague. I have spoken in your interests to some of my friends who were very intimate with him, and they assure me that there is no such picture among his possessions. It is true that the said Zorzo painted a *Notte* for M. Taddeo Contarini, which, according to the information which I have, is not as perfect as you would desire. Another picture of the *Notte* was painted by Zorzo for a certain Vittore Beccaro, which, from what I hear, is finer in design and better finished than that of Contarini. But Beccaro is not at present in Venice, and from what I hear neither picture is for sale, because the owners had them painted for their own pleasure, so that I regret I am unable to satisfy Your Excellency's wish. —Your servant, THADDEUS ALBANUS."[1]   Venice, November 8, 1510.

These interesting letters not only prove the exact date of Giorgione's death, but show the priceless value which the paintings of this short-lived master had already acquired in the eyes of his countrymen.

Another painter who caught something of Giorgione's romantic invention and poetic feeling often visited Mantua in Isabella's life-time.   This was Dosso Dossi, one of Alfonso d'Este's favourite artists and an intimate friend of the poet Ariosto, whose fantastic imagination and magical dreams seem to live again in such pictures as the Circe and the Nymph of the Borghese collection.   In 1511 Dosso spent some time at Mantua and painted a fresco in the palace of San Sebastiano, while the St. William in armour and a Holy Family at Hampton Court both came to England from the Gonzaga collection. And it is of interest to remember that Titian paid his first visit to Mantua in the company of this Ferrarese master.   Finally, among the painters who worked for Isabella, we must not forget to mention Caroto and Francesco Bonsignori, whose names appear so often in the Marchesa's letters.   Both were of Veronese birth, but spent many years at Mantua as followers and assistants of Mantegna, and helped in the decoration of the palaces and churches of the Gonzagas.

In 1513 Bonsignori painted a portrait of the poet Pistoia by Isabella's command, while his altar-piece of the Beata Osanna with the Madonna kneeling at her feet belongs to a somewhat earlier date.   To Caroto, Morelli ascribes the well-known portrait of

[1] Luzio, *Arch. St. d. Arte*, 1888.

Elisabetta Gonzaga, Duchess of Urbino, now in the Uffizi, and Vasari tells us that an admirable head of an old man, bearing a hawk on his wrist, by the same artist, was bought by Isabella for a large sum and placed in the studio, where she had collected "an *infinite* number of rare and precious works of art."[1]

[1] *Vite*, x. 70.

GENEALOGICAL TABLES

TABLE I.—ESTE

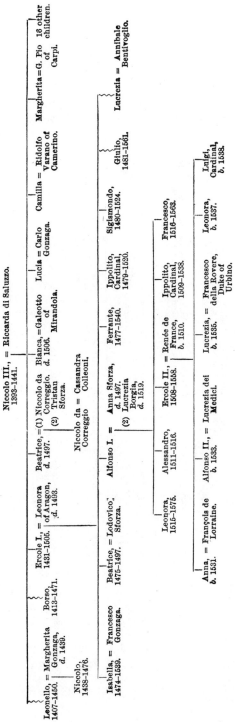

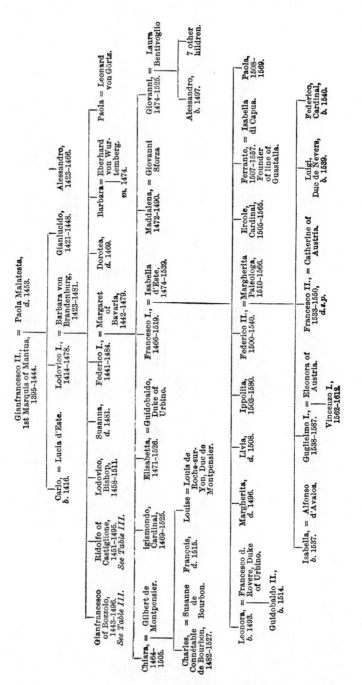

TABLE II.—GONZAGA

TABLE III.—1. GONZAGA DI BOZZOLO E SABBIONETA; 2. GONZAGA DI CASTIGLIONE

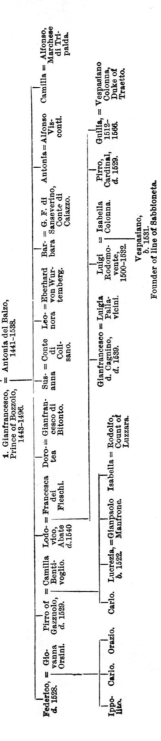
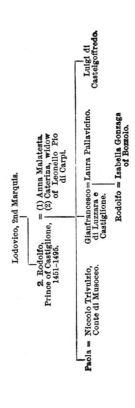

Lodovico, 2nd Marquis of Mantua.

1. Gianfrancesco, = Antonia del Balzo,
Prince of Bozzolo,
1443–1496.
1441–1558.

Federico, = Gio-   Pirro of = Camilla   Lodo- = Francesca   Doro- = Gianfran-   Sus- = Conte   Leo- = Eberhard   Bar- = G. F. di   Antonia = Alfonso   Camilla = Alfonso,
d. 1528.   vanna   Gazzuolo,   Benti-   vico,   dei   tea   cesco di   anna   di   nora   von Wur-   bara   Saneverino,   Vis-   Marchese
  Orsini.   d. 1529.   voglio.   Abate   Fieschi.   Bitonto.   Coli-   temberg.   Conte di   conti.   di Tri-
                            d.1540   sano.   Caiazzo.   palda.

Carlo.   Orazio.   Lucrezia, = Gianpaolo   Isabella = Rodolfo,   Gianfrancesco = Luigia   Luigi = Isabella   Pirro,   Gulila, = Vespasiano
Ippo-   Carlo.   b. 1522.   Manfrone.   Count of   d. Cagnino,   Palla-   Rodomo-   Colonna.   Cardinal,   1512–   Colonna,
lito.   Luzzara.   d. 1539.   vicini.   vente,   d. 1629.   1566.   Duke of
                                                               1500–1632.   Traetto.

Vespasiano,
b. 1631.
Founder of line of Sabbioneta.

Lodovico, 2nd Marquis.

2. Rodolfo,   = (1) Anna Malatesta.
Prince of Castiglione,   (2) Caterina, widow
1451–1495.   of Leonello Pio
                    di Carpi.

Paola = Niccolo Trivulzio,   Gianfrancesco = Laura Pallavicino.   Luigi di
      Conte di Musocco.   di Luzzara e   Castelgoffredo.
                         Castiglione.

Rodolfo = Isabella Gonzaga
             of Bozzolo.

END OF VOL. I.

Printed by BALLANTYNE, HANSON & Co.
Edinburgh & London